SELECTED WORKS

OF

MAO TSE-TUNG

Volume II

FOREIGN LANGUAGES PRESS
PEKING 1967

First Edition   1965
Second Printing   1967

The present volume is an English translation of the
second Chinese edition of the second volume of the
Selected Works of Mao Tse-tung, published by the
People's Publishing House, Peking, in April 1960.

Printed in the People's Republic of China

CONTENTS

THE PERIOD OF THE WAR OF RESISTANCE AGAINST JAPAN (I)

THE PERIOD OF
THE WAR OF RESISTANCE
AGAINST JAPAN (I)

POLICIES, MEASURES AND PERSPECTIVES
FOR RESISTING
THE JAPANESE INVASION

July 23, 1937

I. TWO POLICIES

On July 8, the day after the Lukouchiao Incident,[1] the Central Committee of the Communist Party of China issued a manifesto to the whole nation calling for a war of resistance. The manifesto reads in part:

> Fellow-countrymen! Peiping and Tientsin are in peril! Northern China is in peril! The Chinese nation is in peril! A war of resistance by the whole nation is the only way out. We demand immediate and resolute resistance to the invading Japanese armies and immediate preparations to meet all emergencies. From top to bottom the whole nation must at once abandon any idea of being able to live in submissive peace with the Japanese aggressors. Fellow-countrymen! We should acclaim and support the heroic resistance of Feng Chih-an's troops. We should acclaim and support the declaration of the local authorities of northern China that they will defend the homeland to the death. We demand that General

---

On July 7, 1937, the Japanese imperialists staged the Lukouchiao Incident in their attempt to annex the whole of China by armed force. The Chinese people unanimously demanded war against Japan. Ten days elapsed before Chiang Kai-shek tardily made a public statement at Lushan announcing armed resistance to Japan. He did so under nation-wide popular pressure and as a result of the serious blow the Japanese invasion had dealt to the interests both of the British and U.S. imperialists in China and of the big landlords and the big bourgeoisie whom Chiang Kai-shek directly represented. But at the same time the Chiang Kai-shek government continued to parley with the Japanese aggressors and even accepted the so-called peaceful settlements they concluded with local authorities. It was not until August 13, 1937, when the Japanese aggressors launched a major attack on Shanghai and

13

Sung Cheh-yuan immediately mobilize the entire 29th Army[2] and send it into action at the front. Of the Central Government in Nanking we demand the following: Give effective aid to the 29th Army. Immediately lift the ban on patriotic movements among the masses and let the people give full play to their enthusiasm for armed resistance. Immediately mobilize all the country's land, sea and air forces for action. Immediately weed out all the hidden traitors and Japanese agents in China and so consolidate our rear. We call on the people of the whole country to throw all their strength behind the sacred war of self-defence against Japan. Our slogans are: Armed defence of Peiping, Tientsin and northern China! Defend our homeland to the last drop of our blood! Let the people of the whole country, the government, and the armed forces unite and build up the national united front as our solid Great Wall of resistance to Japanese aggression! Let the Kuomintang and the Communist Party closely co-operate and resist the new attacks of the Japanese aggressors! Drive the Japanese aggressors out of China!

This is a declaration of policy.

On July 17, Mr. Chiang Kai-shek made a statement at Lushan. Setting out as it did a policy of preparing for a war of resistance, the statement was the Kuomintang's first correct declaration on foreign affairs for many years and it has consequently been welcomed by all our countrymen as well as by ourselves. The statement listed four conditions for the settlement of the Lukouchiao Incident:

(1) Any settlement must not infringe China's sovereignty and territorial integrity; (2) there must be no unlawful change in the administrative structure of Hopei and Chahar Provinces; (3) there must be no dismissal and replacement, at the demand of others,

---

thus made it impossible for Chiang Kai-shek to maintain his rule in southeastern China, that he was compelled to embark on armed resistance; but Chiang never ceased his clandestine attempts to make peace with Japan right up to 1944. Throughout the War of Resistance Chiang Kai-shek opposed all-out people's war in which the entire people are mobilized, and pursued the reactionary policy of passively resisting Japan but actively opposing the Communist Party and the people; thus his actions completely violated his own Lushan statement that "once war breaks out, every person, young or old, in the north or in the south, must take up the responsibility of resisting Japan and defending our homeland". The two policies, two sets of measures and two perspectives discussed by Comrade Mao Tse-tung in this article reflect the struggle between the line of the Communist Party and Chiang Kai-shek's line in the War of Resistance.

of local officials appointed by the Central Government; (4) the 29th Army must not be confined to the area in which it is now stationed.

The concluding remarks of the statement read:

> Concerning the Lukouchiao Incident, the government has decided on a policy and a stand to which it will always adhere. We realize that when the whole nation goes to war, sacrifices to the bitter end will be called for, and we should not cherish the faintest hope of an easy way out. Once war breaks out, every person, young or old, in the north or in the south, must take up the responsibility of resisting Japan and defending our homeland.

This, too, is a declaration of policy.

Here we have two historic political declarations on the Lukouchiao Incident, one by the Communist Party and the other by the Kuomintang. They have this point in common: both stand for a resolute war of resistance and oppose compromise and concessions.

This is one kind of policy for meeting Japanese invasion, the correct policy.

But there is the possibility of the adoption of another kind of policy. In recent months the traitors and the pro-Japanese elements in Peiping and Tientsin have been very active, they have been trying to get the local authorities to acquiesce in Japan's demands, they have been undermining the policy of resolute armed resistance and advocating compromise and concessions. These are extremely dangerous signs.

The policy of compromise and concessions is the diametrical opposite of the policy of resolute armed resistance. If it is not speedily reversed, Peiping, Tientsin and the whole of northern China will fall into the hands of the enemy, and the entire nation will be seriously imperilled. Everyone must be on the alert.

Patriotic officers and men of the 29th Army, unite! Oppose compromise and concessions and conduct resolute armed resistance!

Fellow patriots of Peiping, Tientsin and northern China, unite! Oppose compromise and concessions and support resolute armed resistance!

Fellow patriots throughout the country, unite! Oppose compromise and concessions and support resolute armed resistance!

Mr. Chiang Kai-shek and all patriotic members of the Kuomintang! We hope that you will firmly adhere to your policy, fulfil your promises, oppose compromise and concessions, conduct resolute armed resistance, and thus answer the outrages of the enemy with deeds.

Let all the armed forces in the country, including the Red Army, support Mr. Chiang Kai-shek's declaration, oppose compromise and concessions and conduct resolute armed resistance!

We Communists are whole-heartedly and faithfully carrying out our own manifesto, and at the same time we resolutely support Mr. Chiang Kai-shek's declaration; together with the members of the Kuomintang and all our fellow-countrymen, we are ready to defend the homeland to the last drop of our blood; we oppose any hesitation, vacillation, compromise or concessions, and will conduct resolute armed resistance.

II. TWO SETS OF MEASURES

To achieve its purpose the policy of resolute armed resistance calls for a whole set of measures.

What are they? The principal ones are the following:

1. *Mobilize all the armed forces of the whole country.* Mobilize our standing armed forces of well over two million men, including the land, sea and air forces, the Central Army, the local troops and the Red Army, and immediately send the main forces to the national defence lines, while keeping some forces in the rear to maintain order. Entrust the command on the various fronts to generals loyal to the national interests. Call a national defence conference to decide on strategy and to achieve unity of purpose in military operations. Overhaul the political work in the army in order to achieve unity between officers and men and between the army and the people. Establish the principle that guerrilla warfare should carry the responsibility for one aspect of the strategic task, and ensure proper co-ordination between guerrilla and regular warfare. Weed out traitors from the army. Call up an adequate number of reserves and train them for service at the front. Adequately replenish the equipment and supplies of the armed forces. Military plans on these lines must be made, in keeping with the general policy of resolute armed resistance. China's troops are far from few, but unless these plans are executed, they will not be able to defeat the enemy. However, if the political and material factors are combined, our armed forces will become unmatched in East Asia.

2. *Mobilize the whole people.* Lift the ban on patriotic movements, release political prisoners, annul the "Emergency Decree for Dealing with Actions Endangering the Republic"[3] and the "Press Censorship Regulations",[4] grant legal status to existing patriotic organizations, extend these organizations among the workers, peasants, businessmen and intellectuals, arm the people for self-defence and for operations in support of the army. In a word, give the people freedom to express their patriotism. By their combined strength the people and the army will deal a death-blow to Japanese imperialism. Beyond doubt, there can be no victory in a national war without reliance on the great masses of the people. Let us take warning from the fall of Abyssinia.[5] No one who is sincere about waging a resolute war of resistance can afford to ignore this point.

3. *Reform the government apparatus.* Bring representatives of all political parties and groups and public leaders into the government for joint management of the affairs of the state and weed out the hidden pro-Japanese elements and traitors in the government, so that the government can become one with the people. Resistance to Japan is a gigantic task which cannot be performed by a few individuals alone. If they insist on keeping it in their own hands, they will only bungle it. If the government is to be a real government of national defence, it must rely on the people and practise democratic centralism. It must be at once democratic and centralized; it is this kind of government which is the most powerful. The national assembly must be truly representative of the people; it must be the supreme organ of authority, determine the major policies of the state and decide on the policies and plans for resisting Japan and saving the nation.

4. *Adopt an anti-Japanese foreign policy.* Accord the Japanese imperialists no advantages or facilities, but on the contrary confiscate their property, repudiate their loans, weed out their lackeys and expel their spies. Immediately conclude a military and political alliance with the Soviet Union and closely unite with the Soviet Union, the country which is most reliable, most powerful and most capable of helping China to resist Japan. Enlist the sympathy of Britain, the United States and France for our resistance to Japan, and secure their help provided that it entails no loss of our territory or our sovereign rights. We should rely mainly on our own strength to defeat the Japanese aggressors; but foreign aid cannot be dispensed with, and an isolationist policy will only play into the enemy's hands.

5. *Proclaim a programme for improving the livelihood of the people and immediately begin to put it into effect.* Start with the following minimum points: Abolish exorbitant taxes and miscellaneous levies, reduce land rent, restrict usury, increase the workers' pay, improve the livelihood of the soldiers and junior officers, improve the livelihood of office workers, and provide relief for victims of natural calamities. Far from making a mess of the country's finances as some people argue, these new measures will increase the people's purchasing power and lead to thriving commercial and financial conditions. They will add immeasurably to our strength for resisting Japan and consolidate the government's foundations.

6. *Institute education for national defence.* Radically reform the existing educational policy and system. All projects that are not urgent and all measures that are not rational must be discarded. Newspapers, books and magazines, films, plays, literature and art should all serve national defence. Traitorous propaganda must be prohibited.

7. *Adopt financial and economic policies for resisting Japan.* Financial policy should be based on the principle that those with money should contribute money and that the property of the Japanese imperialists and Chinese traitors should be confiscated, and economic policy should be based on the principle of boycotting Japanese goods and promoting home products — everything for the sake of resistance to Japan. Financial strain is the product of wrong measures and can surely be overcome after the adoption of new policies such as these, which serve the interests of the people. It is sheer nonsense to say that a country with so vast a territory and so huge a population is financially and economically helpless.

8. *Unite the entire Chinese people, the government and the armed forces to build up the national united front as our solid Great Wall.* The application of the policy of armed resistance and of the above measures depends on this united front. Here the key is close co-operation between the Kuomintang and the Communist Party. Let the government, the troops, all the political parties and the whole people unite on the basis of such co-operation between the two parties. The slogan "Unity in good faith to meet the national crisis" must not be limited to fine words but must be demonstrated in fine deeds. Unity must be genuine; deception will not do. There must be more large-mindedness and a broader sweep in the conduct of state affairs. Petty niggling, mean tricks, bureaucracy, and Ah Q-ism[6] are of no use at all. They are of no avail against the enemy and simply ridiculous if

practised on one's own countrymen. There are major and minor principles in everything, and the minor principles are all subordinate to the major. Our compatriots must think things over carefully in the light of the major principles, for only then will they be able to orientate their own ideas and actions properly. Today, anyone who has not begun to have some genuine desire for unity ought to examine his conscience in the stillness of the night and feel some shame, even if no one else censures him.

The set of measures for resolute armed resistance described above may be called the Eight-Point Programme.

The policy of resolute armed resistance must be accompanied by this set of measures, or otherwise victory will never be achieved and Japanese aggression against China will never be ended, while China will be helpless against Japan and hardly be able to escape the fate of Abyssinia.

Whoever is sincere about the policy of resolute armed resistance must put this set of measures into practice. And the test of whether or not he is sincere about resolute armed resistance is whether or not he accepts and carries out this set of measures.

There is another set of measures which is contrary to this set in every respect.

Not the total mobilization of the armed forces, but their immobilization or withdrawal.

Not freedom for the people, but oppression.

Not a government of national defence based on democratic centralism, but an autocratic government of bureaucrats, compradors and big landlords.

Not a foreign policy of resisting Japan, but one of fawning on her.

Not the improvement of the people's livelihood, but continued extortions so that they groan under their sufferings and are powerless to resist Japan.

Not education for national defence, but education for national subjugation.

Not financial and economic policies for resisting Japan, but the same old, or even worse, financial and economic policies benefiting the enemy rather than our own country.

Not building up the Anti-Japanese National United Front as our Great Wall, but tearing it down, or talking glibly about unity while never doing anything to advance it.

Measures stem from policy. If the policy is one of non-resistance, all measures will reflect non-resistance; we have been taught this lesson over the last six years. If the policy is one of resolute armed resistance, then it is imperative to apply the appropriate measures — the Eight-Point Programme.

III. TWO PERSPECTIVES

What are the perspectives? This is what everyone is anxious about.

Pursue the first policy and adopt the first set of measures, and the perspective will definitely be the expulsion of Japanese imperialism and the attainment of China's liberation. Can there still be any doubt about it? I think not.

Pursue the second policy and adopt the second set of measures, and the perspective will definitely be the occupation of China by the Japanese imperialists, with the Chinese people being turned into slaves and beasts of burden. Can there still be any doubt about it? Again, I think not.

IV. CONCLUSION

It is imperative to carry out the first policy, to adopt the first set of measures and to strive for the first perspective.

It is imperative to oppose the second policy, to reject the second set of measures and to avert the second perspective.

Let all patriotic members of the Kuomintang and all members of the Communist Party unite and steadfastly carry out the first policy, adopt the first set of measures and strive for the first perspective; let them steadfastly oppose the second policy, reject the second set of measures and avert the second perspective.

Let all patriotic people, patriotic troops and patriotic parties and groups unite as one and steadfastly carry out the first policy, adopt the first set of measures and strive for the first perspective; let them steadfastly oppose the second policy, reject the second set of measures and avert the second perspective.

Long live the national revolutionary war!

Long live the liberation of the Chinese nation!

NOTES

[1] On July 7, 1937, the Japanese invading forces attacked the Chinese garrison at Lukouchiao, some ten kilometres southwest of Peking. Under the influence of the ardent nation-wide anti-Japanese movement, the Chinese troops put up resistance. This incident marked the beginning of the Chinese people's heroic War of Resistance Against Japan which lasted for eight years.

[2] The 29th Army, which was originally part of the Kuomintang's Northwestern Army under Feng Yu-hsiang, was then stationed in Hopei and Chahar Provinces. Sung Cheh-yuan was its commander and Feng Chih-an one of its divisional commanders.

[3] The Kuomintang government promulgated the so-called "Emergency Decree for Dealing with Actions Endangering the Republic" on January 31, 1931, using the trumped-up charge of "endangering the Republic" to persecute and slaughter patriots and revolutionaries. This decree imposed extremely brutal measures of persecution.

[4] "Press Censorship Regulations" was another name for the "General Measures for Press Censorship" issued by the Kuomintang government in August 1934 to stifle the voice of the people. They laid down that "all news copy must be submitted to censorship".

[5] See "The Tasks of the Chinese Communist Party in the Period of Resistance to Japan", *Selected Works of Mao Tse-tung*, Eng. ed., Foreign Languages Press, Peking, 1965, Vol. I, p. 267.

[6] Ah Q is the leading character in *The True Story of Ah Q*, the famous work by the great Chinese writer Lu Hsun. Ah Q typifies all those who compensate themselves for their failures and setbacks in real life by regarding them as moral or spiritual victories.

NOTES

1. ...

2. ...

3. ...

FOR THE MOBILIZATION OF
ALL THE NATION'S FORCES FOR VICTORY
IN THE WAR OF RESISTANCE

August 25, 1937

A. The Lukouchiao Incident of July 7 marked the beginning of the Japanese imperialist all-out invasion of China south of the Great Wall. The fight put up by the Chinese troops at Lukouchiao marked the beginning of China's nation-wide War of Resistance. The ceaseless Japanese attacks, the people's resolute struggle, the national bourgeoisie's tendency towards resistance, the Communist Party's vigorous advocacy and firm application of a national united front policy and the nation-wide support this policy has won — all these have compelled the Chinese authorities to begin changing their policy of non-resistance, as pursued ever since the September 18th Incident of 1931, to a policy of resistance since the Lukouchiao Incident, and have caused the Chinese revolution to develop beyond the stage reached after the December 9th Movement,[1] *i.e.*, the stage of ending the civil war and preparing for resistance, into the stage of actual resistance. The initial changes in the Kuomintang's policy with the Sian Incident and the Third Plenary Session of its Central Executive Committee as their starting point, Mr. Chiang Kai-shek's Lushan statement of July 17 on the question of resistance to Japan, and many of his measures of national defence, all deserve commendation. The troops at the front, whether the land and air forces or the local armed units, have all fought courageously and demonstrated the heroic spirit of the Chinese nation. In the name of the national revolution, the Chinese

---

This was an outline for propaganda and agitation written by Comrade Mao Tse-tung in August 1937 for the propaganda organs of the Central Committee of the Chinese Communist Party. It was approved by the enlarged meeting of the Political Bureau of the Central Committee at Lochuan, northern Shensi.

Communist Party ardently salutes our patriotic troops and fellow-countrymen throughout China.

B. But on the other hand, even after the Lukouchiao Incident of July 7, the Kuomintang authorities are continuing to pursue the wrong policy they have pursued ever since the September 18th Incident, making compromises and concessions,[2] suppressing the zeal of the patriotic troops and clamping down on the patriotic people's national salvation movement. There is no doubt that, having seized Peiping and Tientsin, Japanese imperialism will press ahead with its policy of large-scale offensives, take the second and third steps in its premeditated war plan and launch fierce attacks on the whole of northern China and other areas, relying on its own brute military strength while at the same time drawing support from German and Italian imperialism and exploiting the vacillations of British imperialism and the estrangement of the Kuomintang from the broad masses of the working people. The flames of war are already raging in Chahar and in Shanghai. To save our motherland, to resist the attacks of the powerful invaders, to defend northern China and the seacoast and recover Peiping, Tientsin and northeastern China, the Kuomintang authorities and the whole people must thoroughly learn the lesson of the loss of northeastern China, Peiping and Tientsin, learn and take warning from the fall of Abyssinia, learn from the Soviet Union's past victories over its foreign enemies,[3] learn from Spain's present experience in successfully defending Madrid,[4] and firmly unite to fight to the end in defence of the motherland. Henceforth the task is: "Mobilize all the nation's forces for victory in the War of Resistance", and the key to its accomplishment is a complete and thorough change in Kuomintang policy. The step forward taken by the Kuomintang on the question of resistance is to be commended; it is what the Chinese Communist Party and the people of the whole country have for years been hoping for, and we welcome it. But the Kuomintang has not changed its policies on such matters as the mobilization of the masses and the introduction of political reforms. It is still basically unwilling to lift the ban on the people's anti-Japanese movement or make fundamental changes in the government apparatus, it still has no policy for improving the people's livelihood, and is still not sufficiently sincere in its co-operation with the Communist Party. If, at this critical juncture of life or death for our nation, the Kuomintang continues in the same old groove and does not quickly change its policy, it will bring disaster to the War of Resistance. Some Kuomintang members say, "Let political reforms be instituted after victory." They think the Japanese aggressors can be defeated by the government's efforts alone, but they are wrong. A few battles may be won in a war of resistance fought by the government alone, but it will be impossible to defeat the Japanese aggressors thoroughly. This can be done only by a war of total resistance by the whole nation. Such a war, however, requires a complete and drastic change in Kuomintang policy and the joint efforts of the whole nation from top to bottom to carry out a thoroughgoing programme of resistance to Japan, that is, a national salvation programme formulated in the spirit of the revolutionary Three People's Principles and the Three Great Policies[5] drawn up personally by Dr. Sun Yat-sen during the first period of Kuomintang-Communist co-operation.

C. In all earnestness the Chinese Communist Party proposes to the Kuomintang, to the people of the whole country, to all political parties and groups, to people in all walks of life and to all the armed forces a Ten-Point National Salvation Programme for the purpose of completely defeating the Japanese aggressors. It firmly believes that only by carrying out this programme fully, sincerely and resolutely will it be possible to defend the motherland and defeat the Japanese aggressors. Otherwise, the responsibility will fall on those who procrastinate and allow the situation to deteriorate; once the country's doom is sealed, it will be too late for regrets and lamentations. The ten points are as follows:

1. Overthrow Japanese imperialism.

Sever diplomatic relations with Japan, expel Japanese officials, arrest Japanese agents, confiscate Japanese property in China, repudiate debts to Japan, abrogate treaties signed with Japan and take back all Japanese Concessions.

Fight to the finish in defence of northern China and the seacoast.

Fight to the finish for the recovery of Peiping, Tientsin and northeastern China.

Drive the Japanese imperialists out of China.

Oppose all vacillation and compromise.

2. Mobilize the military strength of the whole nation.

Mobilize all land, sea and air forces for a nation-wide war of resistance.

Oppose a passive, purely defensive strategy and adopt an active, independent strategy.

Set up a permanent council of national defence to deliberate and decide on national defence plans and strategy.

Arm the people and develop anti-Japanese guerrilla warfare in co-ordination with the operations of the main forces.

Reform the political work in the armed forces to achieve unity between officers and men.

Achieve unity between the army and the people and bring the army's militant spirit into play.

Support the Northeast Anti-Japanese United Army and disrupt the enemy's rear.

Give equal treatment to all troops fighting in the War of Resistance.

Establish military zones in all parts of the country, mobilize the whole nation to join in the war and thus effect a gradual change from the mercenary system to one of general military service.

3. Mobilize the people of the whole country.

Let all the people of the country (with the exception of the traitors) have freedom of speech, the press, assembly and association in resisting Japan and saving the nation, and the right to take up arms against the enemy.

Annul all old laws and decrees which restrict the people's patriotic movements and promulgate new, revolutionary laws and decrees.

Release all patriotic and revolutionary political prisoners and lift the ban on political parties.

Let the people of the whole country mobilize, take up arms and join the War of Resistance. Let those with strength contribute strength, those with money contribute money, those with guns contribute guns, and those with knowledge contribute knowledge.

Mobilize the Mongolian, the Hui and all other minority nationalities, in accordance with the principle of national self-determination and autonomy, in the common fight against Japan.

4. Reform the government apparatus.

Call a national assembly which is genuinely representative of the people to adopt a genuinely democratic constitution, to decide on policies for resisting Japan and saving the nation, and to elect a government of national defence.

The government of national defence must draw in the revolutionaries of all parties and mass organizations, and expel the pro-Japanese elements.

The government of national defence shall practise democratic centralism, and shall be at once democratic and centralized.

The government of national defence shall pursue revolutionary policies for resisting Japan and saving the nation.

Institute local self-government, throw out corrupt officials and establish clean government.

5. Adopt an anti-Japanese foreign policy.

Conclude anti-aggression alliances and anti-Japanese pacts for mutual military aid with all countries that are opposed to Japanese aggression, provided that this entails no loss of our territory or of our sovereign rights.

Support the international peace front and oppose the front of aggression of Germany, Japan and Italy.

Unite with the worker and peasant masses of Korea and Japan against Japanese imperialism.

6. Adopt wartime financial and economic policies.

Financial policy should be based on the principle that those with money should contribute money and that the property of the traitors should be confiscated in order to meet war expenditures. Economic policy should consist in readjusting and expanding defence production, developing the rural economy and assuring self-sufficiency in wartime commodities. Encourage the use of Chinese goods and improve local products. Completely prohibit Japanese goods. Suppress profiteering merchants and ban speculation and manipulation of the market.

7. Improve the people's livelihood.

Improve the conditions of workers, office employees and teachers, and of soldiers fighting the Japanese.

Give preferential treatment to the families of the soldiers fighting the Japanese.

Abolish exorbitant taxes and miscellaneous levies.

Reduce rent and interest.

Give relief to the unemployed.

Regulate grain supplies.

Aid the victims of natural calamities.

8. Adopt an anti-Japanese educational policy.

Change the existing educational system and curriculum and put into effect a new system and curriculum aimed at resisting Japan and saving the nation.

9. Weed out traitors and pro-Japanese elements and consolidate the rear.

10. Achieve national unity against Japan.

Build up the Anti-Japanese National United Front of all political parties and groups, people in all walks of life and all armed forces on the basis of Kuomintang-Communist co-operation in order to lead the War of Resistance, unite in good faith and meet the national crisis.

D. It is imperative to discard the policy of resistance by the government alone and to enforce the policy of total resistance by the whole nation. The government must unite with the people, fully restore the revolutionary spirit of Dr. Sun Yat-sen, put the above Ten-Point Programme into effect and strive for complete victory. Together with the masses of the people and the armed forces under its leadership, the Chinese Communist Party will firmly adhere to this programme and stand in the forefront of the War of Resistance, defending the motherland to the last drop of its blood. In keeping with its consistent policy, the Chinese Communist Party is ready to stand side by side with the Kuomintang and the other political parties and groups and unite with them in building the solid Great Wall of the national united front to defeat the infamous Japanese aggressors and strive for a new China which is independent, happy and free. To achieve this goal, we must firmly repudiate the traitors' theories of compromise and capitulation, and combat national defeatism according to which it is impossible to defeat the Japanese aggressors. The Chinese Communist Party firmly believes that the Japanese aggressors can definitely be defeated provided the above Ten-Point Programme is carried out. If our 450 million countrymen all exert themselves, the Chinese nation will certainly achieve final victory!

Down with Japanese imperialism!

Long live the national revolutionary war!

Long live New China, independent, happy and free!

NOTES

[1] The year 1935 witnessed a new upsurge in the popular patriotic movement throughout the country. Students in Peking, under the leadership of the Communist Party of China, held a patriotic demonstration on December 9, putting forward such slogans as "Stop the civil war and unite to resist foreign aggression" and "Down with Japanese imperialism". This movement broke through the long reign of terror imposed by the Kuomintang government in league with the Japanese invaders and very quickly won the people's support throughout the country. It is known as the

"December 9th Movement". The outcome was that new changes manifested themselves in the relations among the various classes in the country, and the Anti-Japanese National United Front proposed by the Communist Party of China became the openly advocated policy of all patriotic people. The Chiang Kai-shek government with its traitorous policy became very isolated.

[2] See the introductory note to "Policies, Measures and Perspectives for Resisting the Japanese Invasion", pp. 13-14 of this volume.

[3] See *History of the Communist Party of the Soviet Union (Bolsheviks), Short Course*, Eng. ed., FLPH, Moscow, 1951, pp. 347-81.

[4] The defence of Madrid, starting in October 1936, lasted for two years and five months. In 1936, fascist Germany and Italy made use of the Spanish fascist warlord Franco to launch a war of aggression against Spain. The Spanish people, led by the Popular Front Government, heroically defended democracy against aggression. The battle of Madrid, the capital of Spain, was the bitterest in the whole war. Madrid fell in March 1939 because Britain, France and other imperialist countries assisted the aggressors by their hypocritical policy of "non-intervention" and because divisions arose within the Popular Front.

[5] The Three People's Principles were the principles and the programme put forward by Sun Yat-sen on the questions of nationalism, democracy and people's livelihood in China's bourgeois-democratic revolution. In the manifesto adopted by the Kuomintang at its First National Congress in 1924 Sun Yat-sen restated the Three People's Principles. Nationalism was interpreted as opposition to imperialism and active support was expressed for the movements of the workers and peasants. Thus the old Three People's Principles were transformed into the new Three People's Principles characterized by the Three Great Policies, that is, alliance with Russia, co-operation with the Communist Party, and assistance to the peasants and workers. The new Three People's Principles provided the political basis for the co-operation between the Communist Party of China and the Kuomintang during the First Revolutionary Civil War period.

COMBAT LIBERALISM

September 7, 1937

We stand for active ideological struggle because it is the weapon for ensuring unity within the Party and the revolutionary organizations in the interest of our fight. Every Communist and revolutionary should take up this weapon.

But liberalism rejects ideological struggle and stands for unprincipled peace, thus giving rise to a decadent, philistine attitude and bringing about political degeneration in certain units and individuals in the Party and the revolutionary organizations.

Liberalism manifests itself in various ways.

To let things slide for the sake of peace and friendship when a person has clearly gone wrong, and refrain from principled argument because he is an old acquaintance, a fellow townsman, a schoolmate, a close friend, a loved one, an old colleague or old subordinate. Or to touch on the matter lightly instead of going into it thoroughly, so as to keep on good terms. The result is that both the organization and the individual are harmed. This is one type of liberalism.

To indulge in irresponsible criticism in private instead of actively putting forward one's suggestions to the organization. To say nothing to people to their faces but to gossip behind their backs, or to say nothing at a meeting but to gossip afterwards. To show no regard at all for the principles of collective life but to follow one's own inclination. This is a second type.

To let things drift if they do not affect one personally; to say as little as possible while knowing perfectly well what is wrong, to be worldly wise and play safe and seek only to avoid blame. This is a third type.

Not to obey orders but to give pride of place to one's own opinions. To demand special consideration from the organization but to reject its discipline. This is a fourth type.

31

To indulge in personal attacks, pick quarrels, vent personal spite or seek revenge instead of entering into an argument and struggling against incorrect views for the sake of unity or progress or getting the work done properly. This is a fifth type.

To hear incorrect views without rebutting them and even to hear counter-revolutionary remarks without reporting them, but instead to take them calmly as if nothing had happened. This is a sixth type.

To be among the masses and fail to conduct propaganda and agitation or speak at meetings or conduct investigations and inquiries among them, and instead to be indifferent to them and show no concern for their well-being, forgetting that one is a Communist and behaving as if one were an ordinary non-Communist. This is a seventh type.

To see someone harming the interests of the masses and yet not feel indignant, or dissuade or stop him or reason with him, but to allow him to continue. This is an eighth type.

To work half-heartedly without a definite plan or direction; to work perfunctorily and muddle along — "So long as one remains a monk, one goes on tolling the bell." This is a ninth type.

To regard oneself as having rendered great service to the revolution, to pride oneself on being a veteran, to disdain minor assignments while being quite unequal to major tasks, to be slipshod in work and slack in study. This is a tenth type.

To be aware of one's own mistakes and yet make no attempt to correct them, taking a liberal attitude towards oneself. This is an eleventh type.

We could name more. But these eleven are the principal types.

They are all manifestations of liberalism.

Liberalism is extremely harmful in a revolutionary collective. It is a corrosive which eats away unity, undermines cohesion, causes apathy and creates dissension. It robs the revolutionary ranks of compact organization and strict discipline, prevents policies from being carried through and alienates the Party organizations from the masses which the Party leads. It is an extremely bad tendency.

Liberalism stems from petty-bourgeois selfishness, it places personal interests first and the interests of the revolution second, and this gives rise to ideological, political and organizational liberalism.

People who are liberals look upon the principles of Marxism as abstract dogma. They approve of Marxism, but are not prepared to practise it or to practise it in full; they are not prepared to replace their liberalism by Marxism. These people have their Marxism, but they have their liberalism as well — they talk Marxism but practise liberalism; they apply Marxism to others but liberalism to themselves. They keep both kinds of goods in stock and find a use for each. This is how the minds of certain people work.

Liberalism is a manifestation of opportunism and conflicts fundamentally with Marxism. It is negative and objectively has the effect of helping the enemy; that is why the enemy welcomes its preservation in our midst. Such being its nature, there should be no place for it in the ranks of the revolution.

We must use Marxism, which is positive in spirit, to overcome liberalism, which is negative. A Communist should have largeness of mind and he should be staunch and active, looking upon the interests of the revolution as his very life and subordinating his personal interests to those of the revolution; always and everywhere he should adhere to principle and wage a tireless struggle against all incorrect ideas and actions, so as to consolidate the collective life of the Party and strengthen the ties between the Party and the masses; he should be more concerned about the Party and the masses than about any private person, and more concerned about others than about himself. Only thus can he be considered a Communist.

All loyal, honest, active and upright Communists must unite to oppose the liberal tendencies shown by certain people among us, and set them on the right path. This is one of the tasks on our ideological front.

URGENT TASKS
FOLLOWING THE ESTABLISHMENT OF
KUOMINTANG-COMMUNIST
CO-OPERATION

September 29, 1937

As far back as 1933, the Chinese Communist Party issued a declaration stating that it was ready to conclude an agreement for resisting Japan with any section of the Kuomintang army on three conditions, namely, that attacks on the Red Army be stopped, that democratic freedoms be granted to the people and that the people be armed. This declaration was made because after the September 18th Incident in 1931, resistance to the Japanese imperialist invasion became the primary task of the Chinese people. But we did not succeed in our objective.

In August 1935, the Chinese Communist Party and the Chinese Red Army called upon all political parties and groups and the people throughout the country to organize an anti-Japanese united army and a government of national defence for a common fight against Japanese imperialism.[1] In December of that year, the Chinese Communist Party adopted a resolution[2] on the formation of an anti-Japanese national united front with the national bourgeoisie. In May 1936, the Red Army published an open telegram[3] demanding that the Nanking government stop the civil war and make common cause against Japan. In August of that year, the Central Committee of the Chinese Communist Party sent a letter[4] to the Central Executive Committee of the Kuomintang demanding that the Kuomintang stop the civil war and form a united front of the two parties to fight jointly against Japanese imperialism. In September of the same year, the Communist Party passed a resolution[5] on the establishment of a unified democratic republic in China. Besides the declaration, the open telegram, the

35

letter and the resolutions, we sent representatives to hold discussions with people from the Kuomintang side on many occasions, and yet all in vain. It was only towards the end of 1936 after the Sian Incident that the plenipotentiary of the Chinese Communist Party and the responsible chief of the Kuomintang reached an agreement on a contemporary issue of vital political importance, namely, cessation of the civil war between the two parties, and brought about the peaceful settlement of the Sian Incident. This was a great event in Chinese history and provided a prerequisite for the renewal of co-operation between the two parties.

On February 10 this year, the Central Committee of the Chinese Communist Party sent a telegram[6] to the Third Plenary Session of the Kuomintang Central Executive Committee on the eve of its meeting, making comprehensive proposals for concrete co-operation between the two parties. In that telegram we demanded that the Kuomintang give the Communist Party guarantees on the following five points: the ending of the civil war, the realization of democratic freedoms, the convening of a national assembly, speedy preparations for resisting Japan, and improvement of the people's livelihood. At the same time the Communist Party offered guarantees to the Kuomintang on the following four points: the elimination of the state of antagonism between the two regimes, the redesignation of the Red Army, the application of the new-democratic system in the revolutionary base areas, and the discontinuance of the confiscation of the land of the landlords. This was likewise an important political step, for without it the establishment of co-operation between the two parties would have been retarded, which would have been wholly detrimental to speedy preparations for resisting Japan.

Since then the two parties have moved a step closer to each other in their negotiations. The Communist Party has made more specific proposals on the question of a common political programme for the two parties, on the question of lifting the ban on the mass movements and releasing political prisoners, and on the question of redesignating the Red Army. So far the common programme has not yet been promulgated, nor has the ban on the mass movements been lifted, nor has the new system in the revolutionary base areas been recognized; however, about a month after the fall of Peiping and Tientsin an order was issued to the effect that the Red Army was to be redesignated as the Eighth Route Army of the National Revolutionary Army (also called the Eighteenth Group Army in the anti-Japanese battle order).

The declaration of the Central Committee of our Party on the establishment of bi-partisan co-operation, which had been conveyed to the Kuomintang as early as July 15, and Chiang Kai-shek's statement recognizing the legal status of the Communist Party of China, which should have been published as agreed simultaneously with the declaration, were finally released to the public (alas after a long delay) by the Kuomintang Central News Agency on September 22 and 23 respectively, when the situation at the front had become critical. The Communist Party's declaration and Chiang Kai-shek's statement announced the establishment of co-operation between the two parties and laid the necessary foundation for the great cause of alliance between the two parties to save the nation. The declaration of the Communist Party not only embodies the principle of unity between the two parties but also embodies the basic principle of the great unity of the people throughout the country. It is good that Chiang Kai-shek, in his statement, recognized the legal status of the Communist Party throughout China and spoke of the necessity of unity to save the nation; however, he has not abandoned his Kuomintang arrogance or made any necessary self-criticism, and we can hardly be satisfied with that. Nevertheless, the united front between the two parties has been proclaimed as established. This has ushered in a new epoch in the history of the Chinese revolution. It will exert a widespread and profound influence on the Chinese revolution and play a decisive role in defeating Japanese imperialism.

Ever since 1924, the relationship between the Kuomintang and the Chinese Communist Party has played a decisive role in the Chinese revolution. The revolution of 1924-27 took place as a result of the co-operation of the two parties on the basis of a definite programme. In a mere two or three years, tremendous successes were achieved in the national revolution to which Dr. Sun Yat-sen had devoted forty years and which he had left unaccomplished; these successes were the establishment of the revolutionary base in Kwangtung and the victory of the Northern Expedition. They were the products of the formation of the united front of the two parties. But at the very moment when the revolution was nearing its triumph, some people who failed to uphold the revolutionary cause disrupted the two-party united front and so brought about the failure of the revolution, and the door was left open for foreign aggression. These were the products of the disruption of the united front of the two parties. Now the newly formed united front between the two parties has ushered in a new period in the Chinese revolution. There are still people who do not understand the historical role of the united front and its great future and regard it as a mere temporary makeshift devised under the pressure of circumstances; nevertheless, through this united front, the wheel of history will propel the Chinese revolution forward to a completely new stage. Whether China can extricate herself from the national and social crisis which is now so grave depends on how this united front will develop. There is already fresh evidence that the prospects are favourable. First, as soon as the policy of the united front was put forward by the Chinese Communist Party, it won the approval of the people everywhere. This is a clear expression of the will of the people. Second, immediately after the Sian Incident was settled peacefully and the two parties ended the civil war, all political parties and groups, people in all walks of life and all armed forces in the country achieved unprecedented unity. This unity, however, still falls far short of meeting the needs of resisting Japan, especially as the problem of unity between the government and the people remains basically unsolved. Third, and most striking of all, is the fact that the nation-wide War of Resistance has started. We are not satisfied with the War of Resistance in its present state because, though national in character, it is still confined to the government and the armed forces. As we pointed out earlier, Japanese imperialism cannot be defeated through a war of resistance of this kind. Nevertheless, for the first time in a hundred years, China is definitely putting up nation-wide resistance to a foreign invader, and this could never have come about without internal peace and without co-operation between the two parties. If the Japanese aggressors were able to take the four north-eastern provinces without firing a single shot during the time when the two-party united front was broken up, then today, when the united front has been re-established, they will not be able to occupy more Chinese territory without paying a price in bloody battles. Fourth, there is the effect abroad. The proposal for the anti-Japanese united front put forward by the Chinese Communist Party has won the support of the workers and peasants and the Communist Parties all over the world. With the establishment of co-operation between the Kuomintang and the Communist Party, the people of various countries, and particularly of the Soviet Union, will help China more actively. China and the Soviet Union have concluded a treaty of non-aggression[7] and the relations between the two countries can be expected to improve still further. From all this evidence we can state with certainty that the growth of the united front will carry China towards a bright and great future, namely, the defeat of Japanese imperialism and the establishment of a unified democratic republic.

However, the united front cannot accomplish this great task if it remains in its present state. The united front of the two parties must be developed further. For in its present state it is not yet broadly based or consolidated.

Should the Anti-Japanese National United Front be confined to the Kuomintang and the Communist Party? No, it should be a united front of the whole nation, with the two parties forming only a part of it. It should be a united front of all parties and groups, people in all walks of life and all armed forces, a united front of all patriots — the workers, peasants, soldiers, intellectuals and businessmen. So far, the united front has in fact been confined to the two parties, while the masses of the workers, peasants, soldiers and urban petty bourgeoisie and a large number of other patriots have not yet been aroused, called into action, organized or armed. This is the most serious problem at present. It is serious because it makes victories at the front impossible. It is no longer possible to conceal the critical situation at the front both in northern China and in Kiangsu and Chekiang Provinces, nor is there any need to do so; the question is how to save the situation. And the only way to save it is to put Dr. Sun Yat-sen's Testament into practice, to "arouse the masses of the people". In his deathbed Testament, Dr. Sun declared he was deeply convinced, from the experience accumulated over forty years, that only thus could the goal of revolution be achieved. What reason is there for obstinately refusing to put this testament into practice? What reason is there for failing to do so at a moment when the fate of the nation is at stake? Everybody knows that autocracy and suppression run counter to the principle of "arousing the masses of the people". Resistance by the government and the army alone can never defeat Japanese imperialism. Early in May this year we warned the ruling Kuomintang in all seriousness that unless the masses of the people were aroused to resist, China would follow the same path to disaster as Abyssinia. This point has been made not only by the Chinese Communists but by progressives throughout the country and by many intelligent members of the Kuomintang itself. Yet the policy of autocratic rule remains unchanged. As a result the government has estranged itself from the people, the army from the masses, and the military command from the rank and file. Unless the united front is reinforced by the participation of the masses, the crisis on the war fronts will inevitably be aggravated, not mitigated.

The present anti-Japanese united front still lacks a political programme to replace the Kuomintang's policy of autocratic rule, a programme accepted by both parties and formally promulgated. In relation to the masses the Kuomintang is continuing the same practices it has followed for the last ten years; there has been no change and on the whole everything has remained the same for the last ten years, from the government apparatus, the army system and the policy towards civilians to financial, economic and educational policies. Changes there are and very great ones too — cessation of civil war and unity against Japan. The two parties have ended the civil war and the nation-wide War of Resistance Against Japan has started, which mean a tremendous change in the Chinese political scene since the Sian Incident. But so far there has been no change in the practices enumerated above, and there is thus a disharmony between the things that have not changed and those that have. The old practices are suited only to compromise abroad and suppression of the revolution at home, and they prove ill-suited in every respect and reveal all their inadequacies when it comes to coping with the Japanese imperialist invasion. It would be another story if we did not want to resist Japan, but since we do and resistance has actually begun, and since a serious crisis has already revealed itself, refusal to change over to new ways will lead to the gravest dangers imaginable. Resistance to Japan requires a broadly based united front, and hence all the people should be mobilized to join it. Resistance to Japan requires a consolidated united front, and this calls for a common programme. The common programme will be the united front's guide to action and will serve also as the tie which, like a cord, closely binds together all the organizations and individuals in the united front, all political parties and groups, people in all walks of life and all armed forces. Only in this way will we be able to speak of firm unity. We are opposed to the old binding rules, because they are unsuited to the national revolutionary war. We look forward to the introduction of new binding rules to replace the old, that is, to the promulgation of a common programme and the establishment of revolutionary order. Nothing else will suit the War of Resistance.

What should the common programme be? It should be the Three People's Principles of Dr. Sun Yat-sen and the Ten-Point Programme for Resisting Japan and Saving the Nation[8] proposed by the Communist Party on August 25 this year.

In its declaration announcing Kuomintang-Communist co-operation, the Chinese Communist Party stated that "the Three People's Principles of Dr. Sun Yat-sen being what China needs today, our Party is ready to fight for their complete realization". Some people find it strange that the Communist Party should be ready to put the Three People's Principles of the Kuomintang into practice; Chu Ching-lai[9] of Shanghai, for instance, has expressed doubts in a local periodical. These people think that communism and the Three People's Principles are incompatible. This is a purely formal approach. Communism will be put into practice at a future stage of the development of the revolution; at the present stage the communists harbour no illusions about being able to realize it but will carry out the national and democratic revolution as required by history. This is the basic reason why the Communist Party has proposed an anti-Japanese national united front and a unified democratic republic. As for the Three People's Principles, at the Kuomintang's First National Congress the Communist Party and the Kuomintang jointly decided to put them into practice during the first two-party united front over ten years ago, and they were put into practice from 1924 to 1927 in large areas of the country through the efforts of all loyal Communists and all loyal members of the Kuomintang. Unfortunately that united front broke up in 1927, and in the subsequent ten years the Kuomintang opposed the application of the Three People's Principles. But as far as the Communist Party is concerned, all its policies in these ten years have been fundamentally in line with the revolutionary spirit of Dr. Sun's Three People's Principles and Three Great Policies. Not a day has passed without the Communist Party's conducting a struggle against imperialism, which means the thoroughgoing application of the Principle of Nationalism; the worker-peasant democratic dictatorship is nothing but the thoroughgoing application of the Principle of Democracy; the Agrarian Revolution is the thoroughgoing application of the Principle of People's Livelihood. Why, then, has the Communist Party announced the abolition of the worker-peasant democratic dictatorship and the discontinuance of confiscating the land of landlords? The reason, as we explained some time ago, is not that there is anything at all wrong with these things, but that the Japanese imperialist armed aggression has led to a change in class relations in the country, and has thereby not only made it necessary to unite all classes of the nation against Japanese imperialism, but also created the possibility of doing so. An anti-fascist united front for the sake of the common struggle against fascism is both necessary and possible not only in China but throughout the world. Therefore we stand for the establishment of a national and democratic united front in China. It is on these grounds that we have proposed a democratic republic based on the alliance of all classes in place of a worker-peasant democratic dictatorship. The Agrarian Revolution put into effect the principle of "land to the tiller", which is precisely what Dr. Sun Yat-sen proposed. We have now discontinued it for the sake of uniting greater numbers of people against Japanese imperialism, but that does not mean China does not need to solve her land problem. We have unequivocally explained our position on the causes of these changes in policy and their timing. It is precisely because the Chinese Communist Party, basing itself on Marxist principles, has constantly adhered to and developed the revolutionary Three People's Principles — the common programme of the first Kuomintang-Communist united front — that, in this hour of national crisis when our country is invaded by a powerful aggressor, the Party has been able to put forward the timely proposal for a national and democratic united front, which is the only policy capable of saving the nation, and to apply this policy with unremitting effort. The question now is not whether it is the Communist Party which believes in or carries out the revolutionary Three People's Principles, but whether it is the Kuomintang which does so. The present task is to restore the revolutionary spirit of Dr. Sun's Three People's Principles throughout the country, and on this basis to work out a definite programme and policy and put them into practice sincerely and not half-heartedly, conscientiously and not perfunctorily, promptly and not tardily; the Chinese Communist Party has been earnestly praying day and night for this to happen. For this very reason, it put forward the Ten-Point Programme for Resisting Japan and Saving the Nation after the Lukouchiao Incident. The Ten-Point Programme is in line both with Marxism and with the genuine revolutionary Three People's Principles. It is an initial programme, the programme for the Chinese revolution at the present stage, which is the stage of the anti-Japanese national revolutionary war; China can be saved only if this programme is put into effect. History will punish those who persist in any course conflicting with this programme.

It is impossible to put this programme into practice throughout the country without the consent of the Kuomintang, because the Kuomintang today is still the biggest party in China and the party in power. We believe that the day will come when intelligent members of the Kuomintang will agree to this programme. For if they do not, the Three People's Principles will for ever remain an empty phrase, and it will be impossible to restore the revolutionary spirit of Dr. Sun Yat-sen, impossible to defeat Japanese imperialism and impossible for the Chinese people to escape becoming the slaves of a foreign power. No really intelligent member of the Kuomintang can possibly want this to happen, and our people will never allow themselves to be turned into slaves. Moreover, in his statement of September 23 Mr. Chiang Kai-shek declared:

> I hold that we who stand for the revolution should put aside personal grudges and prejudices and devote ourselves to the realization of the Three People's Principles. At this critical juncture of life and death, we should all the more let bygones be bygones and together with the whole nation make a completely fresh start, and work strenuously for unity in order to preserve the very life and existence of our country.

This is most true. The urgent task at present is to strive for the realization of the Three People's Principles, to discard personal and factional prejudices, to change the old set of practices, to carry out a revolutionary programme in line with the Three People's Principles immediately and to make a completely fresh start together with the whole nation. Today this is the only course. With further delay it will be too late to repent.

But there must be instruments for carrying out the Three People's Principles and the Ten-Point Programme, and this raises the question of reforming the government and the army. The present government is still a one-party dictatorship of the Kuomintang and not a government of the national democratic united front. In the absence of a government of the national democratic united front, it is impossible to carry out the Three People's Principles and the Ten-Point Programme. The present army system of the Kuomintang is still the old one, and it is impossible to defeat Japanese imperialism with troops organized under this system. The troops are now engaged in resistance and we have great admiration and respect for them all, and especially for those fighting at the front. But the lessons of the War of Resistance in the last three months demonstrate that the Kuomintang army system must be changed, as it is unsuited to the task of completely defeating the Japanese aggressors and to the successful application

of the Three People's Principles and the revolutionary programme.
The change should be based on the principles of unity between officers
and men and unity between the army and the people. The present
army system of the Kuomintang is fundamentally opposed to both
these principles. It prevents the mass of officers and men from giving
their best despite their loyalty and courage, and therefore an immediate
start must be made to reform it. This does not mean that the fighting
has to stop until the system is reformed; it can be reformed while the
fighting is going on. Here the central task is to bring about a change
in the army's political spirit and its political work. The National
Revolutionary Army during the Northern Expedition provides an
admirable precedent, for in general it did establish unity between
officers and men and between the army and the people; a revival of
the spirit of those days is absolutely necessary. China should learn
from the war in Spain where the Republican army has been built up
under extremely adverse circumstances. China is in a better position
than Spain, but she lacks a broadly based and consolidated united
front, she lacks a united front government capable of carrying out
the whole revolutionary programme and large numbers of troops
organized according to a new system. She must remedy these defects.
With regard to the war as a whole, the Red Army led by the Chinese
Communist Party can at present only play a vanguard role, it cannot
yet play a decisive role on a national scale. Nevertheless its political,
military and organizational merits are well worth acquiring by friendly
armies throughout the country. At its inception the Red Army was
not what it is today; it, too, has undergone many reforms, the main
ones being the weeding out of feudal practices within the army and
the application of the principles of unity between officers and men
and unity between the army and the people. Friendly armies throughout the country can draw on this experience.

   Anti-Japanese comrades of the ruling Kuomintang party! Today
we share with you the responsibility for saving the nation from
extinction and ensuring its survival. You have already formed an
anti-Japanese united front with us. That is very good. You have started
resisting Japan. That is also very good. But we do not approve of
your continuing your other policies in the old way. We should all
develop and broaden the united front and draw in the masses of the
people. It is necessary to consolidate the united front and pursue a
common programme. It is essential resolutely to reform the political
and army systems. It is absolutely necessary to have a new govern-

ment, which alone can carry out the revolutionary programme and start to reform the armies on a national scale. This proposal of ours answers the needs of the times. Many people in your party also feel that now is the time to put it into practice. Dr. Sun Yat-sen, in his day, made up his mind and reformed the political and army systems, thereby laying the foundation for the revolution of 1924-27. The responsibility for effecting the same kind of reform now falls on your shoulders. We believe that no loyal and patriotic member of the Kuomintang will consider that our proposal is ill-suited to the needs of the situation. We are firmly convinced that it meets the objective needs.

The fate of our nation is at stake — let the Kuomintang and the Communist Party unite closely! Let all our fellow-countrymen who refuse to become slaves unite closely on the basis of Kuomintang-Communist unity! The urgent task in the Chinese revolution today is to make all the reforms necessary to overcome all difficulties. When this task is accomplished, we can surely defeat Japanese imperialism. If we try hard, our future will be bright.

NOTES

[1] See "The Tasks of the Chinese Communist Party in the Period of Resistance to Japan", Note 2, *Selected Works of Mao Tse-tung*, Eng. ed., FLP, Peking, 1965, Vol. I, pp. 276-77.

[2] For the resolution see *ibid.*, Note 3, pp. 277-78.

[3] For the open telegram see *ibid.*, Note 4, pp. 279-80.

[4] For the contents of the letter see "A Statement on Chiang Kai-shek's Statement", Note 7, *ibid.*, pp. 259-61.

[5] For the resolution see "The Tasks of the Chinese Communist Party in the Period of Resistance to Japan", Note 6, *ibid.*, pp. 280-81.

[6] For the telegram see *ibid.*, Note 7, pp. 281-82.

[7] The Treaty of Non-Aggression Between the Republic of China and the Union of Soviet Socialist Republics was concluded on August 21, 1937.

[8] For the Ten-Point Programme see "For the Mobilization of All the Nation's Forces for Victory in the War of Resistance", pp. 25-28 of this volume.

[9] Chu Ching-lai was a leader of the National Socialist Party (a small clique organized by reactionary landlords, bureaucrats and big bourgeoisie) who later became a member of the traitorous Wang Ching-wei government.

INTERVIEW WITH THE BRITISH JOURNALIST
JAMES BERTRAM

October 25, 1937

THE COMMUNIST PARTY OF CHINA AND
THE WAR OF RESISTANCE

James Bertram: What specific pronouncements has the Chinese Communist Party made before and since the outbreak of the Sino-Japanese war?

Mao Tse-tung: Before the war broke out, the Chinese Communist Party warned the whole nation time and again that war with Japan was inevitable, and that all the Japanese imperialists' talk of a "peaceful settlement" and all the fine phrases of the Japanese diplomats were only so much camouflage to screen their preparations for war. We repeatedly stressed that a victorious war of national liberation cannot be waged unless the united front is strengthened and a revolutionary policy is adopted. The most important point in this revolutionary policy is that the Chinese government must institute democratic reforms in order to mobilize all the people to join the anti-Japanese front. We repeatedly pointed out the error of those who believed in Japan's "peace pledge" and thought that war might be avoided, or of those who believed in the possibility of resisting the Japanese aggressors without mobilizing the masses. Both the outbreak of the war and its course have proved our views to be correct. The day after the Lukouchiao Incident, the Communist Party issued a manifesto to the whole country, calling upon all political parties and groups and all social strata to make common cause in resisting Japanese aggression and strengthening the national united front. Soon afterwards we announced the Ten-Point Programme for Resisting Japan and Saving the Nation, in which we set out the policies that the Chinese

47

government ought to adopt in the War of Resistance. With the institution of Kuomintang-Communist co-operation we issued another important declaration. All this testifies to our firm adherence to the principle of waging the War of Resistance by strengthening the united front and putting a revolutionary policy into effect. In the present period our basic slogan is "Total resistance by the whole nation".

THE WAR SITUATION AND ITS LESSONS

Question: As you see it, what are the results of the war up to the present?

Answer: There are two main aspects. On the one hand, by capturing our cities, seizing our territory, raping, plundering, burning and massacring, the Japanese imperialists have irrevocably brought the Chinese people face to face with the danger of national subjugation. On the other hand, the majority of the Chinese people have consequently become very much aware that the crisis cannot be overcome without greater unity and without resistance by the whole nation. At the same time, the peace-loving countries of the world are being awakened to the necessity of resisting the Japanese menace. These are the results produced by the war so far.

Question: What do you think are Japan's objectives, and how far have they been achieved?

Answer: Japan's plan is to occupy northern China and Shanghai as the first step and then to occupy other regions of China. As to how far the Japanese aggressors have realized their plan, they seized the three provinces of Hopei, Chahar and Suiyuan within a short space of time, and now they are threatening Shansi; the reason is that China's War of Resistance has hitherto been confined to resistance by the government and the army alone. This crisis can be overcome only if resistance is carried out jointly by the people and the government.

Question: In your opinion, has China scored any achievements in the War of Resistance? If there are any lessons to be drawn, what are they?

Answer: I would like to discuss this question with you in some detail. First of all, there have been achievements, and great achievements too. They are to be seen in the following: (1) Never since imperialist aggression began against China has there been anything comparable to the present War of Resistance Against Japan. Geographically, it is truly a war involving the whole country. This war is revolutionary in character. (2) The war has changed a disunited country into a relatively united one. The basis of this unity is Kuomintang-Communist co-operation. (3) The war has the sympathy of world public opinion. Those who once despised China for her nonresistance now respect her for her resistance. (4) The war has inflicted heavy losses on the Japanese aggressors. The daily drain on their resources is reported to be twenty million yen and their casualties are also undoubtedly very heavy, though figures are not yet available. While the Japanese aggressors took the four northeastern provinces with ease and with hardly any exertion, now they cannot occupy Chinese territory without fighting bloody battles. The aggressors expected to be able to gorge themselves in China, but China's protracted resistance will bring about the collapse of Japanese imperialism. Thus China is fighting not only to save herself but also to discharge her great duty in the world anti-fascist front. Here also the revolutionary character of the War of Resistance is manifest. (5) We have learned some lessons from the war. They have been paid for in territory and blood.

As for the lessons, they are likewise great ones. Several months of fighting have disclosed many of China's weaknesses. They are manifest above all in the political sphere. Although geographically the war involves the whole country, it is not being waged by the whole nation. As in the past, the broad masses are restrained by the government from taking part, and so the war is not yet of a mass character. Unless it has a mass character, the war against Japanese imperialist aggression cannot possibly succeed. Some say, "The war is already an all-embracing war." But this is true only in the sense that vast parts of the country are involved. As regards participation, it is still a partial war because it is being waged only by the government and the army, and not by the people. It is precisely here that the chief reason for the great loss of territory and for the many military setbacks during the last few months is to be found. Therefore, although the present armed resistance is a revolutionary one, its revolutionary character is incomplete because it is not yet a mass war. Here, too, the problem of unity is involved. Although the political parties and groups are relatively united as compared with the past, unity still falls far short of what is needed. Most of the political prisoners have not yet been released, and the ban on political parties has not been completely lifted.

Relations are still very bad between the government and the people, between the army and the people, and between officers and men, and here one observes estrangement instead of unity. This is a fundamental problem. Unless it is solved, victory is out of the question. In addition, military blunders are another major reason for our losses in men and territory. The battles fought have been mostly passive, or to put it in military terms, have been battles of "pure defence". We can never win by fighting this way. For the attainment of victory, policies radically different from the present ones are necessary in both the political and the military fields. These are the lessons we have learned.

Question: What, then, are the political and military prerequisites?

Answer: On the political side, first, the present government must be transformed into a united front government in which the representatives of the people play their part. This government must be at once democratic and centralized. It should carry out the necessary revolutionary policies. Secondly, the people must be granted freedom of speech, freedom of the press, and freedom of assembly and association and the right to take up arms against the enemy, so that the war will acquire a mass character. Thirdly, the people's livelihood must be improved through such measures as the abolition of exorbitant taxes and miscellaneous levies, the reduction of rent and interest, better conditions for workers, junior officers and soldiers, preferential treatment for the families of the soldiers fighting the Japanese, and relief for victims of natural calamities and war refugees. Government finance should be based on the principle of equitable distribution of the economic burden, which means that those who have money should contribute money. Fourthly, there should be a positive foreign policy. Fifthly, cultural and educational policy should be changed. Sixthly, traitors must be sternly suppressed. The problem has become extremely serious. The traitors are running wild. At the front they are helping the enemy; in the rear they are creating disturbances, and some of them even put on an anti-Japanese pose and denounce patriotic people as traitors and have them arrested. Effective suppression of the traitors will be possible only when the people are free to co-operate with the government. On the military side, comprehensive reforms are required, the most important of these being to change from pure defence in strategy and tactics to the principle of active attack; to change the armies of the old type into armies of a new type; to change the method of forcible recruitment into one of arousing the people to go to the front; to change the divided command into a unified command; to change the indiscipline which alienates the army from the people into conscious discipline which forbids the slightest violation of the people's interests; to change the present situation in which the regular army is fighting alone into one in which extensive guerrilla warfare by the people is developed in co-ordination with regular army operations; and so on and so forth. All these political and military prerequisites are listed in our published Ten-Point Programme. They all conform to the spirit of Dr. Sun Yat-sen's Three People's Principles, his Three Great Policies and his Testament. The war can be won only when they are carried into effect.

Question: What is the Communist Party doing to carry out this programme?

Answer: We take it as our task tirelessly to explain the situation and to unite with the Kuomintang and all other patriotic parties and groups in the effort to expand and consolidate the Anti-Japanese National United Front, mobilize all forces and achieve victory in the War of Resistance. The Anti-Japanese National United Front is still very limited in scope and it is necessary to broaden it, that is, to "arouse the masses of the people", as called for in Dr. Sun Yat-sen's Testament, by mobilizing the people at the grass roots to join the united front. Consolidation of the united front means carrying out a common programme which will be binding on all political parties and groups in their actions. We agree to accept Dr. Sun's revolutionary Three People's Principles, Three Great Policies and Testament as the common programme of the united front of all political parties and all social classes. But so far this programme has not been accepted by all the parties, and above all the Kuomintang has not agreed to the proclamation of such an over-all programme. Dr. Sun Yat-sen's Principle of Nationalism has been partially put into practice by the Kuomintang, as shown in its resistance to Japan. But neither his Principle of Democracy nor his Principle of People's Livelihood has been applied, and the present serious crisis in the War of Resistance is the result. The war situation having become so critical, it is high time that the Kuomintang applied the Three People's Principles in full, or otherwise it will be too late to repent. It is the duty of the Communist Party to raise its voice and tirelessly and persuasively explain all this to the Kuomintang and the whole nation so that the genuinely revolutionary Three People's Principles, the Three Great Policies and Dr. Sun Yat-sen's Testament are fully and thoroughly applied throughout the country, and the Anti-Japanese National United Front is broadened and consolidated.

THE EIGHTH ROUTE ARMY IN THE WAR
OF RESISTANCE

Question: Please tell me about the Eighth Route Army in which so many people are interested — for instance, about its strategy and tactics, its political work, and so on.

Answer: Indeed a large number of people have become interested in its activities since the Red Army was redesignated as the Eighth Route Army and went to the front. I shall now give you a general account.

First about its field operations. Strategically, the Eighth Route Army is centring them on Shansi. As you know, it has won many victories. Examples are the battle of Pinghsingkuan, the recapture of Chingping, Pinglu and Ningwu, the recovery of Laiyuan and Kuangling, the capture of Tzechingkuan, the cutting of the three main supply routes of the Japanese troops (between Tatung and Yenmenkuan, between Weihsien and Pinghsingkuan, and between Shuohsien and Ningwu), the assault on the rear of the Japanese forces south of Yenmenkuan, the recapture twice over of Pinghsingkuan and Yenmenkuan, and the recent recovery of Chuyang and Tanghsien. The Japanese troops in Shansi are being strategically encircled by the Eighth Route Army and other Chinese troops. We may say with certainty that the Japanese troops will meet with the most stubborn resistance in northern China. If they try to ride roughshod over Shansi, they will certainly encounter greater difficulties than ever.

Next about strategy and tactics. We are doing what the other Chinese troops have not done, *i.e.*, operating chiefly on the enemy's flanks and rear. This way of fighting is vastly different from purely frontal defence. We are not against employing part of the forces in frontal operations, for that is necessary. But the main forces must be used against the enemy's flanks and it is essential to adopt encircling and outflanking tactics in order to attack the enemy independently and with the initiative in our hands, for that is the only way to destroy his forces and preserve our own. Furthermore, the use of some of our armed forces against the enemy's rear is particularly effective, because they can disrupt his supply lines and bases. Even the frontal forces should rely mainly on "counter assault" and not on purely defensive tactics. One important reason for the military setbacks in the last few months has been the use of unsuitable methods of fighting. The methods of fighting employed by the Eighth Route Army are what we call guerrilla and mobile warfare applied independently and with the initiative in our hands. In principle these methods are basically the same as those we used during the civil war, but there are certain differences. For example, at the present stage, in order to facilitate our surprise attacks on the enemy's flanks and rear over an extensive area, we divide our forces more often than we concentrate them. Since the armed forces of the country as a whole are numerically strong, some of them should be used for frontal defence and some dispersed to carry on guerrilla operations, but the main forces should always be concentrated against the enemy's flanks. The first essential in war is to preserve oneself and to destroy the enemy, and for this purpose it is necessary to wage guerrilla and mobile warfare independently and with the initiative in our hands and to avoid all passive and inflexible tactics. If a vast number of troops wage mobile warfare with the Eighth Route Army assisting them by guerrilla warfare, our victory will be certain.

Next about political work. Another highly significant and distinctive feature of the Eighth Route Army is its political work, which is guided by three basic principles. First, the principle of unity between officers and men, which means eradicating feudal practices in the army, prohibiting beating and abuse, building up a conscious discipline, and sharing weal and woe — as a result of which the entire army is closely united. Second, the principle of unity between the army and the people, which means maintaining a discipline that forbids the slightest violation of the people's interests, conducting propaganda among the masses, organizing and arming them, lightening their financial burdens and suppressing the traitors and collaborators who do harm to the army and the people — as a result of which the army is closely united with the people and welcomed everywhere. Third, the principle of disintegrating the enemy troops and giving lenient treatment to prisoners of war. Our victory depends not only upon our military operations but also upon the disintegration of the enemy troops. Although our measures for disintegrating the enemy troops and for treating prisoners of war leniently have not yielded conspicuous results as yet, they will certainly do so in the future. Moreover, in line with the second of the three principles, the Eighth Route Army replenishes its forces not by coercion but by the much more effective method of arousing the people to volunteer for the front.

Although Hopei, Chahar and Suiyuan and part of Shansi have been lost, we are not at all discouraged but are resolutely calling upon the entire army to co-ordinate with the friendly armies and fight with grim determination to defend Shansi and recover the lost territories. The Eighth Route Army will co-ordinate its actions with those of other Chinese troops in order to maintain the resistance in Shansi; this will be very important for the war as a whole, and especially for the war in northern China.

Question: In your opinion, can these good points of the Eighth Route Army also be acquired by the other Chinese armies?

Answer: Certainly they can. In 1924-27 the spirit of the Kuomintang troops was broadly similar to that of the Eighth Route Army today. The Communist Party and the Kuomintang were then co-operating in organizing armed forces of a new type which, beginning with only two regiments, rallied round themselves many other troops and won their first victory when they defeated Chen Chiung-ming. These forces later grew into an army corps and still more troops came under its influence; only then did the Northern Expedition take place. A fresh spirit prevailed among these forces; on the whole there was unity between officers and men and between the army and the people, and the army was filled with a revolutionary militancy. The system of Party representatives and of political departments, adopted for the first time in China, entirely changed the complexion of these armed forces. The Red Army, which was founded in 1927, and the Eighth Route Army of today have inherited this system and developed it. In the revolutionary period of 1924-27, the armed forces which were imbued with this new spirit naturally employed methods of fighting consistent with their political outlook, operating not in a passive and inflexible way but with initiative and with an eagerness to take the offensive, and consequently they were victorious in the Northern Expedition. It is troops of this kind we need on the battle-fields today. We do not necessarily need them in millions; with a nucleus of a few hundred thousand such men, we can defeat Japanese imperialism. We deeply esteem the armies throughout the country for their heroic sacrifices since the War of Resistance began, but there are lessons to be learned from the bloody battles that have been fought.

Question: Japanese army discipline being what it is, will not your policy of giving lenient treatment to prisoners of war prove ineffective?

For instance, the Japanese command may kill the prisoners when you release them and the Japanese army as a whole will not understand the meaning of your policy.

Answer: That is impossible. The more they kill, the more sympathy will be aroused for the Chinese forces among the Japanese soldiers. Such facts cannot be concealed from the rank and file. We will persevere in this policy of ours. For instance, we shall not change it even if the Japanese army carries out its declared intention of using poison-gas against the Eighth Route Army. We shall go on giving lenient treatment to captured Japanese soldiers and to those captured junior officers who have fought us under coercion; we shall not insult or abuse them, but shall set them free after explaining to them the identity of the interests of the people of the two countries. Those who do not want to go back may serve in the Eighth Route Army. If an international brigade appears on the anti-Japanese battle front, they may join it and take up arms against Japanese imperialism.

CAPITULATIONISM IN THE WAR OF RESISTANCE

Question: I understand that while carrying on the war, Japan is spreading peace rumours in Shanghai. What are her real objectives?

Answer: After succeeding in certain of their plans, the Japanese imperialists will once again put up a smokescreen of peace in order to attain three objectives. They are: (1) to consolidate the positions already captured for use as a strategic springboard for further offensives; (2) to split China's anti-Japanese front; and (3) to break up the international front of support for China. The present peace rumours are simply the first smoke-bomb. The danger is that there are certain vacillating elements in China who are ready to succumb to the enemy's wiles and that the traitors and collaborators are manoeuvring among them and spreading all kinds of rumours in their efforts to make China capitulate to the Japanese aggressors.

Question: As you see it, what could this danger lead to?

Answer: There can be only two courses of development: either the Chinese people will overcome capitulationism, or capitulationism will prevail, with the result that the anti-Japanese front will be split and China will be plunged into disorder.

Question: Which of the two is the more likely?

Answer: The whole Chinese people demand that the war be fought to a finish. If a section of the ruling group takes the road of capitulation, the rest who remain firm will certainly oppose it and carry on resistance together with the people. Of course it would be a misfortune for China's anti-Japanese front. But I am sure that the capitulationists cannot win mass support and that the masses will overcome capitulationism, persevere in the war and achieve victory.

Question: May I ask how capitulationism can be overcome?

Answer: Both by words, that is, by exposing the danger of capitulationism, and by deeds, that is, by organizing the masses to stop the capitulationist activities. Capitulationism has its roots in national defeatism or national pessimism, that is, in the idea that having lost some battles, China has no strength left to fight Japan. These pessimists do not realize that failure is the mother of success, that the lessons learned from failures are the basis for future triumphs. They see the defeats but not the successes in the War of Resistance, and in particular they fail to see that our defeats contain the elements of victory, while the enemy's victories contain the elements of defeat. We must show the masses of the people the victorious prospects of the war and help them to understand that our defeats and difficulties are temporary and that, as long as we keep on fighting in spite of all setbacks, the final victory will be ours. Deprived of a mass base, the capitulationists will have no chance to play their tricks, and the anti-Japanese front will be consolidated.

DEMOCRACY AND THE WAR OF RESISTANCE

Question: What is the meaning of "democracy" as put forward by the Communist Party in its programme? Does it not conflict with a "wartime government"?

Answer: Not at all. The Communist Party put forward the slogan of a "democratic republic" as early as August 1936. Politically and organizationally this slogan signifies: (1) The state and government must not belong to a single class but must be based on the alliance of all the anti-Japanese classes to the exclusion of traitors and collaborators, and must include the workers, the peasants and other sections of the petty bourgeoisie. (2) The organizational form of such a government will be democratic centralism, which is at once democratic and centralized, with the two seeming opposites of democracy and centralization united in a definite form. (3) This government will grant the people all the necessary political freedoms, especially the freedom to organize and train and arm themselves for self-defence. In these three respects, it can be seen that a democratic republic in no way conflicts with a wartime government, but is precisely the form of state and government advantageous to the War of Resistance.

Question: Is not "democratic centralism" a self-contradictory term?

Answer: We must look not only at the term but at the reality. There is no impassable gulf between democracy and centralism, both of which are essential for China. On the one hand, the government we want must be truly representative of the popular will; it must have the support of the broad masses throughout the country and the people must be free to support it and have every opportunity of influencing its policies. This is the meaning of democracy. On the other hand, the centralization of administrative power is also necessary, and once the policy measures demanded by the people are transmitted to their own elected government through their representative body, the government will carry them out and will certainly be able to do so smoothly, so long as it does not go against the policy adopted in accordance with the people's will. This is the meaning of centralism. Only by adopting democratic centralism can a government be really strong, and this system must be adopted by China's government of national defence in the anti-Japanese war.

Question: This does not correspond to a war cabinet, does it?

Answer: It does not correspond to some of the war cabinets of the past.

Question: Have there ever been any war cabinets of this kind?

Answer: Yes. Systems of government in wartime may generally be divided into two kinds, as determined by the nature of the war — one kind is democratic centralism and the other absolute centralism. All wars in history may be divided into two kinds according to their nature: just wars and unjust wars. For instance, the Great War in Europe some twenty years ago was an unjust, imperialist war. The governments of the imperialist countries forced the people to fight for the interests of imperialism and thus went against the people's interests, these circumstances necessitating a type of government such as the Lloyd George government in Britain. Lloyd George repressed the British people, forbidding them to speak against the imperialist war and banning organizations or assemblies that expressed popular opinion against the war; even though Parliament remained, it was merely the organ of a group of imperialists, a parliament which rubber-stamped the war budget. The absence of unity between the government and the people in a war gives rise to a government of absolute centralism with all centralism and no democracy. But historically there have also been revolutionary wars, *e.g.*, in France, Russia, and present-day Spain. In such wars the government does not fear popular disapproval, because the people are most willing to wage this kind of war; far from fearing the people, it endeavours to arouse them and encourages them to express their views so that they will actively participate in the war, because the government rests upon the people's voluntary support. China's war of national liberation has the full approval of the people and cannot be won without their participation; therefore democratic centralism becomes a necessity. In the Northern Expedition of 1926-27, too, the victories were achieved through democratic centralism. Thus it can be seen that when the aims of a war directly reflect the interests of the people, the more democratic the government, the more effectively can the war be prosecuted. Such a government need have no fear that the people will oppose the war; rather it should be worried lest the people remain inactive or indifferent to the war. The nature of a war determines the relationship between the government and the people — this is a law of history.

Question: Then what steps are you prepared to take for this system of government to be instituted?

Answer: The key question is co-operation between the Kuomintang and the Communist Party.

Question: Why?

Answer: For the last fifteen years, the relationship between the Kuomintang and the Communist Party has been the decisive political factor in China. The co-operation of the two parties in 1924-27 resulted in the victories of the first revolution. The split between the two parties in 1927 resulted in the unfortunate situation of the last decade. However, the responsibility for the split was not ours; we were compelled to resist the Kuomintang's oppression, and we persisted in holding high the glorious banner of China's liberation. Now the third stage has come, and the two parties must co-operate fully on a definite programme in order to resist Japan and save the nation. Through our ceaseless efforts, the establishment of co-operation has at last been announced, but the point is that both sides must accept a common programme and act upon it. An essential part of such a programme is the setting up of a new system of government.

Question: How can the new system be set up through the co-operation of the two parties?

Answer: We are proposing a reconstruction of the government apparatus and the army system. We propose that a provisional national assembly be convened to meet the present emergency. Delegates to this assembly should be chosen in due proportion from the various anti-Japanese political parties, anti-Japanese armies and anti-Japanese popular and business organizations, as Dr. Sun Yat-sen suggested in 1924. This assembly should function as the supreme organ of state authority to decide on the policies for saving the nation, adopt a constitutional programme and elect the government. We hold that the War of Resistance has reached a critical turning point and that only the immediate convening of such a national assembly vested with authority and representative of the popular will can regenerate China's political life and overcome the present crisis. We are exchanging views with the Kuomintang about this proposal and hope to obtain its agreement.

Question: Has not the National Government announced that the national assembly has been called off?

Answer: It was right to call it off. What has been called off is the national assembly which the Kuomintang was preparing to convene; according to the Kuomintang's stipulations it would not have had the slightest power, and the procedure for its election was entirely in conflict with the popular will. Together with the people of all sections of society, we disapproved of that kind of national assembly. The provisional national assembly we are proposing is radically different from the one that has been called off. The convening of this provisional national assembly will undoubtedly impart a new spirit to the whole country and provide the essential prerequisite for reconstructing the government apparatus and the army and for mobilizing the entire people. On this hinges the favourable turn in the War of Resistance.

THE SITUATION AND TASKS
IN THE ANTI-JAPANESE WAR
AFTER THE FALL OF
SHANGHAI AND TAIYUAN

November 12, 1937

I. THE PRESENT SITUATION IS ONE OF
TRANSITION FROM
A WAR OF PARTIAL RESISTANCE
TO A WAR OF TOTAL RESISTANCE

1. We support any kind of war of resistance, even though partial, against the invasion of Japanese imperialism. For partial resistance is a step forward from non-resistance, and to a certain extent it is revolutionary in character and is a war in defence of the motherland.

2. However, a war of partial resistance by the government alone without the mass participation of the people will certainly fail, as we have already pointed out (at the meeting of Party activists in Yenan in April of this year, at the Party's National Conference in May, and in the resolution[1] of the Political Bureau of the Central Committee in August). For it is not a national revolutionary war in the full sense, not a people's war.

3. We stand for a national revolutionary war in the full sense, a war in which the entire people are mobilized, in other words, total resistance. For only such resistance constitutes a people's war and can achieve the goal of defending the motherland.

This was the outline for a report made by Comrade Mao Tse-tung in Yenan in November 1937 at a meeting of Party activists. It met with immediate opposition from the Right opportunists in the Party, and not until the Sixth Plenary Session of the Sixth Central Committee in October 1938 was the Right deviation basically overcome.

4. Although the war of partial resistance advocated by the Kuomintang also constitutes a national war and is revolutionary in character to a certain extent, its revolutionary character is far from complete. Partial resistance is bound to lead to defeat in the war; it can never successfully defend the motherland.

5. Herein lies the difference in principle between the stand of the Communist Party and the present stand of the Kuomintang with regard to resistance. If Communists forget this difference in principle, they will be unable to guide the War of Resistance correctly, they will be powerless to overcome the Kuomintang's one-sidedness, and they will debase themselves to the point of abandoning their principles and reduce their Party to the level of the Kuomintang. That would be a crime against the sacred cause of the national revolutionary war and the defence of the motherland.

6. In a national revolutionary war in the full sense, in a war of total resistance, it is essential to put into effect the Ten-Point Programme for Resisting Japan and Saving the Nation proposed by the Communist Party, and it is essential to have a government and an army that will enforce this programme in its entirety.

7. The situation after the fall of Shanghai and Taiyuan is as follows:

(1) In northern China, regular warfare in which the Kuomintang played the chief role has ended, and guerrilla warfare in which the Communist Party is playing the chief role has become primary. In Kiangsu and Chekiang Provinces, the Japanese aggressors have broken through the Kuomintang's battle lines and are advancing on Nanking and the Yangtse valley. It is already clear that the Kuomintang's partial resistance cannot last long.

(2) In their own imperialist interests, the governments of Britain, the United States and France have indicated that they will help China, but so far there has been only verbal sympathy and no practical aid whatsoever.

(3) The German and Italian fascists are doing everything to assist Japanese imperialism.

(4) The Kuomintang is still unwilling to make any fundamental change in its one-party dictatorship and autocratic rule over the people, through which it is carrying on partial resistance.

This is one side of the picture.

The other side is seen in the following:

(1) The political influence of the Communist Party and the Eighth Route Army is spreading fast and far, and they are being acclaimed throughout the country as "the saviours of the nation". The Communist Party and the Eighth Route Army are determined to keep up the guerrilla warfare in northern China, so as to defend the whole country, tie down the Japanese aggressors and hinder them from attacking the Central Plains and the Northwest.

(2) The mass movement has developed a step further.

(3) The national bourgeoisie is leaning towards the left.

(4) Forces favouring reforms are growing within the Kuomintang.

(5) The movement to oppose Japan and aid China is spreading among the people of the world.

(6) The Soviet Union is preparing to give practical assistance to China.

This is the other side of the picture.

8. Therefore, the present situation is one of transition from partial to total resistance. While partial resistance cannot last long, total resistance has not yet begun. The transition from one to the other, the gap in time, is fraught with danger.

9. In this period, China's partial resistance may develop in one of three directions:

The first is the ending of partial resistance and its replacement by total resistance. This is what the majority of the nation demands, but the Kuomintang is still undecided.

The second is the ending of armed resistance and its replacement by capitulation. This is what the Japanese aggressors, the collaborators and the pro-Japanese elements demand, but the majority of the Chinese people oppose it.

The third is the coexistence of armed resistance and capitulation in China. This could come about as a result of the intrigues of the Japanese aggressors, the collaborators and the pro-Japanese elements to split China's anti-Japanese front when they find it impossible to attain the second direction. They are now engineering something of this kind. Indeed this danger is very grave.

10. Judging from the present situation, the domestic and international factors which prevent capitulationism from winning out have the upper hand. These factors include: Japan's persistence in its policy of subjugating China, which leaves China no alternative but to fight;

the existence of the Communist Party and the Eighth Route Army; the wishes of the Chinese people; the wishes of the majority of the Kuomintang members; the anxiety of Britain, the United States and France lest capitulation by the Kuomintang damage their interests; the existence of the Soviet Union and its policy of helping China; the high hopes which the Chinese people place (not without foundation) in the Soviet Union. The proper and co-ordinated use of these factors would not only frustrate capitulationism and splitting but also overcome the obstructions to any advance beyond partial resistance.

11. Therefore, the prospect of going over from partial to total resistance does exist. To strive for this prospect is the urgent common task of all Chinese Communists, all progressive members of the Kuomintang, and all the Chinese people.

12. China's anti-Japanese national revolutionary war is now confronting a grave crisis. This crisis may be prolonged, or it may be overcome fairly quickly. Internally, the decisive factors are Kuomintang-Communist co-operation and a change in Kuomintang policy on the basis of this co-operation, and the strength of the worker and peasant masses. Externally, the decisive factor is assistance from the Soviet Union.

13. Political and organizational reform of the Kuomintang is both necessary and possible.[2] The main reasons are Japanese pressure, the Chinese Communist Party's united front policy, the wishes of the Chinese people, and the growth of new forces inside the Kuomintang. Our task is to work for this reform of the Kuomintang as a basis for reforming the government and the army. This reform undoubtedly requires the consent of the Central Executive Committee of the Kuomintang, and we are only in a position to offer suggestions.

14. The government should be reformed. We have proposed the convening of a provisional national assembly, which is likewise both necessary and possible. Undoubtedly this reform also requires the consent of the Kuomintang.

15. The task of reforming the army consists in building up new armies and reforming the old armies. If a new army of 250,000 to 300,000 men imbued with a new political spirit can be built up within six to twelve months, the situation on the anti-Japanese battlefield will begin to mend. Such an army would influence all the old armies and rally them around itself. This would provide the military basis for the turn to the strategic counter-offensive in the War of Resistance. This reform likewise requires the Kuomintang's consent. The Eighth

Route Army ought to have an exemplary role to play in the course of this reform. And the Eighth Route Army itself should be expanded.

II. CAPITULATIONISM MUST BE COMBATED BOTH INSIDE THE PARTY AND THROUGHOUT THE COUNTRY

INSIDE THE PARTY, OPPOSE CLASS CAPITULATIONISM

16. In 1927 Chen Tu-hsiu's capitulationism led to the failure of the revolution. No member of our Party should ever forget this historical lesson written in blood.

17. With regard to the Party's line of an anti-Japanese national united front, the main danger inside the Party before the Lukouchiao Incident was "Left" opportunism, that is, closed-doorism, the reason being chiefly that the Kuomintang had not yet begun to resist Japan.

18. Since the Lukouchiao Incident the main danger inside the Party is no longer "Left" closed-doorism but Right opportunism, that is, capitulationism, the reason being chiefly that the Kuomintang has begun to resist Japan.

19. Already in April at the Yenan meeting of Party activists, then again in May at the National Conference of the Party, and especially in August at the meeting of the Political Bureau of the Central Committee (the Lochuan meeting), we posed the following question: Will the proletariat lead the bourgeoisie in the united front, or the bourgeoisie the proletariat? Will the Kuomintang draw over the Communist Party, or the Communist Party the Kuomintang? In relation to the current specific political task this question means: Is the Kuomintang to be raised to the level of the Ten-Point Programme for Resisting Japan and Saving the Nation, to the level of the total resistance advocated by the Communist Party? Or is the Communist Party to sink to the level of the Kuomintang dictatorship of the landlords and bourgeoisie, to the level of partial resistance?

20. Why must we pose the question so sharply? The answer is:

On the one hand, we have the Chinese bourgeoisie's proneness to compromise; the Kuomintang's superiority in material strength; the declaration and the decisions of the Third Plenary Session of the Central Executive Committee of the Kuomintang, which slander and insult the Communist Party and cry out for "an end to the class struggle"; the Kuomintang's yearning for "the capitulation of the Communist Party" and its widespread propaganda to this end; Chiang Kai-shek's attempts to place the Communist Party under his control; the Kuomintang's policy of restricting and weakening the Red Army and the anti-Japanese democratic base areas; the plan concocted during the Kuomintang's Lushan Training Course[3] in July "to reduce the Communist Party's strength by two-fifths in the course of the War of Resistance"; the attempts of the Kuomintang to seduce Communist cadres with offers of fame and fortune and wine and women; the political capitulation of certain petty-bourgeois radicals (represented by Chang Nai-chi[4]); etc.

On the other hand, we have the uneven theoretical level among Communists; the fact that many of our Party members lack the experience of co-operation between the two parties gained during the Northern Expedition; the fact that a large number of Party members are of petty-bourgeois origin; the reluctance of some Party members to continue a life of bitter struggle; the tendency towards unprincipled accommodation with the Kuomintang in the united front; the emergence of a tendency towards a new type of warlordism in the Eighth Route Army; the emergence of the problem of Communist participation in the Kuomintang government; the emergence of a tendency towards excessive accommodation in the anti-Japanese democratic base areas; etc.

We must sharply pose the question of who is to lead and must resolutely combat capitulationism in view of the grave situation described above.

21. For several months now, and especially since the outbreak of the War of Resistance, the Central Committee and Party organizations at all levels have waged a clear-cut and firm struggle against capitulationist tendencies, actual or potential, have taken various necessary precautions against them and have achieved good results.

The Central Committee has issued a draft resolution[5] on the problem of Communist participation in the government.

A struggle has been started against the tendency towards new warlordism in the Eighth Route Army. This tendency is manifest in certain individuals who, since the redesignation of the Red Army, have become unwilling to submit strictly to Communist Party leadership, have developed individualistic heroism, taken pride in being given appointments by the Kuomintang (*i.e.*, in becoming officials), and so forth. The tendency towards this new type of warlordism has the same root (the reduction of the Communist Party to the level of the Kuomintang) and the same result (the alienation of the masses) as the tendency towards the old type of warlordism, which expressed itself in beating and abusing people, violating discipline, etc.; it is particularly dangerous because it is occurring in the period of the Kuomintang-Communist united front, and it therefore calls for special attention and determined opposition. Both the system of political commissars, which was abolished because of Kuomintang intervention, and the system of political departments, which were renamed "political training offices" for the same reason, have now been restored. We have initiated and staunchly carried out the new strategic principle of "independent guerrilla warfare in the mountain regions with the initiative in our own hands", thus basically ensuring the Eighth Route Army's successes in fighting and in its other tasks. We have rejected the Kuomintang's demand that its members should be sent to the Eighth Route Army units as cadres and have upheld the principle of absolute leadership of the Eighth Route Army by the Communist Party. Similarly, we have introduced the principle of "independence and initiative within the united front" in the revolutionary anti-Japanese base areas. We have corrected the tendency towards "parliamentarism"[6] (of course not the parliamentarism of the Second International, which is absent in the Chinese Party); we have also persisted in our struggle against bandits, enemy spies and saboteurs.

In Sian we have corrected the tendency towards unprincipled accommodation in our relations with the Kuomintang and have developed the mass struggle anew.

In eastern Kansu we have on the whole done the same as in Sian.

In Shanghai we have criticized Chang Nai-chi's line of "issuing fewer calls and offering more suggestions" and begun to correct the tendency towards excessive accommodation in the work of the national salvation movement.

In the guerrilla zones in the south — these representing part of the gains of our decade of sanguinary warfare with the Kuomintang, our strategic strongholds for the anti-Japanese national revolutionary war in the southern provinces, and our forces which the Kuomintang tried to wipe out by "encirclement and suppression" even after the Sian Incident, and which it has tried to weaken by the newer method of "luring the tiger out of the mountains" even after the Lukouchiao Incident — we have taken special care (1) to guard against concentrating our forces regardless of circumstances (which would suit the Kuomintang's desire to destroy these strongholds), (2) to reject Kuomintang appointees, and (3) to be on the alert against the danger of another Ho Ming Incident[7] (*i.e.*, the danger of being surrounded and disarmed by the Kuomintang).

Our attitude in the *Liberation Weekly*[8] has continued to be one of serious and fair criticism.

22. In order to persevere in armed resistance and win final victory as well as to turn partial resistance into total resistance, it is necessary to adhere to the Anti-Japanese National United Front and expand and strengthen it. No views disruptive of the Kuomintang-Communist united front will be tolerated. We must still guard against "Left" closed-doorism. But at the same time we must closely adhere to the principle of independence and initiative in all our united front work. Our united front with the Kuomintang and other parties is based on the execution of a definite programme. Without this basis there can be no united front, and in that case co-operation would become unprincipled and a manifestation of capitulationism. Thus the key to leading the anti-Japanese national revolutionary war to victory is to explain, apply and uphold the principle of "independence and initiative within the united front".

23. What is our purpose in all this? In one respect, it is to hold the ground we have already won, for this ground is our strategic point of departure and its loss would mean the end of everything. But our chief purpose is to extend the ground already won and realize the positive aim of "winning the masses in their millions for the Anti-Japanese National United Front and the overthrow of Japanese imperialism". Holding our ground and extending it are inseparably connected. In the last few months, many more left-wing members of the petty bourgeoisie have become united under our influence, the new forces in the Kuomintang camp have grown, the mass struggle in Shansi has developed, and our Party organizations have expanded in many places.

24. But we must clearly understand that generally speaking the organizational strength of our Party is still quite small in the country as a whole. The strength of the masses in the country as a whole is also very small, because the workers and peasants, the basic sections of the masses, are not yet organized. All this is due to the Kuomintang's policy of control and repression on the one hand and the inadequacy of our own work or even its complete absence on the other. This is the

fundamental weakness of our Party in the present anti-Japanese national revolutionary war. Unless we overcome this weakness, Japanese imperialism cannot be defeated. To this end we must apply the principle of "independence and initiative within the united front" and overcome all tendencies towards capitulation or excessive accommodation.

IN THE COUNTRY AS A WHOLE, OPPOSE NATIONAL CAPITULATIONISM

25. The above points deal with class capitulationism. This tendency would lead the proletariat to accommodate itself to bourgeois reformism and bourgeois lack of thoroughness. Unless it is overcome, we cannot succeed in carrying forward the anti-Japanese national revolutionary war, in turning partial resistance into total resistance and in defending the motherland.

But there is also the other kind of capitulationism, national capitulationism, which would lead China to accommodate herself to the interests of Japanese imperialism, make China a Japanese colony and turn the Chinese people into colonial slaves. This tendency has now appeared in the right wing of the Anti-Japanese National United Front.

26. The left wing of the Anti-Japanese National United Front is composed of the Communist-led masses, which include the proletariat, the peasantry and the urban petty bourgeoisie. Our task is to do our utmost to extend and consolidate this wing. The accomplishment of this task is the basic prerequisite for reforming the Kuomintang, the government and the army, for establishing a unified democratic republic, for turning partial resistance into total resistance and for overthrowing Japanese imperialism.

27. The intermediate section of the Anti-Japanese National United Front is composed of the national bourgeoisie and the upper stratum of the petty bourgeoisie. Those for whom the leading Shanghai newspapers speak are now tending towards the Left,[9] while some members of the Fu Hsing Society have begun to vacillate and some members of the C.C. Clique are also wavering.[10] The armies resisting Japan have learned severe lessons, and some have begun or are preparing to introduce reforms. Our task is to help the intermediate section to move forward and change its stand.

28. The right wing of the Anti-Japanese National United Front consists of the big landlords and big bourgeoisie, and it is the nerve

centre of national capitulationism. It is inevitable that these people should tend towards capitulationism, for they fear both the destruction of their property in the war and the rise of the masses. Many of them are already collaborators, many have become or are ready to become pro-Japanese, many are vacillating, and only a few, owing to special circumstances, are firmly anti-Japanese. Some of them have joined the national united front for the time being under compulsion and with reluctance. Generally speaking, it will not be long before they split away. Indeed many of the worst elements among the big land-lords and big bourgeoisie are at this very moment engineering a split in the Anti-Japanese National United Front. They are manufacturing rumours, and stories such as "the Communists are engaged in insur-rection" and "the Eighth Route Army is in retreat" are sure to multiply daily. Our task is to combat national capitulationism res-olutely and, in the course of this struggle, to expand and consolidate the left wing and help the intermediate section to move forward and change its stand.

THE RELATION BETWEEN CLASS CAPITULATIONISM AND NATIONAL CAPITULATIONISM

29. Class capitulationism is actually the reserve force of national capitulationism in the anti-Japanese national revolutionary war; it is a vile tendency that lends support to the camp of the right wing and leads to defeat in the war. We must fight this tendency inside the Communist Party and the proletariat and extend the fight to all spheres of our work, in order to invigorate the struggle against national capitulationism, and in order to achieve the liberation of the Chinese nation and the emancipation of the toiling masses.

NOTES

[1] This refers to the "Resolution on the Present Situation and the Tasks of the Party" adopted by the Political Bureau of the Central Committee of the Chinese Communist Party at its meeting in Lochuan, northern Shensi, on August 25, 1937. The full text reads as follows:

(1) The military provocation by the Japanese aggressors at Lukouchiao and their occupation of Peiping and Tientsin represent only the beginning of their large-scale invasion of China south of the Great Wall. They have already begun

their national mobilization for war. Their propaganda that they have "no desire to aggravate the situation" is only a smokescreen for further attacks.

(2) Under the pressure of the Japanese aggressors' attacks and the Chinese people's indignation, the Nanking government is beginning to make up its mind to fight. General defence arrangements and actual resistance in some places have already started. Full-scale war between China and Japan is inevitable. The resistance at Lukouchiao on July 7 marked the starting point of China's national war of resistance.

(3) Thus a new stage has opened in China's political situation, the stage of actual resistance. The stage of preparation for resistance is over. In the present stage the central task is to mobilize all the nation's forces for victory in the War of Resistance. The winning of democracy, which was not accomplished in the previous stage because of the Kuomintang's unwillingness and the inadequate mobilization of the people, is a task that must be fulfilled in the course of the struggle for victory in the War of Resistance.

(4) Our differences and disputes with the Kuomintang and other anti-Japanese groups in this new stage are no longer about whether to wage a war of resistance but about how to win victory.

(5) The key to victory in the war now lies in developing the resistance that has already begun into a war of total resistance by the whole nation. Only through such a war of total resistance can final victory be won. The Ten-Point Programme for Resisting Japan and Saving the Nation now proposed by our Party spells out concretely the way to win final victory in the War of Resistance.

(6) A great danger lurks in the present state of resistance. The main reason for this danger is that the Kuomintang is still unwilling to arouse the whole people to take part in the war. Instead, it regards the war as the concern of the government alone, and at every turn fears and restricts the people's participation in the war, prevents the government and the army from forming close ties with the people, denies the people the democratic right to resist Japan and save the nation, and refuses to reform the government apparatus thoroughly and to turn the government into a national defence government of the whole nation. A war of resistance of this kind may achieve partial victories, but never final victory. On the contrary, it may end in grievous failure.

(7) The existence of serious weaknesses in the War of Resistance may lead to many setbacks, retreats, internal splits, betrayals, temporary and partial compromises and other such reverses. Therefore it should be realized that the war will be an arduous and protracted war. But we are confident that, through the efforts of our Party and the whole people, the resistance already started will sweep aside all obstacles and continue to advance and develop. We must overcome all difficulties and firmly fight for the realization of the Ten-Point Programme for victory proposed by our Party. We must firmly oppose all wrong policies which run counter to it and combat national defeatism and the pessimism and despair it engenders.

(8) Together with the people and the armed forces under the leadership of the Party, members of the Communist Party must actively take their stand in the forefront of the struggle, become the core of the nation's resistance and do their utmost to develop the anti-Japanese mass movement. They must never for a moment relax or miss a single opportunity to do propaganda among the masses and to organize and arm them. Victory in the War of Resistance Against Japan will be certain provided the masses in their millions are really organized in the national united front.

[2] In the initial period of the War of Resistance, the Kuomintang and Chiang Kai-shek made a number of promises to introduce various reforms under popular pressure, but very quickly broke them one after another. The possibility that the Kuomintang might introduce the reforms desired by the whole people was not actualized. As Comrade Mao Tse-tung said later in "On Coalition Government":

All the people, including the Communists and other democrats, earnestly hoped that the Kuomintang government would seize the opportunity, at a time when the nation was in peril and the people were filled with enthusiasm, to institute democratic reforms and put Dr. Sun Yat-sen's revolutionary Three People's Principles into practice. But their hopes came to nought. (See *Selected Works of Mao Tse-tung*, Eng. ed., FLP, Peking, 1965, Vol. III, p. 263.)

[3] The Lushan Training Course was set up by Chiang Kai-shek at Lushan, Kiangsi Province, to train high and middle-ranking officials of the Kuomintang party and government to form the core of his reactionary regime.

[4] Chang Nai-chi was then advocating "issuing fewer calls and offering more suggestions". But it would have been useless merely to submit "suggestions" to the Kuomintang, since it was following a policy of oppression. Calls had to be made directly to the masses, in order to arouse them to struggle against the Kuomintang. Otherwise, it would have been impossible to keep up the war against Japan or to resist Kuomintang reaction. Chang Nai-chi was wrong on this point, and gradually he realized his mistake.

[5] This refers to the "Draft Resolution of the Central Committee of the Communist Party of China Concerning the Communist Party's Participation in the Government" which was drawn up on September 25, 1937. The full text reads as follows:

(1) The present situation in the anti-Japanese war urgently requires a united front government representing the whole nation, for only such a government can effectively lead the anti-Japanese national revolutionary war and defeat Japanese imperialism. The Communist Party is ready to participate in such a government, that is, to undertake administrative responsibilities in the government directly and officially and play an active part in it. But such a government does not yet exist. What exists today is still the government of the Kuomintang one-party dictatorship.

(2) The Communist Party of China can participate in the government only when it is changed from a one-party dictatorship of the Kuomintang into a united front government of the whole nation, that is, when the present Kuomintang government (a) accepts the fundamentals of the Ten-Point Programme for Resisting Japan and Saving the Nation proposed by our Party and promulgates an administrative programme in accordance therewith; (b) begins to show by deeds the sincerity of its efforts to carry out this programme and achieves definite results; and (c) permits the legal existence of Communist Party organizations and guarantees the Communist Party freedom to mobilize, organize and educate the masses.

(3) Before the Central Committee of the Party decides to participate in the Central Government, members of the Communist Party must not as a rule participate in any local government or in any administrative councils or committees attached to the administrative organs of the government, central or local. For such participation would only obscure the distinctive features of the Communist Party, prolong the Kuomintang's dictatorship and hinder rather than help the effort to bring a unified democratic government into being.

(4) However, members of the Communist Party may participate in the local governments of certain particular regions, such as battle areas, where the old authorities find it impossible to rule as before and are on the whole willing to put the Communist Party's policies into effect, where the Communist Party is free to operate openly, and where the present emergency makes Communist participation a necessity in the opinion both of the people and of the government. Still more so in the Japanese-occupied areas, the Communist Party should come forward openly as the organizer of the anti-Japanese united front governments.

(5) Before the Communist Party officially joins the government, it is permissible in principle for Party members to participate in representative bodies, such as an all-China national assembly, for the purpose of discussing a democratic constitution and policies to save the nation. Thus, the Communist Party should strive to get its members elected to such assemblies and use them as a forum for propagating the Party's views, so as to mobilize the people and rally them round the Party and promote the establishment of a unified democratic government.

(6) Given a definite common programme and the principle of absolute equality, the Central Committee of the Communist Party or its local branches may form united front organizations with the Central Executive Committee of the Kuomintang or its local headquarters, such as various joint committees (*e.g.*, national revolutionary leagues, committees for mass movements and committees for mobilization in the war zones), and through such joint activities the Communist Party should achieve co-operation with the Kuomintang.

(7) With the redesignation of the Red Army as part of the National Revolutionary Army and the change of the organ of Red political power into the Government of the Special Region, their representatives may, by virtue of the legal status they have acquired, join all the military and mass organizations which further the resistance to Japan and the salvation of the nation.

(8) It is most essential to maintain absolutely independent Communist Party leadership in what was originally the Red Army and in all the guerrilla units, and Communists must not show any vacillation on this matter of principle.

[6] "Parliamentarism" here refers to the proposal of some Party comrades that the system of political power in the revolutionary base areas, the system of people's representative conferences, should be changed into the bourgeois parliamentary system.

[7] The Ho Ming Incident took place after the outbreak of the anti-Japanese war. In October 1934, when the Central Red Army moved northward, Red Army guerrilla units stayed behind and maintained guerrilla warfare in extremely difficult circumstances in fourteen areas in the eight southern provinces of Kiangsi, Fukien, Kwangtung, Hunan, Hupeh, Honan, Chekiang and Anhwei. When the anti-Japanese war began, these units, acting on instructions from the Central Committee of the Chinese Communist Party, entered into negotiations with the Kuomintang for the cessation of civil war and organized themselves into a single army (namely, the New Fourth Army which later stubbornly fought the Japanese on the southern and northern banks of the Yangtse River) and moved to the front to resist Japan. But Chiang Kai-shek plotted to exploit these negotiations for the purpose of wiping out the guerrilla units. Ho Ming was one of the guerrilla leaders in the Fukien-Kwangtung border area which was one of the fourteen guerrilla areas. He was not on the alert against Chiang Kai-shek's plot, with the result that more than one

thousand of the guerrillas under his command were surrounded and disarmed by the Kuomintang forces after they assembled.

[8] Founded in Yenan in 1937, the *Liberation Weekly* was the organ of the Central Committee of the Communist Party of China. It was superseded by the *Liberation Daily* in 1941.

[9] They were that section of the national bourgeoisie for whom newspapers like the Shanghai *Shen Pao* served as a vehicle.

[10] The Fu Hsing Society and the C.C. Clique, two fascist organizations within the Kuomintang, were headed by Chiang Kai-shek and Chen Li-fu respectively. They served the oligarchic interests of the big landlords and the big bourgeoisie. But many petty-bourgeois elements had joined them under compulsion or had been duped into joining. The text refers to the section of the Fu Hsing Society consisting mainly of lower and middle-ranking officers in the Kuomintang army and to the section of the C.C. Clique consisting mainly of members not in power.

PROCLAMATION BY THE GOVERNMENT OF THE SHENSI-KANSU-NINGSIA BORDER REGION AND THE REAR HEADQUARTERS OF THE EIGHTH ROUTE ARMY

May 15, 1938

Be it hereby proclaimed: Ever since the Lukouchiao Incident, all our patriotic countrymen have been firmly waging the War of Resistance. Officers and men at the front are shedding their blood and sacrificing their lives. All political parties and groups have united in good faith. All sections of the people have joined forces to save the nation. This points to a bright future for the Chinese nation and affords a firm guarantee for victory over Japan. All our fellow-countrymen must continue along this line of advance. The army and the people of our Shensi-Kansu-Ningsia Border Region[1] have followed the Government's leadership and devoted their efforts to the cause of national salvation. Whatever they have done has been just and honourable. Under bitter hardships, they have struggled on tirelessly and uncomplainingly. The people throughout the country are unanimous in praising them. For their part the Border Region Government and the Rear Headquarters will encourage the people of the whole region to continue their efforts to the very end. Nobody will be allowed to neglect his duty and nothing will be allowed to undermine the

---

This proclamation was written by Comrade Mao Tse-tung for the Government of the Shensi-Kansu-Ningsia Border Region and the Rear Headquarters of the Eighth Route Army with a view to countering disruptive activities by the Chiang Kai-shek clique. Shortly after the establishment of Kuomintang-Communist co-operation, the Chiang Kai-shek clique began to plot disruption against the revolutionary forces under Communist leadership. The disruption of the Shensi-Kansu-Ningsia Border Region was part of their plot. Comrade Mao Tse-tung maintained that a firm stand was necessary to defend the interests of the revolution. The proclamation dealt a blow at the opportunist stand of some Party members in the anti-Japanese united front with regard to the intrigues of the Chiang clique.

cause of national salvation. However, recent investigations in the
Border Region have disclosed that, disregarding the public interest,
some persons are using various means to force the peasants to return
land and houses that have been distributed to them, to compel debtors
to pay back old cancelled loans,[2] to coerce the people into changing
the democratic system that has been built up, or to disrupt the military,
economic, cultural and mass organizations that have been established.
Some of them are even acting as spies, conspiring with bandits, inciting
our soldiers to mutiny, making surveys and maps of our region,
secretly collecting information, or openly spreading propaganda against
the Border Region Government. Clearly, all these activities are violations of the basic principle of unity for resistance to Japan, run
counter to the will of the people of the Border Region, and are
intended to foment internal dissension, disrupt the united front,
damage the people's interests, undermine the prestige of the Border
Region Government and increase the difficulties of mobilization
against Japan. The reason is that a handful of die-hards are behaving
unscrupulously to the detriment of the national interest. Some are
even serving as tools of the Japanese aggressors, using various guises
to camouflage their conspiratorial activities. For several months,
reports demanding our daily attention have been steadily pouring in
from people in the counties requesting us to put a stop to such activities.
With a view to strengthening the anti-Japanese forces, consolidating
the rear against Japan, and safeguarding the interests of the people, the
Government and the Rear Headquarters find it imperative to proscribe
the above-mentioned activities. Accordingly, we hereby unequivocally
proclaim:

(1) The Government and the Rear Headquarters, in order to
protect the rights already secured by the people, forbid any un-
authorized change in the distribution of land or houses and in the
cancellation of debts made within the areas under the jurisdiction of
the Border Region Government before internal peace was established.

(2) The Government and the Rear Headquarters will protect the
activities of all the military, political, economic, cultural and mass
organizations which were in existence when internal peace was
established and which have since advanced and expanded in accordance with the principle of the united front, will promote their progress,
and stop all intrigues and disruptive activities against them.

(3) The Government and the Rear Headquarters, resolutely
carrying out the Programme of Armed Resistance and National

Reconstruction, will gladly initiate and promote any undertaking that serves the cause of resistance to Japan and national salvation. We welcome sincere assistance from people in every quarter. But to guard against impostors and keep out traitors, we prohibit any person, whatever his activities, from entering and staying in the Border Region unless he secures permission and written authorization from the Government and the Rear Headquarters.

(4) In this tense period of armed resistance, it is right and proper for the people to report any person who tries to sabotage, engage in disruption, stir up sedition or ferret out military secrets within the boundaries of the Border Region. Upon valid evidence, persons so charged may be arrested on the spot. If convicted, offenders will be punished with due severity.

These four regulations must be observed by all members of the armed forces and all civilians throughout the Border Region, and no violation whatsoever will be permitted. Henceforward, should any lawless person dare to plot disruption, the Border Region Government and the Rear Headquarters will enforce these regulations to the letter and will accept no plea of ignorance.

This proclamation is hereby issued with the full force of the law.

NOTES

[1] The Shensi-Kansu-Ningsia Border Region was the revolutionary base area which was gradually built up after 1931 through revolutionary guerrilla war in northern Shensi. When the Central Red Army arrived in northern Shensi after the Long March, it became the central base area of the revolution and the seat of the Central Committee of the Chinese Communist Party. It was named the Shensi-Kansu-Ningsia Border Region after the formation of the Anti-Japanese National United Front in 1937, and it included twenty-three counties along the common borders of the three provinces.

[2] By 1936 most places in the Border Region had carried out the policy of confiscating the land of the landlords and distributing it among the peasants and cancelling the old debts of the peasants. After 1936, in order to facilitate the formation of a broad anti-Japanese national united front, the Chinese Communist Party changed its policy for the country as a whole to one of reduction of rent and interest; at the same time, however, it resolutely protected the gains already secured by the peasants in the land reform.

PROBLEMS OF STRATEGY IN GUERRILLA WAR AGAINST JAPAN

May 1938

CHAPTER I

WHY RAISE THE QUESTION OF STRATEGY IN GUERRILLA WAR?

In the War of Resistance Against Japan, regular warfare is primary and guerrilla warfare supplementary. This point has already been correctly settled. Thus, it seems there are only tactical problems in guerrilla warfare. Why then raise the question of strategy?

If China were a small country in which the role of guerrilla warfare was only to render direct support over short distances to the campaigns of the regular army, there would, of course, be only tactical problems but no strategic ones. On the other hand, if China were a country as strong as the Soviet Union and the invading enemy could either be quickly expelled, or, even though his expulsion were to take some time, he could not occupy extensive areas, then again guerrilla warfare would simply play a supporting role in campaigns, and would naturally involve only tactical but not strategic problems.

The question of strategy in guerrilla war does arise, however, in the case of China, which is neither small nor like the Soviet Union, but which is both a large and a weak country. This large and weak country is being attacked by a small and strong country, but the large

---

In the early days of the War of Resistance Against Japan, many people inside and outside the Party belittled the important strategic role of guerrilla warfare and pinned their hopes on regular warfare alone, and particularly on the operations of the Kuomintang forces. Comrade Mao Tse-tung refuted this view and wrote this article to show the correct road of development for anti-Japanese guerrilla warfare. As a result, the Eighth Route Army and the New Fourth Army, which had just over 40,000 men when the War of Resistance began in 1937, grew to a great army and weak country is in an era of progress; this is the source of the whole problem. It is in these circumstances that vast areas have come under enemy occupation and that the war has become a protracted one. The enemy is occupying vast areas of this large country of ours, but Japan is a small country, she does not have sufficient soldiers and has to leave many gaps in the occupied areas, so that our anti-Japanese guerrilla warfare consists primarily not in interior-line operations in support of the campaigns of the regular troops but in independent operations on exterior lines; furthermore, China is progressive, that is to say, she has a staunch army and broad masses of people, both led by the Communist Party, so that, far from being small-scale, our anti-Japanese guerrilla warfare is in fact large-scale warfare. Hence the emergence of a whole series of problems, such as the strategic defensive, the strategic offensive, etc. The protracted nature of the war and its attendant ruthlessness have made it imperative for guerrilla warfare to undertake many unusual tasks; hence such problems as those of the base areas, the development of guerrilla warfare into mobile warfare, and so on. For all these reasons, China's guerrilla warfare against Japan has broken out of the bounds of tactics to knock at the gates of strategy, and it demands examination from the viewpoint of strategy. The point that merits our particular attention is that such extensive as well as protracted guerrilla warfare is quite new in the entire history of war. This is bound up with the fact that we are now in the Nineteen Thirties and Nineteen Forties and that we now have the Communist Party and the Red Army. Herein lies the heart of the matter. Our enemy is probably still cherishing fond dreams of emulating the Mongol conquest of the Sung Dynasty, the Manchu conquest of the Ming Dynasty, the British occupation of North America and India, the Latin occupation of Central and South America, etc. But such dreams have no practical value in present-day China because there are certain factors present in the China of today which were absent in those historical instances, and one of them is guerrilla warfare, which is quite a new phenomenon. If our enemy overlooks this fact, he will certainly come to grief.

---

of one million by the time Japan surrendered in 1945, established many revolutionary base areas, played a great part in the war and thus, throughout this period, made Chiang Kai-shek afraid to capitulate to Japan or launch a nation-wide civil war. In 1946, when Chiang Kai-shek did launch a nation-wide civil war, the People's Liberation Army, formed out of the Eighth Route and New Fourth Armies, was strong enough to deal with his attacks.

These are the reasons why our anti-Japanese guerrilla warfare, though occupying only a supplementary place in the War of Resistance as a whole, must nevertheless be examined from the viewpoint of strategy.

Why not, then, apply to guerrilla warfare the general strategic principles of the War of Resistance?

The question of strategy in our anti-Japanese guerrilla warfare is indeed closely linked with the question of strategy in the War of Resistance as a whole, because they have much in common. On the other hand, guerrilla warfare is different from regular warfare and has its own peculiarities, and consequently many peculiar elements are involved in the question of strategy in guerrilla warfare. Without modification it is impossible to apply the strategic principles of the War of Resistance in general to guerrilla warfare with its own peculiarities.

CHAPTER II

THE BASIC PRINCIPLE OF WAR IS TO PRESERVE ONESELF AND DESTROY THE ENEMY

Before discussing the question of strategy in guerrilla warfare in concrete terms, a few words are needed on the fundamental problem of war.

All the guiding principles of military operations grow out of the one basic principle: to strive to the utmost to preserve one's own strength and destroy that of the enemy. In a revolutionary war, this principle is directly linked with basic political principles. For instance, the basic political principle of China's War of Resistance Against Japan, *i.e.*, its political aim, is to drive out Japanese imperialism and build an independent, free and happy new China. In terms of military action this principle means the use of armed force to defend our motherland and to drive out the Japanese invaders. To attain this end, the operations of the armed units take the form of doing their utmost to preserve their own strength on the one hand and destroy the enemy's on the other. How then do we justify the encouragement of heroic sacrifice in war? Every war exacts a price, sometimes an extremely high one. Is this not in contradiction with "preserving oneself"? In fact, there is no contradiction at all; to put it more exactly, sacrifice and self-preservation are both opposite and complementary to each other. For such sacrifice is essential not only for destroying the enemy but also for preserving oneself — partial and temporary "non-preservation" (sacrifice, or paying the price) is necessary for the sake of general and permanent preservation. From this basic principle stems the series of principles guiding military operations, all of which — from the principles of shooting (taking cover to preserve oneself, and making full use of fire-power to destroy the enemy) to the principles of strategy — are permeated with the spirit of this basic principle. All technical, tactical and strategic principles represent applications of this basic principle. The principle of preserving oneself and destroying the enemy is the basis of all military principles.

CHAPTER III

SIX SPECIFIC PROBLEMS OF STRATEGY IN GUERRILLA WAR AGAINST JAPAN

Now let us see what policies or principles have to be adopted in guerrilla operations against Japan before we can attain the object of preserving ourselves and destroying the enemy. Since the guerrilla units in the War of Resistance (and in all other revolutionary wars) generally grow out of nothing and expand from a small to a large force, they must preserve themselves and, moreover, they must expand. Hence the question is, what policies or principles have to be adopted before we can attain the object of preserving and expanding ourselves and destroying the enemy?

Generally speaking, the main principles are as follows: (1) the use of initiative, flexibility and planning in conducting offensives within the defensive, battles of quick decision within protracted war, and exterior-line operations within interior-line operations; (2) co-ordination with regular warfare; (3) establishment of base areas; (4) the strategic defensive and the strategic offensive; (5) the development of guerrilla warfare into mobile warfare; and (6) correct relationship of command. These six items constitute the whole of the strategic programme for guerrilla war against Japan and are the means necessary for the preservation and expansion of our forces, for the destruction and expulsion of the enemy, for co-ordination with regular warfare and the winning of final victory.

CHAPTER IV

INITIATIVE, FLEXIBILITY AND PLANNING IN CONDUCTING OFFENSIVES WITHIN THE DEFENSIVE, BATTLES OF QUICK DECISION WITHIN PROTRACTED WAR, AND EXTERIOR-LINE OPERATIONS WITHIN INTERIOR-LINE OPERATIONS

Here the subject may be dealt with under four headings: (1) the relationship between the defensive and the offensive, between protractedness and quick decision, and between the interior and exterior lines; (2) the initiative in all operations; (3) flexible employment of forces; and (4) planning in all operations.

To start with the first.

If we take the War of Resistance as a whole, the fact that Japan is a strong country and is attacking while China is a weak country and is defending herself makes our war strategically a defensive and protracted war. As far as the operational lines are concerned, the Japanese are operating on exterior and we on interior lines. This is one aspect of the situation. But there is another aspect which is just the reverse. The enemy forces, though strong (in arms, in certain qualities of their men, and certain other factors), are numerically small, whereas our forces, though weak (likewise, in arms, in certain qualities of our men, and certain other factors), are numerically very large. Added to the fact that the enemy is an alien nation invading our country while we are resisting his invasion on our own soil, this determines the following strategy. It is possible and necessary to use tactical offensives within the strategic defensive, to fight campaigns and battles of quick decision within a strategically protracted war and to fight campaigns and battles on exterior lines within strategically interior lines. Such is the strategy to be adopted in the War of Resistance as a whole. It holds true both for regular and for guerrilla warfare. Guerrilla warfare is different only in degree and form. Offensives in guerrilla warfare generally take the form of surprise attacks. Although surprise attacks can and should be employed in regular warfare too, the degree of surprise is less. In guerrilla warfare, the need to bring operations to a quick decision is very great, and our exterior-line ring of encirclement of the enemy in campaigns and battles is very small. All these distinguish it from regular warfare.

Thus it can be seen that in their operations guerrilla units have to concentrate the maximum forces, act secretly and swiftly, attack the enemy by surprise and bring battles to a quick decision, and that they must strictly avoid passive defence, procrastination and the dispersal of forces before engagements. Of course, guerrilla warfare includes not only the strategic but also the tactical defensive. The latter embraces, among other things, containing and outpost actions during battles; the disposition of forces for resistance at narrow passes, strategic points, rivers or villages in order to deplete and exhaust the enemy; and action to cover withdrawal. But the basic principle of guerrilla warfare must be the offensive, and guerrilla warfare is more offensive in its character than regular warfare. The offensive, moreover, must take the form of surprise attacks, and to expose ourselves by ostentatiously parading our forces is even less permissible in guerrilla warfare than in regular warfare. From the fact that the enemy is strong and we are weak it necessarily follows that, in guerrilla operations in general even more than in regular warfare, battles must be decided quickly, though on some occasions guerrilla fighting may be kept up for several days, as in an assault on a small and isolated enemy force cut off from help. Because of its dispersed character, guerrilla warfare can spread everywhere, and in many of its tasks, as in harassing, containing and disrupting the enemy and in mass work, its principle is dispersal of forces; but a guerrilla unit, or a guerrilla formation, must concentrate its main forces when it is engaged in destroying the enemy, and especially when it is striving to smash an enemy attack. "Concentrate a big force to strike at a small section of the enemy force" remains a principle of field operations in guerrilla warfare.

Thus it can also be seen that, if we take the War of Resistance as a whole, we can attain the aim of our strategic defensive and finally defeat Japanese imperialism only through the cumulative effect of many offensive campaigns and battles in both regular and guerrilla warfare, namely, through the cumulative effect of many victories in offensive actions. Only through the cumulative effect of many campaigns and battles of quick decision, namely, the cumulative effect of many victories achieved through quick decision in offensive campaigns and battles, can we attain our goal of strategic protractedness, which means gaining time to increase our capacity to resist while hastening or awaiting changes in the international situation and the internal collapse of the enemy, in order to be able to launch a strategic counter-offensive and drive the Japanese invaders out of China. We must concentrate superior forces and fight exterior-line operations in every campaign or battle, whether in the stage of strategic defensive or in that of strategic counter-offensive, in order to encircle and destroy the enemy forces, encircling part if not all of them, destroying part if not all of the forces we have encircled, and inflicting heavy casualties on the encircled forces if we cannot capture them in large numbers. Only through the cumulative effect of many such battles of annihilation can we change the relative position as between the enemy and ourselves, thoroughly smash his strategic encirclement — that is, his scheme of exterior-line operations — and finally, in co-ordination with international forces and the revolutionary struggles of the Japanese people, surround the Japanese imperialists and deal them the *coup de grâce*. These results are to be achieved mainly through regular warfare, with guerrilla warfare making a secondary contribution. What is common to both, however, is the accumulation of many minor victories to make a major victory. Herein lies the great strategic role of guerrilla warfare in the War of Resistance.

Now let us discuss initiative, flexibility and planning in guerrilla warfare.

What is initiative in guerrilla warfare?

In any war, the opponents contend for the initiative, whether on a battlefield, in a battle area, in a war zone or in the whole war, for the initiative means freedom of action for an army. Any army which, losing the initiative, is forced into a passive position and ceases to have freedom of action, faces the danger of defeat or extermination. Naturally, gaining the initiative is harder in strategic defensive and interior-line operations and easier in offensive exterior-line operations. However, Japanese imperialism has two basic weaknesses, namely, its shortage of troops and the fact that it is fighting on foreign soil. Moreover, its underestimation of China's strength and the internal contradictions among the Japanese militarists have given rise to many mistakes in command, such as piecemeal reinforcement, lack of strategic co-ordination, occasional absence of a main direction for attack, failure to grasp opportunities in some operations and failure to wipe out encircled forces, all of which may be considered the third weakness of Japanese imperialism. Thus, despite the advantage of being on the offensive and operating on exterior lines, the Japanese militarists are gradually losing the initiative, because of their shortage of troops (their small territory, small population, inadequate resources, feudal-istic imperialism, etc.), because of the fact that they are fighting on foreign soil (their war is imperialist and barbarous) and because of their stupidities in command. Japan is neither willing nor able to conclude the war at present, nor has her strategic offensive yet come to an end, but, as the general trend shows, her offensive is confined within certain limits, which is the inevitable consequence of her three weaknesses; she cannot go on indefinitely till she swallows the whole of China. Already there are signs that Japan will one day find herself in an utterly passive position. China, on the other hand, was in a rather passive position at the beginning of the war, but, having gained experience, she is now turning to the new policy of mobile warfare, the policy of taking the offensive, seeking quick decisions and operat-ing on exterior lines in campaigns and battles, which, together with the policy of developing widespread guerrilla warfare, is helping China to build up a position of initiative day by day.

The question of the initiative is even more vital in guerrilla war-fare. For most guerrilla units operate in very difficult circumstances, fighting without a rear, with their own weak forces facing the enemy's strong forces, lacking experience (when the units are newly organized), being separated, etc. Nevertheless, it is possible to build up the initia-tive in guerrilla warfare, the essential condition being to seize on the enemy's three weaknesses. Taking advantage of the enemy's shortage of troops (from the viewpoint of the war as a whole), the guerrilla units can boldly use vast areas as their fields of operation; taking advantage of the fact that the enemy is an alien invader and is pursuing a most barbarous policy, the guerrilla units can boldly enlist the support of millions upon millions of people; and taking advantage of the stupidities in the enemy's command, the guerrilla units can give full scope to their resourcefulness. While the regular army must seize on all these weaknesses of the enemy and turn them to good account in order to defeat him, it is even more important for the guerrilla units to do so. As for the guerrilla units' own weaknesses, they can be gradually reduced in the course of the struggle. Moreover, these weaknesses sometimes constitute the very condition for gaining the initiative. For example, it is precisely because the guerrilla units are small that they can mysteriously appear and disappear in their operations behind enemy lines, without the enemy's being able to do anything about them, and thus enjoy a freedom of action such as massive regular armies never can.

When the enemy is making a converging attack from several directions, a guerrilla unit can exercise initiative only with difficulty and can lose it all too easily. In such a case, if its appraisals and dispositions are wrong, it is liable to get into a passive position and consequently fail to smash the converging enemy attack. This may occur even when the enemy is on the defensive and we are on the offensive. For the initiative results from making a correct appraisal of the situation (both our own and that of the enemy) and from making the correct military and political dispositions. A pessimistic appraisal out of accord with the objective conditions and the passive dispositions ensuing from it will undoubtedly result in the loss of the initiative and throw one into a passive position. On the other hand, an over-optimistic appraisal out of accord with the objective conditions and the risky (unjustifiably risky) dispositions ensuing from it will also result in the loss of the initiative and eventually land one in a position similar to that of the pessimists. The initiative is not an innate attribute of genius, but is something an intelligent leader attains through open-minded study and correct appraisal of the objective conditions and through correct military and political dispositions. It follows that the initiative is not ready-made but is something that requires conscious effort.

When forced into a passive position through some incorrect appraisal and disposition or through overwhelming pressure, a guerrilla unit must strive to extricate itself. How this can be done depends on the circumstances. In many cases it is necessary to "move away". The ability to move is the distinctive feature of a guerrilla unit. To move away is the principal method for getting out of a passive position and regaining the initiative. But it is not the sole method. The moment when the enemy is most energetic and we are in the greatest difficulties is often the very moment when things begin to turn against him and in our favour. Frequently a favourable situation recurs and the initiative is regained as a result of "holding out a little longer".

Next, let us deal with flexibility.

Flexibility is a concrete expression of the initiative. The flexible employment of forces is more essential in guerrilla warfare than in regular warfare.

A guerrilla commander must understand that the flexible employment of his forces is the most important means of changing the situation as between the enemy and ourselves and of gaining the initiative. The nature of guerrilla warfare is such that guerrilla forces must be employed flexibly in accordance with the task in hand and with such circumstances as the state of the enemy, the terrain and the local population, and the chief ways of employing the forces are dispersal, concentration and shifting of position. In employing his forces, a guerrilla commander is like a fisherman casting his net, which he should be able to spread wide as well as draw in tight. When casting his net, the fisherman has to ascertain the depth of the water, the speed of the current and the presence or absence of obstructions; similarly, when dispersing his units, a guerrilla commander must take care not to incur losses through ignorance of the situation or through miscalculated action. Just as the fisherman must keep a grip on the cord in order to draw his net in tight, so the guerrilla commander must maintain liaison and communication with all his forces and keep enough of his main forces at hand. Just as a frequent change of position is necessary in fishing, so a frequent shift of position is necessary for a guerrilla unit. Dispersal, concentration and shifting of position are the three ways of flexibly employing forces in guerrilla warfare.

Generally speaking, the dispersal of guerrilla units, or "breaking up the whole into parts", is employed chiefly: (1) when we want to threaten the enemy with a wide frontal attack because he is on the defensive, and there is temporarily no chance to mass our forces for action; (2) when we want to harass and disrupt the enemy throughout an area where his forces are weak; (3) when we are unable to break through the enemy's encirclement and try to slip away by making ourselves less conspicuous; (4) when we are restricted by terrain or supplies; or (5) when we are carrying on mass work over a wide area. But whatever the circumstances, when dispersing for action we should pay attention to the following: (1) we should never make an absolutely even dispersal of forces, but should keep a fairly large part in an area convenient for manoeuvre, so that any possible exigency can be met and there is a centre of gravity for the task being carried out in dispersion; and (2) we should assign to the dispersed units clearly defined tasks, fields of operation, time limits for actions, places for reassembly and ways and means of liaison.

Concentration of forces, or "assembling the parts into a whole", is the method usually applied to destroy an enemy when he is on the offensive and sometimes to destroy some of his stationary forces when he is on the defensive. Concentration of forces does not mean absolute concentration, but the massing of the main forces for use in one important direction while retaining or dispatching part of the forces for use in other directions to contain, harass or disrupt the enemy, or to carry on mass work.

Although the flexible dispersal or concentration of forces according to circumstances is the principal method in guerrilla warfare, we must also know how to shift (or transfer) our forces flexibly. When the enemy feels seriously threatened by guerrillas, he will send troops to attack or suppress them. Hence the guerrilla units will have to take stock of the situation. If advisable, they should fight where they are; if not, they should lose no time in shifting elsewhere. Sometimes, in order to crush the enemy units one by one, guerrilla units which have destroyed an enemy force in one place may immediately shift to another so as to wipe out a second enemy force; sometimes, finding it inadvisable to fight in one place, they may have to disengage quickly and fight the enemy elsewhere. If the enemy's forces in a certain place present a particularly serious threat, the guerrilla units should not linger, but should move off with lightning speed. In general, shifts of position should be made with secrecy and speed. In order to mislead, decoy and confuse the enemy, they should constantly use stratagems, such as making a feint to the east but attacking in the west, appearing now in the south and now in the north, hit-and-run attacks, and night actions.

Flexibility in dispersal, concentration and shifts of position is a concrete expression of the initiative in guerrilla warfare, whereas rigidness and inertia inevitably lead to passivity and cause unnecessary losses. But a commander proves himself wise not just by recognition of the importance of employing his forces flexibly but by skill in dispersing, concentrating or shifting them in good time according to the specific circumstances. This wisdom in sensing changes and choosing the right moment to act is not easily acquired; it can be gained only by those who study with a receptive mind and investigate and ponder diligently. Prudent consideration of the circumstances is essential to prevent flexibility from turning into impulsive action.

Lastly, we come to planning.

Without planning, victories in guerrilla warfare are impossible. Any idea that guerrilla warfare can be conducted in haphazard fashion indicates either a flippant attitude or ignorance of guerrilla warfare.

The operations in a guerrilla zone as a whole, or those of a guerrilla unit or formation, must be preceded by as thorough planning as possible, by preparation in advance for every action. Grasping the situation, setting the tasks, disposing the forces, giving military and political training, securing supplies, putting the equipment in good order, making proper use of the people's help, etc. — all these are part of the work of the guerrilla commanders, which they must carefully consider and conscientiously perform and check up on. There can be no initiative, no flexibility, and no offensive unless they do so. True, guerrilla conditions do not allow as high a degree of planning as do those of regular warfare, and it would be a mistake to attempt very thorough planning in guerrilla warfare. But it is necessary to plan as thoroughly as the objective conditions permit, for it should be understood that fighting the enemy is no joke.

The above points serve to explain the first of the strategic principles of guerrilla warfare, the principle of using initiative, flexibility and planning in conducting offensives within the defensive, battles of quick decision within protracted war, and exterior-line operations within interior-line operations. It is the key problem in the strategy of guerrilla warfare. The solution of this problem provides the major guarantee of victory in guerrilla warfare so far as military command is concerned.

Although a variety of matters have been dealt with here, they all revolve around the offensive in campaigns and battles. The initiative can be decisively grasped only after victory in an offensive. Every offensive operation must be organized on our initiative and not launched under compulsion. Flexibility in the employment of forces revolves around the effort to take the offensive, and planning likewise is necessary chiefly in order to ensure success in offensive operations. Measures of tactical defence are meaningless if they are divorced from their role of giving either direct or indirect support to an offensive. Quick decision refers to the tempo of an offensive, and exterior lines refer to its scope. The offensive is the only means of destroying the enemy and is also the principal means of self-preservation, while pure defence and retreat can play only a temporary and partial role in self-preservation and are quite useless for destroying the enemy.

The principle stated above is basically the same for both regular and guerrilla war; it differs to some degree only in its form of expression. But in guerrilla war it is both important and necessary to note this difference. It is precisely this difference in form which distinguishes the operational methods of guerrilla war from those of regular war.

If we confuse the two different forms in which the principle is expressed, victory in guerrilla war will be impossible.

CHAPTER V

CO-ORDINATION WITH REGULAR WARFARE

The second problem of strategy in guerrilla warfare is its co-ordination with regular warfare. It is a matter of clarifying the relation between guerrilla and regular warfare on the operational level, in the light of the nature of actual guerrilla operations. An understanding of this relation is very important for effectiveness in defeating the enemy.

There are three kinds of co-ordination between guerrilla and regular warfare, co-ordination in strategy, in campaigns and in battles.

Taken as a whole, guerrilla warfare behind the enemy lines, which cripples the enemy, pins him down, disrupts his supply lines and inspires the regular forces and the people throughout the country, is co-ordinated with regular warfare in strategy. Take the case of the guerrilla warfare in the three northeastern provinces. Of course, the question of co-ordination did not arise before the nation-wide War of Resistance, but since the war began the significance of such co-ordination has become obvious. Every enemy soldier the guerrillas kill there, every bullet they make the enemy expend, every enemy soldier they stop from advancing south of the Great Wall, can be reckoned a contribution to the total strength of the resistance. It is, moreover, clear that they are having a demoralizing effect on the whole enemy army and all Japan and a heartening effect on our whole army and people. Still clearer is the role in strategic co-ordination played by the guerrilla warfare along the Peiping-Suiyuan, Peiping-Hankow, Tientsin-Pukow, Tatung-Puchow, Chengting-Taiyuan and Shanghai-Hangchow Railways. Not only are the guerrilla units performing the function of co-ordination with the regular forces in our present strategic defensive, when the enemy is on the strategic offensive; not only will they co-ordinate with the regular forces in disrupting the enemy's hold on the occupied territory, after he concludes his strategic offensive and switches to the safeguarding of his gains; they will also co-ordinate with the regular forces in driving out the enemy forces and recovering all the lost territories, when the regular forces launch the strategic counter-offensive. The great role of guerrilla warfare in strategic co-ordination must not be overlooked. The commanders both of the guerrilla units and of the regular forces must clearly understand this role.

In addition, guerrilla warfare performs the function of co-ordination with regular warfare in campaigns. For instance, in the campaign at Hsinkou, north of Taiyuan, the guerrillas played a re-markable role in co-ordination both north and south of Yenmenkuan by wrecking the Tatung-Puchow Railway and the motor roads running through Pinghsingkuan and Yangfangkou. Or take another instance. After the enemy occupied Fenglingtu, guerrilla warfare, which was already widespread throughout Shansi Province and was conducted mainly by the regular forces, played an even greater role through co-ordination with the defensive campaigns west of the Yellow River in Shensi Province and south of the Yellow River in Honan Province. Again, when the enemy attacked southern Shantung, the guerrilla warfare in the five provinces of northern China contributed a great deal through co-ordination with the campaigns of our army. In per-forming a task of this sort, the leaders of each guerrilla base behind the enemy lines, or the commanders of a guerrilla formation tem-porarily dispatched there, must dispose their forces well and, by adopting different tactics suited to the time and place, move ener-getically against the enemy's most vital and vulnerable spots in order to cripple him, pin him down, disrupt his supply lines, inspire our armies campaigning on the interior lines, and so fulfil their duty of co-ordinating with the campaign. If each guerrilla zone or unit goes it alone without giving any attention to co-ordinating with the campaigns of the regular forces, its role in strategic co-ordination will lose a great deal of its significance, although it will still play some such role in the general strategy. All guerrilla commanders should give this point serious attention. To achieve co-ordination in campaigns, it is absolutely necessary for all larger guerrilla units and guerrilla formations to have radio equipment.

Finally, co-ordination with the regular forces in battles, in actual fighting on the battlefield, is the task of all guerrilla units in the vicinity of an interior-line battlefield. Of course, this applies only to guerrilla units operating close to the regular forces or to units of regulars dispatched on temporary guerrilla missions. In such cases, a guerrilla unit has to perform whatever task it is assigned by the commander of the regular forces, which is usually to pin down some of the enemy's forces, disrupt his supply lines, conduct reconnaissance, or act as guides for the regular forces. Even without such an assignment, the guerrilla unit should carry out these tasks on its own initiative. To sit by idly, neither moving nor fighting, or to move about without fighting, would be an intolerable attitude for a guerrilla unit.

CHAPTER VI

THE ESTABLISHMENT OF BASE AREAS

The third problem of strategy in anti-Japanese guerrilla warfare is the establishment of base areas, which is important and essential because of the protracted nature and ruthlessness of the war. The recovery of our lost territories will have to await the nation-wide strategic counter-offensive; by then the enemy's front will have extended deep into central China and cut it in two from north to south, and a part or even a greater part of our territory will have fallen into the hands of the enemy and become his rear. We shall have to extend guerrilla warfare all over this vast enemy-occupied area, make a front out of the enemy's rear, and force him to fight ceaselessly throughout the territory he occupies. Until such time as our strategic counter-offensive is launched and so long as our lost territories are not recovered, it will be necessary to persist in guerrilla warfare in the enemy's rear, certainly for a fairly long time, though one cannot say definitely for how long. This is why the war will be a protracted one. And in order to safeguard his gains in the occupied areas, the enemy is bound to step up his anti-guerrilla measures and, especially after the halting of his strategic offensive, to embark on relentless suppression of the guerrillas. With ruthlessness thus added to protractedness, it will be impossible to sustain guerrilla warfare behind the enemy lines without base areas.

What, then, are these base areas? They are the strategic bases on which the guerrilla forces rely in performing their strategic tasks and achieving the object of preserving and expanding themselves and destroying and driving out the enemy. Without such strategic bases, there will be nothing to depend on in carrying out any of our strategic tasks or achieving the aim of the war. It is a characteristic of guerrilla warfare behind the enemy lines that it is fought without a rear, for the guerrilla forces are severed from the country's general rear. But guerrilla warfare could not last long or grow without base areas. The base areas, indeed, are its rear.

History knows many peasant wars of the "roving rebel" type, but none of them ever succeeded. In the present age of advanced communications and technology, it would be all the more groundless to imagine that one can win victory by fighting in the manner of roving rebels. However, this roving-rebel idea still exists among impoverished peasants, and in the minds of guerrilla commanders it becomes the view that base areas are neither necessary nor important. Therefore, ridding the minds of guerrilla commanders of this idea is a prerequisite for deciding on a policy of establishing base areas. The question of whether or not to have base areas and of whether or not to regard them as important, in other words, the conflict between the idea of establishing base areas and that of fighting like roving rebels, arises in all guerrilla warfare, and, to a certain extent, our anti-Japanese guerrilla warfare is no exception. Therefore the struggle against the roving-rebel ideology is an inevitable process. Only when this ideology is thoroughly overcome and the policy of establishing base areas is initiated and applied will there be conditions favourable for the maintenance of guerrilla warfare over a long period.

Now that the necessity and importance of base areas have been made clear, let us pass on to the following problems which must be understood and solved when it comes to establishing the base areas. These problems are the types of base areas, the guerrilla zones and the base areas, the conditions for establishing base areas, their consolidation and expansion, and the forms in which we and the enemy encircle one another.

1. THE TYPES OF BASE AREAS

Base areas in anti-Japanese guerrilla warfare are mainly of three types, those in the mountains, those on the plains and those in the river-lake-estuary regions.

The advantage of setting up base areas in mountainous regions is obvious, and those which have been, are being or will be established in the Changpai,[1] Wutai,[2] Taihang,[3] Taishan,[4] Yenshan[5] and Maoshan[6] Mountains all belong to this type. They are all places where anti-Japanese guerrilla warfare can be maintained for the longest time and are important strongholds for the War of Resistance. We must develop guerrilla warfare and set up base areas in all the mountainous regions behind the enemy lines.

Of course, the plains are less suitable than the mountains, but it is by no means impossible to develop guerrilla warfare or establish any base areas there. Indeed, the widespread guerrilla warfare in the plains of Hopei and of northern and northwestern Shantung proves that it is possible to develop guerrilla warfare in the plains. While there is as yet no evidence on the possibility of setting up base areas there and maintaining them for long, it has been proved that the setting up of temporary base areas is possible, and it should be possible to set up base areas for small units or for seasonal use. On the one hand, the enemy does not have enough troops at his disposal and is pursuing a policy of unparalleled brutality, and on the other hand, China has a vast territory and vast numbers of people who are resisting Japan; the objective conditions for spreading guerrilla warfare and setting up temporary base areas in the plains are therefore fulfilled. Given competent military command, it should of course be possible to establish bases for small guerrilla units there, bases which are long-term but not fixed.[7] Broadly speaking, when the strategic offensive of the enemy is brought to a halt and he enters the stage of safeguarding his occupied areas, he will undoubtedly launch savage attacks on all the guerrilla base areas, and those in the plains will naturally be the first to bear the brunt. The large guerrilla formations operating on the plains will be unable to keep on fighting there for long and will gradually have to move up into the mountains as the circumstances require, as for instance, from the Hopei Plain to the Wutai and Taihang Mountains, or from the Shantung Plain to Taishan Mountain and the Shantung Peninsula in the east. But in the circumstances of our national war it is not impossible for numerous small guerrilla units to keep going in various counties over the vast plains and adopt a fluid way of fighting, *i.e.*, by shifting their bases from place to place. It is definitely possible to conduct seasonal guerrilla warfare by taking advantage of the "green curtain" of tall crops in summer and of the frozen rivers in winter. As the enemy has no strength to spare now and will never be able to attend to everything even when he has the strength to spare, it is absolutely necessary for us to decide on the policy, for the present, of spreading guerrilla warfare far and wide and setting up temporary base areas in the plains and, for the future, of preparing to keep up guerrilla warfare by small units, if only seasonally, and of creating base areas which are not fixed.

Objectively speaking, the possibilities of developing guerrilla warfare and establishing base areas are greater in the river-lake-estuary regions than in the plains, though less than in the mountains. The dramatic battles fought by "pirates" and "water-bandits", of which our history is full, and the guerrilla warfare round the Hunghu Lake kept up for several years in the Red Army period, both testify to the possibility of developing guerrilla warfare and of establishing base areas in the river-lake-estuary regions. So far, however, the political parties and the masses who are resisting Japan have given this possibility little attention. Though the subjective conditions are as yet lacking, we should undoubtedly turn our attention to this possibility and start working on it. As one aspect in the development of our nation-wide guerrilla warfare, we should effectively organize guerrilla warfare in the Hungtse Lake region north of the Yangtse River, in the Taihu Lake region south of the Yangtse, and in all river-lake-estuary regions in the enemy-occupied areas along the rivers and on the seacoast, and we should create permanent base areas in and near such places. By overlooking this aspect we are virtually providing the enemy with water transport facilities; this is a gap in our strategic plan for the War of Resistance which must be filled in good time.

2. GUERRILLA ZONES AND BASE AREAS

In guerrilla warfare behind the enemy lines, there is a difference between guerrilla zones and base areas. Areas which are surrounded by the enemy but whose central parts are not occupied or have been recovered, like some counties in the Wutai mountain region (*i.e.*, the Shansi-Chahar-Hopei border area) and also some places in the Taihang and Taishan mountain regions, are ready-made bases for the convenient use of guerrilla units in developing guerrilla warfare. But elsewhere in these areas the situation is different, as for instance in the eastern and northern sections of the Wutai mountain region, which include parts of western Hopei and southern Chahar, and in many places east of Paoting and west of Tsangchow. When guerrilla warfare began, the guerrillas could not completely occupy these places but could only make frequent raids; they are areas which are held by the guerrillas when they are there and by the puppet regime when they are gone, and are therefore not yet guerrilla bases but only what may be called guerrilla zones. Such guerrilla zones will be transformed into base areas when they have gone through the necessary processes of guerrilla warfare, that is, when large numbers of enemy troops have been annihilated or defeated there, the puppet regime has been destroyed, the masses have been roused to activity, anti-Japanese mass organizations have been formed, people's local armed forces have been developed, and anti-Japanese political power has been established. By the expansion of our base areas we mean the addition of areas such as these to the bases already established.

In some places, for example, eastern Hopei, the whole area of guerrilla operations has been a guerrilla zone from the very beginning. The puppet regime is of long standing there, and from the beginning the whole area of operations has been a guerrilla zone both for the people's armed forces that have grown out of local uprisings and for the guerrilla detachments dispatched from the Wutai Mountains. At the outset of their activities, all they could do was to choose some fairly good spots there as temporary rear or base areas. Such places will not be transformed from guerrilla zones into relatively stable base areas until the enemy forces are destroyed and the work of arousing the people is in full swing.

Thus the transformation of a guerrilla zone into a base area is an arduous creative process, and its accomplishment depends on the extent to which the enemy is destroyed and the masses are aroused.

Many regions will remain guerrilla zones for a long time. In these regions the enemy will not be able to set up stable puppet regimes, however much he tries to maintain control, while we, on our part, will not be able to achieve the aim of establishing anti-Japanese political power, however much we develop guerrilla warfare. Examples of this kind are to be found in the enemy-occupied regions along the railway lines, in the neighbourhood of big cities and in certain areas in the plains.

As for the big cities, the railway stops and the areas in the plains which are strongly garrisoned by the enemy, guerrilla warfare can only extend to the fringes and not right into these places which have relatively stable puppet regimes. This is another kind of situation.

Mistakes in our leadership or strong enemy pressure may cause a reversal of the state of affairs described above, *i.e.*, a guerrilla base may turn into a guerrilla zone, and a guerrilla zone may turn into an area under relatively stable enemy occupation. Such changes are possible, and they deserve special vigilance on the part of guerrilla commanders.

Therefore, as a result of guerrilla warfare and the struggle between us and the enemy, the entire enemy-occupied territory will fall into the following three categories: first, anti-Japanese bases held by our guerrilla units and our organs of political power; second, areas held by Japanese imperialism and its puppet regimes; and third, inter-mediate zones contested by both sides, namely, guerrilla zones. Guerrilla commanders have the duty to expand the first and third categories to the maximum and to reduce the second category to the minimum. This is the strategic task of guerrilla warfare.

3. CONDITIONS FOR ESTABLISHING BASE AREAS

The fundamental conditions for establishing a base area are that there should be anti-Japanese armed forces, that these armed forces should be employed to inflict defeats on the enemy and that they should arouse the people to action. Thus the establishment of a base area is first and foremost a matter of building an armed force. Leaders in guerrilla war must devote their energy to building one or more guerrilla units, and must gradually develop them in the course of struggle into guerrilla formations or even into units and formations of regular troops. The building up of an armed force is the key to estab-lishing a base area; if there is no armed force or if the armed force is weak, nothing can be done. This constitutes the first condition.

The second indispensable condition for establishing a base area is that the armed forces should be used in co-ordination with the people to defeat the enemy. All places under enemy control are enemy, and not guerrilla, base areas, and obviously cannot be trans-formed into guerrilla base areas unless the enemy is defeated. Unless we repulse the enemy's attacks and defeat him, even places held by the guerrillas will come under enemy control, and then it will be impossible to establish base areas.

The third indispensable condition for establishing a base area is the use of all our strength, including our armed forces, to arouse the masses for struggle against Japan. In the course of this struggle we must arm the people, *i.e.*, organize self-defence corps and guerrilla units. In the course of this struggle, we must form mass organizations, we must organize the workers, peasants, youth, women, children, merchants and professional people — according to the degree of their political consciousness and fighting enthusiasm — into the various mass organizations necessary for the struggle against Japanese aggression, and we must gradually expand them. Without organization, the people cannot give effect to their anti-Japanese strength. In the course of this struggle, we must weed out the open and the hidden traitors, a task which can be accomplished only by relying on the strength of the people. In this struggle, it is particularly important to arouse the people to establish, or to consolidate, their local organs of anti-Japanese political power. Where the original Chinese organs of political power have not been destroyed by the enemy, we must re-organize and strengthen them with the support of the broad masses, and where they have been destroyed by the enemy, we should rebuild them by the efforts of the masses. They are organs of political power for carrying out the policy of the Anti-Japanese National United Front and should unite all the forces of the people to fight against our sole enemy, Japanese imperialism, and its jackals, the traitors and reactionaries.

A base area for guerrilla war can be truly established only with the gradual fulfilment of the three basic conditions, *i.e.*, only after the anti-Japanese armed forces are built up, the enemy has suffered defeats and the people are aroused.

Mention must also be made of geographical and economic con-ditions. As for the former, we have already discussed three different categories in the earlier section on the types of base areas, and here we need only mention one major requirement, namely, that the area must be extensive. In places surrounded by the enemy on all sides, or on three sides, the mountainous regions naturally offer the best conditions for setting up base areas which can hold out for a long time, but the main thing is that there must be enough room for the guerrillas to manoeuvre, namely, the areas have to be extensive. Given an extensive area, guerrilla warfare can be developed and sustained even in the plains, not to mention the river-lake-estuary regions. By and large, the vastness of China's territory and the enemy's shortage of troops provide guerrilla warfare in China with this con-dition. This is an important, even a primary condition, as far as the possibility of waging guerrilla warfare is concerned, and small countries like Belgium which lack this condition have few or no such possibili-ties.[8] In China, this condition is not something which has to be striven for, nor does it present a problem; it is there physically, waiting only to be exploited.

So far as their physical setting is concerned, the economic conditions resemble the geographical conditions. For now we are discussing the establishment of base areas not in a desert, where no enemy is to be found, but behind the enemy lines; every place the enemy can penetrate already has its Chinese inhabitants and an economic basis for subsistence, so that the question of choice of economic conditions in establishing base areas simply does not arise. Irrespective of the economic conditions, we should do our utmost to develop guerrilla warfare and set up permanent or temporary base areas in all places where Chinese inhabitants and enemy forces are to be found. In a political sense, however, the economic conditions do present a problem, a problem of economic policy which is of immense importance to the establishment of base areas. The economic policy of the guerrilla base areas must follow the principles of the Anti-Japanese National United Front by equitably distributing the financial burden and protecting commerce. Neither the local organs of political power nor the guerrilla units must violate these principles, or otherwise the establishment of base areas and the maintenance of guerrilla warfare would be adversely affected. The equitable distribution of the financial burden means that "those with money should contribute money", while the peasants should supply the guerrilla units with grain within certain limits. The protection of commerce means that the guerrilla units should be highly disciplined and that the confiscation of shops, except those owned by proved traitors, should be strictly prohibited. This is no easy matter, but the policy is set and must be put into effect.

4. THE CONSOLIDATION AND EXPANSION OF BASE AREAS

In order to confine the enemy invaders to a few strongholds, that is, to the big cities and along the main communication lines, the guerrillas must do all they can to extend guerrilla warfare from their base areas as widely as possible and hem in all the enemy's strongholds, thus threatening his existence and shaking his morale while expanding the base areas. This is essential. In this context, we must oppose conservatism in guerrilla warfare. Whether originating in the desire for an easy life or in overestimation of the enemy's strength, conservatism can only bring losses in the War of Resistance and is harmful to guerrilla warfare and to the base areas themselves. At the same time, we must not forget the consolidation of the base areas, the chief task being to arouse and organize the masses and to train guerrilla units and local armed forces. Such consolidation is needed for maintaining protracted warfare and also for expansion, and in its absence energetic expansion is impossible. If we attend only to expansion and forget about consolidation in our guerrilla warfare, we shall be unable to withstand the enemy's attacks, and consequently not only forfeit the possibility of expansion but also endanger the very existence of the base areas. The correct principle is expansion with consolidation, which is a good method and allows us to take the offensive or the defensive as we choose. Given a protracted war, the problem of consolidating and expanding base areas constantly arises for every guerrilla unit. The concrete solution depends, of course, on the circumstances. At one time, the emphasis may be on expansion, *i.e.*, on expanding the guerrilla zones and increasing the number of guerrillas. At another, the emphasis may be on consolidation, *i.e.*, on organizing the masses and training the troops. As expansion and consolidation differ in nature, and as the military dispositions and other tasks will differ accordingly, an effective solution of the problem is possible only if we alternate the emphasis according to time and circumstances.

5. FORMS IN WHICH WE AND THE ENEMY ENCIRCLE ONE ANOTHER

Taking the War of Resistance as a whole, there is no doubt that we are strategically encircled by the enemy, because he is on the strategic offensive and is operating on exterior lines while we are on the strategic defensive and are operating on interior lines. This is the first form of enemy encirclement. We on our part encircle each of the enemy columns advancing on us along separate routes, because we apply the policy of the offensive and of exterior-line operations in campaigns and battles by using numerically preponderant forces against these enemy columns advancing on us from exterior lines. This is the first form of our encirclement of the enemy. Next, if we consider the guerrilla base areas in the enemy's rear, each area taken singly is surrounded by the enemy on all sides, like the Wutai mountain region, or on three sides, like the northwestern Shansi area. This is the second form of enemy encirclement. However, if one considers all the guerrilla base areas together and in their relation to the battle fronts of the regular forces, one can see that we in turn surround a great many enemy forces. In Shansi Province, for instance, we have surrounded the Tatung-Puchow Railway on three sides (the east and

west flanks and the southern end) and the city of Taiyuan on all sides;
and there are many similar instances in Hopei and Shantung Provinces.
This is the second form of our encirclement of the enemy. Thus there
are two forms of encirclement by the enemy forces and two forms of
encirclement by our own — rather like a game of *weichi*.[9] Campaigns
and battles fought by the two sides resemble the capturing of each
other's pieces, and the establishment of strongholds by the enemy and
of guerrilla base areas by us resembles moves to dominate spaces
on the board. It is in the matter of "dominating the spaces" that the
great strategic role of guerrilla base areas in the rear of the enemy
is revealed. We are raising this question in the War of Resistance
in order that the nation's military authorities and the guerrilla commanders in all areas should place on the agenda the development of
guerrilla warfare behind the enemy lines and the establishment of
base areas wherever possible, and carry this out as a strategic task.
If on the international plane we can create an anti-Japanese front in
the Pacific region, with China as one strategic unit, and the Soviet
Union and other countries which may join it as other strategic units,
we shall then have one more form of encirclement against the enemy
than he has against us and bring about exterior-line operations in
the Pacific region by which to encircle and destroy fascist Japan. To
be sure, this is of little practical significance at present, but such a
prospect is not impossible.

CHAPTER VII

THE STRATEGIC DEFENSIVE
AND THE STRATEGIC OFFENSIVE
IN GUERRILLA WAR

The fourth problem of strategy in guerrilla war concerns the
strategic defensive and the strategic offensive. This is the problem
of how the policy of offensive warfare, which we mentioned in our
discussion of the first problem, is to be carried out in practice, when
we are on the defensive and when we are on the offensive in our
guerrilla warfare against Japan.

Within the nation-wide strategic defensive or strategic offensive
(to be more exact, the strategic counter-offensive), small-scale strategic

defensives and offensives take place in and around each guerrilla base area. By strategic defensive we mean our strategic situation and policy when the enemy is on the offensive and we are on the defensive; by strategic offensive we mean our strategic situation and policy when the enemy is on the defensive and we are on the offensive.

1. THE STRATEGIC DEFENSIVE IN GUERRILLA WAR

After guerrilla warfare has broken out and grown to a considerable extent, the enemy will inevitably attack the guerrilla base areas, especially in the period when his strategic offensive against the country as a whole is brought to an end and he adopts the policy of safeguarding his occupied areas. It is essential to recognize the inevitability of such attacks, for otherwise the guerrilla commanders will be caught wholly unprepared, and in the face of heavy enemy attacks they will undoubtedly become alarmed and confused and their forces will be routed.

To wipe out the guerrillas and their base areas, the enemy frequently resorts to converging attacks. For instance, in each of the four or five "punitive expeditions" directed against the Wutai mountain region, the enemy made a planned advance in three, four or even six or seven columns simultaneously. The larger the scale of the guerrilla fighting, the more important the position of the base areas, and the greater the threat to the enemy's strategic centres and vital communication lines, the fiercer will be the enemy's attacks. Therefore, the fiercer the enemy's attacks on a guerrilla area, the greater the indication that the guerrilla warfare there is successful and is being effectively co-ordinated with the regular fighting.

When the enemy launches a converging attack in several columns, the guerrilla policy should be to smash it by counter-attack. It can be easily smashed if each advancing enemy column consists of only one unit, whether big or small, has no follow-up units and is unable to station troops along the route of advance, construct blockhouses or build motor roads. When the enemy launches a converging attack, he is on the offensive and operating on exterior lines, while we are on the defensive and operating on interior lines. As for our dispositions, we should use our secondary forces to pin down several enemy columns, while our main force should launch surprise attacks (chiefly in the form of ambushes) in a campaign or battle against a single enemy column, striking it when it is on the move. The enemy, though strong, will be weakened by repeated surprise attacks and will often withdraw when he is halfway; the guerrilla units can then make more surprise attacks during the pursuit and weaken him still further. The enemy generally occupies the county towns or other towns in our base areas before he stops his offensive or begins to withdraw, and we should encircle these towns, cutting off his grain supply and severing his communications, so that when he cannot hold out and begins to retreat, we can seize the opportunity to pursue and attack him. After smashing one column, we should shift our forces to smash another, and, by smashing them one by one, shatter the converging attack.

A big base area like the Wutai mountain region forms a military area, which is divided into four or five, or even more, military sub-areas, each with its own armed forces operating independently. By employing the tactics described above, these forces have often smashed the enemy's attacks simultaneously or successively.

In our plan of operations against a converging attack by the enemy, we generally place our main force on interior lines. But when we have the strength to spare, we should use our secondary forces (such as the county or the district guerrilla units, or even detachments of the main force) on exterior lines to disrupt the enemy's communications and pin down his reinforcements. Should the enemy stay put in our base area, we may reverse the tactics, namely, leave some of our forces in the base area to invest the enemy while employing the main force to attack the region whence he has come and to step up our activities there, in order to induce him to withdraw and attack our main force; this is the tactic of "relieving the state of Chao by besieging the state of Wei".[10]

In the course of operations against a converging attack, the local anti-Japanese self-defence corps and all the mass organizations should mobilize for action and in every way help our troops to fight the enemy. In fighting the enemy, it is important both to enforce local martial law and, as far as possible, to "strengthen our defence works and clear the fields". The purpose of the former is to suppress traitors and prevent the enemy from getting information, and of the latter to assist our own operations (by strengthening our defence works) and prevent the enemy from getting food (by clearing the fields). "Clearing the fields" means harvesting the crops as soon as they are ripe.

When the enemy retreats, he often burns down the houses in the cities and towns he has occupied and razes the villages along his route, with the purpose of destroying the guerrilla base areas; but in so doing he deprives himself of shelter and food in his next offensive, and the damage recoils upon his own head. This is a concrete illustration of what we mean by one and the same thing having two contradictory aspects.

A guerrilla commander should not think of abandoning his base area and shifting to another, unless it proves impossible, after repeated operations, to smash the enemy's heavy converging attacks. In these circumstances he must guard against pessimism. So long as the leaders do not blunder in matters of principle, it is generally possible to smash the converging attacks and hold on to the base areas in the mountainous regions. It is only in the plains that, when confronted by a heavy converging attack, the guerrilla commander should consider other measures in the light of the specific circumstances, namely, leaving many small units for scattered operations, while temporarily shifting large guerrilla formations to some mountainous region, so that they can return and resume their activities in the plains once the main forces of the enemy move away.

Generally speaking, the Japanese cannot adopt the principle of blockhouse warfare, which the Kuomintang employed in the days of the civil war, because their forces are inadequate in relation to China's vast territory. However, we should reckon with the possibility that they may use it to some extent against those guerrilla base areas which pose a particular threat to their vital positions, but even in such circumstances we should be prepared to keep up guerrilla warfare in those areas. Since we have had the experience of being able to maintain guerrilla warfare during the civil war, there is not the slightest doubt of our greater capacity to do so in a national war. Though, in point of relative military strength, the enemy can throw forces that are vastly superior in quantity as well as in quality against some of our base areas, there remain the insoluble national contradiction between us and the enemy and the unavoidable weaknesses of his command. Our victories are based on thorough work among the masses and flexible tactics in our operations.

2. THE STRATEGIC OFFENSIVE IN GUERRILLA WAR

After we have smashed an enemy offensive and before the enemy starts a new offensive, he is on the strategic defensive and we are on the strategic offensive.

At such times our operational policy is not to attack enemy forces which are entrenched in defensive positions and which we are not sure of defeating, but systematically to destroy or drive out the small enemy units and puppet forces in certain areas, which our guerrilla units are strong enough to deal with, and to expand our areas, arouse the masses for struggle against Japan, replenish and train our troops and organize new guerrilla units. If the enemy still remains on the defensive when these tasks are under way, we can expand our new areas still further and attack weakly garrisoned cities and communication lines and hold them for as long as circumstances permit. These are all tasks of the strategic offensive, and the purpose is to take advantage of the fact that the enemy is on the defensive so that we may effectively build up our own military and mass strength, effectively reduce the enemy's strength and prepare to smash the enemy methodically and vigorously when he mounts an offensive again.

It is essential to rest and train our troops, and the best time for doing so is when the enemy is on the defensive. It is not a question of shutting ourselves off from everything else for rest and training, but of finding time for rest and training while expanding our areas, mopping up small enemy units and arousing the people. This is usually also the time for tackling the difficult problem of getting food supplies, bedding, clothing, etc.

It is also the time for destroying the enemy's communication lines on a large scale, hampering his transport and giving direct support to the regular forces in their campaigns.

At such times the guerrilla base areas, guerrilla zones and guerrilla units are in high spirits, and the areas devastated by the enemy are gradually rehabilitated and revived. The people in the enemy-occupied territories are also delighted, and the fame of the guerrillas resounds everywhere. On the other hand, in the camp of the enemy and his running dogs, the traitors, panic and disintegration are mounting, while there is growing hatred of the guerrillas and their base areas and preparations to deal with them are intensified. During the strategic offensive, therefore, it is impermissible for the guerrilla commanders to become so elated as to underrate the enemy and forget to strengthen unity in their own ranks and to consolidate their base areas and their forces. At such times, they must skilfully watch the enemy's every move for signs of any new offensive against us, so that the moment it comes they can wind up their strategic offensive in good order, turn to the strategic defensive and thereby smash the enemy's offensive.

CHAPTER VIII

DEVELOPMENT OF GUERRILLA WAR
INTO MOBILE WAR

The fifth problem of strategy in guerrilla war against Japan is its development into mobile war, a development which is necessary and possible because the war is protracted and ruthless. If China could speedily defeat the Japanese invaders and recover her lost territories, and if the war were neither protracted nor ruthless, this would not be necessary. But as, on the contrary, the war is protracted and ruthless, guerrilla warfare cannot adapt itself to such a war except by developing into mobile warfare. Since the war is protracted and ruthless, it is possible for the guerrilla units to undergo the necessary steeling and gradually to transform themselves into regular forces, so that their mode of operations is gradually regularized and guerrilla warfare develops into mobile warfare. The necessity and possibility of this development must be clearly recognized by the guerrilla commanders if they are to persist in, and systematically carry out, the policy of turning guerrilla warfare into mobile warfare.

In many places, such as the Wutai mountain region, the present guerrilla warfare owes its growth to the strong detachments sent there by the regular forces. The operations there, though generally of a guerrilla character, have contained an element of mobile warfare from the very beginning. This element will gradually increase as the war goes on. Herein lies the advantage which makes possible the swift expansion of the present anti-Japanese guerrilla warfare and its rapid development to a higher level; thus the conditions for guerrilla warfare are far superior to what they were in the three northeastern provinces.

To transform guerrilla units waging guerrilla warfare into regular forces waging mobile warfare, two conditions are necessary — an increase in numbers, and an improvement in quality. Apart from directly mobilizing the people to join the forces, increased numbers can be attained by amalgamating small units, while better quality depends on steeling the fighters and improving their weapons in the course of the war.

In amalgamating small units, we must, on the one hand, guard against localism, whereby attention is concentrated exclusively on local interests and centralization is impeded, and, on the other, guard against the purely military approach, whereby local interests are brushed aside.

Localism exists among the local guerrilla units and local governments, which are frequently preoccupied with local considerations to the neglect of the general interest, or which prefer to act each on its own because they are unaccustomed to acting in larger groups. The commanders of the main guerrilla units or of the guerrilla formations must take this into account and adopt the method of gradual amalgamation of part of the local units, allowing the localities to keep some of their forces and expand their guerrilla warfare; the commanders should draw these units into joint operations and then bring about their amalgamation without breaking up their original organization or reshuffling their cadres, so that the small groups may integrate smoothly into the larger group.

As against localism, the purely military approach represents the wrong viewpoint held in the main forces by those who are bent on expanding their own strength and who neglect to assist the local armed units. They do not realize that the development of guerrilla warfare into mobile warfare means not the abandonment of guerrilla warfare, but the gradual formation, in the midst of widespread guerrilla warfare, of a main force capable of conducting mobile warfare, a force around which there must still be numerous guerrilla units carrying on extensive guerrilla operations. These guerrilla units are powerful auxiliaries to the main force and serve as inexhaustible reserves for its continuous growth. Therefore, if a commander of a main force has made the mistake of neglecting the interests of the local population and the local government as a result of a purely military approach, he must correct it in order that the expansion of the main force and the multiplication of the local armed units may both receive due attention.

To raise the quality of the guerrilla units it is imperative to raise their political and organizational level and improve their equipment, military technique, tactics and discipline, so that they gradually pattern themselves on the regular forces and shed their guerrilla ways. Politically, it is imperative to get both the commanders and the fighters to realize the necessity of raising the guerrilla units to the level of the regular forces, to encourage them to strive towards this end, and to guarantee its attainment by means of political work. Organizationally, it is imperative gradually to fulfil all the requirements of a regular formation in the following respects — military and political organs, staff and working methods, a regular supply system, a medical service, etc. In the matter of equipment, it is imperative to acquire better and more varied weapons and increase the supply of the necessary communications equipment. In the matter of military technique and tactics, it is imperative to raise the guerrilla units to the level required of a regular formation. In the matter of discipline, it is imperative to raise the level so that uniform standards are observed, every order is executed without fail and all slackness is eliminated. To accomplish all these tasks requires a prolonged effort, and it cannot be done overnight; but that is the direction in which we must develop. Only thus can a main force be built up in each guerrilla base area and mobile warfare emerge for more effective attacks on the enemy. Where detachments or cadres have been sent in by the regular forces, the goal can be achieved more easily. Hence all the regular forces have the responsibility of helping the guerrilla units to develop into regular units.

CHAPTER IX

THE RELATIONSHIP OF COMMAND

The last problem of strategy in guerrilla war against Japan concerns the relationship of command. A correct solution of this problem is one of the prerequisites for the unhampered development of guerrilla warfare.

Since guerrilla units are a lower level of armed organization characterized by dispersed operations, the methods of command in guerrilla warfare do not allow as high a degree of centralization as in regular warfare. If any attempt is made to apply the methods of command in regular warfare to guerrilla warfare, its great flexibility will inevitably be restricted and its vitality sapped. A highly centralized command is in direct contradiction to the great flexibility of guerrilla warfare and must not and cannot be applied to it.

However, guerrilla warfare cannot be successfully developed without some centralized command. When extensive regular warfare and extensive guerrilla warfare are going on at the same time, their operations must be properly co-ordinated; hence the need for a command co-ordinating the two, *i.e.*, for a unified strategic command by the national general staff and the war-zone commanders. In a guerrilla zone or guerrilla base area with many guerrilla units, there are usually one or more guerrilla formations (sometimes together with regular formations) which constitute the main force, a number of other guerrilla units, big and small, which represent the supplementary force, and many armed units composed of people not withdrawn from production; the enemy forces there usually form a unified complex to concert their operations against the guerrillas. Consequently, the problem arises of setting up a unified or centralized command in such guerrilla zones or base areas.

Hence, as opposed both to absolute centralization and to absolute decentralization, the principle of command in guerrilla war should be centralized strategic command and decentralized command in campaigns and battles.

Centralized strategic command includes the planning and direction of guerrilla warfare as a whole by the state, the co-ordination of guerrilla warfare with regular warfare in each war zone, and the unified direction of all the anti-Japanese armed forces in each guerrilla zone or base area. Here lack of harmony, unity and centralization is harmful, and every effort must be made to ensure all three. In general matters, that is, matters of strategy, the lower levels should report to the higher and follow their instructions so as to ensure concerted action. Centralization, however, stops at this point, and it would likewise be harmful to go beyond it and interfere with the lower levels in matters of detail like the specific dispositions for a campaign or battle. For such details must be settled in the light of specific conditions, which change from time to time and from place to place and are quite beyond the knowledge of the distant higher levels of command. This is what is meant by the principle of decentralized command in campaigns and battles. The same principle generally applies in regular operations, especially when communications are inadequate. In a word, it means guerrilla warfare waged independently and with the initiative in our hands within the framework of a unified strategy.

Where a guerrilla base area constitutes a military area divided into sub-areas, each comprising several counties, each of which is again divided into districts, the relationship between the various levels, from the headquarters of the military area and sub-areas down to the county and district governments, is one of consecutive subordination, and every armed force must, according to its nature, be under the direct command of one of these. On the principle that has been enunciated, in the relationship of command at these levels matters of general policy should be centralized in the higher levels, while actual operations should be carried out in the light of the specific circumstances by the lower levels, which should have the right of independent action. If a higher level has something to say about the actual operations undertaken at a lower level, it can and should advance its views as "instructions" but must not issue hard and fast "commands". The more extensive the area, the more complex the situation and the greater the distance between the higher and the lower levels, the more advisable it becomes to allow greater independence to the lower levels in their actual operations and thus give those operations a character conforming more closely to the local requirements, so that the lower levels and the local personnel may develop the ability to work independently, cope with complicated situations, and successfully expand guerrilla warfare. For an armed unit or bigger formation which is engaged in a concentrated operation, the principle to be applied is one of centralization in its internal relationship of command, since the situation is clear to the higher command; but the moment this unit or formation breaks up for dispersed action, the principle of centralization in general matters and of decentralization in details should be applied, for then the specific situation cannot be clear to the higher command.

Absence of centralization where it is needed means negligence by the higher levels or usurpation of authority by the lower levels, neither of which can be tolerated in the relationship between higher and lower levels, especially in the military sphere. If decentralization is not effected where it should be, that means monopolization of power by the higher levels and lack of initiative on the part of the lower levels, neither of which can be tolerated in the relationship between higher and lower levels, especially in the command of guerrilla warfare. The above principles constitute the only correct policy for solving the problem of the relationship of command.

NOTES

[1] The Changpai mountain range is situated on the northeastern border of China. After the Japanese invasion on September 18, 1931, the region became a base area for the anti-Japanese guerrillas led by the Chinese Communist Party.

² The Wutai mountain range is situated on the borders between Shansi, Hopei, and what was then Chahar Province. In October 1937 the Eighth Route Army led by the Chinese Communist Party started building the Shansi-Chahar-Hopei anti-Japanese base area with the Wutai mountain region as its centre.

³ The Taihang mountain range is situated on the borders between Shansi, Hopei and Honan Provinces. In November 1937 the Eighth Route Army started building the southeastern Shansi anti-Japanese base area with the Taihang mountain region as its centre.

⁴ The Taishan Mountain is one of the chief peaks of the Tai-Yi mountain range in central Shantung. In the winter of 1937 the guerrilla forces led by the Communist Party started building the central Shantung anti-Japanese base area with the Tai-Yi mountain region as its centre.

⁵ The Yenshan mountain range is situated on the border of Hopei and what was then Jehol Province. In the summer of 1938 the Eighth Route Army started building the eastern Hopei anti-Japanese base area with the Yenshan mountain region as its centre.

⁶ The Maoshan Mountains are in southern Kiangsu. In June 1938 the New Fourth Army led by the Communist Party started building the southern Kiangsu anti-Japanese base area with the Maoshan mountain region as its centre.

⁷ Experience gained in the War of Resistance proved that it was possible to establish long-term and, in many places, stable base areas in the plains. This was due to their vastness and big populations, the correctness of the Communist Party's policies, the extensive mobilization of the people and the enemy's shortage of troops. Comrade Mao Tse-tung affirmed this possibility more definitely in later directives.

⁸ Ever since the end of World War II, the national and democratic revolutionary movement has been surging forward in Asia, Africa and Latin America. In many countries the people, led by their own revolutionary and progressive forces, have carried on sustained armed struggles to overthrow the dark rule of imperialism and reaction. This demonstrates that in the new historical circumstances — when the socialist camp, the revolutionary forces of the people in the colonial countries and the forces of the people striving for democracy and progress in all countries are taking giant strides forward, when the world capitalist system is weakening still further, and when the colonial rule of imperialism is heading for disintegration — the conditions under which the people of various countries conduct guerrilla warfare today need not be quite the same as those which were necessary in the days of the guerrilla warfare waged by the Chinese people against Japan. In other words, guerrilla war can be victoriously waged in a country which is not large in territory, as for instance, in Cuba, Algeria, Laos and southern Viet Nam.

⁹ *Weichi* is an old Chinese game, in which the two players try to encircle each other's pieces on the board. When a player's pieces are encircled, they are counted as "dead" (captured). But if there is a sufficient number of blank spaces among the encircled pieces, then the latter are still "alive" (not captured).

¹⁰ In 353 B.C. the state of Wei laid siege to Hantan, capital of the state of Chao. The king of the state of Chi, an ally of Chao, ordered his generals Tien Chi and Sun Pin to aid Chao with their troops. Knowing that the crack forces of Wei had entered Chao and left their own territory weakly garrisoned, General Sun Pin attacked the state of Wei whose troops withdrew to defend their own country. Taking advantage of their exhaustion, the troops of Chi engaged and routed them at Kueiling (northeast of the present Hotse County in Shantung). The siege of Hantan, capital of Chao, was thus lifted. Since then Chinese strategists have referred to similar tactics as "relieving the state of Chao by besieging the state of Wei".

ON PROTRACTED WAR

May 1938

STATEMENT OF THE PROBLEM

1. It will soon be July 7, the first anniversary of the great War of Resistance Against Japan. Rallying in unity, persevering in resistance and persevering in the united front, the forces of the whole nation have been valiantly fighting the enemy for almost a year. The people of the whole world are attentively following this war, which has no precedent in the history of the East, and which will go down as a great war in world history too. Every Chinese suffering from the disasters of the war and fighting for the survival of his nation daily yearns for victory. But what actually will be the course of the war? Can we win? Can we win quickly? Many people are talking about a protracted war, but why is it a protracted war? How to carry on a protracted war? Many people are talking about final victory, but why will final victory be ours? How shall we strive for final victory? Not everyone has found answers to these questions; in fact, to this day most people have not done so. Therefore the defeatist exponents of the theory of national subjugation have come forward to tell people that China will be subjugated, that final victory will not be China's. On the other hand, some impetuous friends have come forward to tell people that China will win very quickly without having to exert any great effort. But are these views correct? We have said all along they are not. However, most people have not yet grasped what we have been saying. This is partly because we did not do enough propaganda and explanatory work, and partly because the development

---

This series of lectures was delivered by Comrade Mao Tse-tung from May 26 to June 3, 1938, at the Yenan Association for the Study of the War of Resistance Against Japan.

113

of objective events had not yet fully and clearly revealed their inherent nature and their features to the people, who were thus not in a position to foresee the over-all trend and the outcome and hence to decide on a complete set of policies and tactics. Now things are better; the experience of ten months of war has been quite sufficient to explode the utterly baseless theory of national subjugation and to dissuade our impetuous friends from their theory of quick victory. In these circumstances many people are asking for a comprehensive explanation. All the more so with regard to protracted war, not only because of the opposing theories of national subjugation and quick victory but also because of the shallow understanding of its nature. "Our four hundred million people have been making a concerted effort since the Lukouchiao Incident, and the final victory will belong to China." This formula has a wide currency. It is a correct formula but needs to be given more content. Our perseverance in the War of Resistance and in the united front has been possible because of many factors. Internally, they comprise all the political parties in the country from the Communist Party to the Kuomintang, all the people from the workers and peasants to the bourgeoisie, and all the armed forces from the regular forces to the guerrillas; internationally, they range from the land of socialism to justice-loving people in all countries; in the camp of the enemy, they range from those people in Japan who are against the war to those Japanese soldiers at the front who are against the war. In short, all these forces have contributed in varying degrees to our War of Resistance. Every man with a conscience should salute them. We Communists, together with all the other anti-Japanese political parties and the whole people, have no other course than to strive to unite all forces for the defeat of the diabolical Japanese aggressors. July 1 this year will be the 17th anniversary of the founding of the Communist Party of China. A serious study of protracted war is necessary in order to enable every Communist to play a better and greater part in the War of Resistance. Therefore my lectures will be devoted to such a study. I shall try to speak on all the problems relevant to the protracted war, but I cannot possibly go into everything in one series of lectures.

2. All the experience of the ten months of war proves the error both of the theory of China's inevitable subjugation and of the theory of China's quick victory. The former gives rise to the tendency to compromise and the latter to the tendency to underestimate the enemy.

Both approaches to the problem are subjective and one-sided, or, in a word, unscientific.

3. Before the War of Resistance, there was a great deal of talk about national subjugation. Some said, "China is inferior in arms and is bound to lose in a war." Others said, "If China offers armed resistance, she is sure to become another Abyssinia." Since the beginning of the war, open talk of national subjugation has disappeared, but secret talk, and quite a lot of it too, still continues. For instance, from time to time an atmosphere of compromise arises and the advocates of compromise argue that "the continuance of the war spells subjugation".[1] In a letter from Hunan a student has written:

> In the countryside everything seems difficult. Doing propaganda work on my own, I have to talk to people when and where I find them. The people I have talked to are by no means ignoramuses; they all have some understanding of what is going on and are very interested in what I have to say. But when I run into my own relatives, they always say: "China cannot win; she is doomed." They make one sick! Fortunately, they do not go around spreading their views, otherwise things would really be bad. The peasants would naturally put more stock in what they say.

Such exponents of the theory of China's inevitable subjugation form the social basis of the tendency to compromise. They are to be found everywhere in China, and therefore the problem of compromise is liable to crop up within the anti-Japanese front at any time and will probably remain with us right until the end of the war. Now that Hsuchow has fallen and Wuhan is in danger, it will not be unprofitable, I think, to knock the bottom out of the theory of national subjugation.

4. During these ten months of war all kinds of views which are indicative of impetuosity have also appeared. For instance, at the outset of the war many people were groundlessly optimistic, underestimating Japan and even believing that the Japanese could not get as far as Shansi. Some belittled the strategic role of guerrilla warfare in the War of Resistance and doubted the proposition, "With regard to the whole, mobile warfare is primary and guerrilla warfare supplementary; with regard to the parts, guerrilla warfare is primary and mobile warfare supplementary." They disagreed with the Eighth Route

Army's strategy, "Guerrilla warfare is basic, but lose no chance for mobile warfare under favourable conditions", which they regarded as a "mechanical" approach.[2] During the battle of Shanghai some people said: "If we can fight for just three months, the international situation is bound to change, the Soviet Union is bound to send troops, and the war will be over." They pinned their hopes for the future of the War of Resistance chiefly on foreign aid.[3] After the Taierhchuang victory,[4] some people maintained that the Hsuchow campaign should be fought as a "quasi-decisive campaign" and that the policy of protracted war should be changed. They said such things as, "This campaign marks the last desperate struggle of the enemy," or, "If we win, the Japanese warlords will be demoralized and able only to await their Day of Judgement."[5] The victory at Pinghsingkuan turned some people's heads, and further victory at Taierhchuang has turned more people's heads. Doubts have arisen as to whether the enemy will attack Wuhan. Many people think "probably not", and many others "definitely not". Such doubts may affect all major issues. For instance, is our anti-Japanese strength already sufficient? Some people may answer affirmatively, for our present strength is already sufficient to check the enemy's advance, so why increase it? Or, for instance, is the slogan "Consolidate and expand the Anti-Japanese National United Front" still correct? Some people may answer negatively, for the united front in its present state is already strong enough to repulse the enemy, so why consolidate and expand it? Or, for instance, should our efforts in diplomacy and international propaganda be intensified? Here again the answer may be in the negative. Or, for instance, should we proceed in earnest to reform the army system and the system of government, develop the mass movement, enforce education for national defence, suppress traitors and Trotskyites, develop war industries and improve the people's livelihood? Or, for instance, are the slogans calling for the defence of Wuhan, of Canton and of the Northwest and for the vigorous development of guerrilla warfare in the enemy's rear still correct? The answers might all be in the negative. There are even some people who, the moment a slightly favourable turn occurs in the war situation, are prepared to intensify the "friction" between the Kuomintang and the Communist Party, diverting attention from external to internal matters. This almost invariably occurs whenever a comparatively big battle is won or the enemy's advance comes to a temporary halt. All the above can be termed political and military short-sightedness. Such talk, however plausible, is actually specious and groundless. To sweep away such verbiage should help the victorious prosecution of the War of Resistance.

5. The question now is: Will China be subjugated? The answer is, No, she will not be subjugated, but will win final victory. Can China win quickly? The answer is, No, she cannot win quickly, and the War of Resistance will be a protracted war.

6. As early as two years ago, we broadly indicated the main arguments on these questions. On July 16, 1936, five months before the Sian Incident and twelve months before the Lukouchiao Incident, in an interview with the American correspondent, Mr. Edgar Snow, I made a general estimate of the situation with regard to war between China and Japan and advanced various principles for winning victory. The following excerpts may serve as a reminder:

Question: Under what conditions do you think China can defeat and destroy the forces of Japan?

Answer: Three conditions are required: first, the establishment of an anti-Japanese united front in China; second, the formation of an international anti-Japanese united front; third, the rise of the revolutionary movement of the people in Japan and the Japanese colonies. From the standpoint of the Chinese people, the unity of the people of China is the most important of the three conditions.

Question: How long do you think such a war would last?

Answer: That depends on the strength of China's anti-Japanese united front and many other conditioning factors involving China and Japan. That is to say, apart from China's own strength, which is the main thing, international help to China and the help rendered by the revolution in Japan are also important. If China's anti-Japanese united front is greatly expanded and effectively organized horizontally and vertically, if the necessary help is given to China by those governments and peoples which recognize the Japanese imperialist menace to their own interests and if revolution comes quickly in Japan, the war will speedily be brought to an end and China will speedily win victory. If these conditions are not realized quickly, the war will be prolonged. But in the end, just the same, Japan will certainly be defeated and China will certainly be victorious. Only the sacrifices will be great and there will be a very painful period.

Question: What is your opinion of the probable course of development of such a war, politically and militarily?

Answer: Japan's continental policy is already fixed, and those who think they can halt the Japanese advance by making compromises with Japan at the expense of more Chinese territory and sovereign rights are indulging in mere fantasy. We definitely know that the lower Yangtse valley and our southern seaports are already included in the continental programme of Japanese imperialism. Moreover, Japan wants to occupy the Philippines, Siam, Indo-China, the Malay Peninsula and the Dutch East Indies in order to cut off other countries from China and monopolize the southwestern Pacific. This is Japan's maritime policy. In such a period, China will undoubtedly be in an extremely difficult position. But the majority of the Chinese people believe that such difficulties can be overcome; only the rich in the big port cities are defeatists because they are afraid of losing their property. Many people think it would be impossible for China to continue the war, once her coastline is blockaded by Japan. This is nonsense. To refute them we need only cite the war history of the Red Army. In the present War of Resistance Against Japan, China's position is much superior to that of the Red Army in the civil war. China is a vast country, and even if Japan should succeed in occupying a section of China with as many as 100 to 200 million people, we would still be far from defeated. We would still have ample strength to fight against Japan, while the Japanese would have to fight defensive battles in their rear throughout the war. The heterogeneity and uneven development of China's economy are rather advantageous in the war of resistance. For example, to sever Shanghai from the rest of China would definitely not be as disastrous to China as would be the severance of New York from the rest of the United States. Even if Japan blockades the Chinese coastline, it is impossible for her to blockade China's Northwest, Southwest and West. Thus, once more the central point of the problem is the unity of the entire Chinese people and the building up of a nation-wide anti-Japanese front. This is what we have long been advocating.

Question: If the war drags on for a long time and Japan is not completely defeated, would the Communist Party agree to the negotiation of a peace with Japan and recognize her rule in northeastern China?

Answer: No. Like the people of the whole country, the Chinese Communist Party will not allow Japan to retain an inch of Chinese territory.

Question: What, in your opinion, should be the main strategy and tactics to be followed in this "war of liberation"?

Answer: Our strategy should be to employ our main forces to operate over an extended and fluid front. To achieve success, the Chinese troops must conduct their warfare with a high degree of mobility on extensive battlefields, making swift advances and withdrawals, swift concentrations and dispersals. This means large-scale mobile warfare, and not positional warfare depending exclusively on defence works with deep trenches, high fortresses and successive rows of defensive positions. It does not mean the abandonment of all the vital strategic points, which should be defended by positional warfare as long as profitable. But the pivotal strategy must be mobile warfare. Positional warfare is also necessary, but strategically it is auxiliary and secondary. Geographically the theatre of the war is so vast that it is possible for us to conduct mobile warfare most effectively. In the face of the vigorous actions of our forces, the Japanese army will have to be cautious. Its war-machine is ponderous and slow-moving, with limited efficiency. If we concentrate our forces on a narrow front for a defensive war of attrition, we would be throwing away the advantages of our geography and economic organization and repeating the mistake of Abyssinia. In the early period of the war, we must avoid any major decisive battles, and must first employ mobile warfare gradually to break the morale and combat effectiveness of the enemy troops.

Besides employing trained armies to carry on mobile warfare, we must organize great numbers of guerrilla units among the peasants. One should know that the anti-Japanese volunteer units in the three northeastern provinces are only a minor demonstration of the latent power of resistance that can be mobilized from the peasants of the whole country. The Chinese peasants have very great latent power; properly organized and directed, they can keep the Japanese army busy twenty-four hours a day and worry it to death. It must be remembered that the war will be fought in China, that is to say, the Japanese army will be entirely surrounded by the hostile Chinese people, it will be forced to move in all its provisions and guard them, it must use large numbers of troops to protect its lines of communications and constantly guard against attacks, and it needs large forces to garrison Manchuria and Japan as well.

In the course of the war, China will be able to capture many Japanese soldiers and seize many weapons and munitions with which to arm herself; at the same time China will win foreign aid to reinforce the equipment of her troops gradually. Therefore China will be able to conduct positional warfare in the latter period of the war and make positional attacks on the Japanese-occupied areas. Thus Japan's economy will crack under the strain of China's long resistance and the morale of the Japanese forces will break under the trial of innumerable battles. On the Chinese side, however, the growing latent power of resistance will be constantly brought into play and large numbers of revolutionary people will be pouring into the front lines to fight for their freedom. The combination of all these and other factors will enable us to make the final and decisive attacks on the fortifications and bases in the Japanese-occupied areas and drive the Japanese forces of aggression out of China.

The above views have been proved correct in the light of the experience of the ten months of war and will also be borne out in the future.

7. As far back as August 25, 1937, less than two months after the Lukouchiao Incident, the Central Committee of the Chinese Communist Party clearly pointed out in its "Resolution on the Present Situation and the Tasks of the Party":

The military provocation by the Japanese aggressors at Lukouchiao and their occupation of Peiping and Tientsin represent only the beginning of their large-scale invasion of China south of the Great Wall. They have already begun their national mobilization for war. Their propaganda that they have "no desire to aggravate the situation" is only a smokescreen for further attacks.

The resistance at Lukouchiao on July 7 marked the starting point of China's national War of Resistance.

Thus a new stage has opened in China's political situation, the stage of actual resistance. The stage of preparation for resistance is over. In the present stage the central task is to mobilize all the nation's forces for victory in the War of Resistance.

The key to victory in the war now lies in developing the resistance that has already begun into a war of total resistance by the whole nation. Only through such a war of total resistance can final victory be won.

The existence of serious weaknesses in the War of Resistance may lead to many setbacks, retreats, internal splits, betrayals, temporary and partial compromises and other such reverses. Therefore it should be realized that the war will be an arduous and protracted war. But we are confident that, through the efforts of our Party and the whole people, the resistance already started will sweep aside all obstacles and continue to advance and develop.

The above thesis, too, has been proved correct in the light of the experience of the ten months of war and will also be borne out in the future.

8. Epistemologically speaking, the source of all erroneous views on war lies in idealist and mechanistic tendencies on the question. People with such tendencies are subjective and one-sided in their approach to problems. They either indulge in groundless and purely subjective talk, or, basing themselves upon a single aspect or a temporary manifestation, magnify it with similar subjectivity into the whole of the problem. But there are two categories of erroneous views, one comprising fundamental, and therefore consistent, errors which are hard to correct, and the other comprising accidental, and therefore temporary, errors which are easy to correct. Since both are wrong, both need to be corrected. Therefore, only by opposing idealist and mechanistic tendencies and taking an objective and all-sided view in making a study of war can we draw correct conclusions on the question of war.

THE BASIS OF THE PROBLEM

9. Why is the War of Resistance Against Japan a protracted war? Why will the final victory be China's? What is the basis for these statements?

The war between China and Japan is not just any war, it is specifically a war of life and death between semi-colonial and semi-feudal China and imperialist Japan, fought in the Nineteen Thirties. Herein lies the basis of the whole problem. The two sides in the war have many contrasting features, which will be considered in turn below.

10. *The Japanese side.* First, Japan is a powerful imperialist country, which ranks first in the East in military, economic and political-organizational power, and is one of the five or six foremost imperialist countries of the world. These are the basic factors in Japan's war of aggression. The inevitability of the war and the impossibility of quick victory for China are due to Japan's imperialist system and her great military, economic and political-organizational power. Secondly, however, the imperialist character of Japan's social economy determines the imperialist character of her war, a war that is retrogressive and barbarous. In the Nineteen Thirties, the internal and external contradictions of Japanese imperialism have driven her not only to embark on an adventurist war unparalleled in scale but also to approach her final collapse. In terms of social development, Japan is no longer a thriving country; the war will not lead to the prosperity sought by her ruling classes but to the very reverse, the doom of Japanese imperialism. This is what we mean by the retrogressive nature of Japan's war. It is this reactionary quality, coupled with the military-feudal character of Japanese imperialism, that gives rise to the peculiar barbarity of Japan's war. All of which will arouse to the utmost the class antagonisms within Japan, the antagonism between the Japanese and the Chinese nations, and the antagonism between Japan and most other countries of the world. The reactionary and barbarous character of Japan's war constitutes the primary reason for her inevitable defeat. Thirdly, Japan's war is conducted on the basis of her great military, economic and political-organizational power, but at the same time it rests on an inadequate natural endowment. Japan's military, economic and political-organizational power is great but quantitatively inadequate. Japan is a comparatively small country, deficient in manpower and in military, financial and material resources, and she cannot stand a long war. Japan's rulers are endeavouring to resolve this difficulty through war, but again they will get the very reverse of what they desire; that is to say, the war they have launched to resolve this difficulty will eventually aggravate it and even exhaust Japan's original resources. Fourthly and lastly, while Japan can get international support from the fascist countries, the international opposition she is bound to encounter will be greater than her international support. This opposition will gradually grow and eventually not only cancel out the support but even bear down upon Japan herself. Such is the law that an unjust cause finds meagre support, and such is the con-

sequence of the very nature of Japan's war. To sum up, Japan's advantage lies in her great capacity to wage war, and her disadvantages lie in the reactionary and barbarous nature of her war, in the inadequacy of her manpower and material resources, and in her meagre international support. These are the characteristics on the Japanese side.

11. *The Chinese side.* First, we are a semi-colonial and semi-feudal country. The Opium War,[6] the Taiping Revolution,[7] the Reform Movement of 1898,[8] the Revolution of 1911[9] and the Northern Expedition[10] — the revolutionary or reform movements which aimed at extricating China from her semi-colonial and semi-feudal state — all met with serious setbacks, and China remains a semi-colonial and semi-feudal country. We are still a weak country and manifestly inferior to the enemy in military, economic and political-organizational power. Here again one can find the basis for the inevitability of the war and the impossibility of quick victory for China. Secondly, however, China's liberation movement, with its cumulative development over the last hundred years, is now different from that of any previous period. Although the domestic and foreign forces opposing it have caused it serious setbacks, at the same time they have tempered the Chinese people. Although China today is not so strong as Japan militarily, economically, politically and culturally, yet there are factors in China more progressive than in any other period of her history. The Communist Party of China and the army under its leadership represent these progressive factors. It is on the basis of this progress that China's present war of liberation can be protracted and can achieve final victory. By contrast with Japanese imperialism, which is declining, China is a country rising like the morning sun. China's war is progressive, hence its just character. Because it is a just war, it is capable of arousing the nation to unity, of evoking the sympathy of the people in Japan and of winning the support of most countries in the world. Thirdly, and again by contrast with Japan, China is a very big country with vast territory, rich resources, a large population and plenty of soldiers, and is capable of sustaining a long war. Fourthly and lastly, there is broad international support for China stemming from the progressive and just character of her war, which is again exactly the reverse of the meagre support for Japan's unjust cause. To sum up, China's disadvantage lies in her military weakness, and her advantages lie in the progressive and just character of her

war, her great size and her abundant international support. These are China's characteristics.

12. Thus it can be seen that Japan has great military, economic and political-organizational power, but that her war is reactionary and barbarous, her manpower and material resources are inadequate, and she is in an unfavourable position internationally. China, on the contrary, has less military, economic and political-organizational power, but she is in her era of progress, her war is progressive and just, she is moreover a big country, a factor which enables her to sustain a protracted war, and she will be supported by most countries. The above are the basic, mutually contradictory characteristics of the Sino-Japanese war. They have determined and are determining all the political policies and military strategies and tactics of the two sides; they have determined and are determining the protracted character of the war and its outcome, namely, that the final victory will go to China and not to Japan. The war is a contest between these characteristics. They will change in the course of the war, each according to its own nature; and from this everything else will follow. These characteristics exist objectively and are not invented to deceive people; they constitute all the basic elements of the war, and are not incomplete fragments; they permeate all major and minor problems on both sides and all stages of the war, and they are not matters of no consequence. If anyone forgets these characteristics in studying the Sino-Japanese war, he will surely go wrong; and even though some of his ideas win credence for a time and may seem right, they will inevitably be proved wrong by the course of the war. On the basis of these characteristics we shall now proceed to explain the problems to be dealt with.

REFUTATION OF THE THEORY OF NATIONAL SUBJUGATION

13. The theorists of national subjugation, who see nothing but the contrast between the enemy's strength and our weakness, used to say, "Resistance will mean subjugation," and now they are saying, "The continuance of the war spells subjugation." We shall not be able to convince them merely by stating that Japan, though strong, is small, while China, though weak, is large. They can adduce historical

instances, such as the destruction of the Sung Dynasty by the Yuan and the destruction of the Ming Dynasty by the Ching, to prove that a small but strong country can vanquish a large but weak one and, moreover, that a backward country can vanquish an advanced one. If we say these events occurred long ago and do not prove the point, they can cite the British subjugation of India to prove that a small but strong capitalist country can vanquish a large but weak and backward country. Therefore, we have to produce other grounds before we can silence and convince all the subjugationists, and supply everyone engaged in propaganda with adequate arguments to persuade those who are still confused or irresolute and so strengthen their faith in the War of Resistance.

14. What then are the grounds we should advance? The characteristics of the epoch. These characteristics are concretely reflected in Japan's retrogression and paucity of support and in China's progress and abundance of support.

15. Our war is not just any war, it is specifically a war between China and Japan fought in the Nineteen Thirties. Our enemy, Japan, is first of all a moribund imperialist power; she is already in her era of decline and is not only different from Britain at the time of the subjugation of India, when British capitalism was still in the era of its ascendency, but also different from what she herself was at the time of World War I twenty years ago. The present war was launched on the eve of the general collapse of world imperialism and, above all, of the fascist countries; that is the very reason the enemy has launched this adventurist war, which is in the nature of a last desperate struggle. Therefore, it is an inescapable certainty that it will not be China but the ruling circles of Japanese imperialism which will be destroyed as a result of the war. Moreover, Japan has undertaken this war at a time when many countries have been or are about to be embroiled in war, when we are all fighting or preparing to fight against barbarous aggression, and China's fortunes are linked with those of most of the countries and peoples of the world. This is the root cause of the opposition Japan has aroused and will increasingly arouse among those countries and peoples.

16. What about China? The China of today cannot be compared with the China of any other historical period. She is a semi-colony and a semi-feudal society, and she is consequently considered a weak country. But at the same time, China is historically in her era of progress; this is the primary reason for her ability to defeat Japan.

When we say that the War of Resistance Against Japan is progressive, we do not mean progressive in the ordinary or general sense, nor do we mean progressive in the sense that the Abyssinian war against Italy, or the Taiping Revolution or the Revolution of 1911 were progressive, we mean progressive in the sense that China is progressive today. In what way is the China of today progressive? She is progressive because she is no longer a completely feudal country and because we already have some capitalism in China, we have a bourgeoisie and a proletariat, we have vast numbers of people who have awakened or are awakening, we have a Communist Party, we have a politically progressive army — the Chinese Red Army led by the Communist Party — and we have the tradition and the experience of many decades of revolution, and especially the experience of the seventeen years since the founding of the Chinese Communist Party. This experience has schooled the people and the political parties of China and forms the very basis for the present unity against Japan. If it is said that without the experience of 1905 the victory of 1917 would have been impossible in Russia, then we can also say that without the experience of the last seventeen years it would be impossible to win our War of Resistance. Such is the internal situation.

In the existing international situation, China is not isolated in the war, and this fact too is without precedent in history. In the past, China's wars, and India's too, were wars fought in isolation. It is only today that we meet with world-wide popular movements, extraordinary in breadth and depth, which have arisen or are arising and which are supporting China. The Russian Revolution of 1917 also received international support, and thus the Russian workers and peasants won; but that support was not so broad in scale and deep in nature as ours today. The popular movements in the world today are developing on a scale and with a depth that are unprecedented. The existence of the Soviet Union is a particularly vital factor in present-day international politics, and the Soviet Union will certainly support China with the greatest enthusiasm; there was nothing like this twenty years ago. All these factors have created and are creating important conditions indispensable to China's final victory. Large-scale direct assistance is as yet lacking and will come only in the future, but China is progressive and is a big country, and these are the factors enabling her to protract the war and to promote as well as await international help.

17. There is the additional factor that while Japan is a small country with a small territory, few resources, a small population and a limited number of soldiers, China is a big country with vast territory, rich resources, a large population and plenty of soldiers, so that, besides the contrast between strength and weakness, there is the contrast between a small country, retrogression and meagre support and a big country, progress and abundant support. This is the reason why China will never be subjugated. It follows from the contrast between strength and weakness that Japan can ride roughshod over China for a certain time and to a certain extent, that China must unavoidably travel a hard stretch of road, and that the War of Resistance will be a protracted war and not a war of quick decision; nevertheless, it follows from the other contrast — a small country, retrogression and meagre support versus a big country, progress and abundant support — that Japan cannot ride roughshod over China indefinitely but is sure to meet final defeat, while China can never be subjugated but is sure to win final victory.

18. Why was Abyssinia vanquished? First, she was not only weak but also small. Second, she was not as progressive as China; she was an old country passing from the slave to the serf system, a country without any capitalism or bourgeois political parties, let alone a Communist Party, and with no army such as the Chinese army, let alone one like the Eighth Route Army. Third, she was unable to hold out and wait for international assistance and had to fight her war in isolation. Fourth, and most important of all, there were mistakes in the direction of her war against Italy. Therefore Abyssinia was subjugated. But there is still quite extensive guerrilla warfare in Abyssinia, which, if persisted in, will enable the Abyssinians to recover their country when the world situation changes.

19. If the subjugationists quote the history of the failure of liberation movements in modern China to prove their assertions first that "resistance will mean subjugation", and then that "the continuance of the war spells subjugation", here again our answer is, "Times are different." China herself, the internal situation in Japan and the international environment are all different now. It is a serious matter that Japan is stronger than before while China in her unchanged semi-colonial and semi-feudal position is still fairly weak. It is also a fact that for the time being Japan can still control her people at home and exploit international contradictions in order to invade China. But during a long war, these things are bound to change in the

opposite direction. Such changes are not yet accomplished facts, but they will become so in future. The subjugationists dismiss this point. As for China, we already have new people, a new political party, a new army and a new policy of resistance to Japan, a situation very different from that of over a decade ago, and what is more, all these will inevitably make further progress. It is true that historically the liberation movements met with repeated setbacks with the result that China could not accumulate greater strength for the present War of Resistance — this is a very painful historical lesson, and never again should we destroy any of our revolutionary forces. Yet even on the present basis, by exerting great efforts we can certainly forge ahead gradually and increase the strength of our resistance. All such efforts should converge on the great Anti-Japanese National United Front. As for international support, though direct and large-scale assistance is not yet in sight, it is in the making, the international situation being fundamentally different from before. The countless failures in the liberation movement of modern China had their subjective and objective causes, but the situation today is entirely different. Today, although there are many difficulties which make the War of Resistance arduous — such as the enemy's strength and our weakness, and the fact that his difficulties are just starting, while our own progress is far from sufficient — nevertheless many favourable conditions exist for defeating the enemy; we need only add our subjective efforts, and we shall be able to overcome the difficulties and win through to victory. These are favourable conditions such as never existed before in any period of our history, and that is why the War of Resistance Against Japan, unlike the liberation movements of the past, will not end in failure.

COMPROMISE OR RESISTANCE?
CORRUPTION OR PROGRESS?

20. It has been fully explained above that the theory of national subjugation is groundless. But there are many people who do not subscribe to this theory; they are honest patriots, who are nevertheless deeply worried about the present situation. Two things are worrying them, fear of a compromise with Japan and doubts about the possibility of political progress. These two vexing questions are

being widely discussed and no key has been found to their solution. Let us now examine them.

21. As previously explained, the question of compromise has its social roots, and as long as these roots exist the question is bound to arise. But compromise will not avail. To prove the point, again we need only look for substantiation to Japan, China, and the international situation. First take Japan. At the very beginning of the War of Resistance, we estimated that the time would come when an atmosphere conducive to compromise would arise, in other words, that after occupying northern China, Kiangsu and Chekiang, Japan would probably resort to the scheme of inducing China to capitulate. True enough, she did resort to the scheme, but the crisis soon passed, one reason being that the enemy everywhere pursued a barbarous policy and practised naked plunder. Had China capitulated, every Chinese would have become a slave without a country. The enemy's predatory policy, the policy of subjugating China, has two aspects, the material and the spiritual, both of which are being applied universally to all Chinese, not only to the people of the lower strata but also to members of the upper strata; of course the latter are treated a little more politely, but the difference is only one of degree, not of principle. In the main the enemy is transplanting into the interior of China the same old measures he adopted in the three northeastern provinces. Materially, he is robbing the common people even of their food and clothing, making them cry out in hunger and cold; he is plundering the means of production, thus ruining and enslaving China's national industries. Spiritually, he is working to destroy the national consciousness of the Chinese people. Under the flag of the "Rising Sun" all Chinese are forced to be docile subjects, beasts of burden forbidden to show the slightest trace of Chinese national spirit. This barbarous enemy policy will be carried deeper into the interior of China. Japan with her voracious appetite is unwilling to stop the war. As was inevitable, the policy set forth in the Japanese cabinet's statement of January 16, 1938[11] is still being obstinately carried out, which has enraged all strata of the Chinese people. This rage is engendered by the reactionary and barbarous character of Japan's war — "there is no escape from fate", and hence an absolute hostility has crystallized. It is to be expected that on some future occasion the enemy will once again resort to the scheme of inducing China to capitulate and that certain subjugationists will again crawl out and most probably collude with certain foreign elements (to be found in Britain, the United States and France, and

especially among the upper strata in Britain) as partners in crime. But the general trend of events will not permit capitulation; the obstinate and peculiarly barbarous character of Japan's war has decided this aspect of the question.

22. Second, let us take China. There are three factors contributing to China's perseverance in the War of Resistance. In the first place, the Communist Party, which is the reliable force leading the people to resist Japan. Next, the Kuomintang, which depends on Britain and the United States and hence will not capitulate to Japan unless they tell it to. Finally, the other political parties and groups, most of which oppose compromise and support the War of Resistance. With unity among these three, whoever compromises will be standing with the traitors, and anybody will have the right to punish him. All those unwilling to be traitors have no choice but to unite and carry on the War of Resistance to the end; therefore compromise can hardly succeed.

23. Third, take the international aspect. Except for Japan's allies and certain elements in the upper strata of other capitalist countries, the whole world is in favour of resistance, and not of compromise by China. This factor reinforces China's hopes. Today the people throughout the country cherish the hope that international forces will gradually give China increasing help. It is not a vain hope; the existence of the Soviet Union in particular encourages China in her War of Resistance. The socialist Soviet Union, now strong as never before, has always shared China's joys and sorrows. In direct contrast to all the members of the upper strata in the capitalist countries who seek nothing but profits, the Soviet Union considers it its duty to help all weak nations and all revolutionary wars. That China is not fighting her war in isolation has its basis not only in international support in general but in Soviet support in particular. China and the Soviet Union are in close geographical proximity, which aggravates Japan's crisis and facilitates China's War of Resistance. Geographical proximity to Japan increases the difficulties of China's resistance. Proximity to the Soviet Union, on the other hand, is a favourable condition for the War of Resistance.

24. Hence we may conclude that the danger of compromise exists but can be overcome. Even if the enemy can modify his policy to some extent, he cannot alter it fundamentally. In China the social roots of compromise are present, but the opponents of compromise are in the majority. Internationally, also, some forces favour compromise but the main forces favour resistance. The combination of these three

factors makes it possible to overcome the danger of compromise and persist to the end in the War of Resistance.

25. Let us now answer the second question. Political progress at home and perseverance in the War of Resistance are inseparable. The greater the political progress, the more we can persevere in the war, and the more we persevere in the war, the greater the political progress. But, fundamentally, everything depends on our perseverance in the War of Resistance. The unhealthy phenomena in various fields under the Kuomintang regime are very serious, and the accumulation of these undesirable factors over the years has caused great anxiety and vexation among the broad ranks of our patriots. But there is no ground for pessimism, since experience in the War of Resistance has already proved that the Chinese people have made as much progress in the last ten months as in many years in the past. Although the cumulative effects of long years of corruption are seriously retarding the growth of the people's strength to resist Japan, thus reducing the extent of our victories and causing us losses in the war, yet the over-all situation in China, in Japan and in the world is such that the Chinese people cannot but make progress. This progress will be slow because of the factor of corruption, which impedes progress. Progress and the slow pace of progress are two characteristics of the present situation, and the second ill accords with the urgent needs of the war, which is a source of great concern to patriots. But we are in the midst of a revolutionary war, and revolutionary war is an antitoxin which not only eliminates the enemy's poison but also purges us of our own filth. Every just, revolutionary war is endowed with tremendous power, which can transform many things or clear the way for their transformation. The Sino-Japanese war will transform both China and Japan; provided China perseveres in the War of Resistance and in the united front, the old Japan will surely be transformed into a new Japan and the old China into a new China, and people and everything else in both China and Japan will be transformed during and after the war. It is proper for us to regard the anti-Japanese war and our national reconstruction as interconnected. To say that Japan can also be transformed is to say that the war of aggression by her rulers will end in defeat and may lead to a revolution by the Japanese people. The day of triumph of the Japanese people's revolution will be the day Japan is transformed. All this is closely linked with China's War of Resistance and is a prospect we should take into account.

THE THEORY OF NATIONAL SUBJUGATION
IS WRONG
AND THE THEORY OF QUICK VICTORY
IS LIKEWISE WRONG

26. In our comparative study of the enemy and ourselves with respect to the basic contradictory characteristics, such as relative strength, relative size, progress or reaction, and the relative extent of support, we have already refuted the theory of national subjugation, and we have explained why compromise is unlikely and why political progress is possible. The subjugationists stress the contradiction between strength and weakness and puff it up until it becomes the basis of their whole argument on the question, neglecting all the other contradictions. Their preoccupation with the contrast in strength shows their one-sidedness, and their exaggeration of this one side of the matter into the whole shows their subjectivism. Thus, if one looks at the matter as a whole, it will be seen that they have no ground to stand on and are wrong. As for those who are neither subjugationists nor confirmed pessimists, but who are in a pessimistic frame of mind for the moment simply because they are confused by the disparity between our strength and that of the enemy at a given time and in certain respects or by the corruption in the country, we should point out to them that their approach also tends to be one-sided and subjective. But in their case correction is relatively easy; once they are alerted, they will understand, for they are patriots and their error is only momentary.

27. The exponents of quick victory are likewise wrong. Either they completely forget the contradiction between strength and weakness, remembering only the other contradictions, or they exaggerate China's advantages beyond all semblance of reality and beyond recognition, or they presumptuously take the balance of forces at one time and place for the whole situation, as in the old saying, "A leaf before the eye shuts out Mount Tai." In a word, they lack the courage to admit that the enemy is strong while we are weak. They often deny this point and consequently deny one aspect of the truth. Nor do they have the courage to admit the limitations of our advantages, and thus they deny another aspect of the truth. The result is that they make mistakes, big and small, and here again it is subjectivism and one-sidedness that are doing the mischief. These friends have their

hearts in the right place, and they, too, are patriots. But while "the gentlemen's aspirations are indeed lofty", their views are wrong, and to act according to them would certainly be to run into a brick wall. For if appraisal does not conform to reality, action cannot attain its objective; and to act notwithstanding would mean the army's defeat and the nation's subjugation, so that the result would be the same as with the defeatists. Hence this theory of quick victory will not do either.

28. Do we deny the danger of national subjugation? No, we do not. We recognize that China faces two possible prospects, liberation or subjugation, and that the two are in violent conflict. Our task is to achieve liberation and to avert subjugation. The conditions for liberation are China's progress, which is basic, the enemy's difficulties, and international support. We differ from the subjugationists. Taking an objective and all-sided view, we recognize the two possibilities of national subjugation and liberation, stress that liberation is the dominant possibility, point out the conditions for its achievement, and strive to secure them. The subjugationists, on the other hand, taking a subjective and one-sided view, recognize only one possibility, that of subjugation; they do not admit the possibility of liberation, and still less point out the conditions necessary for liberation or strive to secure them. Moreover, while acknowledging the tendency to compromise and the corruption, we see other tendencies and phenomena which, we indicate, will gradually prevail and are already in violent conflict with the former; in addition, we point out the conditions necessary for the healthy tendencies and phenomena to prevail, and we strive to overcome the tendency to compromise and to change the state of corruption. Therefore, contrary to the pessimists, we are not at all down-hearted.

29. Not that we would not like a quick victory; everybody would be in favour of driving the "devils" out overnight. But we point out that, in the absence of certain definite conditions, quick victory is something that exists only in one's mind and not in objective reality, and that it is a mere illusion, a false theory. Accordingly, having made an objective and comprehensive appraisal of all the circumstances concerning both the enemy and ourselves, we point out that the only way to final victory is the strategy of protracted war, and we reject the groundless theory of quick victory. We maintain that we must strive to secure all the conditions indispensable to final victory, and the more fully and the earlier these conditions are secured, the

surer we shall be of victory and the earlier we shall win it. We believe that only in this way can the course of the war be shortened, and we reject the theory of quick victory, which is just idle talk and an effort to get things on the cheap.

WHY A PROTRACTED WAR?

30. Let us now examine the problem of protracted war. A correct answer to the question "Why a protracted war?" can be arrived at only on the basis of all the fundamental contrasts between China and Japan. For instance, if we say merely that the enemy is a strong imperialist power while we are a weak semi-colonial and semi-feudal country, we are in danger of falling into the theory of national subjugation. For neither in theory nor in practice can a struggle become protracted by simply pitting the weak against the strong. Nor can it become protracted by simply pitting the big against the small, the progressive against the reactionary, or abundant support against meagre support. The annexation of a small country by a big one or of a big country by a small one is a common occurrence. It often happens that a progressive country which is not strong is destroyed by a big, reactionary country, and the same holds for everything that is progressive but not strong. Abundant or meagre support is an important but a subsidiary factor, and the degree of its effect depends upon the fundamental factors on both sides. Therefore when we say that the War of Resistance Against Japan is a protracted war, our conclusion is derived from the interrelations of all the factors at work on both sides. The enemy is strong and we are weak, and the danger of subjugation is there. But in other respects the enemy has shortcomings and we have advantages. The enemy's advantage can be reduced and his shortcomings aggravated by our efforts. On the other hand, our advantages can be enhanced and our shortcoming remedied by our efforts. Hence, we can win final victory and avert subjugation, while the enemy will ultimately be defeated and will be unable to avert the collapse of his whole imperialist system.

31. Since the enemy has advantages only in one respect but shortcomings in all others and we have shortcomings in only one respect but advantages in all others, why has this produced not a balance, but, on the contrary, a superior position for him and an inferior

position for us at the present time? Quite clearly, we cannot consider the question in such a formal way. The fact is that the disparity between the enemy's strength and our own is now so great that the enemy's shortcomings have not developed, and for the time being cannot develop, to a degree sufficient to offset his strength, while our advantages have not developed, and for the time being cannot develop, to a degree sufficient to compensate for our weakness. Therefore there can as yet be no balance, only imbalance.

32. Although our efforts in persevering in the War of Resistance and the united front have somewhat changed the enemy's strength and superiority as against our weakness and inferiority, there has as yet been no basic change. Hence during a certain stage of the war, to a certain degree the enemy will be victorious and we shall suffer defeat. But why is it that in this stage the enemy's victories and our defeats are definitely restricted in degree and cannot be transcended by complete victory or complete defeat? The reason is that, first, from the very beginning the enemy's strength and our weakness have been relative and not absolute, and that, second, our efforts in persevering in the War of Resistance and in the united front have further accentuated this relativeness. In comparison with the original situation, the enemy is still strong, but unfavourable factors have reduced his strength, although not yet to a degree sufficient to destroy his superiority, and similarly we are still weak, but favourable factors have compensated for our weakness, although not yet to a degree sufficient to transform our inferiority. Thus it turns out that the enemy is relatively strong and we are relatively weak, that the enemy is in a relatively superior and we are in a relatively inferior position. On both sides, strength and weakness, superiority and inferiority, have never been absolute, and besides, our efforts in persevering in resistance to Japan and in the united front during the war have brought about further changes in the original balance of forces between us and the enemy. Therefore, in this stage the enemy's victory and our defeat are definitely restricted in degree, and hence the war becomes protracted.

33. But circumstances are continually changing. In the course of the war, provided we employ correct military and political tactics, make no mistakes of principle and exert our best efforts, the enemy's disadvantages and China's advantages will both grow as the war is drawn out, with the inevitable result that there will be a continual change in the difference in comparative strength and hence in the relative position of the two sides. When a new stage is reached, a great

change will take place in the balance of forces, resulting in the enemy's defeat and our victory.

34. At present the enemy can still manage to exploit his strength, and our War of Resistance has not yet fundamentally weakened him. The insufficiency in his manpower and material resources is not yet such as to prevent his offensive; on the contrary, they can still sustain his offensive to a certain extent. The reactionary and barbarous nature of his war, a factor which intensifies both class antagonisms within Japan and the resistance of the Chinese nation, has not yet brought about a situation which radically impedes his advance. The enemy's international isolation is increasing but is not yet complete. In many countries which have indicated they will help us, the capitalists dealing in munitions and war materials and bent solely on profit are still furnishing Japan with large quantities of war supplies,[12] and their governments[13] are still reluctant to join the Soviet Union in practical sanctions against Japan. From all this it follows that our War of Resistance cannot be won quickly and can only be a protracted war. As for China, although there has been some improvement with regard to her weakness in the military, economic, political and cultural spheres in the ten months of resistance, it is still a long way from what is required to prevent the enemy's offensive and prepare our counter-offensive. Moreover, quantitatively speaking, we have had to sustain certain losses. Although all the factors favourable to us are having a positive effect, it will not be sufficient to halt the enemy's offensive and to prepare for our counter-offensive unless we make an immense effort. Neither the abolition of corruption and the acceleration of progress at home, nor the curbing of the pro-Japanese forces and the expansion of the anti-Japanese forces abroad, are yet accomplished facts. From all this it follows that our war cannot be won quickly but can only be a protracted war.

THE THREE STAGES OF THE PROTRACTED WAR

35. Since the Sino-Japanese war is a protracted one and final victory will belong to China, it can reasonably be assumed that this protracted war will pass through three stages. The first stage covers the period of the enemy's strategic offensive and our strategic defensive. The second stage will be the period of the enemy's strategic con-

solidation and our preparation for the counter-offensive. The third stage will be the period of our strategic counter-offensive and the enemy's strategic retreat. It is impossible to predict the concrete situation in the three stages, but certain main trends in the war may be pointed out in the light of present conditions. The objective course of events will be exceedingly rich and varied, with many twists and turns, and nobody can cast a horoscope for the Sino-Japanese war; nevertheless it is necessary for the strategic direction of the war to make a rough sketch of its trends. Although our sketch may not be in full accord with the subsequent facts and will be amended by them, it is still necessary to make it in order to give firm and purposeful strategic direction to the protracted war.

36. The first stage has not yet ended. The enemy's design is to occupy Canton, Wuhan and Lanchow and link up these three points. To accomplish this aim the enemy will have to use at least fifty divisions, or about one and a half million men, spend from one and a half to two years, and expend more than ten thousand million yen. In penetrating so deeply, he will encounter immense difficulties, with consequences disastrous beyond imagination. As for attempting to occupy the entire length of the Canton-Hankow Railway and the Sian-Lanchow Highway, he will have to fight perilous battles and even so may not fully accomplish his design. But in drawing up our operational plan we should base ourselves on the assumption that the enemy may occupy the three points and even certain additional areas, as well as link them up, and we should make dispositions for a protracted war, so that even if he does so, we shall be able to cope with him. In this stage the form of fighting we should adopt is primarily mobile warfare, supplemented by guerrilla and positional warfare. Through the subjective errors of the Kuomintang military authorities, positional warfare was assigned the primary role in the first phase of this stage, but it is nevertheless supplementary from the point of view of the stage as a whole. In this stage, China has already built up a broad united front and achieved unprecedented unity. Although the enemy has used and will continue to use base and shameless means to induce China to capitulate in the attempt to realize his plan for a quick decision and to conquer the whole country without much effort, he has failed so far, nor is he likely to succeed in the future. In this stage, in spite of considerable losses, China will make considerable progress, which will become the main basis for her continued resistance in the second stage. In the present stage the Soviet Union

has already given substantial aid to China. On the enemy side, there are already signs of flagging morale, and his army's momentum of attack is less in the middle phase of this stage than it was in the initial phase, and it will diminish still further in the concluding phase. Signs of exhaustion are beginning to appear in his finances and economy; war-weariness is beginning to set in among his people and troops; and within the clique at the helm of the war, "war frustrations" are beginning to manifest themselves and pessimism about the prospects of the war is growing.

37. The second stage may be termed one of strategic stalemate. At the tail end of the first stage, the enemy will be forced to fix certain terminal points to his strategic offensive owing to his shortage of troops and our firm resistance, and upon reaching them he will stop his strategic offensive and enter the stage of safeguarding his occupied areas. In the second stage, the enemy will attempt to safeguard the occupied areas and to make them his own by the fraudulent method of setting up puppet governments, while plundering the Chinese people to the limit; but again he will be confronted with stubborn guerrilla warfare. Taking advantage of the fact that the enemy's rear is unguarded, our guerrilla warfare will develop extensively in the first stage, and many base areas will be established, seriously threatening the enemy's consolidation of the occupied areas, and so in the second stage there will still be widespread fighting. In this stage, our form of fighting will be primarily guerrilla warfare, supplemented by mobile warfare. China will still retain a large regular army, but she will find it difficult to launch the strategic counter-offensive immediately because, on the one hand, the enemy will adopt a strategically defensive position in the big cities and along the main lines of communication under his occupation and, on the other hand, China will not yet be adequately equipped technically. Except for the troops engaged in frontal defence against the enemy, our forces will be switched in large numbers to the enemy's rear in comparatively dispersed dispositions, and, basing themselves on all the areas not actually occupied by the enemy and co-ordinating with the people's local armed forces, they will launch extensive, fierce guerrilla warfare against enemy-occupied areas, keeping the enemy on the move as far as possible in order to destroy him in mobile warfare, as is now being done in Shansi Province. The fighting in the second stage will be ruthless, and the country will suffer serious devastation. But the guerrilla warfare will be successful, and if it is well conducted the

enemy may be able to retain only about one-third of his occupied territory, with the remaining two-thirds in our hands, and this will constitute a great defeat for the enemy and a great victory for China. By then the enemy-occupied territory as a whole will fall into three categories: first, the enemy base areas; second, our base areas for guerrilla warfare; and, third, the guerrilla areas contested by both sides. The duration of this stage will depend on the degree of change in the balance of forces between us and the enemy and on the changes in the international situation; generally speaking, we should be prepared to see this stage last a comparatively long time and to weather its hardships. It will be a very painful period for China; the two big problems will be economic difficulties and the disruptive activities of the traitors. The enemy will go all out to wreck China's united front, and the traitor organizations in all the occupied areas will merge into a so-called "unified government". Owing to the loss of big cities and the hardships of war, vacillating elements within our ranks will clamour for compromise, and pessimism will grow to a serious extent. Our tasks will then be to mobilize the whole people to unite as one man and carry on the war with unflinching perseverance, to broaden and consolidate the united front, sweep away all pessimism and ideas of compromise, promote the will to hard struggle and apply new wartime policies, and so to weather the hardships. In the second stage, we will have to call upon the whole country resolutely to maintain a united government, we will have to oppose splits and systematically improve fighting techniques, reform the armed forces, mobilize the entire people and prepare for the counter-offensive. The international situation will become still more unfavourable to Japan and the main international forces will incline towards giving more help to China, even though there may be talk of "realism" of the Chamberlain type which accommodates itself to *faits accomplis*. Japan's threat to Southeast Asia and Siberia will become greater, and there may even be another war. As regards Japan, scores of her divisions will be inextricably bogged down in China. Widespread guerrilla warfare and the people's anti-Japanese movement will wear down this big Japanese force, greatly reducing it and also disintegrating its morale by stimulating the growth of homesickness, war-weariness and even anti-war sentiment. Though it would be wrong to say that Japan will achieve no results at all in her plunder of China, yet, being short of capital and harassed by guerrilla warfare, she cannot possibly achieve rapid or substantial results. This second stage will be the transitional

stage of the entire war; it will be the most trying period but also the
pivotal one. Whether China becomes an independent country or is
reduced to a colony will be determined not by the retention or loss
of the big cities in the first stage but by the extent to which the whole
nation exerts itself in the second. If we can persevere in the War of
Resistance, in the united front and in the protracted war, China will
in that stage gain the power to change from weakness to strength. It will
be the second act in the three-act drama of China's War of Resistance.
And through the efforts of the entire cast it will become possible to
perform a most brilliant last act.

38. The third stage will be the stage of the counter-offensive to
recover our lost territories. Their recovery will depend mainly upon
the strength which China has built up in the preceding stage and which
will continue to grow in the third stage. But China's strength alone
will not be sufficient, and we shall also have to rely on the support
of international forces and on the changes that will take place inside
Japan, or otherwise we shall not be able to win; this adds to China's
tasks in international propaganda and diplomacy. In the third stage,
our war will no longer be one of strategic defensive, but will turn into
a strategic counter-offensive manifesting itself in strategic offensives;
and it will no longer be fought on strategically interior lines, but will
shift gradually to strategically exterior lines. Not until we fight our
way to the Yalu River can this war be considered over. The third
stage will be the last in the protracted war, and when we talk of
persevering in the war to the end, we mean going all the way through
this stage. Our primary form of fighting will still be mobile warfare,
but positional warfare will rise to importance. While positional defence
cannot be regarded as important in the first stage because of the
prevailing circumstances, positional attack will become quite important in the third stage because of the changed conditions and the
requirements of the task. In the third stage guerrilla warfare will again
provide strategic support by supplementing mobile and positional
warfare, but it will not be the primary form as in the second stage.

39. It is thus obvious that the war is protracted and consequently
ruthless in nature. The enemy will not be able to gobble up the whole
of China but will be able to occupy many places for a considerable
time. China will not be able to oust the Japanese quickly, but the
greater part of her territory will remain in her hands. Ultimately the
enemy will lose and we will win, but we shall have a hard stretch
of road to travel.

40. The Chinese people will become tempered in the course of this long and ruthless war. The political parties taking part in the war will also be steeled and tested. The united front must be persevered in; only by persevering in the united front can we persevere in the war; and only by persevering in the united front and in the war can we win final victory. Only thus can all difficulties be overcome. After travelling the hard stretch of road we shall reach the highway to victory. This is the natural logic of the war.

41. In the three stages the changes in relative strength will proceed along the following lines. In the first stage, the enemy is superior and we are inferior in strength. With regard to our inferiority we must reckon on changes of two different kinds from the eve of the War of Resistance to the end of this stage. The first kind is a change for the worse. China's original inferiority will be aggravated by war losses, namely, decreases in territory, population, economic strength, military strength and cultural institutions. Towards the end of the first stage, the decrease will probably be considerable, especially on the economic side. This point will be exploited by some people as a basis for their theories of national subjugation and of compromise. But the second kind of change, the change for the better, must also be noted. It includes the experience gained in the war, the progress made by the armed forces, the political progress, the mobilization of the people, the development of culture in a new direction, the emergence of guerrilla warfare, the increase in international support, etc. What is on the downgrade in the first stage is the old quantity and the old quality, the manifestations being mainly quantitative. What is on the upgrade is the new quantity and the new quality, the manifestations being mainly qualitative. It is the second kind of change that provides a basis for our ability to fight a protracted war and win final victory.

42. In the first stage, changes of two kinds are also occurring on the enemy's side. The first kind is a change for the worse and manifests itself in hundreds of thousands of casualties, the drain on arms and ammunition, deterioration of troop morale, popular discontent at home, shrinkage of trade, the expenditure of over ten thousand million yen, condemnation by world opinion, etc. This trend also provides a basis for our ability to fight a protracted war and win final victory. But we must likewise reckon with the second kind of change on the enemy's side, a change for the better, that is, his expansion in territory, population and resources. This too is a basis for the protracted nature of our War of Resistance and the impossibility of quick victory, but

at the same time certain people will use it as a basis for their theories of national subjugation and of compromise. However, we must take into account the transitory and partial character of this change for the better on the enemy's side. Japan is an imperialist power heading for collapse, and her occupation of China's territory is temporary. The vigorous growth of guerrilla warfare in China will restrict her actual occupation to narrow zones. Moreover, her occupation of Chinese territory has created and intensified contradictions between Japan and other foreign countries. Besides, generally speaking, such occupation involves a considerable period in which Japan will make capital outlays without drawing any profits, as is shown by the experience in the three northeastern provinces. All of which again gives us a basis for demolishing the theories of national subjugation and of compromise and for establishing the theories of protracted war and of final victory.

43. In the second stage, the above changes on both sides will continue to develop. While the situation cannot be predicted in detail, on the whole Japan will continue on the downgrade and China on the upgrade.[14] For example, Japan's military and financial resources will be seriously drained by China's guerrilla warfare, popular discontent will grow in Japan, the morale of her troops will deteriorate further, and she will become more isolated internationally. As for China, she will make further progress in the political, military and cultural spheres and in the mobilization of the people; guerrilla warfare will develop further; there will be some new economic growth on the basis of the small industries and the widespread agriculture in the interior; international support will gradually increase; and the whole picture will be quite different from what it is now. This second stage may last quite a long time, during which there will be a great reversal in the balance of forces, with China gradually rising and Japan gradually declining. China will emerge from her inferior position, and Japan will lose her superior position; first the two countries will become evenly matched, and then their relative positions will be reversed. Thereupon, China will in general have completed her preparations for the strategic counter-offensive and will enter the stage of the counter-offensive and the expulsion of the enemy. It should be reiterated that the change from inferiority to superiority and the completion of preparations for the counter-offensive will involve three things, namely, an increase in China's own strength, an increase in Japan's difficulties, and an increase in international support; it is the combination of all these forces that will bring about

China's superiority and the completion of her preparations for the counter-offensive.

44. Because of the unevenness in China's political and economic development, the strategic counter-offensive of the third stage will not present a uniform and even picture throughout the country in its initial phase but will be regional in character, rising here and subsiding there. During this stage, the enemy will not relax his divisive tricks to break China's united front, hence the task of maintaining internal unity in China will become still more important, and we shall have to ensure that the strategic counter-offensive does not collapse halfway through internal dissension. In this period the international situation will become very favourable to China. China's task will be to take advantage of it in order to attain complete liberation and establish an independent democratic state, which at the same time will mean helping the world anti-fascist movement.

45. China moving from inferiority to parity and then to superiority, Japan moving from superiority to parity and then to inferiority; China moving from the defensive to stalemate and then to the counter-offensive, Japan moving from the offensive to the safeguarding of her gains and then to retreat — such will be the course of the Sino-Japanese war and its inevitable trend.

46. Hence the questions and the conclusions are as follows: Will China be subjugated? The answer is, No, she will not be subjugated, but will win final victory. Can China win quickly? The answer is, No, she cannot win quickly, and the war must be a protracted one. Are these conclusions correct? I think they are.

47. At this point, the exponents of national subjugation and of compromise will again rush in and say, "To move from inferiority to parity China needs a military and economic power equal to Japan's, and to move from parity to superiority she will need a military and economic power greater than Japan's. But this is impossible, hence the above conclusions are not correct."

48. This is the so-called theory that "weapons decide everything",[15] which constitutes a mechanical approach to the question of war and a subjective and one-sided view. Our view is opposed to this; we see not only weapons but also people. Weapons are an important factor in war, but not the decisive factor; it is people, not things, that are decisive. The contest of strength is not only a contest of military and economic power, but also a contest of human power and morale. Military and economic power is necessarily wielded by

people. If the great majority of the Chinese, of the Japanese and of the people of other countries are on the side of our War of Resistance Against Japan, how can Japan's military and economic power, wielded as it is by a small minority through coercion, count as superiority? And if not, then does not China, though wielding relatively inferior military and economic power, become the superior? There is no doubt that China will gradually grow in military and economic power, provided she perseveres in the War of Resistance and in the united front. As for our enemy, weakened as he will be by the long war and by internal and external contradictions, his military and economic power is bound to change in the reverse direction. In these circumstances, is there any reason why China cannot become the superior? And that is not all. Although we cannot as yet count the military and economic power of other countries as being openly and to any great extent on our side, is there any reason why we will not be able to do so in the future? If Japan's enemy is not just China, if in future one or more other countries make open use of their considerable military and economic power defensively or offensively against Japan and openly help us, then will not our superiority be still greater? Japan is a small country, her war is reactionary and barbarous, and she will become more and more isolated internationally; China is a large country, her war is progressive and just, and she will enjoy more and more support internationally. Is there any reason why the long-term development of these factors should not definitely change the relative position between the enemy and ourselves?

49. The exponents of quick victory, however, do not realize that war is a contest of strength, and that before a certain change has taken place in the relative strength of the belligerents, there is no basis for trying to fight strategically decisive battles and shorten the road to liberation. Were their ideas to be put into practice, we should inevitably run our heads into a brick wall. Or perhaps they are just talking for their own pleasure without really intending to put their ideas into practice. In the end Mr. Reality will come and pour a bucket of cold water over these chatterers, showing them up as mere windbags who want to get things on the cheap, to have gains without pains. We have had this kind of idle chatter before and we have it now, though not very much so far; but there may be more as the war develops into the stage of stalemate and then of counter-offensive. But in the meantime, if China's losses in the first stage are fairly heavy and the second stage drags on very long, the theories of

national subjugation and of compromise will gain great currency. Therefore, our fire should be directed mainly against them and only secondarily against the idle chatter about quick victory.

50. That the war will be protracted is certain, but nobody can predict exactly how many months or years it will last, as this depends entirely upon the degree of the change in the balance of forces. All those who wish to shorten the war have no alternative but to work hard to increase our own strength and reduce that of the enemy. Specifically, the only way is to strive to win more battles and wear down the enemy's forces, develop guerrilla warfare to reduce enemy-occupied territory to a minimum, consolidate and expand the united front to rally the forces of the whole nation, build up new armies and develop new war industries, promote political, economic and cultural progress, mobilize the workers, peasants, businessmen, intellectuals and other sections of the people, disintegrate the enemy forces and win over their soldiers, carry on international propaganda to secure foreign support, and win the support of the Japanese people and other oppressed peoples. Only by doing all this can we reduce the duration of the war. There is no magic short-cut.

A WAR OF JIG-SAW PATTERN

51. We can say with certainty that the protracted War of Resistance Against Japan will write a splendid page unique in the war history of mankind. One of the special features of this war is the interlocking "jig-saw" pattern which arises from such contradictory factors as the barbarity of Japan and her shortage of troops on the one hand, and the progressiveness of China and the extensiveness of her territory on the other. There have been other wars of jig-saw pattern in history, the three years' civil war in Russia after the October Revolution being a case in point. But what distinguishes this war in China is its especially protracted and extensive character, which will set a record in history. Its jig-saw pattern manifests itself as follows.

52. *Interior and exterior lines.* The anti-Japanese war as a whole is being fought on interior lines; but as far as the relation between the main forces and the guerrilla units is concerned, the former are on the interior lines while the latter are on the exterior lines, presenting a remarkable spectacle of pincers around the enemy. The same can be

said of the relationship between the various guerrilla areas. From its own viewpoint each guerrilla area is on interior lines and the other areas are on exterior lines; together they form many battle fronts, which hold the enemy in pincers. In the first stage of the war, the regular army operating strategically on interior lines is withdrawing, but the guerrilla units operating strategically on exterior lines will advance with great strides over wide areas to the rear of the enemy — they will advance even more fiercely in the second stage — thereby presenting a remarkable picture of both withdrawal and advance.

53. *Possession and non-possession of a rear area.* The main forces, which extend the front lines to the outer limits of the enemy's occupied areas, are operating from the rear area of the country as a whole. The guerrilla units, which extend the battle lines into the enemy rear, are separated from the rear area of the country as a whole. But each guerrilla area has a small rear of its own, upon which it relies to establish its fluid battle lines. The case is different with the guerrilla detachments which are dispatched by a guerrilla area for short-term operations in the rear of the enemy in the same area; such detachments have no rear, nor do they have a battle line. "Operating without a rear area" is a special feature of revolutionary war in the new era, wherever a vast territory, a progressive people, and an advanced political party and army are to be found; there is nothing to fear but much to gain from it, and far from having doubts about it we should promote it.

54. *Encirclement and counter-encirclement.* Taking the war as a whole, there is no doubt that we are strategically encircled by the enemy because he is on the strategic offensive and operating on exterior lines while we are on the strategic defensive and operating on interior lines. This is the first form of enemy encirclement. We on our part can encircle one or more of the enemy columns advancing on us along separate routes, because we apply the policy of fighting campaigns and battles from tactically exterior lines by using numerically preponderant forces against these enemy columns advancing on us from strategically exterior lines. This is the first form of our counter-encirclement of the enemy. Next, if we consider the guerrilla base areas in the enemy's rear, each area taken singly is surrounded by the enemy on all sides, like the Wutai Mountains, or on three sides, like the northwestern Shansi area. This is the second form of enemy encirclement. However, if one considers all the guerrilla base areas together and in their relation to the positions of the regular

forces, one can see that we in turn surround a great many enemy forces. In Shansi Province, for instance, we have surrounded the Tatung-Puchow Railway on three sides (the east and west flanks and the southern end) and the city of Taiyuan on all sides; and there are many similar instances in Hopei and Shantung Provinces. This is the second form of our counter-encirclement of the enemy. Thus there are two forms of encirclement by the enemy forces and two forms of encirclement by our own — rather like a game of *weichi*.[16] Campaigns and battles fought by the two sides resemble the capturing of each other's pieces, and the establishment of enemy strongholds (such as Taiyuan) and our guerrilla base areas (such as the Wutai Mountains) resembles moves to dominate spaces on the board. If the game of *weichi* is extended to include the world, there is yet a third form of encirclement as between us and the enemy, namely, the interrelation between the front of aggression and the front of peace. The enemy encircles China, the Soviet Union, France and Czechoslovakia with his front of aggression, while we counter-encircle Germany, Japan and Italy with our front of peace. But our encirclement, like the hand of Buddha, will turn into the Mountain of Five Elements lying athwart the Universe, and the modern Sun Wu-kungs[17] — the fascist aggressors — will finally be buried underneath it, never to rise again. Therefore, if on the international plane we can create an anti-Japanese front in the Pacific region, with China as one strategic unit, with the Soviet Union and other countries which may join it as other strategic units, and with the Japanese people's movement as still another strategic unit, and thus form a gigantic net from which the fascist Sun Wu-kungs can find no escape, then that will be our enemy's day of doom. Indeed, the day when this gigantic net is formed will undoubtedly be the day of the complete overthrow of Japanese imperialism. We are not jesting; this is the inevitable trend of the war.

55. *Big areas and little areas.* There is a possibility that the enemy will occupy the greater part of Chinese territory south of the Great Wall, and only the smaller part will be kept intact. That is one aspect of the situation. But within this greater part, which does not include the three northeastern provinces, the enemy can actually hold only the big cities, the main lines of communication and some of the plains — which may rank first in importance, but will probably constitute only the smaller part of the occupied territory in size and population, while the greater part will be taken up by the guerrilla areas that will grow up everywhere. That is another aspect of the

situation. If we go beyond the provinces south of the Great Wall and include Mongolia, Sinkiang, Chinghai and Tibet, then the unoccupied area will constitute the greater part of China's territory, and the enemy-occupied area will become the smaller part, even with the three northeastern provinces. That is yet another aspect of the situation. The area kept intact is undoubtedly important, and we should devote great efforts to developing it, not only politically, militarily and economically but, what is also important, culturally. The enemy has transformed our former cultural centres into culturally backward areas, and we on our part must transform the former culturally backward areas into cultural centres. At the same time, the work of developing extensive guerrilla areas behind the enemy lines is also extremely important, and we should attend to every aspect of this work, including the cultural. All in all, big pieces of China's territory, namely, the rural areas, will be transformed into regions of progress and light, while the small pieces, namely, the enemy-occupied areas and especially the big cities, will temporarily become regions of backwardness and darkness.

56. Thus it can be seen that the protracted and far-flung War of Resistance Against Japan is a war of a jig-saw pattern militarily, politically, economically and culturally. It is a marvellous spectacle in the annals of war, a heroic undertaking by the Chinese nation, a magnificent and earth-shaking feat. This war will not only affect China and Japan, strongly impelling both to advance, but will also affect the whole world, impelling all nations, especially the oppressed nations such as India, to march forward. Every Chinese should consciously throw himself into this war of a jig-saw pattern, for this is the form of war by which the Chinese nation is liberating itself, the special form of war of liberation waged by a big semi-colonial country in the Nineteen Thirties and the Nineteen Forties.

FIGHTING FOR PERPETUAL PEACE

57. The protracted nature of China's anti-Japanese war is inseparably connected with the fight for perpetual peace in China and the whole world. Never has there been a historical period such as the present in which war is so close to perpetual peace. For several thousand years since the emergence of classes, the life of mankind

has been full of wars; each nation has fought countless wars, either internally or with other nations. In the imperialist epoch of capitalist society, wars are waged on a particularly extensive scale and with a peculiar ruthlessness. The first great imperialist war of twenty years ago was the first of its kind in history, but not the last. Only the war which has now begun comes close to being the final war, that is, comes close to the perpetual peace of mankind. By now one-third of the world's population has entered the war. Look! Italy, then Japan; Abyssinia, then Spain, then China. The population of the countries at war now amounts to almost 600 million, or nearly a third of the total population of the world. The characteristics of the present war are its uninterruptedness and its proximity to perpetual peace. Why is it uninterrupted? After attacking Abyssinia, Italy attacked Spain, and Germany joined in; then Japan attacked China. What will come next? Undoubtedly Hitler will fight the great powers. "Fascism is war"[18] — this is perfectly true. There will be no interruption in the development of the present war into a world war; mankind will not be able to avoid the calamity of war. Why then do we say the present war is near to perpetual peace? The present war is the result of the development of the general crisis of world capitalism which began with World War I; this general crisis is driving the capitalist countries into a new war and, above all, driving the fascist countries into new war adventures. This war, we can foresee, will not save capitalism, but will hasten its collapse. It will be greater in scale and more ruthless than the war of twenty years ago, all nations will inevitably be drawn in, it will drag on for a very long time, and mankind will suffer greatly. But, owing to the existence of the Soviet Union and the growing political consciousness of the people of the world, great revolutionary wars will undoubtedly emerge from this war to oppose all counter-revolutionary wars, thus giving this war the character of a struggle for perpetual peace. Even if later there should be another period of war, perpetual world peace will not be far off. Once man has eliminated capitalism, he will attain the era of perpetual peace, and there will be no more need for war. Neither armies, nor warships, nor military aircraft, nor poison gas will then be needed. Thereafter and for all time, mankind will never again know war. The revolutionary wars which have already begun are part of the war for perpetual peace. The war between China and Japan, two countries which have a combined population of over 500 million, will take an important place in this war for perpetual peace, and out of it will come the liberation of the Chinese nation. The liberated new China of the future will be inseparable from the liberated new world of the future. Hence our War of Resistance Against Japan takes on the character of a struggle for perpetual peace.

58. History shows that wars are divided into two kinds, just and unjust. All wars that are progressive are just, and all wars that impede progress are unjust. We Communists oppose all unjust wars that impede progress, but we do not oppose progressive, just wars. Not only do we Communists not oppose just wars, we actively participate in them. As for unjust wars, World War I is an instance in which both sides fought for imperialist interests; therefore the Communists of the whole world firmly opposed that war. The way to oppose a war of this kind is to do everything possible to prevent it before it breaks out and, once it breaks out, to oppose war with war, to oppose unjust war with just war, whenever possible. Japan's war is an unjust war that impedes progress, and the peoples of the world, including the Japanese people, should oppose it and are opposing it. In our country the people and the government, the Communist Party and the Kuomintang, have all raised the banner of righteousness in the national revolutionary war against aggression. Our war is sacred and just, it is progressive and its aim is peace. The aim is peace not just in one country but throughout the world, not just temporary but perpetual peace. To achieve this aim we must wage a life-and-death struggle, be prepared for any sacrifice, persevere to the end and never stop short of the goal. However great the sacrifice and however long the time needed to attain it, a new world of perpetual peace and brightness already lies clearly before us. Our faith in waging this war is based upon the new China and the new world of perpetual peace and brightness for which we are striving. Fascism and imperialism wish to perpetuate war, but we wish to put an end to it in the not too distant future. The great majority of mankind should exert their utmost efforts for this purpose. The 450 million people of China constitute one quarter of the world's population, and if by their concerted efforts they overthrow Japanese imperialism and create a new China of freedom and equality, they will most certainly be making a tremendous contribution to the struggle for perpetual world peace. This is no vain hope, for the whole world is approaching this point in the course of its social and economic development, and provided that the majority of mankind work together, our goal will surely be attained in several decades.

MAN'S DYNAMIC ROLE IN WAR

59. We have so far explained why the war is a protracted war and why the final victory will be China's, and in the main dealt with what protracted war is and what it is not. Now we shall turn to the question of what to do and what not to do. How to conduct protracted war and how to win the final victory? These are the questions answered below. We shall therefore successively discuss the following problems: man's dynamic role in war, war and politics, political mobilization for the War of Resistance, the object of war, offence within defence, quick decisions within a protracted war, exterior lines within interior lines, initiative, flexibility, planning, mobile warfare, guerrilla warfare, positional warfare, war of annihilation, war of attrition, the possibilities of exploiting the enemy's mistakes, the question of decisive engagements in the anti-Japanese war, and the army and the people as the foundation of victory. Let us start with the problem of man's dynamic role.

60. When we say we are opposed to a subjective approach to problems, we mean that we must oppose ideas which are not based upon or do not correspond to objective facts, because such ideas are fanciful and fallacious and will lead to failure if acted on. But whatever is done has to be done by human beings; protracted war and final victory will not come about without human action. For such action to be effective there must be people who derive ideas, principles or views from the objective facts, and put forward plans, directives, policies, strategies and tactics. Ideas, etc. are subjective, while deeds or actions are the subjective translated into the objective, but both represent the dynamic role peculiar to human beings. We term this kind of dynamic role "man's conscious dynamic role", and it is a characteristic that distinguishes man from all other beings. All ideas based upon and corresponding to objective facts are correct ideas, and all deeds or actions based upon correct ideas are correct actions. We must give full scope to these ideas and actions, to this dynamic role. The anti-Japanese war is being waged to drive out imperialism and transform the old China into a new China; this can be achieved only when the whole Chinese people are mobilized and full scope is given to their conscious dynamic role in resisting Japan. If we just sit by and take no action, only subjugation awaits us and there will be neither protracted war nor final victory.

61. It is a human characteristic to exercise a conscious dynamic role. Man strongly displays this characteristic in war. True, victory or defeat in war is decided by the military, political, economic and geographical conditions on both sides, the nature of the war each side is waging and the international support each enjoys, but it is not decided by these alone; in themselves, all these provide only the possibility of victory or defeat but do not decide the issue. To decide the issue, subjective effort must be added, namely, the directing and waging of war, man's conscious dynamic role in war.

62. In seeking victory, those who direct a war cannot overstep the limitations imposed by the objective conditions; within these limitations, however, they can and must play a dynamic role in striving for victory. The stage of action for commanders in a war must be built upon objective possibilities, but on that stage they can direct the performance of many a drama, full of sound and colour, power and grandeur. Given the objective material foundations, the commanders in the anti-Japanese war should display their prowess and marshal all their forces to crush the national enemy, transform the present situation in which our country and society are suffering from aggression and oppression, and create a new China of freedom and equality; here is where our subjective faculties for directing war can and must be exercised. We do not want any of our commanders in the war to detach himself from the objective conditions and become a blundering hothead, but we decidedly want every commander to become a general who is both bold and sagacious. Our commanders should have not only the boldness to overwhelm the enemy but also the ability to remain masters of the situation throughout the changes and vicissitudes of the entire war. Swimming in the ocean of war, they must not flounder but make sure of reaching the opposite shore with measured strokes. Strategy and tactics, as the laws for directing war, constitute the art of swimming in the ocean of war.

WAR AND POLITICS

63. "War is the continuation of politics." In this sense war is politics and war itself is a political action; since ancient times there has never been a war that did not have a political character. The anti-Japanese war is a revolutionary war waged by the whole nation, and

victory is inseparable from the political aim of the war — to drive out Japanese imperialism and build a new China of freedom and equality — inseparable from the general policy of persevering in the War of Resistance and in the united front, from the mobilization of the entire people, and from the political principles of the unity between officers and men, the unity between army and people and the disintegration of the enemy forces, and inseparable from the effective application of united front policy, from mobilization on the cultural front, and from the efforts to win international support and the support of the people inside Japan. In a word, war cannot for a single moment be separated from politics. Any tendency among the anti-Japanese armed forces to belittle politics by isolating war from it and advocating the idea of war as an absolute is wrong and should be corrected.

64. But war has its own particular characteristics and in this sense it cannot be equated with politics in general. "War is the continuation of politics by other . . . means."[19] When politics develops to a certain stage beyond which it cannot proceed by the usual means, war breaks out to sweep the obstacles from the way. For instance, the semi-independent status of China is an obstacle to the political growth of Japanese imperialism, hence Japan has unleashed a war of aggression to sweep away that obstacle. What about China? Imperialist oppression has long been an obstacle to China's bourgeois-democratic revolution, hence many wars of liberation have been waged in the effort to sweep it away. Japan is now using war for the purpose of oppressing China and completely blocking the advance of the Chinese revolution, and therefore China is compelled to wage the War of Resistance in her determination to sweep away this obstacle. When the obstacle is removed, our political aim will be attained and the war concluded. But if the obstacle is not completely swept away, the war will have to continue till the aim is fully accomplished. Thus anyone who seeks a compromise before the task of the anti-Japanese war is fulfilled is bound to fail, because even if a compromise were to occur for one reason or another, the war would break out again, since the broad masses of the people would certainly not submit but would continue the war until its political objective was achieved. It can therefore be said that politics is war without bloodshed while war is politics with bloodshed.

65. From the particular characteristics of war there arise a particular set of organizations, a particular series of methods and a particular kind of process. The organizations are the armed forces and

everything that goes with them. The methods are the strategy and tactics for directing war. The process is the particular form of social activity in which the opposing armed forces attack each other or defend themselves against one another, employing strategy and tactics favourable to themselves and unfavourable to the enemy. Hence war experience is a particular kind of experience. All who take part in war must rid themselves of their customary ways and accustom themselves to war before they can win victory.

POLITICAL MOBILIZATION FOR
THE WAR OF RESISTANCE

66. A national revolutionary war as great as ours cannot be won without extensive and thoroughgoing political mobilization. Before the anti-Japanese war there was no political mobilization for resistance to Japan, and this was a great drawback, as a result of which China has already lost a move to the enemy. After the war began, political mobilization was very far from extensive, let alone thoroughgoing. It was the enemy's gunfire and the bombs dropped by enemy aeroplanes that brought news of the war to the great majority of the people. That was also a kind of mobilization, but it was done for us by the enemy, we did not do it ourselves. Even now the people in the remoter regions beyond the noise of the guns are carrying on quietly as usual. This situation must change, or otherwise we cannot win in our life-and-death struggle. We must never lose another move to the enemy; on the contrary, we must make full use of this move, political mobilization, to get the better of him. This move is crucial; it is indeed of primary importance, while our inferiority in weapons and other things is only secondary. The mobilization of the common people throughout the country will create a vast sea in which to drown the enemy, create the conditions that will make up for our inferiority in arms and other things, and create the prerequisites for overcoming every difficulty in the war. To win victory, we must persevere in the War of Resistance, in the united front and in the protracted war. But all these are inseparable from the mobilization of the common people. To wish for victory and yet neglect political mobilization is like wishing to "go south by driving the chariot north", and the result would inevitably be to forfeit victory.

67. What does political mobilization mean? First, it means telling the army and the people about the political aim of the war. It is necessary for every soldier and civilian to see why the war must be fought and how it concerns him. The political aim of the war is "to drive out Japanese imperialism and build a new China of freedom and equality"; we must proclaim this aim to everybody, to all soldiers and civilians, before we can create an anti-Japanese upsurge and unite hundreds of millions as one man to contribute their all to the war. Secondly, it is not enough merely to explain the aim to them; the steps and policies for its attainment must also be given, that is, there must be a political programme. We already have the Ten-Point Programme for Resisting Japan and Saving the Nation and also the Programme of Armed Resistance and National Reconstruction; we should popularize both of them in the army and among the people and mobilize everyone to carry them out. Without a clear-cut, concrete political programme it is impossible to mobilize all the armed forces and the whole people to carry the war against Japan through to the end. Thirdly, how should we mobilize them? By word of mouth, by leaflets and bulletins, by newspapers, books and pamphlets, through plays and films, through schools, through the mass organizations and through our cadres. What has been done so far in the Kuomintang areas is only a drop in the ocean, and moreover it has been done in a manner ill-suited to the people's tastes and in a spirit uncongenial to them; this must be drastically changed. Fourthly, to mobilize once is not enough; political mobilization for the War of Resistance must be continuous. Our job is not to recite our political programme to the people, for nobody will listen to such recitations; we must link the political mobilization for the war with developments in the war and with the life of the soldiers and the people, and make it a continuous movement. This is a matter of immense importance on which our victory in the war primarily depends.

THE OBJECT OF WAR

68. Here we are not dealing with the political aim of war; the political aim of the War of Resistance Against Japan has been defined above as "to drive out Japanese imperialism and build a new China of freedom and equality". Here we are dealing with the elementary object of war, war as "politics with bloodshed", as mutual

slaughter by opposing armies. The object of war is specifically "to preserve oneself and destroy the enemy" (to destroy the enemy means to disarm him or "deprive him of the power to resist", and does not mean to destroy every member of his forces physically). In ancient warfare, the spear and the shield were used, the spear to attack and destroy the enemy, and the shield to defend and preserve oneself. To the present day, all weapons are still an extension of the spear and the shield. The bomber, the machine-gun, the long-range gun and poison gas are developments of the spear, while the air-raid shelter, the steel helmet, the concrete fortification and the gas mask are developments of the shield. The tank is a new weapon combining the functions of both spear and shield. Attack is the chief means of destroying the enemy, but defence cannot be dispensed with. In attack the immediate object is to destroy the enemy, but at the same time it is self-preservation, because if the enemy is not destroyed, you will be destroyed. In defence the immediate object is to preserve yourself, but at the same time defence is a means of supplementing attack or preparing to go over to the attack. Retreat is in the category of defence and is a continuation of defence, while pursuit is a continuation of attack. It should be pointed out that destruction of the enemy is the primary object of war and self-preservation the secondary, because only by destroying the enemy in large numbers can one effectively preserve oneself. Therefore attack, the chief means of destroying the enemy, is primary, while defence, a supplementary means of destroying the enemy and a means of self-preservation, is secondary. In actual warfare the chief role is played by defence much of the time and by attack for the rest of the time, but if war is taken as a whole, attack remains primary.

69. How do we justify the encouragement of heroic sacrifice in war? Does it not contradict "self-preservation"? No, it does not; sacrifice and self-preservation are both opposite and complementary to each other. War is politics with bloodshed and exacts a price, sometimes an extremely high price. Partial and temporary sacrifice (non-preservation) is incurred for the sake of general and permanent preservation. This is precisely why we say that attack, which is basically a means of destroying the enemy, also has the function of self-preservation. It is also the reason why defence must be accompanied by attack and should not be defence pure and simple.

70. The object of war, namely, the preservation of oneself and the destruction of the enemy, is the essence of war and the basis of

all war activities, an essence which pervades all war activities, from the technical to the strategic. The object of war is the underlying principle of war, and no technical, tactical, or strategic concepts or principles can in any way depart from it. What for instance is meant by the principle of "taking cover and making full use of fire-power" in shooting? The purpose of the former is self-preservation, of the latter the destruction of the enemy. The former gives rise to such techniques as making use of the terrain and its features, advancing in spurts, and spreading out in dispersed formation. The latter gives rise to other techniques, such as clearing the field of fire and organizing a fire-net. As for the assault force, the containing force and the reserve force in a tactical operation, the first is for annihilating the enemy, the second for preserving oneself, and the third is for either purpose according to circumstances — either for annihilating the enemy (in which case it reinforces the assault force or serves as a pursuit force), or for self-preservation (in which case it reinforces the containing force or serves as a covering force). Thus, no technical, tactical, or strategical principles or operations can in any way depart from the object of war, and this object pervades the whole of a war and runs through it from beginning to end.

71. In directing the anti-Japanese war, leaders at the various levels must lose sight neither of the contrast between the fundamental factors on each side nor of the object of this war. In the course of military operations these contrasting fundamental factors unfold themselves in the struggle by each side to preserve itself and destroy the other. In our war we strive in every engagement to win a victory, big or small, and to disarm a part of the enemy and destroy a part of his men and *matériel*. We must accumulate the results of these partial destructions of the enemy into major strategic victories and so achieve the final political aim of expelling the enemy, protecting the motherland and building a new China.

OFFENCE WITHIN DEFENCE,
QUICK DECISIONS WITHIN A PROTRACTED WAR,
EXTERIOR LINES WITHIN INTERIOR LINES

72. Now let us examine the specific strategy of the War of Resistance Against Japan. We have already said that our strategy

for resisting Japan is that of protracted war, and indeed this is perfectly right. But this strategy is general, not specific. Specifically, how
should the protracted war be conducted? We shall now discuss this
question. Our answer is as follows. In the first and second stages
of the war, i.e., in the stages of the enemy's offensive and preservation
of his gains, we should conduct tactical offensives within the strategic
defensive, campaigns and battles of quick decision within the strategically protracted war, and campaigns and battles on exterior lines
within strategically interior lines. In the third stage, we should launch
the strategic counter-offensive.

73. Since Japan is a strong imperialist power and we are a weak
semi-colonial and semi-feudal country, she has adopted the policy of
the strategic offensive while we are on the strategic defensive. Japan
is trying to execute the strategy of a war of quick decision; we should
consciously execute the strategy of protracted war. Japan is using
dozens of army divisions of fairly high combat effectiveness (now
numbering thirty) and part of her navy to encircle and blockade
China from both land and sea, and is using her air force to bomb
China. Her army has already established a long front stretching from
Paotow to Hangchow and her navy has reached Fukien and Kwang-
tung; thus exterior-line operations have taken shape on a vast scale.
On the other hand, we are in the position of operating on interior lines.
All this is due to the fact that the enemy is strong while we are weak.
This is one aspect of the situation.

74. But there is another and exactly opposite aspect. Japan, though
strong, does not have enough soldiers. China, though weak, has a
vast territory, a large population and plenty of soldiers. Two important
consequences follow. First, the enemy, employing his small forces
against a vast country, can only occupy some big cities and main lines
of communication and part of the plains. Thus there are extensive
areas in the territory under his occupation which he has had to leave
ungarrisoned, and which provide a vast arena for our guerrilla warfare.
Taking China as a whole, even if the enemy manages to occupy the
line connecting Canton, Wuhan and Lanchow and its adjacent areas,
he can hardly seize the regions beyond, and this gives China a general
rear and vital bases from which to carry on the protracted war to final
victory. Secondly, in pitting his small forces against large forces, the
enemy is encircled by our large forces. The enemy is attacking us along
several routes, strategically he is on exterior lines while we are on
interior lines, strategically he is on the offensive while we are on the

defensive; all this looks very much to our disadvantage. However, we can make use of our two advantages, namely, our vast territory and large forces, and, instead of stubborn positional warfare, carry on flexible mobile warfare, employing several divisions against one enemy division, several tens of thousands of our men against ten thousand of his, several columns against one of his columns, and suddenly encircling and attacking a single column from the exterior lines of the battlefield. In this way, while the enemy is on exterior lines and on the offensive in strategic operations, he will be forced to fight on interior lines and on the defensive in campaigns and battles. And for us, interior lines and the defensive in strategic operations will be transformed into exterior lines and the offensive in campaigns and battles. This is the way to deal with one or indeed with any advancing enemy column. Both the consequences discussed above follow from the fact that the enemy is small while we are big. Moreover, the enemy forces, though small, are strong (in arms and in training) while our forces, though large, are weak (in arms and in training but not in morale), and in campaigns and battles, therefore, we should not only employ large forces against small and operate from exterior against interior lines, but also follow the policy of seeking quick decisions. In general, to achieve quick decision, we should attack a moving and not a stationary enemy. We should concentrate a big force under cover beforehand alongside the route which the enemy is sure to take, and while he is on the move, advance suddenly to encircle and attack him before he knows what is happening, and thus quickly conclude the battle. If we fight well, we may destroy the entire enemy force or the greater part or some part of it, and even if we do not fight so well, we may still inflict heavy casualties. This applies to any and every one of our battles. If each month we could win one sizable victory like that at Pinghsingkuan or Taierhchuang, not to speak of more, it would greatly demoralize the enemy, stimulate the morale of our own forces and evoke international support. Thus our strategically protracted war is translated in the field into battles of quick decision. The enemy's war of strategic quick decision is bound to change into protracted war after he is defeated in many campaigns and battles.

75. In a word, the above operational principle for fighting campaigns and battles is one of "quick-decision offensive warfare on exterior lines". It is the opposite of our strategic principle of "protracted defensive warfare on interior lines", and yet it is the

indispensable principle for carrying out this strategy. If we should use "protracted defensive warfare on interior lines" as the principle for campaigns and battles too, as we did at the beginning of the War of Resistance, it would be totally unsuited to the circumstances in which the enemy is small while we are big and the enemy is strong while we are weak; in that case we could never achieve our strategic objective of a protracted war and we would be defeated by the enemy. That is why we have always advocated the organization of the forces of the entire country into a number of large field armies, each counterposed to one of the enemy's field armies but having two, three or four times its strength, and so keeping the enemy engaged in extensive theatres of war in accordance with the principle outlined above. This principle of "quick-decision offensive warfare on exterior lines" can and must be applied in guerrilla as well as in regular warfare. It is applicable not only to any one stage of the war but to its entire course. In the stage of strategic counter-offensive, when we are better equipped technically and are no longer in the position of the weak fighting the strong, we shall be able to capture prisoners and booty on a large scale all the more effectively if we continue to employ superior numbers in quick-decision offensive battles from exterior lines. For instance, if we employ two, three or four mechanized divisions against one mechanized enemy division, we can be all the more certain of destroying it. It is common sense that several hefty fellows can easily beat one.

76. If we resolutely apply "quick-decision offensive warfare on exterior lines" on a battlefield, we shall not only change the balance of forces on that battlefield, but also gradually change the general situation. On the battlefield we shall be on the offensive and the enemy on the defensive, we shall be employing superior numbers on exterior lines and the enemy inferior numbers on interior lines, and we shall seek quick decisions, while the enemy, try as he may, will not be able to protract the fighting in the expectation of reinforcements; for all these reasons, the enemy's position will change from strong to weak, from superior to inferior, while that of our forces will change from weak to strong, from inferior to superior. After many such battles have been victoriously fought, the general situation between us and the enemy will change. That is to say, through the accumulation of victories on many battlefields by quick-decision offensive warfare on exterior lines, we shall gradually strengthen ourselves and weaken the enemy, which will necessarily affect the general balance of forces and bring about changes in it. When that happens, these changes, together with

other factors on our side and together with the changes inside the enemy camp and a favourable international situation, will turn the over-all situation between us and the enemy first into one of parity and then into one of superiority for us. That will be the time for us to launch the counter-offensive and drive the enemy out of the country.

77. War is a contest of strength, but the original pattern of strength changes in the course of war. Here the decisive factor is subjective effort — winning more victories and committing fewer errors. The objective factors provide the possibility for such change, but in order to turn this possibility into actuality both correct policy and subjective effort are essential. It is then that the subjective plays the decisive role.

INITIATIVE, FLEXIBILITY AND PLANNING

78. In quick-decision offensive campaigns and battles on exterior lines, as discussed above, the crucial point is the "offensive"; "exterior lines" refers to the sphere of the offensive and "quick-decision" to its duration. Hence the name "quick-decision offensive warfare on exterior lines". It is the best principle for waging a protracted war and it is also the principle for what is known as mobile warfare. But it cannot be put into effect without initiative, flexibility and planning. Let us now study these three questions.

79. We have already discussed man's conscious dynamic role, so why do we talk about the initiative again? By conscious dynamic role we mean conscious action and effort, a characteristic distinguishing man from other beings, and this human characteristic manifests itself most strongly in war; all this has been discussed already. The initiative here means an army's freedom of action as distinguished from an enforced loss of freedom. Freedom of action is the very life of an army and, once it is lost, the army is close to defeat or destruction. The disarming of a soldier is the result of his losing freedom of action through being forced into a passive position. The same is true of the defeat of an army. For this reason both sides in war do all they can to gain the initiative and avoid passivity. It may be said that the quick-decision offensive warfare on exterior lines which we advocate and the flexibility and planning necessary for its execution are designed to gain the initiative and thus force the enemy into a passive position and achieve the object of preserving ourselves and destroying the enemy. But initiative

or passivity is inseparable from superiority or inferiority in the capacity
to wage war. Consequently it is also inseparable from the correctness
or incorrectness of the subjective direction of war. In addition, there
is the question of exploiting the enemy's misconceptions and unpreparedness in order to gain the initiative and force the enemy into
passivity. These points are analysed below.

80. Initiative is inseparable from superiority in capacity to wage
war, while passivity is inseparable from inferiority in capacity to wage
war. Such superiority or inferiority is the objective basis of initiative
or passivity. It is natural that the strategic initiative can be better
maintained and exercised through a strategic offensive, but to maintain the initiative always and everywhere, that is, to have the absolute
initiative, is possible only when there is absolute superiority matched
against absolute inferiority. When a strong, healthy man wrestles with
an invalid, he has the absolute initiative. If Japan were not riddled
with insoluble contradictions, if, for instance, she could throw in a
huge force of several million or ten million men all at once, if her
financial resources were several times what they are, if she had
no opposition from her own people or from other countries, and if
she did not pursue the barbarous policies which arouse the desperate
resistance of the Chinese people, then she would be able to maintain
absolute superiority and have the absolute initiative always and everywhere. In history, such absolute superiority rarely appears in the early
stages of a war or a campaign but is to be found towards its end.
For instance, on the eve of Germany's capitulation in World War I,
the Entente countries became absolutely superior and Germany
absolutely inferior, so that Germany was defeated and the Entente
countries were victorious; this is an example of absolute superiority
and inferiority towards the end of a war. Again, on the eve of the
Chinese victory at Taierhchuang, the isolated Japanese forces there
were reduced after bitter fighting to absolute inferiority while our
forces achieved absolute superiority, so that the enemy was defeated
and we were victorious; this is an example of absolute superiority and
inferiority towards the end of a campaign. A war or campaign may
also end in a situation of relative superiority or of parity, in which
case there is compromise in the war or stalemate in the campaign. But
in most cases it is absolute superiority and inferiority that decide victory
and defeat. All this holds for the end of a war or a campaign, and not
for the beginning. The outcome of the Sino-Japanese war, it can be
predicted, will be that Japan will become absolutely inferior and be

defeated and that China will become absolutely superior and gain victory. But at present superiority or inferiority is not absolute on either side, but is relative. With the advantages of her military, economic and political-organizational power, Japan enjoys superiority over us with our military, economic and political-organizational weakness, which creates the basis for her initiative. But since quantitatively her military and other power is not great and she has many other disadvantages, her superiority is reduced by her own contradictions. Upon her invasion of China, her superiority has been reduced still further because she has come up against our vast territory, large population, great numbers of troops and resolute nation-wide resistance. Hence, Japan's general position has become one of only relative superiority, and her ability to exercise and maintain the initiative, which is thereby restricted, has likewise become relative. As for China, though placed in a somewhat passive position strategically because of her inferior strength, she is nevertheless quantitatively superior in territory, population and troops, and also superior in the morale of her people and army and their patriotic hatred of the enemy; this superiority, together with other advantages, reduces the extent of her inferiority in military, economic and other power, and changes it into a relative strategic inferiority. This also reduces the degree of China's passivity so that her strategic position is one of only relative passivity. Any passivity, however, is a disadvantage, and one must strive hard to shake it off. Militarily, the way to do so is resolutely to wage quick-decision offensive warfare on exterior lines, to launch guerrilla warfare in the rear of the enemy and so secure overwhelming local superiority and initiative in many campaigns of mobile and guerrilla warfare. Through such local superiority and local initiative in many campaigns, we can gradually create strategic superiority and strategic initiative and extricate ourselves from strategic inferiority and passivity. Such is the interrelation between initiative and passivity, between superiority and inferiority.

81. From this we can also understand the relationship between initiative or passivity and the subjective directing of war. As already explained, it is possible to escape from our position of relative strategic inferiority and passivity, and the method is to create local superiority and initiative in many campaigns, so depriving the enemy of local superiority and initiative and plunging him into inferiority and passivity. These local successes will add up to strategic superiority and initiative for us and strategic inferiority and passivity for the enemy. Such a change depends upon correct subjective direction. Why? Because while

we seek superiority and the initiative, so does the enemy; viewed from this angle, war is a contest in subjective ability between the commanders of the opposing armies in their struggle for superiority and for the initiative on the basis of material conditions such as military forces and financial resources. Out of the contest there emerge a victor and a vanquished; leaving aside the contrast in objective material conditions, the victor will necessarily owe his success to correct subjective direction and the vanquished his defeat to wrong subjective direction. We admit that the phenomenon of war is more elusive and is characterized by greater uncertainty than any other social phenomenon, in other words, that it is more a matter of "probability". Yet war is in no way supernatural, but a mundane process governed by necessity. That is why Sun Wu Tzu's axiom, "Know the enemy and know yourself, and you can fight a hundred battles with no danger of defeat",[20] remains a scientific truth. Mistakes arise from ignorance about the enemy and about ourselves, and moreover the peculiar nature of war makes it impossible in many cases to have full knowledge about both sides; hence the uncertainty about military conditions and operations, and hence mistakes and defeats. But whatever the situation and the moves in a war, one can know their general aspects and essential points. It is possible for a commander to reduce errors and give generally correct direction, first through all kinds of reconnaissance and then through intelligent inference and judgement. Armed with the weapon of "generally correct direction", we can win more battles and transform our inferiority into superiority and our passivity into initiative. This is how initiative or passivity is related to the correct or incorrect subjective direction of a war.

82. The thesis that incorrect subjective direction can change superiority and initiative into inferiority and passivity, and that correct subjective direction can effect a reverse change, becomes all the more convincing when we look at the record of defeats suffered by big and powerful armies and of victories won by small and weak armies. There are many such instances in Chinese and foreign history. Examples in China are the Battle of Chengpu between the states of Tsin and Chu,[21] the Battle of Chengkao between the states of Chu and Han,[22] the Battle in which Han Hsin defeated the Chao armies,[23] the Battle of Kunyang between the states of Hsin and Han,[24] the Battle of Kuantu between Yuan Shao and Tsao Tsao,[25] the Battle of Chihpi between the states of Wu and Wei,[26] the Battle of Yiling between the states of Wu and Shu,[27] the Battle of Feishui between the states

of Chin and Tsin,[28] etc. Among examples to be found abroad are most of Napoleon's campaigns and the civil war in the Soviet Union after the October Revolution. In all these instances, victory was won by small forces over big and by inferior over superior forces. In every case, the weaker force, pitting local superiority and initiative against the enemy's local inferiority and passivity, first inflicted one sharp defeat on the enemy and then turned on the rest of his forces and smashed them one by one, thus transforming the over-all situation into one of superiority and initiative. The reverse was the case with the enemy who originally had superiority and held the initiative; owing to subjective errors and internal contradictions, it sometimes happened that he completely lost an excellent or fairly good position in which he enjoyed superiority and initiative, and became a general without an army or a king without a kingdom. Thus it can be seen that although superiority or inferiority in the capacity to wage war is the objective basis determining initiative or passivity, it is not in itself actual initiative or passivity; it is only through a struggle, a contest of ability, that actual initiative or passivity can emerge. In the struggle, correct subjective direction can transform inferiority into superiority and passivity into initiative, and incorrect subjective direction can do the opposite. The fact that every ruling dynasty was defeated by revolutionary armies shows that mere superiority in certain respects does not guarantee the initiative, much less the final victory. The inferior side can wrest the initiative and victory from the superior side by securing certain conditions through active subjective endeavour in accordance with the actual circumstances.

83. To have misconceptions and to be caught unawares may mean to lose superiority and initiative. Hence, deliberately creating misconceptions for the enemy and then springing surprise attacks upon him are two ways — indeed two important means — of achieving superiority and seizing the initiative. What are misconceptions? "To see every bush and tree on Mount Pakung as an enemy soldier"[29] is an example of misconception. And "making a feint to the east but attacking in the west" is a way of creating misconceptions among the enemy. When the mass support is sufficiently good to block the leakage of news, it is often possible by various ruses to succeed in leading the enemy into a morass of wrong judgements and actions so that he loses his superiority and the initiative. The saying, "There can never be too much deception in war", means precisely this. What does "being caught unawares" mean? It means being unprepared. Without

preparedness superiority is not real superiority and there can be no initiative either. Having grasped this point, a force which is inferior but prepared can often defeat a superior enemy by surprise attack. We say an enemy on the move is easy to attack precisely because he is then off guard, that is, unprepared. These two points — creating misconceptions among the enemy and springing surprise attacks on him — mean transferring the uncertainties of war to the enemy while securing the greatest possible certainty for ourselves and thereby gaining superiority, the initiative and victory. Excellent organization of the masses is the prerequisite for attaining all this. Therefore it is extremely important to arouse all the people who are opposed to the enemy, to arm themselves to the last man, make widespread raids on the enemy and also prevent the leakage of news and provide a screen for our own forces; in this way the enemy will be kept in the dark about where and when our forces will attack, and an objective basis will be created for misconceptions and unpreparedness on his part. It was largely owing to the organized, armed masses of the people that the weak and small force of the Chinese Red Army was able to win many battles in the period of the Agrarian Revolutionary War. Logically, a national war should win broader mass support than an agrarian revolutionary war; however, as a result of past mistakes[30] the people are in an unorganized state, cannot be promptly drawn in to serve the cause and are sometimes even made use of by the enemy. The resolute rallying of the people on a broad scale is the only way to secure inexhaustible resources to meet all the requirements of the war. Moreover, it will definitely play a big part in carrying out our tactics of defeating the enemy by misleading him and catching him unawares. We are not Duke Hsiang of Sung and have no use for his asinine ethics.[31] In order to achieve victory we must as far as possible make the enemy blind and deaf by sealing his eyes and ears and drive his commanders to distraction by creating confusion in their minds. The above concerns the way in which the initiative or passivity is related to the subjective direction of the war. Such subjective direction is indispensable for defeating Japan.

84. By and large, Japan has held the initiative in the stage of her offensive by reason of her military power and her exploitation of our subjective errors, past and present. But her initiative is beginning to wane to some extent because of her many inherent disadvantages and of the subjective errors she too has committed in the course of the war (of which more later) and also because of our many advantages.

The enemy's defeat at Taierhchuang and his predicament in Shansi prove this clearly. The widespread development of guerrilla warfare in the enemy's rear has placed his garrisons in the occupied areas in a completely passive position. Although he is still on the offensive strategically and still holds the initiative, his initiative will end when his strategic offensive ends. The first reason why the enemy will not be able to maintain the initiative is that his shortage of troops renders it impossible for him to carry on the offensive indefinitely. Our offensive warfare in campaigns and our guerrilla warfare behind the enemy lines, together with other factors, constitute the second reason why he will have to cease his offensive at a certain limit and will not be able to keep his initiative. The existence of the Soviet Union and changes in the international situation constitute the third reason. Thus it can be seen that the enemy's initiative is limited and can be shattered. If, in military operations, China can keep up offensive warfare by her main forces in campaigns and battles, vigorously develop guerrilla warfare in the enemy's rear and mobilize the people on a broad scale politically, we can gradually build up a position of strategic initiative.

85. Let us now discuss flexibility. What is flexibility? It is the concrete realization of the initiative in military operations; it is the flexible employment of armed forces. The flexible employment of armed forces is the central task in directing a war, a task most difficult to perform well. In addition to organizing and educating the army and the people, the business of war consists in the employment of troops in combat, and all these things are done to win the fight. Of course it is difficult to organize an army, etc., but it is even more difficult to employ it, particularly when the weak are fighting the strong. To do so requires subjective ability of a very high order and requires the overcoming of the confusion, obscurity and uncertainty peculiar to war and the discovery of order, clarity and certainty in it; only thus can flexibility in command be realized.

86. The basic principle of field operations for the War of Resistance Against Japan is quick-decision offensive warfare on exterior lines. There are various tactics or methods for giving effect to this principle, such as dispersion and concentration of forces, diverging advance and converging attack, the offensive and the defensive, assault and containment, encirclement and outflanking, advance and retreat. It is easy to understand these tactics, but not at all easy to employ and vary them flexibly. Here the three crucial links are the time, the place and the troops. No victory can be won

unless the time, the place and the troops are well chosen. For example, in attacking an enemy force on the move, if we strike too early, we expose ourselves and give the enemy a chance to prepare, and if we strike too late, the enemy may have encamped and concentrated his forces, presenting us with a hard nut to crack. This is the question of the time. If we select a point of assault on the left flank which actually turns out to be the enemy's weak point, victory will be easy; but if we select the right flank and hit a snag, nothing will be achieved. This is the question of the place. If a particular unit of our forces is employed for a particular task, victory may be easy; but if another unit is employed for the same task, it may be hard to achieve results. This is the question of the troops. We should know not only how to employ tactics but how to vary them. For flexibility of command the important task is to make changes such as from the offensive to the defensive or from the defensive to the offensive, from advance to retreat or from retreat to advance, from containment to assault or from assault to containment, from encirclement to outflanking or from outflanking to encirclement, and to make such changes properly and in good time according to the circumstances of the troops and terrain on both sides. This is true of command in campaigns and strategic command as well as of command in battles.

87. The ancients said: "Ingenuity in varying tactics depends on mother wit"; this "ingenuity", which is what we mean by flexibility, is the contribution of the intelligent commander. Flexibility does not mean recklessness; recklessness must be rejected. Flexibility consists in the intelligent commander's ability to take timely and appropriate measures on the basis of objective conditions after "judging the hour and sizing up the situation" (the "situation" includes the enemy's situation, our situation and the terrain), and this flexibility is "ingenuity in varying tactics". On the basis of this ingenuity, we can win more victories in quick-decision offensive warfare on exterior lines, change the balance of forces in our favour, gain the initiative over the enemy, and overwhelm and crush him so that the final victory will be ours.

88. Let us now discuss the question of planning. Because of the uncertainty peculiar to war, it is much more difficult to prosecute war according to plan than is the case with other activities. Yet, since "preparedness ensures success and unpreparedness spells failure", there can be no victory in war without advance planning and preparations. There is no absolute certainty in war, and yet it is not without some

degree of relative certainty. We are comparatively certain about our own situation. We are very uncertain about the enemy's, but here too there are signs for us to read, clues to follow and sequences of phenomena to ponder. These form what we call a degree of relative certainty, which provides an objective basis for planning in war. Modern technical developments (telegraphy, radio, aeroplanes, motor vehicles, railways, steamships, etc.) have added to the possibilities of planning in war. However, complete or stable planning is difficult because there is only very limited and transient certainty in war; such planning must change with the movement (flow or change) of the war and vary in degree according to the scale of the war. Tactical plans, such as plans for attack or defence by small formations or units, often have to be changed several times a day. A plan of campaign, that is, of action by large formations, can generally stand till the conclusion of the campaign, in the course of which, however, it is often changed partially or sometimes even wholly. A strategic plan based on the over-all situation of both belligerents is still more stable, but it too is applicable only in a given strategic stage and has to be changed when the war moves towards a new stage. The making and changing of tactical, campaign and strategic plans in accordance with scope and circumstance is a key factor in directing a war; it is the concrete expression of flexibility in war, in other words, it is also ingenuity in varying one's tactics. Commanders at all levels in the anti-Japanese war should take note.

89. Because of the fluidity of war, some people categorically deny that war plans or policies can be relatively stable, describing such plans or policies as "mechanical". This view is wrong. In the preceding section we fully recognized that, because the circumstances of war are only relatively certain and the flow (movement or change) of war is rapid, war plans or policies can be only relatively stable and have to be changed or revised in good time in accordance with changing circumstances and the flow of the war; otherwise we would become mechanists. But one must not deny the need for war plans or policies that are relatively stable over given periods; to negate this is to negate everything, including the war itself as well as the negator himself. As both military conditions and operations are relatively stable, we must grant the relative stability of the war plans and policies resulting from them. For example, since both the circumstances of the war in northern China and the dispersed nature of the Eighth Route Army's operations are relatively stable for a particular stage, it is absolutely

necessary during this stage to acknowledge the relative stability of the Eighth Route Army's strategic principle of operation, namely, "Guerrilla warfare is basic, but lose no chance for mobile warfare under favourable conditions." The period of validity of a plan for a campaign is shorter than that of a strategic plan, and for a tactical plan it is shorter still, but each is stable over a given period. Anyone denying this point would have no way of handling warfare and would become a relativist in war with no settled views, for whom one course is just as wrong or just as right as another. No one denies that even a plan valid for a given period is fluid; otherwise, one plan would never be abandoned in favour of another. But it is fluid within limits, fluid within the bounds of the various war operations undertaken for carrying it out, but not fluid as to its essence; in other words, it is quantitatively but not qualitatively fluid. Within such a given period of time, this essence is definitely not fluid, which is what we mean by relative stability within a given period. In the great river of absolute fluidity throughout the war there is relative stability at each particular stretch — such is our fundamental view regarding war plans or policies.

90. Having dealt with protracted defensive warfare on interior lines in strategy and with quick-decision offensive warfare on exterior lines in campaigns and battles, and also with the initiative, flexibility and planning, we can now sum up briefly. The anti-Japanese war must have a plan. War plans, which are the concrete application of strategy and tactics, must be flexible so that they can be adapted to the circumstances of the war. We should always seek to transform our inferiority into superiority and our passivity into the initiative so as to change the situation as between the enemy and ourselves. All these find expression in quick-decision offensive warfare on exterior lines in campaigns and battles and protracted defensive warfare on interior lines in strategy.

MOBILE WARFARE, GUERRILLA WARFARE AND POSITIONAL WARFARE

91. A war will take the form of mobile warfare when its content is quick-decision offensive warfare on exterior lines in campaigns and battles within the framework of the strategy of interior lines, protracted

war and defence. Mobile warfare is the form in which regular armies wage quick-decision offensive campaigns and battles on exterior lines along extensive fronts and over big areas of operation. At the same time, it includes "mobile defence", which is conducted when necessary to facilitate such offensive battles; it also includes positional attack and positional defence in a supplementary role. Its characteristics are regular armies, superiority of forces in campaigns and battles, the offensive, and fluidity.

92. China has a vast territory and an immense number of soldiers, but her troops are inadequately equipped and trained; the enemy's forces, on the other hand, are inadequate in number, but better equipped and trained. In this situation, there is no doubt that we must adopt offensive mobile warfare as our primary form of warfare, supplementing it by others and integrating them all into mobile warfare. We must oppose "only retreat, never advance", which is flightism, and at the same time oppose "only advance, never retreat", which is desperate recklessness.

93. One of the characteristics of mobile warfare is fluidity, which not only permits but requires a field army to advance and to withdraw in great strides. However, it has nothing in common with flightism of the Han Fu-chu brand.[32] The primary requirement of war is to destroy the enemy, and the other requirement is self-preservation. The object of self-preservation is to destroy the enemy, and to destroy the enemy is in turn the most effective means of self-preservation. Hence mobile warfare is in no way an excuse for people like Han Fu-chu and can never mean moving only backward, and never forward; that kind of "moving" which negates the basic offensive character of mobile warfare would, in practice, "move" China out of existence despite her vastness.

94. However, the other view, which we call the desperate recklessness of "only advance, never retreat", is also wrong. The mobile warfare we advocate, the content of which is quick-decision offensive warfare on exterior lines in campaigns and battles, includes positional warfare in a supplementary role, "mobile defence" and retreat, without all of which mobile warfare cannot be fully carried out. Desperate recklessness is military short-sightedness, originating often from fear of losing territory. A man who acts with desperate recklessness does not know that one characteristic of mobile warfare is fluidity, which not only permits but requires a field army to advance and to withdraw in great strides. On the positive side, in order to

draw the enemy into a fight unfavourable to him but favourable to us, it is usually necessary that he should be on the move and that we should have a number of advantages, such as favourable terrain, a vulnerable enemy, a local population that can prevent the leakage of information, and the enemy's fatigue and unpreparedness. This requires that the enemy should advance, and we should not grudge a temporary loss of part of our territory. For the temporary loss of part of our territory is the price we pay for the permanent preservation of all our territory, including the recovery of lost territory. On the negative side, whenever we are forced into a disadvantageous position which fundamentally endangers the preservation of our forces, we should have the courage to retreat, so as to preserve our forces and hit the enemy when new opportunities arise. In their ignorance of this principle, the advocates of desperate action will contest a city or a piece of ground even when the position is obviously and definitely unfavourable; as a result, they not only lose the city or ground but fail to preserve their forces. We have always advocated the policy of "luring the enemy in deep", precisely because it is the most effective military policy for a weak army strategically on the defensive to employ against a strong army.

95. Among the forms of warfare in the anti-Japanese war mobile warfare comes first and guerrilla warfare second. When we say that in the entire war mobile warfare is primary and guerrilla warfare supplementary, we mean that the outcome of the war depends mainly on regular warfare, especially in its mobile form, and that guerrilla warfare cannot shoulder the main responsibility in deciding the outcome. It does not follow, however, that the role of guerrilla warfare is unimportant in the strategy of the war. Its role in the strategy of the war as a whole is second only to that of mobile warfare, for without its support we cannot defeat the enemy. In saying this we also have in mind the strategic task of developing guerrilla warfare into mobile warfare. Guerrilla warfare will not remain the same throughout this long and cruel war, but will rise to a higher level and develop into mobile warfare. Thus the strategic role of guerrilla warfare is twofold, to support regular warfare and to transform itself into regular warfare. Considering the unprecedented extent and duration of guerrilla warfare in China's War of Resistance, it is all the more important not to underestimate its strategic role. Guerrilla warfare in China, therefore, has not only its tactical but also its peculiar strategic problems. I have already discussed this in "Problems

of Strategy in Guerrilla War Against Japan". As indicated above, the forms of warfare in the three strategic stages of the War of Resistance are as follows. In the first stage mobile warfare is primary, while guerrilla and positional warfare are supplementary. In the second stage guerrilla warfare will advance to the first place and will be supplemented by mobile and positional warfare. In the third stage mobile warfare will again become the primary form and will be supplemented by positional and guerrilla warfare. But the mobile warfare of the third stage will no longer be undertaken solely by the original regular forces; part, possibly quite an important part, will be undertaken by forces which were originally guerrillas but which will have progressed from guerrilla to mobile warfare. From the viewpoint of all three stages in China's War of Resistance Against Japan, guerrilla warfare is definitely indispensable. Our guerrilla war will present a great drama unparalleled in the annals of war. For this reason, out of the millions of China's regular troops, it is absolutely necessary to assign at least several hundred thousand to disperse through all enemy-occupied areas, arouse the masses to arm themselves, and wage guerrilla warfare in co-ordination with the masses. The regular forces so assigned should shoulder this sacred task conscientiously, and they should not think their status lowered because they fight fewer big battles and for the time being do not appear as national heroes. Any such thinking is wrong. Guerrilla warfare does not bring as quick results or as great renown as regular warfare, but "a long road tests a horse's strength and a long task proves a man's heart", and in the course of this long and cruel war guerrilla warfare will demonstrate its immense power; it is indeed no ordinary undertaking. Moreover, such regular forces can conduct guerrilla warfare when dispersed and mobile warfare when concentrated, as the Eighth Route Army has been doing. The principle of the Eighth Route Army is, "Guerrilla warfare is basic, but lose no chance for mobile warfare under favourable conditions." This principle is perfectly correct; the views of its opponents are wrong.

96. At China's present technical level, positional warfare, defensive or offensive, is generally impracticable, and this is where our weakness manifests itself. Moreover, the enemy is also exploiting the vastness of our territory to bypass our fortified positions. Hence positional warfare cannot be an important, still less the principal, means for us. But in the first and second stages of the war, it is possible and essential, within the scope of mobile warfare, to employ localized

positional warfare in a supplementary role in campaigns. Semi-positional "mobile defence" is a still more essential part of mobile warfare undertaken for the purpose of resisting the enemy at every step, thereby depleting his forces and gaining extra time. China must strive to increase her supplies of modern weapons so that she can fully carry out the tasks of positional attack in the stage of the strategic counter-offensive. In this third stage positional warfare will undoubtedly play a greater role, for then the enemy will be holding fast to his positions, and we shall not be able to recover our lost territory unless we launch powerful positional attacks in support of mobile warfare. Nevertheless, in the third stage too, we must exert our every effort to make mobile warfare the primary form of warfare. For the art of directing war and the active role of man are largely nullified in positional warfare such as that fought in Western Europe in the second half of World War I. It is only natural that the war should be taken "out of the trenches", since the war is being fought in the vast expanses of China and since our side will remain poorly equipped technically for quite a long time. Even during the third stage, when China's technical position will be better, she will hardly surpass her enemy in that respect, and so will have to concentrate on highly mobile warfare, without which she cannot achieve final victory. Hence, throughout the War of Resistance China will not adopt positional warfare as primary; the primary or important forms are mobile warfare and guerrilla warfare. These two forms of warfare will afford full play to the art of directing war and to the active role of man — what a piece of good fortune out of our misfortune!

WAR OF ATTRITION AND WAR OF ANNIHILATION

97. As we have said before, the essence, or the object, of war is to preserve oneself and destroy the enemy. Since there are three forms of warfare, mobile, positional and guerrilla, for achieving this object, and since they differ in degrees of effectiveness, there arises the broad distinction between war of attrition and war of annihilation.

98. To begin with, we may say that the anti-Japanese war is at once a war of attrition and a war of annihilation. Why? Because the enemy is still exploiting his strength and retains strategic superiority and strategic initiative, and therefore, unless we fight campaigns and

battles of annihilation, we cannot effectively and speedily reduce his strength and break his superiority and initiative. We still have our weakness and have not yet rid ourselves of strategic inferiority and passivity; therefore, unless we fight campaigns and battles of annihilation, we cannot win time to improve our internal and international situation and alter our unfavourable position. Hence campaigns of annihilation are the means of attaining the objective of strategic attrition. In this sense war of annihilation *is* war of attrition. It is chiefly by using the method of attrition through annihilation that China can wage protracted war.

99. But the objective of strategic attrition may also be achieved by campaigns of attrition. Generally speaking, mobile warfare performs the task of annihilation, positional warfare performs the task of attrition, and guerrilla warfare performs both simultaneously; the three forms of warfare are thus distinguished from one another. In this sense war of annihilation is different from war of attrition. Campaigns of attrition are supplementary but necessary in protracted war.

100. Speaking theoretically and in terms of China's needs, in order to achieve the strategic objective of greatly depleting the enemy's forces, China in her defensive stage should not only exploit the function of annihilation, which is fulfilled primarily by mobile warfare and partially by guerrilla warfare, but also exploit the function of attrition, which is fulfilled primarily by positional warfare (which itself is supplementary) and partially by guerrilla warfare. In the stage of stalemate we should continue to exploit the functions of annihilation and attrition fulfilled by guerrilla and mobile warfare for further large-scale depletion of the enemy's forces. All this is aimed at protracting the war, gradually changing the general balance of forces and preparing the conditions for our counter-offensive. During the strategic counter-offensive, we should continue to employ the method of attrition through annihilation so as finally to expel the enemy.

101. But as a matter of fact, it was our experience in the last ten months that many or even most of the mobile warfare campaigns became campaigns of attrition, and guerrilla warfare did not adequately fulfil its proper function of annihilation in certain areas. The positive aspect is that at least we depleted the enemy's forces, which is important both for the protracted warfare and for our final victory, and did not shed our blood in vain. But the drawbacks are first, that we did not sufficiently deplete the enemy, and second, that we were

unable to avoid rather heavy losses and captured little war booty. Although we should recognize the objective cause of this situation, namely, the disparity between us and the enemy in technical equipment and in the training of troops, in any case it is necessary, both theoretically and practically, to urge that our main forces should fight vigorous battles of annihilation whenever circumstances are favourable. And although our guerrilla units have to wage battles of pure attrition in performing specific tasks such as sabotage and harassment, it is necessary to advocate and vigorously carry out campaigns and battles of annihilation whenever circumstances are favourable, so as greatly to deplete the enemy's forces and greatly replenish our own.

102. The "exterior lines", the "quick-decision" and the "offensive" in quick-decision offensive warfare on exterior lines and the "mobility" in mobile warfare find their main operational expression in the use of encircling and outflanking tactics; hence the necessity for concentrating superior forces. Therefore concentration of forces and the use of encircling and outflanking tactics are the prerequisites for mobile warfare, that is, for quick-decision offensive warfare on exterior lines. All this is aimed at annihilating the enemy forces.

103. The strength of the Japanese army lies not only in its weapons but also in the training of its officers and men — its degree of organization, its self-confidence arising from never having been defeated, its superstitious belief in the Mikado and in supernatural beings, its arrogance, its contempt for the Chinese people and other such characteristics, all of which stem from long years of indoctrination by the Japanese warlords and from the Japanese national tradition. This is the chief reason why we have taken very few prisoners, although we have killed and wounded a great many enemy troops. It is a point that has been underestimated by many people in the past. To destroy these enemy characteristics will be a long process. The first thing to do is to give the matter serious attention, and then patiently and systematically to work at it in the political field and in the fields of international propaganda and the Japanese people's movement; in the military sphere war of annihilation is of course one of the means. In these enemy characteristics pessimists may find a basis for the theory of national subjugation, and passively minded military men a basis for opposition to war of annihilation. We, on the contrary, maintain that these strong points of the Japanese army can be destroyed and that their destruction has already begun.

The chief method of destroying them is to win over the Japanese soldiers politically. We should understand, rather than hurt, their pride and channel it in the proper direction and, by treating prisoners of war leniently, lead the Japanese soldiers to see the anti-popular character of the aggression committed by the Japanese rulers. On the other hand, we should demonstrate to the Japanese soldiers the indomitable spirit and the heroic, stubborn fighting capacity of the Chinese army and the Chinese people, that is, we should deal them blows in battles of annihilation. Our experience in the last ten months of military operations shows that it is possible to annihilate enemy forces — witness the Pinghsingkuan and Taierhchuang campaigns. The Japanese army's morale is beginning to sag, its soldiers do not understand the aim of the war, they are engulfed by the Chinese armies and by the Chinese people, in assault they show far less courage than the Chinese soldiers, and so on; all these are objective factors favourable to waging battles of annihilation, and they will, moreover, steadily develop as the war becomes protracted. From the viewpoint of destroying the enemy's overweening arrogance through battles of annihilation, such battles are one of the prerequisites for shortening the war and accelerating the emancipation of the Japanese soldiers and the Japanese people. Cats make friends with cats, and nowhere in the world do cats make friends with mice.

104. On the other hand, it must be admitted that for the present we are inferior to the enemy in technical equipment and in troop training. Therefore, it is often difficult to achieve the maximum in annihilation, such as capturing the whole or the greater part of an enemy force, especially when fighting on the plains. In this connection the excessive demands of the theorists of quick victory are wrong. What should be demanded of our forces in the anti-Japanese war is that they should fight battles of annihilation as far as possible. In favourable circumstances, we should concentrate superior forces in every battle and employ encircling and outflanking tactics — encircle part if not all of the enemy forces, capture part if not all of the encircled forces, and inflict heavy casualties on part of the encircled forces if we cannot capture them. In circumstances which are unfavourable for battles of annihilation, we should fight battles of attrition. In favourable circumstances, we should employ the principle of concentration of forces, and in unfavourable circumstances that of their dispersion. As for the relationship of command in campaigns, we should apply the principle of centralized command in the former and

that of decentralized command in the latter. These are the basic
principles of field operations for the War of Resistance Against Japan.

THE POSSIBILITIES OF EXPLOITING
THE ENEMY'S MISTAKES

105. The enemy command itself provides a basis for the possibility of defeating Japan. History has never known an infallible general,
and the enemy makes mistakes just as we ourselves can hardly avoid
making them; hence, the possibility exists of exploiting the enemy's
errors. In the ten months of his war of aggression the enemy has already
made many mistakes in strategy and tactics. There are five major ones.

First, piecemeal reinforcement. This is due to the enemy's
underestimation of China and also to his shortage of troops. The
enemy has always looked down on us. After grabbing the four
northeastern provinces at small cost, he occupied eastern Hopei
and northern Chahar, all by way of strategic reconnaissance. The
conclusion the enemy came to was that the Chinese nation is a
heap of loose sand. Thus, thinking that China would crumble
at a single blow, he mapped out a plan of "quick decision",
attempting with very small forces to send us scampering in panic.
He did not expect to find such great unity and such immense
powers of resistance as China has shown during the past ten
months, forgetting as he did that China is already in an era of
progress and already has an advanced political party, an advanced
army and an advanced people. Meeting with setbacks, the enemy
then increased his forces piecemeal from about a dozen to thirty
divisions. If he wants to advance, he will have to augment his
forces still further. But because of Japan's antagonism with the
Soviet Union and her inherent shortage of manpower and finances,
there are inevitable limits to the maximum number of men she
can throw in and to the furthest extent of her advance.

Second, absence of a main direction of attack. Before the
Taierhchuang campaign, the enemy had divided his forces more
or less evenly between northern and central China and had again
divided them inside each of these areas. In northern China,
for instance, he divided his forces among the Tientsin-Pukow,

the Peiping-Hankow and the Tatung-Puchow Railways, and along each of these lines he suffered some casualties and left some garrisons in the places occupied, after which he lacked the forces for further advances. After the Taierhchuang defeat, from which he learned a lesson, the enemy concentrated his main forces in the direction of Hsuchow, and so temporarily corrected this mistake.

Third, lack of strategic co-ordination. On the whole co-ordination exists within the groups of enemy forces in northern China and in central China, but there is glaring lack of co-ordination between the two. When his forces on the southern section of the Tientsin-Pukow Railway attacked Hsiaopengpu, those on the northern section made no move, and when his forces on the northern section attacked Taierhchuang, those on the southern section made no move. After the enemy came to grief at both places, the Japanese minister of war arrived on an inspection tour and the chief of general staff turned up to take charge, and for the moment, it seemed, there was co-ordination. The landlord class, the bourgeoisie and the warlords of Japan have very serious internal contradictions, which are growing, and the lack of military co-ordination is one of the concrete manifestations of this fact.

Fourth, failure to grasp strategic opportunities. This failure was conspicuously shown in the enemy's halt after the occupation of Nanking and Taiyuan, chiefly because of his shortage of troops and his lack of a strategic pursuit force.

Fifth, encirclement of large, but annihilation of small, numbers. Before the Taierhchuang campaign, in the campaigns of Shanghai, Nanking, Tsangchow, Paoting, Nankow, Hsinkou and Linfen, many Chinese troops were routed but few were taken prisoner, which shows the stupidity of the enemy command.

These five errors — piecemeal reinforcement, absence of a main direction of attack, lack of strategic co-ordination, failure to grasp opportunities, and encirclement of large, but annihilation of small, numbers — were all points of incompetence in the Japanese command before the Taierhchuang campaign. Although the enemy has since made some improvements, he cannot possibly avoid repeating his errors because of his shortage of troops, his internal contradictions and other factors. In addition, what he gains at one point he loses at another. For instance, when he concentrated his forces in northern China on Hsuchow, he left a great vacuum in the occupied areas in northern China, which gave us full scope for developing guerrilla warfare. These mistakes were of the enemy's own making and not induced by us. On our part, we can deliberately make the enemy commit errors, that is, we can mislead him and manoeuvre him into the desired position by ingenious and effective moves with the help of a well-organized local population, for example, by "making a feint to the east but attacking in the west". This possibility has already been discussed. All the above shows that in the enemy's command, too, we can find some basis for victory. Of course, we should not take it as an important basis for our strategic planning; on the contrary, the only reliable course is to base our planning on the assumption that the enemy will make few mistakes. Besides, the enemy can exploit our mistakes just as we can exploit his. It is the duty of our command to allow him the minimum of opportunities for doing so. Actually, the enemy command has committed errors, will again commit errors in the future, and can be made to do so through our endeavours. All these errors we can exploit, and it is the business of our generals in the War of Resistance to do their utmost to seize upon them. However, although much of the enemy's strategic and campaign command is incompetent, there are quite a few excellent points in his battle command, that is, in his unit and small formation tactics, and here we should learn from him.

THE QUESTION OF DECISIVE ENGAGEMENTS IN THE ANTI-JAPANESE WAR

106. The question of decisive engagements in the anti-Japanese war should be approached from three aspects: we should resolutely fight a decisive engagement in every campaign or battle in which we are sure of victory; we should avoid a decisive engagement in every campaign or battle in which we are not sure of victory; and we should absolutely avoid a strategically decisive engagement on which the fate of the whole nation is staked. The characteristics differentiating our War of Resistance Against Japan from many other wars are also revealed in this question of decisive engagements. In the first and second stages of the war, which are marked by the enemy's strength

and our weakness, the enemy's objective is to have us concentrate our main forces for a decisive engagement. Our objective is exactly the opposite. We want to choose conditions favourable to us, concentrate superior forces and fight decisive campaigns or battles only when we are sure of victory, as in the battles at Pinghsingkuan, Taierhchuang and other places; we want to avoid decisive engagements under unfavourable conditions when we are not sure of victory, this being the policy we adopted in the Changteh and other campaigns. As for fighting a strategically decisive engagement on which the fate of the whole nation is staked, we simply must not do so, as witness the recent withdrawal from Hsuchow. The enemy's plan for a "quick decision" was thus foiled, and now he cannot help fighting a protracted war with us. These principles are impracticable in a country with a small territory, and hardly practicable in a country that is very backward politically. They are practicable in China because she is a big country and is in an era of progress. If strategically decisive engagements are avoided, then "as long as the green mountains are there, one need not worry about firewood", for even though some of our territory may be lost, we shall still have plenty of room for manoeuvre and thus be able to promote and await domestic progress, international support and the internal disintegration of the enemy; that is the best policy for us in the anti-Japanese war. Unable to endure the arduous trials of a protracted war and eager for an early triumph, the impetuous theorists of quick victory clamour for a strategically decisive engagement the moment the situation takes a slightly favourable turn. To do what they want would be to inflict incalculable damage on the entire war, spell finis to the protracted war, and land us in the enemy's deadly trap; actually, it would be the worst policy. Undoubtedly, if we are to avoid decisive engagements, we shall have to abandon territory, and we must have the courage to do so when (and only when) it becomes completely unavoidable. At such times we should not feel the slightest regret, for this policy of trading space for time is correct. History tells us how Russia made a courageous retreat to avoid a decisive engagement and then defeated Napoleon, the terror of his age. Today China should do likewise.

107. Are we not afraid of being denounced as "non-resisters"? No, we are not. Not to fight at all but to compromise with the enemy — that is non-resistance, which should not only be denounced but must never be tolerated. We must resolutely fight the War of Resistance, but in order to avoid the enemy's deadly trap, it is

absolutely necessary that we should not allow our main forces to be finished off at one blow, which would make it difficult to continue the War of Resistance — in brief, it is absolutely necessary to avoid national subjugation. To have doubts on this point is to be short-sighted on the question of the war and is sure to lead one into the ranks of the subjugationists. We have criticized the desperate recklessness of "only advance, never retreat" precisely because, if it became the fashion, this doctrine would make it impossible to continue the War of Resistance and would lead to the danger of ultimate national subjugation.

108. We are for decisive engagements whenever circumstances are favourable, whether in battles or in major or minor campaigns, and in this respect we should never tolerate passivity. Only through such decisive engagements can we achieve the objective of annihilating or depleting the enemy forces, and every soldier in the anti-Japanese war should resolutely play his part. For this purpose considerable partial sacrifices are necessary; to avoid any sacrifice whatsoever is the attitude of cowards and of those afflicted by the fear of Japan and must be firmly opposed. The execution of Li Fu-ying, Han Fu-chu and other flightists was justified. Within the scope of correct war planning, encouraging the spirit and practice of heroic self-sacrifice and dauntless advance in battle is absolutely necessary and insepa-rable from the waging of protracted war and the achievement of final victory. We have strongly condemned the flightism of "only retreat, never advance" and have supported the strict enforcement of discipline, because it is only through heroic decisive engagements, fought under a correct plan, that we can vanquish the powerful enemy; flightism, on the contrary, gives direct support to the theory of national subjugation.

109. Is it not self-contradictory to fight heroically first and then abandon territory? Will not our heroic fighters have shed their blood in vain? That is not at all the way questions should be posed. To eat and then to empty your bowels — is this not to eat in vain? To sleep and then to get up — is this not to sleep in vain? Can questions be posed in such a way? I would suppose not. To keep on eating, to keep on sleeping, to keep on fighting heroically all the way to the Yalu River without a stop — these are subjectivist and formalist illusions, not realities of life. As everybody knows, although in fighting and shed-ding our blood in order to gain time and prepare the counter-offensive we have had to abandon some territory, in fact we have gained time,

we have achieved the objective of annihilating and depleting enemy forces, we have acquired experience in fighting, we have aroused hitherto inactive people and improved our international standing. Has our blood been shed in vain? Certainly not. Territory has been given up in order to preserve our military forces and indeed to preserve territory, because if we do not abandon part of our territory when conditions are unfavourable but blindly fight decisive engagements without the least assurance of winning, we shall lose our military forces and then be unable to avoid the loss of all our territory, to say nothing of recovering territory already lost. A capitalist must have capital to run his business, and if he loses it all he is no longer a capitalist. Even a gambler must have money to stake, and if he risks it all on a single throw and his luck fails, he cannot gamble any more. Events have their twists and turns and do not follow a straight line, and war is no exception; only formalists are unable to comprehend this truth.

110. I think the same will also hold true for the decisive engagements in the stage of strategic counter-offensive. Although by then the enemy will be in the inferior and we in the superior position, the principle of "fighting profitable decisive engagements and avoiding unprofitable ones" will still apply and will continue to apply until we have fought our way to the Yalu River. This is how we will be able to maintain our initiative from beginning to end, and as for the enemy's "challenges" and other people's "taunts", we should imperturbably brush them aside and ignore them. In the War of Resistance only those generals who show this kind of firmness can be deemed courageous and wise. This is beyond the ken of those who "jump whenever touched". Even though we are in a more or less passive position strategically in this first stage of the war, we should have the initiative in every campaign; and of course we should have the initiative throughout the later stages. We are for protracted war and final victory, we are not gamblers who risk everything on a single throw.

THE ARMY AND THE PEOPLE ARE
THE FOUNDATION OF VICTORY

111. Japanese imperialism will never relax in its aggression against and repression of revolutionary China; this is determined by its

imperialist nature. If China did not resist, Japan would easily seize all China without firing a single shot, as she did the four northeastern provinces. Since China is resisting, it is an inexorable law that Japan will try to repress this resistance until the force of her repression is exceeded by the force of China's resistance. The Japanese landlord class and bourgeoisie are very ambitious, and in order to drive south to Southeast Asia and north to Siberia, they have adopted the policy of breaking through in the centre by first attacking China. Those who think that Japan will know where to stop and be content with the occupation of northern China and of Kiangsu and Chekiang Provinces completely fail to perceive that imperialist Japan, which has developed to a new stage and is approaching extinction, differs from the Japan of the past. When we say that there is a definite limit both to the number of men Japan can throw in and to the extent of her advance, we mean that with her available strength, Japan can only commit part of her forces against China and only penetrate China as far as their capacity allows, for she also wants to attack in other directions and has to defend herself against other enemies; at the same time China has given proof of progress and capacity for stubborn resistance, and it is inconceivable that there should be fierce attacks by Japan without inevitable resistance by China. Japan cannot occupy the whole of China, but she will spare no effort to suppress China's resistance in all the areas she can reach, and will not stop until internal and external developments push Japanese imperialism to the brink of the grave. There are only two possible outcomes to the political situation in Japan. Either the downfall of her entire ruling class occurs rapidly, political power passes to the people and war thus comes to an end, which is impossible at the moment; or her landlord class and bourgeoisie become more and more fascist and maintain the war until the day of their downfall, which is the very road Japan is now travelling. There can be no other outcome. Those who hope that the moderates among the Japanese bourgeoisie will come forward and stop the war are only harbouring illusions. The reality of Japanese politics for many years has been that the bourgeois moderates of Japan have fallen captive to the landlords and the financial magnates. Now that Japan has launched war against China, so long as she does not suffer a fatal blow from Chinese resistance and still retains sufficient strength, she is bound to attack Southeast Asia or Siberia, or even both. She will do so once war breaks out in Europe; in their wishful calculations, the rulers of Japan have it worked out on a grandiose scale. Of course, it is possible that Japan will have to drop her original plan of invading Siberia and adopt a mainly defensive attitude towards the Soviet Union on account of Soviet strength and of the serious extent to which Japan herself has been weakened by her war against China. But in that case, so far from relaxing her aggression against China she will intensify it, because then the only way left to her will be to gobble up the weak. China's task of persevering in the War of Resistance, the united front and the protracted war will then become all the more weighty, and it will be all the more necessary not to slacken our efforts in the slightest.

112. Under the circumstances the main prerequisites for China's victory over Japan are nation-wide unity and all-round progress on a scale ten or even a hundred times greater than in the past. China is already in an era of progress and has achieved a splendid unity, but her progress and unity are still far from adequate. That Japan has occupied such an extensive area is due not only to her strength but also to China's weakness; this weakness is entirely the cumulative effect of the various historical errors of the last hundred years, and especially of the last ten years, which have confined progress to its present bounds. It is impossible to vanquish so strong an enemy without making an extensive and long-term effort. There are many things we have to exert ourselves to do; here I will deal only with two fundamental aspects, the progress of the army and the progress of the people.

113. The reform of our military system requires its modernization and improved technical equipment, without which we cannot drive the enemy back across the Yalu River. In our employment of troops we need progressive, flexible strategy and tactics, without which we likewise cannot win victory. Nevertheless, soldiers are the foundation of an army; unless they are imbued with a progressive political spirit, and unless such a spirit is fostered through progressive political work, it will be impossible to achieve genuine unity between officers and men, impossible to arouse their enthusiasm for the War of Resistance to the full, and impossible to provide a sound basis for the most effective use of all our technical equipment and tactics. When we say that Japan will finally be defeated despite her technical superiority, we mean that the blows we deliver through annihilation and attrition, apart from inflicting losses, will eventually shake the morale of the enemy army whose weapons are not in the hands of politically conscious soldiers. With us, on the contrary, officers and men are at one on the

political aim of the War of Resistance. This gives us the foundation for political work among all the anti-Japanese forces. A proper measure of democracy should be put into effect in the army, chiefly by abolishing the feudal practice of bullying and beating and by having officers and men share weal and woe. Once this is done, unity will be achieved between officers and men, the combat effectiveness of the army will be greatly increased, and there will be no doubt of our ability to sustain the long, cruel war.

114. The richest source of power to wage war lies in the masses of the people. It is mainly because of the unorganized state of the Chinese masses that Japan dares to bully us. When this defect is remedied, then the Japanese aggressor, like a mad bull crashing into a ring of flames, will be surrounded by hundreds of millions of our people standing upright, the mere sound of their voices will strike terror into him, and he will be burned to death. China's armies must have an uninterrupted flow of reinforcements, and the abuses of press-ganging and of buying substitutes,[33] which now exist at the lower levels, must immediately be banned and replaced by widespread and enthusiastic political mobilization, which will make it easy to enlist millions of men. We now have great difficulties in raising money for the war, but once the people are mobilized, finances too will cease to be a problem. Why should a country as large and populous as China suffer from lack of funds? The army must become one with the people so that they see it as their own army. Such an army will be invincible, and an imperialist power like Japan will be no match for it.

115. Many people think that it is wrong methods that make for strained relations between officers and men and between the army and the people, but I always tell them that it is a question of basic attitude (or basic principle), of having respect for the soldiers and the people. It is from this attitude that the various policies, methods and forms ensue. If we depart from this attitude, then the policies, methods and forms will certainly be wrong, and the relations between officers and men and between the army and the people are bound to be unsatisfactory. Our three major principles for the army's political work are, first, unity between officers and men; second, unity between the army and the people; and third, the disintegration of the enemy forces. To apply these principles effectively, we must start with this basic attitude of respect for the soldiers and the people, and of

respect for the human dignity of prisoners of war once they have laid down their arms. Those who take all this as a technical matter and not one of basic attitude are indeed wrong, and they should correct their view.

116. At this moment when the defence of Wuhan and other places has become urgent, it is a task of the utmost importance to arouse the initiative and enthusiasm of the whole army and the whole people to the full in support of the war. There is no doubt that the task of defending Wuhan and other places must be seriously posed and seriously performed. But whether we can be certain of holding them depends not on our subjective desires but on concrete conditions. Among the most important of these conditions is the political mobilization of the whole army and people for the struggle. If a strenuous effort is not made to secure all the necessary conditions, indeed even if one of these conditions is missing, disasters like the loss of Nanking and other places are bound to be repeated. China will have her Madrids in places where the conditions are present. So far China has not had a Madrid, and from now on we should work hard to create several, but it all depends on the conditions. The most fundamental of these is extensive political mobilization of the whole army and people.

117. In all our work we must persevere in the Anti-Japanese National United Front as the general policy. For only with this policy can we persevere in the War of Resistance and in protracted warfare, bring about a widespread and profound improvement in the relations between officers and men and between the army and the people, arouse to the full the initiative and enthusiasm of the entire army and the entire people in the fight for the defence of all the territory still in our hands and for the recovery of what we have lost, and so win final victory.

118. This question of the political mobilization of the army and the people is indeed of the greatest importance. We have dwelt on it at the risk of repetition precisely because victory is impossible without it. There are, of course, many other conditions indispensable to victory, but political mobilization is the most fundamental. The Anti-Japanese National United Front is a united front of the whole army and the whole people, it is certainly not a united front merely of the headquarters and members of a few political parties; our basic objective in initiating the Anti-Japanese National United Front is to mobilize the whole army and the whole people to participate in it.

CONCLUSIONS

119. What are our conclusions? They are:

"Under what conditions do you think China can defeat and destroy the forces of Japan?" "Three conditions are required: first, the establishment of an anti-Japanese united front in China; second, the formation of an international anti-Japanese united front; third, the rise of the revolutionary movement of the people in Japan and the Japanese colonies. From the standpoint of the Chinese people, the unity of the people of China is the most important of the three conditions."

"How long do you think such a war would last?" "That depends on the strength of China's anti-Japanese united front and many other conditioning factors involving China and Japan."

"If these conditions are not realized quickly, the war will be prolonged. But in the end, just the same, Japan will certainly be defeated and China will certainly be victorious. Only the sacrifices will be great and there will be a very painful period."

"Our strategy should be to employ our main forces to operate over an extended and fluid front. To achieve success, the Chinese troops must conduct their warfare with a high degree of mobility on extensive battlefields."

"Besides employing trained armies to carry on mobile warfare, we must organize great numbers of guerrilla units among the peasants."

"In the course of the war, China will be able to . . . reinforce the equipment of her troops gradually. Therefore China will be able to conduct positional warfare in the latter period of the war and make positional attacks on the Japanese-occupied areas. Thus Japan's economy will crack under the strain of China's long resistance and the morale of the Japanese forces will break under the trial of innumerable battles. On the Chinese side, however, the growing latent power of resistance will be constantly brought into play and large numbers of revolutionary people will be pouring into the front lines to fight for their freedom. The combination of all these and other factors will enable us to make the final and decisive attacks on the fortifications and bases in the Japanese-occupied areas and drive the Japanese forces of aggression out of China." (From an interview with Edgar Snow in July 1936.)

"Thus a new stage has opened in China's political situation. . . . In the present stage the central task is to mobilize all the nation's forces for victory in the War of Resistance."

"The key to victory in the war now lies in developing the resistance that has already begun into a war of total resistance by the whole nation. Only through such a war of total resistance can final victory be won."

"The existence of serious weaknesses in the War of Resistance may lead to setbacks, retreats, internal splits, betrayals, temporary and partial compromises and other such reverses. Therefore it should be realized that the war will be arduous and protracted. But we are confident that, through the efforts of our Party and the whole people, the resistance already started will sweep aside all obstacles and continue to advance and develop." ("Resolution on the Present Situation and the Tasks of the Party", adopted by the Central Committee of the Communist Party of China, August 1937.)

These are our conclusions. In the eyes of the subjugationists the enemy are supermen and we Chinese are worthless, while in the eyes of the theorists of quick victory we Chinese are supermen and the enemy are worthless. Both are wrong. We take a different view; the War of Resistance Against Japan is a protracted war, and the final victory will be China's. These are our conclusions.

120. My lectures end here. The great War of Resistance Against Japan is unfolding, and many people are hoping for a summary of experience to facilitate the winning of complete victory. What I have discussed is simply the general experience of the past ten months, and it may perhaps serve as a kind of summary. The problem of protracted war deserves wide attention and discussion; what I have given is only an outline, which I hope you will examine and discuss, amend and amplify.

NOTES

[1] This theory of national subjugation was the view held by the Kuomintang. The Kuomintang was unwilling to resist Japan and fought Japan only under compulsion. After the Lukouchiao Incident (July 7, 1937), the Chiang Kai-shek clique reluctantly took part in the War of Resistance, while the Wang Ching-wei clique became the representatives of the theory of national subjugation, was ready to capitulate to Japan

and in fact subsequently did so. However, the idea of national subjugation not only existed in the Kuomintang, but also affected certain sections of the middle strata of society and even certain backward elements among the labouring people. As the corrupt and impotent Kuomintang government lost one battle after another and the Japanese troops advanced unchecked to the vicinity of Wuhan in the first year of the War of Resistance, some backward people became profoundly pessimistic.

² These views were to be found within the Communist Party. During the first six months of the War of Resistance, there was a tendency to take the enemy lightly among some members of the Party, who held the view that Japan could be defeated at a single blow. It was not that they felt our own forces to be so strong, since they well knew that the troops and the organized people's forces led by the Communist Party were still small, but that the Kuomintang had begun to resist Japan. In their opinion, the Kuomintang was quite powerful, and, in co-ordination with the Communist Party, could deal Japan telling blows. They made this erroneous appraisal because they saw only one aspect of the Kuomintang, that it was resisting Japan, but overlooked the other aspect, that it was reactionary and corrupt.

³ Such was the view of Chiang Kai-shek and company. Though they were compelled to resist Japan, Chiang Kai-shek and the Kuomintang pinned their hopes solely on prompt foreign aid and had no confidence in their own strength, much less in the strength of the people.

⁴ Taierhchuang is a town in southern Shantung where the Chinese army fought a battle in March 1938 against the Japanese invaders. By pitting 400,000 men against Japan's 70,000 to 80,000, the Chinese army defeated the Japanese.

⁵ This view was put forward in an editorial in the *Ta Kung Pao*, then the organ of the Political Science Group in the Kuomintang. Indulging in wishful thinking, this clique hoped that a few more victories of the Taierhchuang type would stop Japan's advance and that there would be no need to mobilize the people for a protracted war, which would threaten the security of its own class. This wishful thinking then pervaded the Kuomintang as a whole.

⁶ For many decades, beginning with the end of the 18th century, Britain exported an increasing quantity of opium to China. This traffic not only subjected the Chinese people to drugging but also plundered China of her silver. It aroused fierce opposition in China. In 1840, under the pretext of safeguarding its trade with China, Britain launched armed aggression against her. The Chinese troops led by Lin Tse-hsu put up resistance, and the people in Canton spontaneously organized the "Quell-the-British Corps", which dealt serious blows to the British forces of aggression. In 1842, however, the corrupt Ching regime signed the Treaty of Nanking with Britain. This treaty provided for the payment of indemnities and the cession of Hongkong to Britain, and stipulated that Shanghai, Foochow, Amoy, Ningpo and Canton were to be opened to British trade and that tariff rates for British goods imported into China were to be jointly fixed by China and Britain.

⁷ The Taiping Revolution, or the Movement of the Taiping Heavenly Kingdom, was the mid-19th century revolutionary peasant movement against the feudal rule and national oppression of the Ching Dynasty. In January 1851 Hung Hsiu-chuan, Yang Hsiu-ching and other leaders launched an uprising in Chintien Village in Kueiping County, Kwangsi Province, and proclaimed the founding of the Taiping Heavenly Kingdom. Proceeding northward from Kwangsi, their peasant army attacked and occupied Hunan and Hupeh in 1852. In 1853 it marched through Kiangsi and Anhwei and captured Nanking. A section of the forces then continued the drive north and pushed on to the vicinity of Tientsin. However, the Taiping army failed

to build stable base areas in the places it occupied; moreover, after establishing its capital in Nanking, its leading group committed many political and military errors. Therefore it was unable to withstand the combined onslaughts of the counter-revolutionary forces of the Ching government and the British, U.S. and French aggressors, and was finally defeated in 1864.

8 The Reform Movement of 1898, whose leading spirits were Kang Yu-wei, Liang Chi-chao and Tan Szu-tung, represented the interests of the liberal bourgeoisie and the enlightened landlords. The movement was favoured and supported by Emperor Kuang Hsu, but had no mass basis. Yuan Shih-kai, who had an army behind him, betrayed the reformers to Empress Dowager Tzu Hsi, the leader of the die-hards, who seized power again and had Emperor Kuang Hsu imprisoned and Tan Szu-tung and five others beheaded. Thus the movement ended in tragic defeat.

9 The Revolution of 1911 was the bourgeois revolution which overthrew the autocratic regime of the Ching Dynasty. On October 10 of that year, a section of the Ching Dynasty's New Army who were under revolutionary influence staged an uprising in Wuchang, Hupeh Province. The existing bourgeois and petty-bourgeois revolutionary societies and the broad masses of the workers, peasants and soldiers responded enthusiastically, and very soon the rule of the Ching Dynasty crumbled. In January 1912, the Provisional Government of the Republic of China was set up in Nanking, with Sun Yat-sen as the Provisional President. Thus China's feudal monarchic system which had lasted for more than two thousand years was brought to an end. The idea of a democratic republic had entered deep in the hearts of the people. But the bourgeoisie which led the revolution was strongly conciliationist in nature. It did not mobilize the peasant masses on an extensive scale to crush the feudal rule of the landlord class in the countryside, but instead handed state power over to the Northern warlord Yuan Shih-kai under imperialist and feudal pressure. As a result, the revolution ended in defeat.

10 The Northern Expedition was the punitive war against the Northern war-lords launched by the revolutionary army which marched north from Kwangtung Province in May-July 1926. The Northern Expeditionary Army, with the Communist Party of China taking part in its leadership and under the Party's influence (the political work in the army was at that time mostly under the charge of Communist Party members), gained the warm support of the broad masses of workers and peasants. In the second half of 1926 and the first half of 1927 it occupied most of the provinces along the Yangtse and Yellow Rivers and defeated the Northern warlords. In April 1927 this revolutionary war failed as a result of betrayal by the reactionary clique under Chiang Kai-shek within the revolutionary army.

11 On January 16, 1938, the Japanese cabinet declared in a policy statement that Japan would subjugate China by force. At the same time it tried by threats and blandishments to make the Kuomintang government capitulate, declaring that if the Kuomintang government "continued to plan resistance", the Japanese government would foster a new puppet regime in China and no longer accept the Kuomintang as "the other party" in negotiations.

12 The capitalists referred to here are chiefly those of the United States.

13 By "their governments" Comrade Mao Tse-tung is here referring to the governments of the imperialist countries — Britain, the United States and France.

14 Comrade Mao Tse-tung's prediction that there would be an upswing in China during the stage of stalemate in the War of Resistance Against Japan was completely confirmed in the case of the Liberated Areas under the leadership of the Chinese Communist Party. But there was actually a decline instead of an upswing in the Kuomintang

areas, because the ruling clique headed by Chiang Kai-shek was passive in resisting Japan and active in opposing the Communist Party and the people. This roused opposition among the broad masses of the people and raised their political consciousness.

[15] According to the theory that "weapons decide everything", China which was inferior to Japan in regard to arms was bound to be defeated in the war. This view was current among all the leaders of the Kuomintang reaction, Chiang Kai-shek included.

[16] See "Problems of Strategy in Guerrilla War Against Japan", Note 9, p. 112 of this volume.

[17] Sun Wu-kung is the monkey king in the Chinese novel *Hsi Yu Chi (Pilgrimage to the West)*, written in the 16th century. He could cover 108,000 *li* by turning a somersault. Yet once in the palm of the Buddha, he could not escape from it, however many somersaults he turned. With a flick of his palm Buddha transformed his fingers into the five-peak Mountain of Five Elements, and buried Sun Wu-kung.

[18] *"Fascism is unbridled chauvinism and predatory war,"* said Comrade Georgi Dimitrov in his report to the Seventh World Congress of the Communist International in August 1935, entitled "The Fascist Offensive and the Tasks of the Communist International" (see *Selected Articles and Speeches*, Eng. ed., Lawrence & Wishart, London, 1951, p. 44). In July 1937, Comrade Dimitrov published an article entitled *Fascism Is War*.

[19] V. I. Lenin, *Socialism and War*, Eng. ed., FLPH, Moscow, 1950, p. 19.

[20] *Sun Tzu*, Chapter 3, "The Strategy of Attack".

[21] Chengpu, situated in the southwest of the present Chuancheng County in Shantung Province, was the scene of a great battle between the states of Tsin and Chu in 632 B.C. At the beginning of the battle the Chu troops got the upper hand. The Tsin troops, after making a retreat of 90 *li*, chose the right and left flanks of the Chu troops, their weak spots, and inflicted heavy defeats on them.

[22] The ancient town of Chengkao, in the northwest of the present Chengkao County, Honan Province, was of great military importance. It was the scene of battles fought in 203 B.C. between Liu Pang, King of Han, and Hsiang Yu, King of Chu. At first Hsiang Yu captured Hsingyang and Chengkao and Liu Pang's troops were almost routed. Liu Pang waited until the opportune moment when Hsiang Yu's troops were in midstream crossing the Szeshui River, and then crushed them and recaptured Chengkao.

[23] In 204 B.C., Han Hsin, a general of the state of Han, led his men in a big battle with Chao Hsieh at Chinghsing. Chao Hsieh's army, said to be 200,000 strong, was several times that of Han. Deploying his troops with their backs to a river, Han Hsin led them in valiant combat, and at the same time dispatched some units to attack and occupy the enemy's weakly garrisoned rear. Caught in a pincer, Chao Hsieh's troops were utterly defeated.

[24] The ancient town of Kunyang, in the north of the present Yehhsien County, Honan Province, was the place where Liu Hsiu, founder of the Eastern Han Dynasty, defeated the troops of Wang Mang, Emperor of the Hsin Dynasty, in A.D. 23. There was a huge numerical disparity between the two sides, Liu Hsiu's forces totalling 8,000 to 9,000 men as against Wang Mang's 400,000. But taking advantage of the negligence of Wang Mang's generals, Wang Hsun and Wang Yi, who underestimated the enemy, Liu Hsiu with only three thousand picked troops put Wang Mang's main forces to rout. He followed up this victory by crushing the rest of the enemy troops.

[25] Kuantu was in the northeast of the present Chungmou County, Honan Province, and the scene of the battle between the armies of Tsao Tsao and Yuan Shao in A.D.

200. Yuan Shao had an army of 100,000, while Tsao Tsao had only a meagre force and was short of supplies. Taking advantage of the lack of vigilance on the part of Yuan Shao's troops, who belittled the enemy, Tsao Tsao dispatched his light-footed soldiers to spring a surprise attack on them and set their supplies on fire. Yuan Shao's army was thrown into confusion and its main force wiped out.

26 The state of Wu was ruled by Sun Chuan, and the state of Wei by Tsao Tsao. Chihpi is situated on the south bank of the Yangtse River, to the northeast of Chiayu, Hupeh Province. In A.D. 208 Tsao Tsao led an army of over 500,000 men, which he proclaimed to be 800,000 strong, to launch an attack on Sun Chuan. The latter, in alliance with Tsao Tsao's antagonist Liu Pei, mustered a force of 30,000. Knowing that Tsao Tsao's army was plagued by epidemics and was unaccustomed to action afloat, the allied forces of Sun Chuan and Liu Pei set fire to Tsao Tsao's fleet and crushed his army.

27 Yiling, to the east of the present Ichang, Hupeh Province, was the place where Lu Sun, a general of the state of Wu, defeated the army of Liu Pei, ruler of Shu, in A.D. 222. Liu Pei's troops scored successive victories at the beginning of the war and penetrated five or six hundred *li* into the territory of Wu as far as Yiling. Lu Sun, who was defending Yiling, avoided battle for over seven months until Liu Pei "was at his wits' end and his troops were exhausted and demoralized". Then he crushed Liu Pei's troops by taking advantage of a favourable wind to set fire to their tents.

28 Hsieh Hsuan, a general of Eastern Tsin Dynasty, defeated Fu Chien, ruler of the state of Chin, in A.D. 383 at the Feishui River in Anhwei Province. Fu Chien had an infantry force of more than 600,000, a cavalry force of 270,000 and a guards corps of more than 30,000, while the land and river forces of Eastern Tsin numbered only 80,000. When the armies lined up on opposite banks of the Feishui River, Hsieh Hsuan, taking advantage of the overconfidence and conceit of the enemy troops, requested Fu Chien to move his troops back so as to leave room for the Eastern Tsin troops to cross the river and fight it out. Fu Chien complied, but when he ordered withdrawal, his troops got into a panic and could not be stopped. Seizing the opportunity, the Eastern Tsin troops crossed the river, launched an offensive and crushed the enemy.

29 In A.D. 383, Fu Chien, the ruler of the state of Chin, belittled the forces of Tsin and attacked them. The Tsin troops defeated the enemy's advance units at Lochien, Shouyang County, Anhwei Province, and pushed forward by land and water. Ascending the city wall of Shouyang, Fu Chien observed the excellent alignment of the Tsin troops and, mistaking the woods and bushes on Mount Pakung for enemy soldiers, was frightened by the enemy's apparent strength.

30 Comrade Mao Tse-tung is here referring to the fact that Chiang Kai-shek and Wang Ching-wei, having betrayed the first national democratic united front of the Kuomintang and the Communist Party in 1927, launched a ten-year war against the people, and thus made it impossible for the Chinese people to be organized on a large scale. For this the Kuomintang reactionaries headed by Chiang Kai-shek must be held responsible.

31 Duke Hsiang of Sung ruled in the Spring and Autumn Era. In 638 B.C., the state of Sung fought with the powerful state of Chu. The Sung forces were already deployed in battle positions when the Chu troops were crossing the river. One of the Sung officers suggested that, as the Chu troops were numerically stronger, this was the moment for attack. But the Duke said, "No, a gentleman should never attack one who is unprepared." When the Chu troops had crossed the river but had not yet completed their battle alignment, the officer again proposed an immediate attack,

and once again the Duke said, "No, a gentleman should never attack an army which has not yet completed its battle alignment." The Duke gave the order for attack only after the Chu troops were fully prepared. As a result, the Sung troops met with a disastrous defeat and the Duke himself was wounded.

[32] Han Fu-chu, a Kuomintang warlord, was for several years governor of Shantung. When the Japanese invaders thrust southward to Shantung along the Tientsin-Pukow Railway after occupying Peiping and Tientsin in 1937, Han Fu-chu fled all the way from Shantung to Honan without fighting a single battle.

[33] The Kuomintang expanded its army by press-ganging. Its military and police seized people everywhere, roping them up and treating them like convicts. Those who had money would bribe the Kuomintang officials or pay for substitutes.

THE ROLE OF
THE CHINESE COMMUNIST PARTY
IN THE NATIONAL WAR

October 1938

Comrades, the prospects ahead of us are bright. Not only is it necessary for us to defeat Japanese imperialism and build a new China, but we are certainly capable of achieving these aims. However, there is a difficult road ahead between the present and the bright future. In the struggle for a new China, the Chinese Communist Party and the whole people must fight the Japanese aggressors in a planned way and can defeat them only through a long war. We have already said a good deal about the various problems relating to the war. We have summed up the experience gained since its outbreak and appraised the present situation, defined the urgent tasks confronting the whole nation and explained the reasons for sustaining a long war by means of a long-term national united front against Japan and the methods for doing so, and we have analysed the international situation. What problems then remain? Comrades, there is one more problem, namely, what role the Chinese Communist Party should play in the national war, or how Communists should understand their own role, strengthen themselves and close their ranks in order to be able to lead this war to victory and not to defeat.

This report was made by Comrade Mao Tse-tung to the Sixth Plenary Session of the Sixth Central Committee of the Party. The session endorsed the line of the Political Bureau headed by Comrade Mao Tse-tung and was a very important one. In discussing the question of the role of the Chinese Communist Party in the national war he helped all comrades clearly to understand and conscientiously to shoulder the Party's great and historic responsibility of leading the War of Resistance Against Japan. The plenary session decided on the line of persisting in the anti-Japanese united front, but at the same time pointed out that there had to be struggle as well as unity within the united front and that the proposition, "Everything through the united front", did not suit Chinese conditions. Thus the error of accommoda-

PATRIOTISM AND INTERNATIONALISM

Can a Communist, who is an internationalist, at the same time be a patriot? We hold that he not only can be but must be. The specific content of patriotism is determined by historical conditions. There is the "patriotism" of the Japanese aggressors and of Hitler, and there is our patriotism. Communists must resolutely oppose the "patriotism" of the Japanese aggressors and of Hitler. The Communists of Japan and Germany are defeatists with regard to the wars being waged by their countries. To bring about the defeat of the Japanese aggressors and of Hitler by every possible means is in the interests of the Japanese and the German people, and the more complete the defeat the better. This is what the Japanese and German Communists should be doing and what they are doing. For the wars launched by the Japanese aggressors and Hitler are harming their own people as well as the people of the world. China's case is different, because she is the victim of aggression. Chinese Communists must therefore combine patriotism with internationalism. We are at once internationalists and patriots, and our slogan is, "Fight to defend the motherland against the aggressors." For us defeatism is a crime and to strive for victory in the War of Resistance is an inescapable duty. For only by fighting in defence of the motherland can we defeat the aggressors and achieve national liberation. And only by achieving national liberation will it be possible for the proletariat and other working people to achieve their own emancipation. The victory of China and the defeat of the invading imperialists will help the people of other countries. Thus in wars of national liberation patriotism is applied internationalism. For this reason Communists must use their initiative to the full, march bravely and resolutely to the battle front

---

tionism in regard to the united front was criticized; this problem was dealt with by Comrade Mao Tse-tung in "The Question of Independence and Initiative Within the United Front", which was part of his concluding speech at the same session. Affirming that it was extremely important for the whole Party to devote itself to organizing the people's armed struggle against Japan, the session decided that the war zones and the enemy's rear should be the Party's main fields of work and repudiated the erroneous ideas of those who pinned their hopes of victory on the Kuomintang armies and who would have entrusted the fate of the people to legal struggles under the reactionary Kuomintang rule. This problem was dealt with by Comrade Mao Tse-tung in "Problems of War and Strategy", which was also part of his concluding speech at the session.

of the war of national liberation and train their guns on the Japanese aggressors. For this reason, immediately after the Incident of September 18, 1931, our Party issued its call to resist the Japanese aggressors by a war of national defence, and later proposed a national united front against Japan, ordered the Red Army to reorganize as part of the anti-Japanese National Revolutionary Army and to march to the front, and instructed Party members to take their place in the forefront of the war and defend the motherland to the last drop of their blood. These are good patriotic actions and, far from running counter to internationalism, are its application in China. Only those who are politically muddle-headed or have ulterior motives talk nonsense about our having made a mistake and abandoned internationalism.

COMMUNISTS SHOULD SET AN EXAMPLE IN THE NATIONAL WAR

For the above reasons Communists should show a high degree of initiative in the national war, and show it concretely, that is, they should play an exemplary vanguard role in every sphere. Our war is being waged under adverse circumstances. National consciousness, national self-respect and national self-confidence are not sufficiently developed among the broad masses, the majority of the people are unorganized, China's military power is weak, the economy is backward, the political system is undemocratic, corruption and pessimism exist, and a lack of unity and solidarity is to be found within the united front; these are among the adverse circumstances. Therefore, Communists must consciously shoulder the great responsibility of uniting the entire nation so as to put an end to all such undesirable phenomena. Here the exemplary vanguard role of the Communists is of vital importance. Communists in the Eighth Route and New Fourth Armies should set an example in fighting bravely, carrying out orders, observing discipline, doing political work and fostering internal unity and solidarity. In their relations with friendly parties and armies, Communists should take a firm stand of unity for resistance to Japan, uphold the programme of the united front and set an example in carrying out the tasks of resistance; they should be true in word and

resolute in deed, free from arrogance and sincere in consulting and
co-operating with the friendly parties and armies, and they should
be models in inter-party relations within the united front. Every Communist engaged in government work should set an example of absolute
integrity, of freedom from favouritism in making appointments and
of hard work for little remuneration. Every Communist working
among the masses should be their friend and not a boss over them,
an indefatigable teacher and not a bureaucratic politician. At no time
and in no circumstances should a Communist place his personal
interests first; he should subordinate them to the interests of the nation
and of the masses. Hence, selfishness, slacking, corruption, seeking the
limelight, and so on, are most contemptible, while selflessness, working
with all one's energy, whole-hearted devotion to public duty, and quiet
hard work will command respect. Communists should work in harmony
with all progressives outside the Party and endeavour to unite the
entire people to do away with whatever is undesirable. It must be
realized that Communists form only a small section of the nation,
and that there are large numbers of progressives and activists outside
the Party with whom we must work. It is entirely wrong to think
that we alone are good and no one else is any good. As for people
who are politically backward, Communists should not slight or despise
them, but should befriend them, unite with them, convince them and
encourage them to go forward. The attitude of Communists towards
any person who has made mistakes in his work should be one of
persuasion in order to help him change and start afresh and not one
of exclusion, unless he is incorrigible. Communists should set an
example in being practical as well as far-sighted. For only by being
practical can they fulfil the appointed tasks, and only far-sightedness
can prevent them from losing their bearings in the march forward.
Communists should therefore set an example in study; at all times
they should learn from the masses as well as teach them. Only by
learning from the people, from actual circumstances and from the
friendly parties and armies, and by knowing them well, can we be
practical in our work and far-sighted as to the future. In a long war
and in adverse circumstances, the dynamic energy of the whole nation
can be mobilized in the struggle to overcome difficulties, defeat the
enemy and build a new China only if the Communists play an
exemplary vanguard role to the best of their ability together with all
the advanced elements among the friendly parties and armies and
among the masses.

UNITE THE WHOLE NATION AND COMBAT ENEMY AGENTS IN ITS MIDST

The one and only policy for overcoming difficulties, defeating the enemy and building a new China is to consolidate and expand the Anti-Japanese National United Front and mobilize the dynamic energy of the whole nation. However, there are already enemy agents playing a disruptive role within our national united front, namely, the traitors, Trotskyites and pro-Japanese elements. Communists must always be on the look-out for them, expose their criminal activities with factual evidence and warn the people not to be duped by them. Communists must sharpen their political vigilance towards these enemy agents. They must understand that the expansion and consolidation of the national united front is inseparable from the exposure and weeding out of enemy agents. It is entirely wrong to pay attention only to the one side and forget the other.

EXPAND THE COMMUNIST PARTY AND PREVENT INFILTRATION BY ENEMY AGENTS

To overcome the difficulties, defeat the enemy and build a new China, the Communist Party must expand its organization and become a great mass party by opening its doors to the masses of workers, peasants and young activists who are truly devoted to the revolution, who believe in the Party's principles, support its policies and are willing to observe its discipline and work hard. Here no tendency towards closed-doorism should be tolerated. But at the same time, there must be no slackening of vigilance against infiltration by enemy agents. The Japanese imperialist secret services are ceaselessly trying to disrupt our Party and to smuggle undercover traitors, Trotskyites, pro-Japanese elements, degenerates and careerists into its ranks in the guise of activists. Not for a moment must we relax our vigilance and our strict precautions against such persons. We must not close our doors for fear of enemy agents, our set policy being boldly to expand our Party. But while boldly enlarging our membership, we must not relax our vigilance against enemy agents and careerists who will avail themselves of this opportunity to sneak in. We shall make mistakes if we only pay attention to the one side and forget the other.

The only correct policy is: "Expand the Party boldly but do not let a single undesirable in."

MAINTAIN BOTH THE UNITED FRONT AND THE INDEPENDENCE OF THE PARTY

It is only by firmly maintaining the national united front that the difficulties can be overcome, the enemy defeated and a new China built. This is beyond all doubt. At the same time, every party and group in the united front must preserve its ideological, political and organizational independence; this holds good for the Kuomintang, the Communist Party or any other party or group. In inter-party relations, the Principle of Democracy in the Three People's Principles permits both the union of all parties and groups and the independent existence of each. To speak of unity alone while denying independence is to abandon the Principle of Democracy, and to this neither the Communist Party nor any other party would agree. There is no doubt that independence within the united front is relative and not absolute, and that to regard it as absolute would undermine the general policy of unity against the enemy. But this relative independence must not be denied; ideologically, politically and organizationally, each party must have its relative independence, that is, relative freedom. Also, the general policy of unity against the enemy would be undermined if this relative freedom were denied or voluntarily abandoned. This should be clearly understood by all members of the Communist Party as well as of the friendly parties.

The same is true of the relationship between the class struggle and the national struggle. It is an established principle that in the War of Resistance everything must be subordinated to the interests of resistance. Therefore, the interests of the class struggle must be subordinated to, and must not conflict with, the interests of the War of Resistance. But classes and the class struggle are facts, and those people who deny the fact of class struggle are wrong. The theory which attempts to deny this fact is utterly wrong. We do not deny the class struggle, we adjust it. The policy of mutual help and mutual concessions which we advocate is applicable not only to party relations but also to class relations. Unity against Japan requires an appropriate policy of adjustment in class relations, a policy which does not leave the labouring people without political and material safeguards but also gives consideration to the interests of the rich, thereby meeting the demands of solidarity against the enemy. It is bad for the War of Resistance to pay attention only to the one side and neglect the other.

CONSIDER THE SITUATION AS A WHOLE, THINK IN TERMS OF THE MAJORITY, AND WORK TOGETHER WITH OUR ALLIES

In leading the masses in struggle against the enemy, Communists must consider the situation as a whole, think in terms of the majority of the people and work together with their allies. They must grasp the principle of subordinating the needs of the part to the needs of the whole. If a proposal appears feasible for a partial situation but not for the situation as a whole, then the part must give way to the whole. Conversely, if the proposal is not feasible for the part but is feasible in the light of the situation as a whole, again the part must give way to the whole. This is what is meant by considering the situation as a whole. Communists must never separate themselves from the majority of the people or neglect them by leading only a few progressive contingents in an isolated and rash advance, but must forge close links between the progressive elements and the broad masses. This is what is meant by thinking in terms of the majority. Wherever there are democratic parties or individuals willing to co-operate with us, the proper attitude for Communists is to talk things over with them and work together with them. It is wrong to indulge in arbitrary decisions and peremptory actions and to ignore our allies. A good Communist must be good at considering the situation as a whole, good at thinking in terms of the majority and good at working with his allies. We have had serious shortcomings in this respect, and we must still give the matter attention.

CADRES POLICY

The Chinese Communist Party is a party leading a great revolutionary struggle in a nation several hundred million strong, and it cannot fulfil its historic task without a large number of leading cadres who combine ability with political integrity. In the last seventeen years our Party has trained a good many competent leaders, so that we have a framework of cadres in military, political, cultural, Party and mass work; all honour is due to the Party and to the nation for this achievement. But the present framework is not yet strong enough to support the vast edifice of our struggle, and it is still necessary to train capable people on a large scale. Many activists have come forward, and are continuing to come forward, in the great struggle of the Chinese people. We have the responsibility for organizing and training them and for taking good care and making proper use of them. Cadres are a decisive factor, once the political line is determined.[1] Therefore, it is our fighting task to train large numbers of new cadres in a planned way.

Our concern should extend to non-Party cadres as well as to Party cadres. There are many capable people outside the Party whom we must not ignore. The duty of every Communist is to rid himself of aloofness and arrogance and to work well with non-Party cadres, give them sincere help, have a warm, comradely attitude towards them and enlist their initiative in the great cause of resisting Japan and reconstructing the nation.

We must know how to judge cadres. We must not confine our judgement to a short period or a single incident in a cadre's life, but should consider his life and work as a whole. This is the principal method of judging cadres.

We must know how to use cadres well. In the final analysis, leadership involves two main responsibilities: to work out ideas, and to use cadres well. Such things as drawing up plans, making decisions, and giving orders and directives, are all in the category of "working out ideas". To put the ideas into practice, we must weld the cadres together and encourage them to go into action; this comes into the category of "using the cadres well". Throughout our national history there have been two sharply contrasting lines on the subject of the use of cadres, one being to "appoint people on their merit", and the other to "appoint people by favouritism". The former is the honest and the latter the dishonest way. The criterion the Communist Party should apply in its cadres policy is whether or not a cadre is resolute in carrying out the Party line, keeps to Party discipline, has close ties with the masses, has the ability to find his bearings independently, and is active, hard-working and unselfish. This is what "appointing people on their merit" means. The cadres policy of Chang Kuo-tao was the exact opposite. Following the line of "appointing people by favouritism", he gathered personal favourites round himself to form a small clique, and in the end he turned traitor to the Party and decamped. This is an important lesson for us. Taking warning from it and from similar historical lessons, the Central Committee and the leaders at all levels must make it their major responsibility to adhere to the honest and fair way in cadres policy and reject the dishonest and unfair way, and so consolidate the unity of the Party.

We must know how to take good care of cadres. There are several ways of doing so.

First, give them guidance. This means allowing them a free hand in their work so that they have the courage to assume responsibility and, at the same time, giving them timely instructions so that, guided by the Party's political line, they are able to make full use of their initiative.

Second, raise their level. This means educating them by giving them the opportunity to study so that they can enhance their theoretical understanding and their working ability.

Third, check up on their work, and help them sum up their experience, carry forward their achievements and correct their mistakes. To assign work without checking up and to take notice only when serious mistakes are made — that is not the way to take care of cadres.

Fourth, in general, use the method of persuasion with cadres who have made mistakes, and help them correct their mistakes. The method of struggle should be confined to those who make serious mistakes and nevertheless refuse to accept guidance. Here patience is essential. It is wrong lightly to label people "opportunists" or lightly to begin "waging struggles" against them.

Fifth, help them with their difficulties. When cadres are in difficulty as a result of illness, straitened means or domestic or other troubles, we must be sure to give them as much care as possible.

This is how to take good care of cadres.

PARTY DISCIPLINE

In view of Chang Kuo-tao's serious violations of discipline, we must affirm anew the discipline of the Party, namely:

    (1) the individual is subordinate to the organization;

    (2) the minority is subordinate to the majority;

    (3) the lower level is subordinate to the higher level; and

    (4) the entire membership is subordinate to the Central Committee.

Whoever violates these articles of discipline disrupts Party unity. Experience proves that some people violate Party discipline through not knowing what it is, while others, like Chang Kuo-tao, violate it knowingly and take advantage of many Party members' ignorance to achieve their treacherous purposes. Hence it is necessary to educate members in Party discipline so that the rank and file will not only observe discipline themselves, but will exercise supervision over the leaders so that they, too, observe it, thus preventing the recurrence of cases like Chang Kuo-tao's. If we are to ensure the development of inner-Party relations along the right lines, besides the four most important articles of discipline mentioned above we must work out a set of fairly detailed Party rules which will serve to unify the actions of the leading bodies at all levels.

PARTY DEMOCRACY

In the present great struggle, the Chinese Communist Party demands that all its leading bodies and all its members and cadres should give the fullest expression to their initiative, which alone can ensure victory. This initiative must be demonstrated concretely in the ability of the leading bodies, the cadres and the Party rank and file to work creatively, in their readiness to assume responsibility, in the exuberant vigour they show in their work, in their courage and ability to raise questions, voice opinions and criticize defects, and in the comradely supervision that is maintained over the leading bodies and the leading cadres. Otherwise, "initiative" will be an empty thing. But the exercise of such initiative depends on the spread of democracy in Party life. It cannot be brought into play if there is not enough democracy in Party life. Only in an atmosphere of democracy can large numbers of able people be brought forward. Ours is a country in which small-scale production and the patriarchal system prevail, and taking the country as a whole there is as yet no democratic life;

consequently, this state of affairs is reflected in our Party by insufficient democracy in Party life. This phenomenon hinders the entire Party from exercising its initiative to the full. Similarly, it has led to insufficient democracy in the united front and in the mass movements. For these reasons, education in democracy must be carried on within the Party so that members can understand the meaning of democratic life, the meaning of the relationship between democracy and centralism, and the way in which democratic centralism should be put into practice. Only in this way can we really extend democracy within the Party and at the same time avoid ultra-democracy and the *laissez-faire* which destroys discipline.

It is also essential to extend democracy in our Party organizations in the army to the degree necessary to stimulate the initiative of the Party members and increase the combat effectiveness of the troops. However, there cannot be as much democracy in the Party organizations in the army as in the local Party organizations. Both in the army and in the local organizations, inner-Party democracy is meant to strengthen discipline and increase combat effectiveness, not to weaken them.

The extension of democracy in the Party should be seen as an essential step in its consolidation and development, and as an important weapon enabling it to be most active in the great struggle, to prove equal to its tasks, create fresh strength and surmount the difficulties of the war.

OUR PARTY HAS CONSOLIDATED ITSELF
AND GROWN STRONG
THROUGH THE STRUGGLE ON TWO FRONTS

Broadly speaking, in the last seventeen years our Party has learned to use the Marxist-Leninist weapon of ideological struggle against incorrect ideas within the Party on two fronts — against Right opportunism and against "Left" opportunism.

Before the Fifth Plenary Session of the Sixth Central Committee,[2] our Party fought Chen Tu-hsiu's Right opportunism and Comrade Li Li-san's "Left" opportunism. It made great progress thanks to the victories achieved in these two inner-Party struggles. After the Fifth Plenary Session there were two further historic inner-Party struggles, namely, the struggles at the Tsunyi Meeting and in connection with the expulsion of Chang Kuo-tao.

The Tsunyi Meeting corrected serious errors of a "Left" opportunist character — errors of principle committed in the fight against the enemy's fifth "encirclement and suppression" campaign — and united the Party and the Red Army; it enabled the Central Committee of the Party and the main forces of the Red Army to bring the Long March to a triumphant conclusion, to advance to a forward position in the resistance to Japan and to carry out the new policy of the Anti-Japanese National United Front. By combating Chang Kuo-tao's Right opportunism, the Pasi and Yenan Meetings (the fight against the Chang Kuo-tao line began at the Pasi Meeting[3] and ended at the Yenan Meeting[4]) succeeded in bringing all the Red forces together and in strengthening the unity of the whole Party for the heroic struggle against Japan. Both kinds of opportunist mistakes arose during the revolutionary civil war, and their characteristic was that they were errors related to the war.

What are the lessons which have been derived from these two inner-Party struggles? They are:

(1) The tendency to "Left" impetuosity, which disregards both the subjective and the objective factors, is extremely harmful to a revolutionary war and, for that matter, to any revolutionary movement — it was among the serious errors of principle which were manifested in the struggle against the enemy's fifth "encirclement and suppression" campaign, and which arose from ignorance of the characteristics of China's revolutionary war.

(2) The opportunism of Chang Kuo-tao, however, was Right opportunism in the revolutionary war and was a combination of a retreatist line, warlordism and anti-Party activity. It was only with the overcoming of this brand of opportunism that large numbers of cadres and Party members in the Fourth Front Army of the Red Army, men of intrinsically fine quality and with a long record of heroic struggle, were able to free themselves from its toils and return to the correct line of the Central Committee.

(3) Striking results were achieved in the great organizational work of the ten years of the Agrarian Revolutionary War — in army building, government work, mass work and Party building. Had it not been for the support rendered by such organizational work to the heroic fighting at the front, we could not have kept

up the bitter struggle against Chiang Kai-shek. However, in the latter part of that period serious errors of principle were made in the Party's policy concerning cadres and organization, errors which showed themselves in the tendency towards sectarianism, in punitiveness and in the policy of ideological struggle carried to excess. They were due both to our failure to eliminate the vestiges of the former Li Li-san line and to the political mistakes in matters of principle committed at the time. These errors, too, were corrected at the Tsunyi Meeting, and the Party was thus able to make the turn to a correct cadres policy and to correct organizational principles. As for Chang Kuo-tao's organizational line, it violated all Party principles, disrupted Party discipline and carried factional activity to the point of opposition to the Party, the Central Committee and the Communist International. The Central Committee did everything possible to overcome Chang Kuo-tao's iniquitous and erroneous line and to frustrate his anti-Party activity, and also tried to save Chang Kuo-tao himself. But as he stubbornly refused to correct his mistakes and resorted to double-dealing, and subsequently even betrayed the Party and threw himself into the arms of the Kuomintang, the Party had to take firm measures and expel him. This disciplinary action won the support not only of all Party members but of all people loyal to the cause of national liberation. The Communist International also endorsed the decision and denounced Chang Kuo-tao as a deserter and renegade.

These lessons, these achievements, have furnished us with the prerequisites for uniting the whole Party, for strengthening its ideological, political and organizational unity, and for successfully waging the War of Resistance. Our Party has consolidated itself and grown strong through the struggle on the two fronts.

THE PRESENT STRUGGLE ON TWO FRONTS

From now on, it is of paramount importance to wage a political struggle against Rightist pessimism in the War of Resistance, although it is still necessary to keep an eye on "Left" impetuosity. On questions of the united front and of Party and mass organization, we must continue the fight against the "Left" tendency towards closed-doorism if we are to achieve co-operation with the various other anti-Japanese parties and groups, expand the Communist Party and broaden the mass movement. At the same time, we must take care to combat the Right opportunist tendency towards co-operation and expansion which are unconditional in character, or otherwise they will both be hindered and be turned into capitulationist co-operation and unprincipled expansion.

Ideological struggle on the two fronts must suit the concrete circumstances of each case, and we must never approach a problem subjectively or permit the bad old habit of "sticking labels" on people to continue.

In the struggle against deviations, we must give serious attention to opposing double-faced behaviour. As Chang Kuo-tao's career shows, the greatest danger of such behaviour is that it may develop into factional activity. To comply in public but oppose in private, to say yes and mean no, to say nice things to a person's face but play tricks behind his back — these are all forms of double-dealing. Only by sharpening the vigilance of cadres and Party members against such behaviour can we strengthen Party discipline.

STUDY

Generally speaking, all Communist Party members who can do so should study the theory of Marx, Engels, Lenin and Stalin, study our national history and study current movements and trends; moreover, they should help to educate members with less schooling. The cadres in particular should study these subjects carefully, while members of the Central Committee and senior cadres should give them even more attention. No political party can possibly lead a great revolutionary movement to victory unless it possesses revolutionary theory and a knowledge of history and has a profound grasp of the practical movement.

The theory of Marx, Engels, Lenin and Stalin is universally applicable. We should regard it not as a dogma, but as a guide to action. Studying it is not merely a matter of learning terms and phrases but of learning Marxism-Leninism as the science of revolution. It is not just a matter of understanding the general laws derived by Marx,

Engels, Lenin and Stalin from their extensive study of real life and revolutionary experience, but of studying their standpoint and method in examining and solving problems. Our Party's mastery of Marxism-Leninism is now rather better than it used to be, but is still far from being extensive or deep. Ours is the task of leading a great nation of several hundred million in a great and unprecedented struggle. For us, therefore, the spreading and deepening of the study of Marxism-Leninism present a big problem demanding an early solution which is possible only through concentrated effort. Following on this plenary session of the Central Committee, I hope to see an all-Party emulation in study which will show who has really learned something, and who has learned more and learned better. So far as shouldering the main responsibility of leadership is concerned, our Party's fighting capacity will be much greater and our task of defeating Japanese imperialism will be more quickly accomplished if there are one or two hundred comrades with a grasp of Marxism-Leninism which is systematic and not fragmentary, genuine and not hollow.

Another of our tasks is to study our historical heritage and use the Marxist method to sum it up critically. Our national history goes back several thousand years and has its own characteristics and innumerable treasures. But in these matters we are mere schoolboys. Contemporary China has grown out of the China of the past; we are Marxist in our historical approach and must not lop off our history. We should sum up our history from Confucius to Sun Yat-sen and take over this valuable legacy. This is important for guiding the great movement of today. Being Marxists, Communists are internationalists, but we can put Marxism into practice only when it is integrated with the specific characteristics of our country and acquires a definite national form. The great strength of Marxism-Leninism lies precisely in its integration with the concrete revolutionary practice of all countries. For the Chinese Communist Party, it is a matter of learning to apply the theory of Marxism-Leninism to the specific circumstances of China. For the Chinese Communists who are part of the great Chinese nation, flesh of its flesh and blood of its blood, any talk about Marxism in isolation from China's characteristics is merely Marxism in the abstract, Marxism in a vacuum. Hence to apply Marxism concretely in China so that its every manifestation has an indubitably Chinese character, *i.e.*, to apply Marxism in the light of China's specific characteristics, becomes a problem which it is urgent for the whole Party to understand and solve. Foreign stereotypes must be abolished, there must be less singing of empty, abstract tunes, and dogmatism must be laid to rest; they must be replaced by the fresh, lively Chinese style and spirit which the common people of China love. To separate internationalist content from national form is the practice of those who do not understand the first thing about internationalism. We, on the contrary, must link the two closely. In this matter there are serious errors in our ranks which should be conscientiously overcome.

What are the characteristics of the present movement? What are its laws? How is it to be directed? These are all practical questions. To this day we do not yet understand everything about Japanese imperialism, or about China. The movement is developing, new things have yet to emerge, and they are emerging in an endless stream. To study this movement in its entirety and in its development is a great task claiming our constant attention. Whoever refuses to study these problems seriously and carefully is no Marxist.

Complacency is the enemy of study. We cannot really learn anything until we rid ourselves of complacency. Our attitude towards ourselves should be "to be insatiable in learning" and towards others "to be tireless in teaching".

UNITY AND VICTORY

Unity within the Chinese Communist Party is the fundamental prerequisite for uniting the whole nation to win the War of Resistance and build a new China. Seventeen years of tempering have taught the Chinese Communist Party many ways of attaining internal unity, and ours is now a much more seasoned Party. Thus we are able to form a powerful nucleus for the whole people in the struggle to win victory in the War of Resistance and to build a new China. Comrades, so long as we are united, we can certainly reach this goal.

NOTES

[1] In his report to the 17th Congress of the C.P.S.U.(B.) in January 1934, Stalin said: ". . . after the correct political line has been laid down, organizational work decides everything, including the fate of the political line itself, its success or failure."

(See *Problems of Leninism*, Eng. ed., FLPH, Moscow, 1954, p. 644.) He also dealt with the question of "proper selection of personnel". In his address in May 1935 delivered in the Kremlin Palace to the graduates from the Red Army Academies, Stalin put forward and explained the slogan: "Cadres decide everything." (*Ibid.*, pp. 661-62.) In his report to the 18th Congress of the C.P.S.U.(B.) in March 1939, Stalin said: "After a correct political line has been worked out and tested in practice, the Party cadres become the decisive force in the leadership exercised by the Party and the state." (*Ibid.*, p. 784.)

[2] The period referred to was that from the emergency meeting of the Political Bureau of the Fifth Central Committee of the Chinese Communist Party in August 1927 to the Fifth Plenary Session of the Sixth Central Committee in January 1934.

[3] The Pasi Meeting was called by the Political Bureau of the Central Committee in August 1935 at Pasi, northwest of the county town of Sungpan, on the borders of northwestern Szechuan and southeastern Kansu. Chang Kuo-tao, leading a section of the Red Army, had broken away from the Central Committee, and was challenging its orders and attempting to undermine it. At this meeting the Central Committee decided to leave the danger zone for northern Shensi with those forces of the Red Army which obeyed its orders. However, Chang Kuo-tao led the Red Army units he had deceived southward to the area of Tienchuan, Lushan, the Big and Small Chinchuan and Ahpa, where he established a bogus central committee and came out publicly against the Party.

[4] The Yenan Meeting was the enlarged meeting of the Political Bureau of the Central Committee of the Party held in Yenan in April 1937. Prior to this meeting large numbers of cadres and soldiers in the Red Army units under Chang Kuo-tao who had already become aware of his deception marched northward towards the Shensi-Kansu border area. On their way, however, some units acted on mistaken orders and switched westward to the area of Kanchow, Liangchow and Suchow, all in Kansu Province. Most of these were wiped out by the enemy and the rest made their way to Sinkiang and only later returned to the Shensi-Kansu border area. The other units had long since reached the Shensi-Kansu border area and joined forces with the Central Red Army. Chang Kuo-tao himself also turned up in northern Shensi and attended the Yenan Meeting. The meeting systematically and conclusively condemned his opportunism and rebellion against the Party. He feigned acquiescence but actually made preparations for his final betrayal of the Party.

THE QUESTION OF
INDEPENDENCE AND INITIATIVE
WITHIN THE UNITED FRONT

November 5, 1938

HELP AND CONCESSIONS SHOULD BE POSITIVE, NOT NEGATIVE

All political parties and groups in the united front must help each other and make mutual concessions for the sake of long-term co-operation, but such help and concessions should be positive, not negative. We must consolidate and expand our own Party and army, and at the same time should assist friendly parties and armies to consolidate and expand; the people want the government to satisfy their political and economic demands, and at the same time give the government every possible help to prosecute the War of Resistance; the factory workers demand better conditions from the owners, and at the same time work hard in the interests of resistance; for the sake of unity against foreign aggression, the landlords should reduce rent and interest, and at the same time the peasants should pay rent and interest. All these principles and policies of mutual assistance are positive, not negative or one-sided. The same should be true of mutual concessions. Each side should refrain from undermining the other and from organizing secret party branches within the other's party, government and army. For our part we organize no secret party

This is part of Comrade Mao Tse-tung's concluding speech at the Sixth Plenary Session of the Sixth Central Committee of the Party. At the time, the issue of independence and initiative within the united front was one of the outstanding questions concerning the anti-Japanese united front, a question on which there were differences of opinion between Comrade Mao Tse-tung and Chen Shao-yu. In essence what was involved was proletarian leadership in the united front. In his report of

213

branches inside the Kuomintang and its government or army, and
so set the Kuomintang's mind at rest, to the advantage of the War
of Resistance. The saying, "Refrain from doing some things in order
to be able to do other things",[1] exactly meets the case. A national
war of resistance would have been impossible without the reorganization of the Red Army, the change in the administrative system in the
Red areas, and the abandonment of the policy of armed insurrection.
By giving way on the latter we have achieved the former; negative
measures have yielded positive results. "To fall back the better to
leap forward"[2] — that is Leninism. To regard concessions as something purely negative is contrary to Marxism-Leninism. There are
indeed instances of purely negative concessions — the Second International's doctrine of collaboration between labour and capital[3]
resulted in the betrayal of a whole class and a whole revolution. In
China, Chen Tu-hsiu and then Chang Kuo-tao were both capitulators;
capitulationism must be strenuously opposed. When we make concessions, fall back, turn to the defensive or halt our advance in our
relations with either allies or enemies, we should always see these
actions as part of our whole revolutionary policy, as an indispensable
link in the general revolutionary line, as one turn in a zigzag course.
In a word, they are positive.

December 1947 ("The Present Situation and Our Tasks") Comrade Mao Tse-tung
briefly summed up these differences:

　　　During the War of Resistance, our Party combated ideas similar to those
of the capitulationists [referring to Chen Tu-hsiu's capitulationism in the period
of the First Revolutionary Civil War], that is, such ideas as making concessions
to the Kuomintang's anti-popular policies, having more confidence in the Kuomintang than in the masses, not daring to arouse and give full rein to mass
struggles, not daring to expand the Liberated Areas and the people's armies in
the Japanese-occupied areas, and handing over the leadership in the War of
Resistance to the Kuomintang. Our Party waged a resolute struggle against such
impotent and degenerate ideas, which run counter to the principles of Marxism-
Leninism, resolutely carried out its political line of "developing the progressive
forces, winning over the middle forces and isolating the die-hard forces", and
resolutely expanded the Liberated Areas and the People's Liberation Army.
Not only did this ensure our Party's ability to defeat Japanese imperialism in
the period of its aggression, but also, in the period after the Japanese surrender
when Chiang Kai-shek launched his counter-revolutionary war, it ensured our
Party's ability to switch smoothly and without loss to the course of opposing
Chiang Kai-shek's counter-revolutionary war with a people's revolutionary war
and to win great victories in a short time. All Party comrades must keep these
lessons of history firmly in mind.

THE IDENTITY BETWEEN THE NATIONAL
AND THE CLASS STRUGGLE

To sustain a long war by long-term co-operation or, in other words, to subordinate the class struggle to the present national struggle against Japan — such is the fundamental principle of the united front. Subject to this principle, the independent character of the parties and classes and their independence and initiative within the united front should be preserved, and their essential rights should not be sacrificed to co-operation and unity, but on the contrary must be firmly upheld within certain limits. Only thus can co-operation be promoted, indeed only thus can there be any co-operation at all. Otherwise co-operation will turn into amalgamation and the united front will inevitably be sacrificed. In a struggle that is national in character, the class struggle takes the form of national struggle, which demonstrates the identity between the two. On the one hand, for a given historical period the political and economic demands of the various classes must not be such as to disrupt co-operation; on the other hand, the demands of the national struggle (the need to resist Japan) should be the point of departure for all class struggle. Thus there is identity in the united front between unity and independence and between the national struggle and the class struggle.

"EVERYTHING THROUGH THE UNITED FRONT"
IS WRONG

The Kuomintang is the party in power, and so far has not allowed the united front to assume an organizational form. Behind the enemy lines, the idea of "everything through" is impossible, for there we have to act independently and with the initiative in our own hands while keeping to the agreements which the Kuomintang has approved (for instance, the Programme of Armed Resistance and National Reconstruction). Or we may act first and report afterwards, anticipating what the Kuomintang might agree to. For instance, the appointment of administrative commissioners and the dispatch of troops to Shantung Province would never have occurred if we had tried to get these things done "through the united front". It is said that the French Communist

Party once put forward a similar slogan, but that was probably because in France, where a joint committee of the parties already existed and the Socialist Party was unwilling to act in accordance with the jointly agreed programme and wanted to have its own way, the Communist Party had to put forward such a slogan in order to restrain the Socialist Party, and certainly it did not do so to shackle itself. In the case of China, the Kuomintang has deprived all other political parties of equal rights and is trying to compel them to take its orders. If this slogan is meant to be a demand that everything done by the Kuomintang must go through us, it is both ridiculous and impossible. If we have to secure the Kuomintang's consent beforehand for everything we do, what if the Kuomintang does not consent? Since the policy of the Kuomintang is to restrict our growth, there is no reason whatever for us to propose such a slogan, which simply binds us hand and foot. At present there are things for which we should secure prior consent from the Kuomintang, such as the expansion of our three divisions into three army corps — this is to report first and act afterwards. There are other things which the Kuomintang can be told after they have become accomplished facts, such as the expansion of our forces to over 200,000 men — this is to act first and report afterwards. There are also things, such as the convening of the Border Region assembly, which we shall do without reporting for the time being, knowing that the Kuomintang will not agree. There are still other things which, for the time being, we shall neither do nor report, for they are likely to jeopardize the whole situation. In short, we must not split the united front, but neither should we allow ourselves to be bound hand and foot, and hence the slogan of "everything through the united front" should not be put forward. If "everything must be submitted to the united front" is interpreted as "everything must be submitted to" Chiang Kai-shek and Yen Hsi-shan, then that slogan, too, is wrong. Our policy is one of independence and initiative within the united front, a policy both of unity and of independence.

NOTES

[1] A quotation from *Mencius*.

[2] V. I. Lenin, "Conspectus of Hegel's Book *Lectures on the History of Philosophy*", *Collected Works*, Russ. ed., Moscow, 1958, Vol. XXXVIII, p. 275.

[3] "The doctrine of collaboration between labour and capital" is the reactionary doctrine of the Second International, which advocates such collaboration in the capitalist countries and opposes the revolutionary overthrow of bourgeois rule and the establishment of the dictatorship of the proletariat.

PROBLEMS OF WAR AND STRATEGY

November 6, 1938

I. CHINA'S CHARACTERISTICS AND REVOLUTIONARY WAR

The seizure of power by armed force, the settlement of the issue by war, is the central task and the highest form of revolution. This Marxist-Leninist principle of revolution holds good universally, for China and for all other countries.

But while the principle remains the same, its application by the party of the proletariat finds expression in varying ways according to the varying conditions. Internally, capitalist countries practise bourgeois democracy (not feudalism) when they are not fascist or not at war; in their external relations, they are not oppressed by, but themselves oppress, other nations. Because of these characteristics, it is the task of the party of the proletariat in the capitalist countries to educate the workers and build up strength through a long period of legal struggle, and thus prepare for the final overthrow of capitalism. In these countries, the question is one of a long legal struggle, of utilizing parliament as a platform, of economic and political strikes, of organizing trade unions and educating the workers. There the form of organization is legal and the form of struggle bloodless (non-military). On the issue of war, the Communist Parties in the capitalist countries oppose the imperialist wars waged by their own

---

This article is part of Comrade Mao Tse-tung's concluding speech at the Sixth Plenary Session of the Sixth Central Committee of the Party. In his "Problems of Strategy in Guerrilla War Against Japan" and "On Protracted War", Comrade Mao Tse-tung had already settled the question of the Party's leading role in the War of Resistance Against Japan. But some comrades, committing Right opportunist errors, denied that the Party must maintain its independence and initiative in the united front, and so doubted and even opposed the Party's line on the war and on strategy.

countries; if such wars occur, the policy of these Parties is to bring
about the defeat of the reactionary governments of their own countries.
The one war they want to fight is the civil war for which they are
preparing.[1] But this insurrection and war should not be launched
until the bourgeoisie becomes really helpless, until the majority of
the proletariat are determined to rise in arms and fight, and until
the rural masses are giving willing help to the proletariat. And when
the time comes to launch such an insurrection and war, the first step
will be to seize the cities, and then advance into the countryside,
and not the other way about. All this has been done by Communist
Parties in capitalist countries, and it has been proved correct by the
October Revolution in Russia.

China is different however. The characteristics of China are that
she is not independent and democratic but semi-colonial and semi-
feudal, that internally she has no democracy but is under feudal
oppression and that in her external relations she has no national independence but is oppressed by imperialism. It follows that we have
no parliament to make use of and no legal right to organize the workers
to strike. Basically, the task of the Communist Party here is not to
go through a long period of legal struggle before launching insurrection
and war, and not to seize the big cities first and then occupy the
countryside, but the reverse.

When imperialism is not making armed attacks on our country,
the Chinese Communist Party either wages civil war jointly with the
bourgeoisie against the warlords (lackeys of imperialism), as in 1924-27
in the wars in Kwangtung Province[2] and the Northern Expedition,
or unites with the peasants and the urban petty bourgeoisie to wage
civil war against the landlord class and the comprador bourgeoisie
(also lackeys of imperialism), as in the War of Agrarian Revolution
of 1927-36. When imperialism launches armed attacks on China, the
Party unites all classes and strata in the country opposing the foreign
aggressors to wage a national war against the foreign enemy, as it is
doing in the present War of Resistance Against Japan.

In order to overcome this Right opportunism, bring the whole Party to a clearer understanding of the prime importance of the problems of war and strategy in the Chinese
revolution and mobilize it for serious work in this connection, Comrade Mao Tse-tung
again stressed the importance of the subject at this plenary session, approaching it
from the viewpoint of the history of China's political struggles, and analysed the
development of the Party's military work and the specific changes in its strategy.
The result was unanimity of thought in the Party leadership and unanimity of action
throughout the Party.

All this shows the difference between China and the capitalist countries. In China war is the main form of struggle and the army is the main form of organization. Other forms such as mass organization and mass struggle are also extremely important and indeed indispensable and in no circumstances to be overlooked, but their purpose is to serve the war. Before the outbreak of a war all organization and struggle are in preparation for the war, as in the period from the May 4th Movement of 1919 to the May 30th Movement of 1925. After war breaks out, all organization and struggle are co-ordinated with the war either directly or indirectly, as, for instance, in the period of the Northern Expedition when all organization and struggle in the rear areas of the revolutionary army were co-ordinated with the war directly, and those in the Northern warlord areas were co-ordinated with the war indirectly. Again in the period of the War of Agrarian Revolution all organization and struggle inside the Red areas were co-ordinated with the war directly, and outside the Red areas indirectly. Yet again in the present period, the War of Resistance, all organization and struggle in the rear areas of the anti-Japanese forces and in the areas occupied by the enemy are directly or indirectly co-ordinated with the war.

"In China the armed revolution is fighting the armed counter-revolution. That is one of the specific features and one of the advantages of the Chinese revolution."[3] This thesis of Comrade Stalin's is perfectly correct and is equally valid for the Northern Expedition, the War of Agrarian Revolution, and the present War of Resistance Against Japan. They are all revolutionary wars, all directed against counter-revolutionaries and all waged mainly by the revolutionary people, differing only in the sense that a civil war differs from a national war, and that a war conducted by the Communist Party differs from a war it conducts jointly with the Kuomintang. Of course, these differences are important. They indicate the breadth of the main forces in the war (an alliance of the workers and peasants, or of the workers, peasants and bourgeoisie) and whether our antagonist in the war is internal or external (whether the war is against domestic or foreign foes, and, if domestic, whether against the Northern warlords or against the Kuomintang); they also indicate that the content of China's revolutionary war differs at different stages of its history. But all these wars are instances of armed revolution fighting armed counter-revolution, they are all revolutionary wars, and all exhibit the specific features and advantages of the Chinese revolution. The thesis that revolutionary war "is one of the specific features and one of the advantages of the Chinese revolution" fits China's conditions perfectly. The main task of the party of the Chinese proletariat, a task confronting it almost from its very inception, has been to unite with as many allies as possible and, according to the circumstances, to organize armed struggles for national and social liberation against armed counter-revolution, whether internal or external. Without armed struggle the proletariat and the Communist Party would have no standing at all in China, and it would be impossible to accomplish any revolutionary task.

Our Party did not grasp this point fully during the first five or six years after it was founded, that is, from 1921 to its participation in the Northern Expedition in 1926. It did not then understand the supreme importance of armed struggle in China, or seriously prepare for war and organize armed forces, or apply itself to the study of military strategy and tactics. During the Northern Expedition it neglected to win over the army but laid one-sided stress on the mass movement, with the result that the whole mass movement collapsed the moment the Kuomintang turned reactionary. For a long time after 1927 many comrades continued to make it the Party's central task to prepare for insurrections in the cities and to work in the White areas. It was only after our victory in repelling the enemy's third "encirclement and suppression" campaign in 1931 that some comrades fundamentally changed their attitude on this question. But this was not true of the whole Party, and there were other comrades who did not think along the lines presented here.

Experience tells us that China's problems cannot be settled without armed force. An understanding of this point will help us in successfully waging the War of Resistance Against Japan from now on. The fact that the whole nation is rising in armed resistance in the war against Japan should inculcate a better understanding of the importance of this question in the whole Party, and every Party member should be prepared to take up arms and go to the front at any moment. Moreover, our present session has clearly defined the direction for our efforts by deciding that the Party's main fields of work are in the battle zones and in the enemy's rear. This is also an excellent antidote against the tendency of some Party members to be willing only to work in Party organizations and in the mass movement but to be unwilling to study or participate in warfare, and against the failure of some schools to encourage students to go to the front, and other such phenomena. In most of China, Party organizational work and mass work are directly linked with armed struggle; there is not, and cannot be, any Party work or mass work that is isolated and stands by itself. Even in rear areas remote from the battle zones (like Yunnan, Kweichow and Szechuan) and in enemy-occupied areas (like Peiping, Tientsin, Nanking and Shanghai), Party organizational work and mass work are co-ordinated with the war, and should and must exclusively serve the needs of the front. In a word, the whole Party must pay great attention to war, study military matters and prepare itself for fighting.

II. THE WAR HISTORY OF THE KUOMINTANG

It will be useful for us to look at the history of the Kuomintang and see what attention it pays to war.

From the start, when he organized a small revolutionary group, Sun Yat-sen staged armed insurrections against the Ching Dynasty.[4] The period of *Tung Meng Hui* (the Chinese Revolutionary League) was replete with armed insurrections,[5] right up to the armed overthrow of the Ching Dynasty by the Revolution of 1911. Then, during the period of the Chinese Revolutionary Party, he carried out a military campaign against Yuan Shih-kai.[6] Subsequent events such as the southern movement of the naval units,[7] the northern expedition from Kweilin[8] and the founding of the Whampoa Military Academy[9] were also among Sun Yat-sen's military undertakings.

After Sun Yat-sen came Chiang Kai-shek, who brought the Kuomintang's military power to its zenith. He values the army as his very life and has had the experience of three wars, namely, the Northern Expedition, the Civil War and the War of Resistance Against Japan. For the last ten years Chiang Kai-shek has been a counter-revolutionary. He has created a huge "Central Army" for counter-revolutionary purposes. He has held firmly to the vital point that whoever has an army has power and that war decides everything. In this respect we ought to learn from him. In this respect both Sun Yat-sen and Chiang Kai-shek are our teachers.

Since the Revolution of 1911, all the warlords have clung to their armies for dear life, setting great store by the principle, "Whoever has an army has power."

Tan Yen-kai,[10] a clever bureaucrat who had a chequered career in Hunan, was never a civil governor pure and simple but always insisted on being both the military governor and the civil governor. Even when he became President of the National Government first in Canton and then in Wuhan, he was concurrently the commander of the Second Army. There are many such warlords who understand this peculiarity of China's.

There have also been parties in China, notably the Progressive Party,[11] which did not want to have an army; yet even this party recognized that it could not get government positions without some warlord backing. Among its successive patrons have been Yuan Shih-kai,[12] Tuan Chi-jui[13] and Chiang Kai-shek (to whom the Political Science Group,[14] formed out of a section of the Progressive Party, has attached itself).

A few small political parties with a short history, e.g., the Youth Party,[15] have no army, and so have not been able to get anywhere.

In other countries there is no need for each of the bourgeois parties to have an armed force under its direct command. But things are different in China, where, because of the feudal division of the country, those landlord or bourgeois groupings or parties which have guns have power, and those which have more guns have more power. Placed in such an environment, the party of the proletariat should see clearly to the heart of the matter.

Communists do not fight for personal military power (they must in no circumstances do that, and let no one ever again follow the example of Chang Kuo-tao), but they must fight for military power for the Party, for military power for the people. As a national war of resistance is going on, we must also fight for military power for the nation. Where there is naivety on the question of military power, nothing whatsoever can be achieved. It is very difficult for the labouring people, who have been deceived and intimidated by the reactionary ruling classes for thousands of years, to awaken to the importance of having guns in their own hands. Now that Japanese imperialist oppression and the nation-wide resistance to it have pushed our labouring people into the arena of war, Communists should prove themselves the most politically conscious leaders in this war. Every Communist must grasp the truth, "Political power grows out of the barrel of a gun." Our principle is that the Party commands the gun, and the gun must never be allowed to command the Party. Yet, having guns, we can create Party organizations, as witness the powerful Party organizations which the Eighth Route Army has created in northern China. We can also create cadres, create schools, create culture, create mass movements. Everything in Yenan has been created by having guns. All things grow out of the barrel of a gun. According to the Marxist theory of the state, the army is the chief component of state power. Whoever wants to seize and retain state power must have a strong army. Some people ridicule us as advocates of the "omnipotence of war". Yes, we are advocates of the omnipotence of revolutionary war; that is good, not bad, it is Marxist. The guns of the Russian Communist Party created socialism. We shall create a democratic republic. Experience in the class struggle in the era of imperialism teaches us that it is only by the power of the gun that the working class and the labouring masses can defeat the armed bourgeoisie and landlords; in this sense we may say that only with guns can the whole world be transformed. We are advocates of the abolition of war, we do not want war; but war can only be abolished through war, and in order to get rid of the gun it is necessary to take up the gun.

III. THE WAR HISTORY OF THE CHINESE COMMUNIST PARTY

Our Party failed to grasp the importance of engaging itself directly in preparations for war and in the organization of armed forces for a period of three or four years, that is, from 1921 (when the Chinese Communist Party was founded) to 1924 (when the First National Congress of the Kuomintang was held), and it still lacked adequate understanding of this issue in the 1924-27 period and even later; nevertheless, after 1924, when it began to participate in the Whampoa Military Academy, it entered a new stage and began to see the importance of military affairs. Through helping the Kuomintang in the wars in Kwangtung Province and participating in the Northern Expedition, the Party gained leadership over some armed forces.[16] Then, having learned a bitter lesson from the failure of the revolution, the Party organized the Nanchang Uprising,[17] the Autumn Harvest Uprising[18] and the Canton Uprising, and entered on a new period, the founding of the Red Army. That was the crucial period in which our Party arrived at a thorough understanding of the importance of the army. Had there been no Red Army and no war fought

by the Red Army in this period, that is, had the Communist Party
adopted Chen Tu-hsiu's liquidationism, the present War of Resistance would have been inconceivable or could not have been sustained
for long.

At its emergency meeting held on August 7, 1927, the Central
Committee of the Party combated Right opportunism in the political
sphere, thus enabling the Party to take a big stride forward. At its
fourth plenary session in January 1931, the Sixth Central Committee
nominally combated "Left" opportunism in the political sphere, but
in fact itself committed the error of "Left" opportunism anew. The
two meetings differed in their content and historical role, but neither
of them dealt seriously with the problems of war and strategy, a
fact which showed that war had not yet been made the centre of
gravity in the Party's work. After the central leadership of the Party
moved into the Red areas in 1933, this situation underwent a radical
change, but mistakes in principle were again committed on the problem
of war (and all other major problems), bringing serious losses to the
revolutionary war. The Tsunyi Meeting of 1935, on the other hand, was
mainly a fight against opportunism in the military sphere and gave
top priority to the question of war, and this was a reflection of the
war conditions of the time. Today we can say with confidence that
in the struggles of the past seventeen years the Chinese Communist
Party has forged not only a firm Marxist political line but also a
firm Marxist military line. We have been able to apply Marxism in
solving not only political but also military problems; we have trained
not only a large core of cadres capable of running the Party and the
state, but also a large core of cadres capable of running the army.
These achievements are the flower of the revolution, watered by the
blood of countless martyrs, a glory that belongs not only to the Chinese
Communist Party and the Chinese people, but also to the Communist
Parties and the peoples of the whole world. There are only three
armies in the whole world which belong to the proletariat and the
labouring people, the armies led by the Communist Parties of the
Soviet Union, of China and of Spain, and as yet Communist Parties
in other countries have had no military experience; hence our army
and our military experience are all the more precious.

In order to carry the present War of Resistance Against Japan
to victory, it is extremely important to expand and consolidate the
Eighth Route Army, the New Fourth Army and all the guerrilla forces
led by our Party. Acting on this principle, the Party should dispatch

a sufficient number of its best members and cadres to the front. Everything must serve victory at the front, and the organizational task must be subordinated to the political task.

IV. CHANGES IN THE PARTY'S MILITARY STRATEGY IN THE CIVIL WAR AND THE NATIONAL WAR

The changes in our Party's military strategy are worth studying. Let us deal separately with the two processes, the civil war and the national war.

The civil war can be roughly divided into two strategic periods. Guerrilla warfare was primary in the first period and regular warfare in the second. But this regular warfare was of the Chinese type, regular only in its concentration of forces for mobile warfare and in a certain degree of centralization and planning in command and organization; in other respects it retained a guerrilla character and, as regular warfare, was on a low level and not comparable with the regular warfare of foreign armies or, in some ways, even with that of the Kuomintang army. Thus, in a sense, this type of regular warfare was only guerrilla warfare raised to a higher level.

The War of Resistance Against Japan can also be roughly divided into two strategic periods, so far as our Party's military tasks are concerned. In the first period (comprising the stages of the strategic defensive and strategic stalemate) it is guerrilla warfare which is primary, while in the second (the stage of the strategic counter-offensive) it is regular warfare which will be primary. However, the guerrilla warfare of the first period of the War of Resistance differs considerably in content from that of the first period of the civil war, because the dispersed guerrilla tasks are being carried out by the regular (*i.e.*, regular to a certain degree) Eighth Route Army. Likewise, the regular warfare of the second period of the War of Resistance will be different from that of the second period of the civil war because we can assume that, given up-to-date equipment, a great change will take place both in the army and in its operations. Our army will then attain a high degree of centralization and organization, and its operations will lose much of their guerrilla character and attain a high degree of regularity; what is now on a low level will then be raised to a higher level, and the Chinese type of regular warfare will change into the general type. That will be our task in the stage of the strategic counter-offensive.

Thus we see that the two processes, the civil war and the War of Resistance Against Japan, and their four strategic periods, contain three changes in strategy. The first was the change from guerrilla warfare to regular warfare in the civil war. The second was the change from regular warfare in the civil war to guerrilla warfare in the War of Resistance. And the third will be the change from guerrilla warfare to regular warfare in the War of Resistance.

The first of the three changes encountered great difficulties. It involved a twofold task. On the one hand, we had to combat the Right tendency of localism and guerrilla-ism, which consisted in clinging to guerrilla habits and refusing to make the turn to regularization, a tendency which arose because our cadres underestimated the changes in the enemy's situation and our own tasks. In the Central Red Area it was only after much painstaking education that this tendency was gradually corrected. On the other hand, we also had to combat the "Left" tendency of over-centralization and adventurism which put undue stress on regularization, a tendency which arose because some of the leading cadres overestimated the enemy, set the tasks too high and mechanically applied foreign experience regardless of the actual conditions. For three long years (before the Tsunyi Meeting) this tendency imposed enormous sacrifices on the Central Red Area, and it was corrected only after we had learned lessons for which we paid in blood. Its correction was the achievement of the Tsunyi Meeting.

The second change in strategy took place in the autumn of 1937 (after the Lukouchiao Incident), at the juncture of the two different wars. We faced a new enemy, Japanese imperialism, and had as our ally our former enemy, the Kuomintang (which was still hostile to us), and the theatre of war was the vast expanse of northern China (which was temporarily our army's front but would soon be the enemy's rear and would remain so for a long time). In this special situation, our change in strategy was an extremely serious one. In this special situation we had to transform the regular army of the past into a guerrilla army (in respect to its dispersed operations, and not to its sense of organization or to its discipline), and transform the mobile warfare of the past into guerrilla warfare, so that we could adapt ourselves to the kind of enemy facing us and to the tasks before us. But this change was, to all appearances, a step backward and therefore necessarily very difficult. Both underestimation and morbid fear of Japan, tendencies likely to occur at such a time, did actually occur among the Kuomintang. When the Kuomintang changed over from civil war to national war, it suffered many needless losses mainly because of its underestimation of the enemy, but also because of its morbid fear of Japan (as exemplified by Han Fu-chu and Liu Chih[19]). On the other hand, we have effected the change fairly smoothly and, instead of suffering losses, have won big victories. The reason is that the great majority of our cadres accepted the correct guidance of the Central Committee in good time and skilfully sized up the actual situation, even though there were serious arguments between the Central Committee and some of the army cadres. The extreme importance of this change for persevering in, developing and winning the War of Resistance as a whole, as well as for the future of the Communist Party of China, can be seen immediately if we think of the historic significance of anti-Japanese guerrilla warfare in determining the fate of the national liberation struggle in China. In its extraordinary breadth and protractedness, China's anti-Japanese guerrilla war is without precedent, not only in the East but perhaps in the whole history of mankind.

The third change, from guerrilla to regular warfare against Japan, belongs to the future development of the war, which will presumably give rise to new circumstances and new difficulties. We need not discuss it now.

V. THE STRATEGIC ROLE OF GUERRILLA WARFARE AGAINST JAPAN

In the anti-Japanese war as a whole, regular warfare is primary and guerrilla warfare supplementary, for only regular warfare can decide the final outcome of the war. Of the three strategic stages (the defensive, the stalemate and the counter-offensive) in the entire process of the war in the country as a whole, the first and last are stages in which regular warfare is primary and guerrilla warfare supplementary. In the intermediate stage guerrilla warfare will become primary and regular warfare supplementary, because the enemy will be holding on to the areas he has occupied and we will be preparing for the counter-offensive but will not yet be ready to launch it. Though this stage will possibly be the longest, it is still only one of the three stages in the entire war. If we take the war as a whole, therefore, regular warfare is primary and guerrilla warfare supplementary. Unless we understand this, unless we recognize that regular warfare will decide the final outcome of the war, and unless we pay attention to building a regular army and to studying and directing regular warfare, we shall be unable to defeat Japan. This is one aspect of the matter.

All the same, guerrilla warfare has its important strategic place throughout the war. Without guerrilla warfare and without due attention to building guerrilla units and guerrilla armies and to studying and directing guerrilla warfare, we shall likewise be unable to defeat Japan. The reason is that, since the greater part of China will be converted into the enemy's rear, in the absence of the most extensive and persistent guerrilla warfare the enemy will entrench himself securely without any fear of attacks from behind, will inflict heavy losses on our main forces fighting at the front and will launch increasingly fierce offensives; thus it will be difficult for us to bring about a stalemate, and the very continuation of the War of Resistance may be jeopardized. But even if things do not turn out that way, other unfavourable circumstances will ensue, such as the inadequate building up of strength for our counter-offensive, the absence of supporting actions during the counter-offensive, and the possibility that the enemy will be able to replace his losses. If these circumstances arise and are not overcome by the timely development of extensive and persistent guerrilla warfare, it will likewise be impossible to defeat Japan. Hence, though guerrilla warfare occupies a supplementary place in the war as a whole, it does have an extremely important place in strategy. In waging the War of Resistance Against Japan it is undoubtedly a grave error to neglect guerrilla warfare. This is the other aspect of the matter.

Given a big country, guerrilla warfare is possible; hence there was guerrilla warfare in the past too. But guerrilla warfare can be persevered in only when led by the Communist Party. That is why guerrilla warfare generally failed in the past and why it can be victorious only in modern times and only in big countries in which Communist Parties have emerged, as in the Soviet Union during its civil war and in China at present. Considering the present circumstances and the general situation with respect to the war, the division of labour between the Kuomintang and the Communist Party in the anti-Japanese war, in which the former carries on frontal regular warfare and the latter carries on guerrilla warfare behind the enemy lines, is both necessary and proper, and is a matter of mutual need, mutual co-ordination and mutual assistance.

It can thus be understood how important and necessary it was for our Party to change its military strategy from the regular warfare of the latter period of the civil war to the guerrilla warfare of the first period of the War of Resistance. The favourable effects of this change can be summed up in the following eighteen points:

(1) reduction of the areas occupied by the enemy forces;

(2) expansion of the base areas of our own forces;

(3) in the stage of the defensive, co-ordination with operations at the regular front, so as to pin down the enemy;

(4) in the stage of stalemate, maintenance of a firm hold on the base areas behind the enemy lines, so as to facilitate the training and reorganization of troops at the regular front;

(5) in the stage of the counter-offensive, co-ordination with the regular front in recovering lost territory;

(6) the quickest and most effective expansion of our forces;

(7) the widest expansion of the Communist Party, so that a Party branch may be organized in every village;

(8) the broadest development of the mass movements, so that all the people behind the enemy lines, except for those in his strongholds, may be organized;

(9) the most extensive establishment of organs of anti-Japanese democratic political power;

(10) the widest development of anti-Japanese cultural and educational work;

(11) the most extensive improvement of the people's livelihood;

(12) the most effective disintegration of the enemy troops;

(13) the most extensive and enduring impact on popular feeling and stimulation of morale throughout the country;

(14) the most extensive impetus to progress in the friendly armies and parties;

(15) adaptation to the situation in which the enemy is strong and we are weak, so that we suffer fewer losses and win more victories;

(16) adaptation to the fact that China is large and Japan small, so as to make the enemy suffer more losses and win fewer victories;

(17) the quickest and most effective training of large numbers of cadres for leadership; and

(18) the most effective solution of the problem of provisions.

It is also beyond doubt that in the long course of struggle the guerrilla units and guerrilla warfare will not remain as they are but will develop to a higher stage and evolve gradually into regular units and regular warfare. Through guerrilla warfare, we shall build up our strength and turn ourselves into a decisive element in the crushing of Japanese imperialism.

VI. PAY GREAT ATTENTION TO THE STUDY OF MILITARY MATTERS

All the issues between two hostile armies depend on war for their solution, and China's survival or extinction depends on her victory or defeat in the present war. Hence our study of military theory, of strategy and tactics and of army political work brooks not a moment's delay. Though our study of tactics is still inadequate, our comrades who are engaged in military work have achieved a great deal in the last ten years and, on the basis of Chinese conditions, have brought forth much that is new; the shortcoming here is that there has been no general summing-up. But so far only a few people have taken up the study of the problems of strategy and the theory of war. First-rate results have been achieved in the study of our political work, which, in wealth of experience and in the number and quality of its innovations, ranks second only to that of the Soviet Union; here too the shortcoming is insufficient synthesis and systematization. The popularization of military knowledge is an urgent task for the Party and the whole country. We must now pay great attention to all these things, but most of all to the theory of war and strategy. I deem it imperative that we arouse interest in the study of military theory and direct the attention of the whole membership to the study of military matters.

NOTES

[1] See V. I. Lenin, "The War and Russian Social-Democracy" (*Collected Works*, Eng. ed., Progress Publishers, Moscow, 1964, Vol. XXI, pp. 27-34), "The Conference of the R.S.D.L.P. Groups Abroad" (*ibid.*, pp. 158-64), "The Defeat of One's Own

Government in the Imperialist War" (*ibid.*, pp. 275-80), "The Defeat of Russia and the Revolutionary Crisis" (*ibid.*, pp. 378-82). These articles, written in 1914-15, deal specifically with the imperialist war of that time. See also *History of the Communist Party of the Soviet Union (Bolsheviks), Short Course*, Eng. ed., FLPH, Moscow, 1951, pp. 258-67.

[2] In 1924, Dr. Sun Yat-sen, in alliance with the Communist Party and the revolutionary workers and peasants, defeated the "Merchants' Corps", an armed force of the compradors and landlords which engaged in counter-revolutionary activities in Canton in collaboration with the British imperialists. The revolutionary army, which had been founded on the basis of co-operation between the Kuomintang and the Communist Party, set out from Canton early in 1925, fought the Eastern Campaign and, with the support of the peasants, defeated the troops of the warlord Chen Chiung-ming. It then returned to Canton and overthrew the Yunnan and Kwangsi warlords who had entrenched themselves there. That autumn it conducted the Second Eastern Campaign and finally wiped out Chen Chiung-ming's forces. These campaigns, in which members of the Communist Party and the Communist Youth League fought heroically in the van, brought about the political unification of Kwangtung Province and paved the way for the Northern Expedition.

[3] J. V. Stalin, "The Prospects of the Revolution in China", *Works*, Eng. ed., FLPH, Moscow, 1954, Vol. VIII, p. 379.

[4] In 1894, Dr. Sun Yat-sen formed a small revolutionary organization in Honolulu called the *Hsing Chung Hui* (Society for China's Regeneration). With the support of the secret societies among the people, he staged two armed insurrections in Kwangtung Province against the Ching government after its defeat in the Sino-Japanese war in 1895, one at Canton in 1895 and the other at Huichow in 1900.

[5] *Tung Meng Hui*, or the Chinese Revolutionary League (a united front organization of the bourgeoisie, the petty bourgeoisie and a section of the landed gentry opposed to the Ching government), was formed in 1905 through the merging of the *Hsing Chung Hui* (see note above) and two other groups, the *Hua Hsing Hui* (Society for China's Regeneration) and the *Kuang Fu Hui* (Society for Breaking the Foreign Yoke). It put forward a programme of bourgeois revolution advocating "the expulsion of the Tartars (Manchus), the recovery of China, the establishment of a republic and the equalization of landownership". In the period of the Chinese Revolutionary League, Dr. Sun Yat-sen, allying himself with the secret societies and a part of the New Army of the Ching government, launched a number of armed insurrections against the Ching regime, notably those at Pinghsiang (Kiangsi Province), Liuyang and Liling (Hunan Province) in 1906, at Huangkang, Chaochow and Chinchow (Kwangtung Province), and at Chennankuan (Kwangsi Province) in 1907, at Hokou (Yunnan Province) in 1908 and at Canton in 1911. The last was followed in the same year by the Wuchang Uprising which resulted in the overthrow of the Ching Dynasty.

[6] In 1912, the Chinese Revolutionary League was reorganized into the Kuomintang and made a compromise with the Northern warlord regime headed by Yuan Shih-kai. In 1913 Yuan's troops marched southward to suppress the forces which had emerged in the provinces of Kiangsi, Anhwei and Kwangtung in the course of the 1911 revolution. Armed resistance was organized by Dr. Sun Yat-sen but it was soon crushed. In 1914, realizing the error of the Kuomintang's policy of compromise, Dr. Sun formed the *Chung Hua Ke Ming Tang* (Chinese Revolutionary Party) in Tokyo, Japan, in order to distinguish his organization from the Kuomintang of the time. The new party was actually an alliance of the political representatives of a section of the petty bourgeoisie and a section of the bourgeoisie against Yuan Shih-kai. Through this

alliance, Dr. Sun Yat-sen staged a minor insurrection in Shanghai in 1914. In 1915, when Yuan Shih-kai proclaimed himself emperor, Tsai Ngo and others set out from Yunnan to take action against him, and Dr. Sun was also very active in advocating and promoting armed opposition to Yuan Shih-kai.

[7] In 1917 Dr. Sun Yat-sen went from Shanghai to Canton at the head of a naval force which was under his influence. Using Kwangtung as a base and co-operating with the Southwestern warlords who were opposed to the Northern warlord Tuan Chi-jui, he set up a military government opposed to Tuan Chi-jui.

[8] In 1921 Dr. Sun Yat-sen planned a northern expedition from Kweilin, Kwangsi Province. But his plan was frustrated by the mutiny of his subordinate, Chen Chiung-ming, who was in league with the Northern warlords.

[9] The Whampoa Military Academy, located at Whampoa near Canton, was established by Dr. Sun Yat-sen in 1924 after the reorganization of the Kuomintang with the help of the Chinese Communist Party and the Soviet Union. Before Chiang Kai-shek's betrayal of the revolution in 1927, the academy was run jointly by the Kuomintang and the Communist Party. Comrades Chou En-lai, Yeh Chien-ying, Yun Tai-ying, Hsiao Chu-nu and others held responsible posts in the academy at one time or another. Many of the cadets were members of the Communist Party or the Communist Youth League, and they formed the revolutionary core of the academy.

[10] Tan Yen-kai was a native of Hunan who had been a *Hanlin*, a member of the highest official scholastic body under the Ching Dynasty. He was a careerist who first advocated a constitutional monarchy and then took part in the Revolution of 1911. His later adherence to the Kuomintang reflected the contradiction between the Hunan landlords and the Northern warlords.

[11] The Progressive Party was organized by Liang Chi-chao and others under the aegis of Yuan Shih-kai during the first years of the Republic.

[12] Yuan Shih-kai was the head of the Northern warlords in the last years of the Ching Dynasty. After the Ching Dynasty was overthrown by the Revolution of 1911, he usurped the presidency of the Republic and organized the first government of the Northern warlords, which represented the big landlord and big comprador classes. He did this by relying on counter-revolutionary armed force and on the support of the imperialists and by taking advantage of the conciliationist character of the bourgeoisie, which was then leading the revolution. In 1915 he wanted to make himself emperor and, to gain the support of the Japanese imperialists, accepted the Twenty-one Demands with which Japan aimed at obtaining exclusive control of all China. In December of the same year an uprising against his assumption of the throne took place in Yunnan Province and promptly won nation-wide response and support. Yuan Shih-kai died in Peking in June 1916.

[13] Tuan Chi-jui was an old subordinate of Yuan Shih-kai and head of the Anhwei clique of Northern warlords. After Yuan's death he more than once controlled the Peking government.

[14] The extremely right-wing Political Science Group was formed in 1916 by a section of the Progressive Party and a section of the Kuomintang. It gambled now on the Southern, now on the Northern, warlords in order to grab government posts. During the Northern Expedition of 1926-27, its pro-Japanese members, such as Huang Fu, Chang Chun and Yang Yung-tai, began to collaborate with Chiang Kai-shek and, using their reactionary political experience, helped him build up a counter-revolutionary regime.

[15] The Youth Party, also called the Chinese Youth Party or the *Étatiste* Party, was formed by a handful of unscrupulous fascist politicians. They made counter-

revolutionary careers for themselves by opposing the Communist Party and the Soviet Union and received subsidies from the various groups of reactionaries in power and from the imperialists.

[16] Comrade Mao Tse-tung is here referring mainly to the independent regiment commanded by General Yeh Ting, a Communist, during the Northern Expedition. See "The Struggle in the Chingkang Mountains", Note 14, *Selected Works of Mao Tse-tung*, Eng. ed., FLP, Peking, 1965, Vol. I, p. 104.

[17] Nanchang, capital of Kiangsi Province, was the scene of the famous uprising on August 1, 1927 led by the Communist Party of China in order to combat the counter-revolution of Chiang Kai-shek and Wang Ching-wei and to continue the revolution of 1924-27. More than thirty thousand troops took part in the uprising which was led by Comrades Chou En-lai, Chu Teh, Ho Lung and Yeh Ting. The insurrectionary army withdrew from Nanchang on August 5 as planned, but suffered a defeat when approaching Chaochow and Swatow in Kwangtung Province. Led by Comrades Chu Teh, Chen Yi and Lin Piao, part of the troops later fought their way to the Chingkang Mountains and joined forces with the First Division of the First Workers' and Peasants' Revolutionary Army under Comrade Mao Tse-tung.

[18] The famous Autumn Harvest Uprising under the leadership of Comrade Mao Tse-tung was launched in September 1927 by the people's armed forces of Hsiushui, Pinghsiang, Pingkiang and Liuyang Counties on the Hunan-Kiangsi border, who formed the First Division of the First Workers' and Peasants' Revolutionary Army. Comrade Mao Tse-tung led this force to the Chingkang Mountains where a revolutionary base was established.

[19] Han Fu-chu was a Kuomintang warlord in Shantung Province. Liu Chih, another warlord, who commanded Chiang Kai-shek's personal troops in Honan Province, was responsible for the defence of the Paoting area in Hopei after the outbreak of the War of Resistance Against Japan. Both of them fled before the Japanese without firing a shot.

THE MAY 4TH MOVEMENT

May 1939

The May 4th Movement twenty years ago marked a new stage in China's bourgeois-democratic revolution against imperialism and feudalism. The cultural reform movement which grew out of the May 4th Movement was only one of the manifestations of this revolution. With the growth and development of new social forces in that period, a powerful camp made its appearance in the bourgeois-democratic revolution, a camp consisting of the working class, the student masses and the new national bourgeoisie. Around the time of the May 4th Movement, hundreds of thousands of students courageously took their place in the van. In these respects the May 4th Movement went a step beyond the Revolution of 1911.

If we trace China's bourgeois-democratic revolution back to its formative period, we see that it has passed through a number of stages in its development: the Opium War, the War of the Taiping Heavenly Kingdom, the Sino-Japanese War of 1894,[1] the Reform Movement of 1898,[2] the Yi Ho Tuan Movement,[3] the Revolution of 1911, the May 4th Movement, the Northern Expedition, and the War of the Agrarian Revolution. The present War of Resistance Against Japan is yet another stage, and is the greatest, most vigorous and most dynamic stage of all. The bourgeois-democratic revolution can be considered accomplished only when the forces of foreign imperialism and domestic feudalism have basically been overthrown and an independent democratic state has been established. From the Opium War onwards each stage in the development of the revolution has had its own distinguishing characteristics. But the most important feature differentiating them is whether they came before or after the emergence of the Communist Party. However, taken as a whole, all

Comrade Mao Tse-tung wrote this article for newspapers in Yenan to commemorate the twentieth anniversary of the May 4th Movement.

the stages bear the character of a bourgeois-democratic revolution. The aim of this democratic revolution is to establish a social system hitherto unknown in Chinese history, namely, a democratic social system having a feudal society (during the last hundred years a semi-colonial and semi-feudal society) as its precursor and a socialist society as its successor. If anyone asks why a Communist should strive to bring into being first a bourgeois-democratic society and then a socialist society, our answer is: we are following the inevitable course of history.

China's democratic revolution depends on definite social forces for its accomplishment. These social forces are the working class, the peasantry, the intelligentsia and the progressive section of the bourgeoisie, that is, the revolutionary workers, peasants, soldiers, students and intellectuals, and businessmen, with the workers and peasants as the basic revolutionary forces and the workers as the class which leads the revolution. It is impossible to accomplish the anti-imperialist and anti-feudal democratic revolution without these basic revolutionary forces and without the leadership of the working class. Today, the principal enemies of the revolution are the Japanese imperialists and the Chinese traitors, and the fundamental policy in the revolution is the policy of the Anti-Japanese National United Front, consisting of all workers, peasants, soldiers, students and intellectuals, and businessmen who are against Japanese aggression. Final victory in the War of Resistance will be won when this united front is greatly consolidated and developed.

In the Chinese democratic revolutionary movement, it was the intellectuals who were the first to awaken. This was clearly demonstrated both in the Revolution of 1911 and in the May 4th Movement, and in the days of the May 4th Movement the intellectuals were more numerous and more politically conscious than in the days of the Revolution of 1911. But the intellectuals will accomplish nothing if they fail to integrate themselves with the workers and peasants. In the final analysis, the dividing line between revolutionary intellectuals and non-revolutionary or counter-revolutionary intellectuals is whether or not they are willing to integrate themselves with the workers and peasants and actually do so. Ultimately it is this alone, and not professions of faith in the Three People's Principles or in Marxism, that distinguishes one from the other. A true revolutionary must be one who is willing to integrate himself with the workers and peasants and actually does so.

It is now twenty years since the May 4th Movement and almost two years since the outbreak of the anti-Japanese war. The young people and the cultural circles of the whole country bear a heavy responsibility in the democratic revolution and the War of Resistance. I hope they will understand the character and the motive forces of the Chinese revolution, make their work serve the workers and peasants, go into their midst and become propagandists and organizers among them. Victory will be ours when the entire people arises against Japan. Young people of the whole country, bestir yourselves!

NOTES

[1] The Sino-Japanese War of 1894 was started by Japanese imperialism for the purpose of invading Korea and China. Many Chinese soldiers and some patriotic generals put up a heroic fight. But China suffered defeat because of the corruption of the Ching government and its failure to prepare resistance. In 1895 the Ching government concluded the shameful Treaty of Shimonoseki with Japan.

[2] For the Reform Movement of 1898 see "On Protracted War", Note 8, p. 191 of this volume.

[3] The Yi Ho Tuan Movement was the anti-imperialist armed struggle which took place in northern China in 1900. The broad masses of peasants, handicraftsmen and other people took part in this movement. Getting in touch with one another through religious and other channels, they organized themselves on the basis of secret societies and waged a heroic struggle against the joint forces of aggression of the eight imperialist powers — the United States, Britain, Japan, Germany, Russia, France, Italy and Austria. The movement was put down with indescribable savagery after the joint forces of aggression occupied Tientsin and Peking.

THE ORIENTATION
OF THE YOUTH MOVEMENT

May 4, 1939

Today is the twentieth anniversary of the May 4th Movement, and the youth of Yenan are all gathered here for this commemoration meeting. I shall therefore take the occasion to speak on some questions concerning the orientation of the youth movement in China.

First, May 4 has now been designated as China's Youth Day,[1] and rightly so. Twenty years have elapsed since the May 4th Movement, yet it is only this year that the day has been designated as the national Youth Day, and this is a most significant fact. For it indicates that the Chinese people's democratic revolution against imperialism and feudalism will soon reach a turning point. This revolution encountered repeated failures over several decades, but now there must be a change, a change towards victory and not another failure. The Chinese revolution is now going forward, forward to victory. The repeated failures of the past cannot and must not be allowed to recur, and they must be turned into victory. But has the change already taken place? No. It has not, nor have we yet won victory. But victory can be won. It is precisely in the present War of Resistance Against Japan that we are striving to reach the turning point from failure to victory. The May 4th Movement was directed against a government of national betrayal, a government which conspired with imperialism and sold out the interests of the nation, a government which oppressed the people. Was it not necessary to oppose such a government? If it was not, then the May 4th Movement was simply a mistake. It is obvious that such a government must be opposed, that a government of national betrayal must be overthrown. Just consider, long before the

This speech was delivered by Comrade Mao Tse-tung at a mass meeting of youth in Yenan to commemorate the twentieth anniversary of the May 4th Movement. It represented a development in his ideas on the question of the Chinese revolution.

May 4th Movement Dr. Sun Yat-sen was already a rebel against the government of his day; he opposed and overthrew the Ching government. Was he right in doing so? In my opinion he was quite right. For the government he opposed did not resist imperialism but conspired with it, and was not a revolutionary government but one that suppressed the revolution. The May 4th Movement was a revolutionary movement precisely because it opposed a government of national betrayal. The youth of China should see the May 4th Movement in this light. Today, when the whole nation has militantly risen to resist Japan, we are determined to defeat Japanese imperialism, and we shall not tolerate any traitors or allow the revolution to fail again, for we have taken warning from its failures in the past. With few exceptions, the whole youth of China is awakened and determined to win, and this is reflected in the designation of May 4th as Youth Day. We are advancing along the road to victory and, provided the whole people make a concerted effort, the Chinese revolution will definitely triumph through the War of Resistance.

Secondly, what is the Chinese revolution directed against? What are the targets of the revolution? As everybody knows, imperialism is one target and feudalism the other. What are the targets of the revolution at this moment? One is Japanese imperialism, and the other the Chinese collaborators. To make our revolution we must overthrow Japanese imperialism and the Chinese traitors. Who are the makers of the revolution? What is its main force? The common people of China. The motive forces of the revolution are the proletariat, the peasantry and all members of other classes who are willing to oppose imperialism and feudalism; these are the revolutionary forces opposing imperialism and feudalism. But who, among so many, are the basic force, the backbone of the revolution? The workers and the peasants, forming 90 per cent of the country's population. What is the nature of the Chinese revolution? What kind of revolution are we making today? Today we are making a bourgeois-democratic revolution, and nothing we do goes beyond its scope. By and large, we should not destroy the bourgeois system of private property for the present; what we want to destroy is imperialism and feudalism. This is what we mean by the bourgeois-democratic revolution. But its accomplishment is already beyond the capacity of the bourgeoisie and must depend on the efforts of the proletariat and the broad masses of the people. What is the goal of this revolution? To overthrow imperialism and feudalism and to establish a people's democratic republic. A people's democratic republic means a republic based on the revolutionary Three People's Principles. It will be different both from the semi-colonial and semi-feudal state of the present and from the socialist system of the future. Capitalists have no place in a socialist society, but they should still be allowed in a people's democracy. Will there always be a place for capitalists in China? No, definitely not in the future. This is true not only of China but of the whole world. In the future no country, whether it be Britain, the United States, France, Japan, Germany, or Italy, will have any place for capitalists, and China will be no exception. The Soviet Union is a country which has already established socialism, and beyond all doubt the whole world will follow its example. China will certainly go over to socialism in the future; that is an irresistible law. But at the present stage our task is not to put socialism into practice, but to destroy imperialism and feudalism, change China's present semi-colonial and semi-feudal status, and establish people's democracy. This is what the youth of the whole country must strive for.

Thirdly, what are the lessons of the Chinese revolution? This question is also an important one for our youth to understand. Strictly speaking, China's bourgeois-democratic revolution against imperialism and feudalism was begun by Dr. Sun Yat-sen and has been going on for more than fifty years; as for foreign capitalist aggression against China, it has been going on for almost a hundred years. During that century, there was first the Opium War against British aggression, then came the War of the Taiping Heavenly Kingdom, then the Sino-Japanese War of 1894, the Reform Movement of 1898, the Yi Ho Tuan Movement, the Revolution of 1911, the May 4th Movement, the Northern Expedition, and the war waged by the Red Army — although these struggles differed from each other, their common purpose was to repel foreign enemies or change existing conditions. However, it was only with Dr. Sun Yat-sen that a more or less clearly defined bourgeois-democratic revolution began. In the last fifty years the revolution started by Dr. Sun Yat-sen has had both its successes and its failures. Was not the Revolution of 1911 a success? Didn't it send the emperor packing? Yet it was a failure in the sense that while it sent the emperor packing, it left China under imperialist and feudal oppression, so that the anti-imperialist and anti-feudal revolutionary task remained unaccomplished. What was the aim of the May 4th Movement? Its aim likewise was to overthrow imperialism and feudalism, but it, too, failed, and China still remained under the rule

of imperialism and feudalism. The same is true of the revolution
known as the Northern Expedition; it scored successes, but it too
failed. From the time the Kuomintang turned against the Communist Party,[2] China again fell under the domination of imperialism
and feudalism. The inevitable result was the ten years' war waged
by the Red Army. But these ten years of struggle fulfilled the revolutionary task only in parts of China and not in the country as a
whole. If we are to sum up the revolution during the past decades,
we may say that it has won only temporary and partial victories and
not permanent and nation-wide victory. As Dr. Sun Yat-sen said,
"The revolution is not yet completed, all my comrades must struggle
on." The question now is: Why, after decades of struggle, has the
Chinese revolution not yet attained its goal? What are the reasons?
I think there are two: first, the enemy forces have been too strong;
second, our own forces have been too weak. Because one side was
strong and the other side weak, the revolution did not succeed. In
saying that the enemy forces have been too strong, we mean that the
forces of imperialism (the primary factor) and of feudalism have been
too strong. In saying that our own forces have been too weak, we
mean weak in the military, political, economic and cultural fields;
but our weaknesses and our consequent failure to fulfil the anti-
imperialist and anti-feudal task are chiefly due to the fact that the
labouring people, the workers and peasants, constituting 90 per cent
of the population, have not yet been mobilized. If we are to sum up
the experience of the revolution of the past decades, we may say
that the people throughout the country have not been fully mobilized
and that the reactionaries have invariably opposed and sabotaged
such mobilization. Only by mobilizing and organizing the workers
and peasants, who comprise 90 per cent of the population, is it possible
to overthrow imperialism and feudalism. Dr. Sun Yat-sen said in
his Testament:

> For forty years I have devoted myself to the cause of the
> national revolution with the aim of winning freedom and equality
> for China. My experiences during these forty years have firmly
> convinced me that to achieve this aim we must arouse the masses
> of the people and unite in a common struggle with those nations
> of the world which treat us as equals.

It is now more than ten years since Dr. Sun died, and if we add these
on, the total is over fifty years. What is the lesson of the revolution

during these years? Fundamentally, it is, "arouse the masses of the people". You should carefully study this lesson, and so should all China's youth. They must know that only by mobilizing the masses of workers and peasants, who form 90 per cent of the population, can we defeat imperialism and feudalism. Unless we mobilize the workers and peasants of the whole country, it will be impossible for us to defeat Japan and build a new China.

Fourthly, to return to the youth movement. On this very day twenty years ago there occurred in China the great historical event known as the May 4th Movement, in which the students participated; it was a movement of tremendous significance. What role have China's young people played since the May 4th Movement? In a way they have played a vanguard role — a fact recognized by everybody except the die-hards. What is a vanguard role? It means taking the lead and marching in the forefront of the revolutionary ranks. In the anti-imperialist and anti-feudal ranks of the Chinese people, there is a contingent composed of the country's young intellectuals and students. It is a contingent of considerable size and, even if the many who have given their lives are not included, it now numbers several million. It is an army on one of the fronts against imperialism and feudalism, and an important army too. But this army is not enough; we cannot defeat the enemy by relying on it alone, for when all is said and done it is not the main force. What then is the main force? The workers and peasants. Our young intellectuals and students must go among the workers and peasants, who make up 90 per cent of the population, and mobilize and organize them. Without this main force of workers and peasants, we cannot win the fight against imperialism and feudalism, we cannot win it by relying only on the contingent of young intellectuals and students. Therefore, the young intellectuals and students throughout the country must unite with the broad masses of workers and peasants and become one with them, and only then can a mighty force be created. A force of hundreds of millions of people! Only with this huge force can the enemy's strongholds be taken and his last fortresses smashed. In assessing the youth movement of the past from this viewpoint, we should call attention to a wrong tendency. In the youth movement of the last few decades, a section of the young people have been unwilling to unite with the workers and peasants and have opposed their movements; this is a counter-current in the youth movement. In fact, these people are not at all bright in their refusal to unite with the masses who make up

90 per cent of the population and in going so far as to oppose them
outright. Is this a good tendency? I think not, because in opposing
the workers and peasants they are in fact opposing the revolution;
that is why we say it is a counter-current in the youth movement. A
youth movement of that kind would come to no good. A few days
ago I wrote a short article in which I noted:

> In the final analysis, the dividing line between revolutionary
> intellectuals and non-revolutionary or counter-revolutionary intel-
> lectuals is whether or not they are willing to integrate themselves
> with the workers and peasants and actually do so.

Here I advanced a criterion which I regard as the only valid one.
How should we judge whether a youth is a revolutionary? How can
we tell? There can only be one criterion, namely, whether or not he
is willing to integrate himself with the broad masses of workers and
peasants and does so in practice. If he is willing to do so and actually
does so, he is a revolutionary; otherwise he is a non-revolutionary
or a counter-revolutionary. If today he integrates himself with the
masses of workers and peasants, then today he is a revolutionary;
if tomorrow he ceases to do so or turns round to oppress the common
people, then he becomes a non-revolutionary or a counter-revolutionary.
Some young people talk glibly about their belief in the Three People's
Principles or in Marxism, but this does not prove anything. Doesn't
Hitler profess belief in "socialism"? Twenty years ago even Mussolini
was a "socialist"! And what does their "socialism" amount to?
Fascism! Didn't Chen Tu-hsiu once "believe" in Marxism? What did
he do later? He went over to the counter-revolution. Didn't Chang
Kuo-tao "believe" in Marxism? Where is he now? He has run away
and landed in the mire. Some people style themselves "followers
of the Three People's Principles" or even old stalwarts of these Principles; but what have they done? It turns out that their Principle
of Nationalism means conspiring with imperialism, that their Principle
of Democracy means oppressing the common people, and that their
Principle of People's Livelihood means sucking the people's blood.
They affirm the Three People's Principles with their lips but deny
them in their hearts. So when we assess a person and judge whether
he is a true or false adherent of the Three People's Principles, whether
he is a true or false Marxist, we need only find out how he stands
in relation to the broad masses of workers and peasants, and then
we shall know him for what he is. This is the only criterion, there is

no other. I hope that the youth of our country will never allow themselves to be carried away by this sinister counter-current but will clearly recognize the workers and peasants as their friends and march forward to a bright future.

Fifthly, the present War of Resistance Against Japan marks a new stage — the greatest, most dynamic and most vigorous stage — in the Chinese revolution. In this stage the youth shoulder tremendous responsibilities. Our revolutionary movement has gone through many stages of struggle in the last decades, but at no stage has it been so broad as in the present War of Resistance. When we maintain that the Chinese revolution now has features distinguishing it from the revolution in the past and that it will make the turn from failure to victory, we mean that the masses of the Chinese people have made progress, of which the progress of the youth is a clear proof. Hence the anti-Japanese war must and certainly will triumph. As everybody knows, the basic policy in this war is the Anti-Japanese National United Front, whose aim it is to overthrow Japanese imperialism and the Chinese collaborators, transform the old China into a new China, and liberate the whole nation from its semi-colonial and semi-feudal status. The present lack of unity in the Chinese youth movement is a serious weakness. You should continue to strive for unity, because unity is strength. You must help the youth of the whole country to understand the present situation, to achieve unity and to resist Japan to the end.

Sixthly and lastly, I want to speak about the youth movement in Yenan. It is the model for the youth movement throughout the country. The direction it is taking is in fact the orientation for the youth movement of the entire country. Why? Because it is the correct orientation. You see, in the matter of unity the youth of Yenan have acquitted themselves well, indeed very well. The youth of Yenan have achieved solidarity and unity. The young intellectuals and students, the young workers and peasants in Yenan are all united. Large numbers of revolutionary youth from all over the country, and even from Chinese communities abroad, have come to study in Yenan. Most of you attending this meeting today have come to Yenan from thousands of miles away; whether your surname is Chang or Li, whether you are a man or a woman, a worker or a peasant, you are all of one mind. Should this not be regarded as a model for the whole country? The youth in Yenan, besides being united among themselves, have integrated themselves with the masses of workers and peasants, and more than anything else this makes you a model for the whole country. What have you been doing? You have been learning the theory of revolution and studying the principles and methods for resisting Japan and saving the nation. You have been carrying out the campaign for production and have reclaimed thousands of *mou* of waste land. Confucius never reclaimed land or tilled the soil. When he ran his school, he had quite a number of students, "seventy worthies and three thousand disciples" — quite a flourishing school! But he had far fewer students than there are in Yenan, and what is more, they would have disliked production campaigns. When a student asked him how to plough the fields, Confucius answered, "I don't know, I am not as good at that as a farmer." Confucius was next asked how to grow vegetables, and he answered, "I don't know, I am not as good at that as a vegetable gardener." In ancient times the youth of China who studied under a sage neither learned revolutionary theory nor took part in labour. Today, there is little revolutionary theory taught and there are no such things as production movements in the schools over vast regions of our country. It is only here in Yenan and in the anti-Japanese base areas behind the enemy lines that the young people are fundamentally different; they are really the vanguard in resisting Japan and saving the nation because their political orientation and their methods of work are correct. That is why I say the youth movement in Yenan is the model for the youth movement throughout the country.

Our meeting today is highly significant. I have said all I wanted. I hope you will all study the lessons of the Chinese revolution in the last fifty years, develop its good points and discard its mistakes, so that the youth will be at one with the people of the whole country and the revolution will make the turn from failure to victory. When the youth and the whole nation are mobilized, organized and united, Japanese imperialism will be overthrown. Each young person must shoulder his responsibility. You must each be different from before and resolve to unite the youth and organize the people of the whole country for the overthrow of Japanese imperialism and the transformation of the old China into a new China. This is what I expect of all of you.

NOTES

[1] May 4 was first adopted as China's Youth Day by the youth organization of the Shensi-Kansu-Ningsia Border Region. Under the pressure of the patriotic upsurge of the broad masses of young people, the Kuomintang government expressed its

agreement. But it subsequently proclaimed March 29 as its own Youth Day (in commemoration of the revolutionary martyrs who died during an uprising at Canton in 1911) because, fearing that the youth would turn revolutionary, it regarded the decision to observe May 4 as dangerous. However, May 4 continued to be observed as Youth Day in the revolutionary base areas under the leadership of the Communist Party, and was officially proclaimed China's Youth Day by the Administrative Council of the Central People's Government in December 1949 after the founding of the People's Republic of China.

[2] "The Kuomintang turned against the Communist Party" here refers to the counter-revolutionary coups staged in 1927 by Chiang Kai-shek in Shanghai and Nanking and by Wang Ching-wei in Wuhan.

OPPOSE CAPITULATIONIST ACTIVITY

June 30, 1939

Ever since the Chinese nation was confronted with the Japanese aggression, the first and foremost question has been to fight or not to fight. This question aroused serious controversy in the period from the Incident of September 18, 1931 to the Lukouchiao Incident of July 7, 1937. The conclusion reached by all patriotic political parties and groups and by all our patriotic fellow-countrymen was: "To fight is to survive, not to fight is to perish." The conclusion reached by all the capitulationists was: "To fight is to perish, not to fight is to survive." For a time, the roaring guns of the resistance at Lukouchiao decided the issue. They proclaimed the first conclusion right and the second wrong. But why was the question settled only temporarily and not once and for all? Because the Japanese imperialists adopted the policy of inducing China to capitulate, the international capitulationists[1] tried to bring about a compromise, and certain people within our anti-Japanese front wavered. Now the issue has been raised again, worded in a slightly different way as a question of "peace or war". Thus a controversy has arisen inside China between those who favour continuing the war and those who favour making peace. Their respective positions remain the same: the conclusion of the war group is "to fight is to survive, to make peace is to perish"; the conclusion of the peace group is "to make peace is to survive, to fight is to perish". The former comprises all patriotic parties and all patriots and they make up the great majority of the nation, while the latter, *i.e.*, the capitulationists, constitutes only a small wavering minority within the anti-Japanese front. Consequently, the peace group has to resort to lying propaganda, and, above all, to anti-Communist propaganda. For example, it has fabricated and released a spate of false news, false reports, false documents and false resolutions, such as: "the Communist Party engages in disruptive activities", "the Eighth Route Army and the

251

New Fourth Army are merely moving about without fighting and refuse to obey orders", "a separatist regime has been formed in the Shensi-Kansu-Ningsia Border Region and is expanding beyond its confines", "the Communist Party is plotting to overthrow the government", and even, "the Soviet Union is plotting aggression against China". Its purpose is to make peace, or in other words to capitulate, by covering up the real facts and confusing public opinion. The peace group, the group of capitulationists, is doing all this because it cannot wreck Kuomintang-Communist co-operation, split the Anti-Japanese National United Front and surrender to Japan unless it combats the Communist Party, which is the initiator and champion of the united front. Second, it hopes that Japanese imperialism will make concessions. It believes that Japan is well-nigh exhausted and will change her basic policy, voluntarily withdrawing from central, southern and even northern China, and that China can thus win without doing any more fighting. Third, it pins its hopes on international pressure. Many people in the peace group bank on the exertion of pressure by the big powers not only on Japan, so that she will make some concessions and thereby facilitate a peace settlement, but also on the Chinese government, so that they can say to the war group: "Look! In the present international climate, we have to make peace!" and "A Pacific international conference[2] would be to China's advantage. It would not be another Munich,[3] but a step towards China's rejuvenation!" This forms the sum total of the views, tactics and schemes of the peace group, the Chinese capitulationists. The drama is being acted out not only by Wang Ching-wei himself, but, what is more serious, by many others like him who are concealed within the anti-Japanese front and are collaborating with him in a kind of duet[4] or joint performance, with some wearing the white make-up of the stage villain and others the red make-up of the hero.

We Communists openly proclaim that, at all times, we stand with those who favour continuing the war and resolutely oppose those who favour making peace. We have but one desire, that is, together with all other patriotic parties and all other patriots, to strengthen unity and strengthen the national united front and Kuomintang-Communist co-operation, put the Three People's Principles into effect, carry the War of Resistance through to the end, fight all the way to the Yalu River and recover all our lost territories.[5] We firmly denounce the Wang Ching-weis, both overt and covert, who are creating an anti-Communist climate, engineering "friction"[6] between the Kuomintang and the Communist Party, and even trying to provoke another civil war between the two parties. We say to them: In essence, your divisive schemes are nothing but preparations for capitulation, and your divisive and capitulationist policy simply reveals your general plan of selling out the interests of the nation for the selfish interests of a few individuals. People have eyes and will see through your scheming. We categorically repudiate the absurd view that a Pacific conference would not be an Eastern Munich. Of course, the so-called Pacific conference would be an Eastern Munich, a preparation for turning China into another Czechoslovakia. We firmly denounce the groundless assertion that Japanese imperialism may come to its senses and make concessions. Japanese imperialism will never change its basic policy of subjugating China. Japan's honeyed words after the fall of Wuhan — for instance, the suggestion that she would abandon the policy of "not accepting the National Government as the opposite party in negotiations"[7] and would instead recognize it as such, or that she would withdraw her troops from central and southern China on certain conditions — are nothing but cunning bait to hook the fish, so that whoever swallows the bait must expect to be well and truly cooked. The international capitulationists are likewise pursuing a cunning policy to induce China to surrender. They have countenanced Japanese aggression against China, while they themselves "sit on top of the mountain to watch the tigers fight", waiting for the opportune moment to engineer a so-called Pacific conference for mediation in order to profit at others' expense. Anyone who pins his hopes on such schemers will likewise find that he has been badly duped.

What was once a question of whether or not to fight has now become a question of whether to continue the war or to make peace, but essentially it is the same question, the most important and fundamental of all questions. In the last six months, with Japan pressing on with her policy of inducing China to capitulate, with the international capitulationists intensifying their activities and, above all, with some people in our anti-Japanese front wavering more than ever, a great clamour has arisen around the question of peace or war, so that capitulation has become the main danger in the present political situation. And the first and most important move the capitulationists are making to prepare for it is to fight communism, that is, to break up Kuomintang-Communist co-operation and the unity of the anti-Japanese front. In these circumstances, all patriotic parties and all patriots must keep a close watch over the capitulationists' activities and must understand the main characteristics of the present situation, namely, that capitulation is the chief danger and that anti-communism is the preparatory step to capitulation, and they must do their utmost to oppose capitulation and a split. No group of people must ever be allowed to undermine or betray the war against Japanese imperialism, a war which has cost the whole nation two full years of bloodshed. No group of people must ever be allowed to disrupt or split the Anti-Japanese National United Front which has been forged by the common effort of the whole nation.

Fight on and persist in unity, and China will survive.

Make peace and persist in splitting, and China will perish.

Which to reject and which to accept? Our countrymen must quickly make their choice.

We Communists will definitely fight on and persist in unity.

All patriotic parties and all patriots will fight on and persist in unity.

Even if the capitulationists who are plotting surrender and a split should get the upper hand for a while, they will eventually be unmasked and punished by the people. The historical task of the Chinese nation is to achieve liberation through united resistance. What the capitulationists desire is the exact opposite, but however much they may have the upper hand, however jubilant they may be, fancying that nobody dare harm them, they cannot escape punishment by the whole people.

Oppose capitulation and a split — this is the urgent task now confronting all the patriotic political parties and groups and all our patriotic fellow-countrymen.

People of the whole country, unite! Persist in resistance and unity, and suppress all plots for capitulation and a split!

NOTES

[1] "The international capitulationists" were the British and U.S. imperialists who were plotting to compromise with Japan by sacrificing China.

[2] The projected Pacific international conference was dubbed a Far Eastern Munich because the British, U.S. and French imperialists, in collaboration with the Chinese group which favoured making peace, were plotting to reach a compromise with Japan by selling out China. It was Chiang Kai-shek who used the absurd argument, which Comrade Mao Tse-tung refutes in this article, that such a conference would not constitute an Eastern Munich.

³ In September 1938, the heads of the British, French, German and Italian governments met in Munich, Germany, and concluded the Munich Agreement under which Britain and France betrayed Czechoslovakia to Germany in exchange for a German attack on the Soviet Union. In 1938 and 1939, British and U.S. imperialism made several moves to reach a compromise with Japanese imperialism by sacrificing China. At the time when Comrade Mao Tse-tung wrote this article in June 1939, talks were being held between Britain and Japan in another attempt to carry out this scheme. It was called an "Eastern Munich" because of its similarity to the Munich conspiracy of Britain, France, Germany and Italy.

⁴ The duet was being acted by Chiang Kai-shek and Wang Ching-wei. While Wang Ching-wei was the ringleader of the open capitulationists, Chiang was the ringleader of those hiding in the anti-Japanese front.

⁵ At the Fifth Plenary Session of the Kuomintang's Fifth Central Executive Committee in January 1939, Chiang Kai-shek openly declared that what he meant by "to the very end" in the slogan "Carry the War of Resistance through to the very end" was merely "to restore the *status quo* before the Lukouchiao Incident", an interpretation that would have meant abandoning vast areas of northern and northeastern China to Japanese occupation. Therefore, to counter Chiang Kai-shek's capitulationist policy, Comrade Mao Tse-tung specially stressed that "to the very end" meant "to fight all the way to the Yalu River and recover all our lost territories".

⁶ The term "friction" was widely used at the time to refer to the various kinds of reactionary political and military actions of the Kuomintang reactionaries undertaken to wreck the Anti-Japanese National United Front and to oppose the Communist Party and the progressive forces, such as massacres and large-scale attacks on the Eighth Route and New Fourth Armies.

⁷ Subsequent to the Japanese occupation of Nanking on December 13, 1937, the Japanese government issued a statement on January 16, 1938, saying that Japan would "not accept the National Government as the opposite party in negotiations, and expects a new government to be established". After Japanese troops occupied Canton and Wuhan in October 1938, the Japanese government, taking advantage of Chiang Kai-shek's vacillation, changed its policy in order to induce him to capitulate. It issued another statement on November 3, which read in part: "As for the National Government, provided it abandons its hitherto erroneous policy and gets new men to carry out rehabilitation and to maintain peace and order, the Empire will not decline to negotiate with it."

THE REACTIONARIES MUST BE PUNISHED

August 1, 1939

Today, the First of August, we are gathered here for a memorial meeting. Why are we holding this memorial meeting? Because the reactionaries have killed our revolutionary comrades, killed fighters against Japan. Who should be killed in these times? The Chinese traitors and the Japanese imperialists. China has been fighting Japanese imperialism for two years, but the outcome is not yet decided. The traitors are still very active, and very few of them have been killed. Yet our revolutionary comrades, all warriors against Japan, have been killed. Killed by whom? Killed by the troops. Why did the troops kill fighters against Japan? They were carrying out orders; certain people gave them the order to kill. Who gave them the order to kill? The reactionaries.[1] Comrades! Logically, who would want to kill fighters against Japan? First, the Japanese imperialists, and next, the Chinese collaborators and traitors such as Wang Ching-wei. But the scene of the killing was not Shanghai, Peiping, Tientsin or Nanking, or any other place occupied by the Japanese aggressors and Chinese collaborators; it took place in Pingkiang, in the rear of the War of Resistance, and among the victims were Comrades Tu Cheng-kun and Lo Tzu-ming, responsible comrades of the Pingkiang Liaison Office of the New Fourth Army. Obviously, the killing was perpetrated by a gang of Chinese reactionaries acting on the orders of the Japanese imperialists and Wang Ching-wei. Preparing to capitulate, these reactionaries obsequiously carried out the orders of the Japanese and Wang Ching-wei, and the first people they killed were the most resolute fighters against Japan. This is no trivial matter; we must raise our voices against it, we must denounce it!

This speech was delivered by Comrade Mao Tse-tung at a memorial meeting held by the people of Yenan for the martyrs of Pingkiang.

The whole nation is now resisting Japan and has forged a great union of the people for the purpose of resistance. But within this great union there are reactionaries and capitulators. What are they doing? They are killing fighters against Japan, holding back progress and working in collusion with the Japanese aggressors and Chinese collaborators to pave the way for capitulation.

Has anyone taken action on this serious case of the murder of anti-Japanese comrades? The murder was committed at 3 p.m. on June 12, today is August 1, but in all this time have we seen anyone step forward and take action? No. Who should have done so? Action should have been taken under the law of the land by the administrators of the law. If such a thing had happened in the Shensi-Kansu-Ningsia Border Region, our high court would have acted long ago. But although nearly two months have elapsed since the Pingkiang massacre, the law and its administrators have done nothing. What is the reason? The reason is, China is not unified.[2]

China must be unified; there can be no victory without unification. But what does unification mean? It means that everybody should resist Japan, that all should unite and strive for progress and that there should be due rewards and punishments. Who ought to be rewarded? Those who resist Japan, those who uphold unity, those who are progressive. And who ought to be punished? The collaborators and reactionaries who undermine resistance, unity and progress. Is our country now unified? It is not. The Pingkiang massacre proves it. It shows that there is no unification where there should be. We have long demanded the unification of the whole country. First, unification on the basis of the War of Resistance. But now, instead of being rewarded, Tu Cheng-kun, Lo Tzu-ming and the other comrades who were resisting the Japanese have been brutally murdered, whereas scoundrels who oppose resistance, prepare to capitulate and commit murder go unpunished. That is not unification. We must oppose these scoundrels and capitulators, and arrest the murderers. Second, unification on the basis of unity. Those who stand for unity ought to be rewarded and those who undermine it ought to be punished. But now, Comrades Tu Cheng-kun, Lo Tzu-ming and the others who upheld unity have been punished, have been brutally murdered, whereas the scoundrels who undermine unity are allowed to go scot-free. That is not unification. Third, unification on the basis of progress. The whole country must go forward; the backward must try to keep pace with the progressive, and the progressive must not be held back to the pace of the backward. The butchers at Pingkiang killed progressive people. Hundreds of Communists and patriots have been assassinated since the outbreak of the War of Resistance, the Pingkiang massacre being only the most recent example. It will be disastrous for China if this continues; all who resist Japan may be murdered. What do these murders mean? They mean that the Chinese reactionaries, acting under orders from the Japanese imperialists and Wang Ching-wei, are preparing to capitulate, and that is why they begin by killing fighters against Japan, by killing Communists and patriots. If this is not stopped, China will perish at the hands of these reactionaries. These murders, therefore, concern the whole country, they are of the gravest importance, and we must demand that the National Government punish these reactionaries with the utmost severity.

Comrades must also realize that Japanese imperialism has recently intensified its disruptive activities, that international imperialism has become more active in helping Japan,[3] and that the traitors in China, both the overt and the covert Wang Ching-weis, are more active than ever in sabotaging the War of Resistance, wrecking unity and turning the clock back. They want to surrender the greater part of our country, cause an internal split and engineer a civil war. At the present time certain secret measures known as "Measures for Restricting the Activities of Alien Parties"[4] are being extensively enforced. They are reactionary to the core, helpful to Japanese imperialism and detrimental to resistance, unity and progress. Which are the "alien parties"? The Japanese imperialists, Wang Ching-wei and the traitors. How can the Communist Party and all the other anti-Japanese political parties, which are united in resistance to Japan, be called "alien parties"? Yet the capitulators, reactionaries and die-hards are deliberately creating friction and disunity within the anti-Japanese ranks. Is this kind of activity right or wrong? It is absolutely wrong! (*Unanimous applause.*) When it comes to restriction, what sort of people should be restricted? The Japanese imperialists, Wang Ching-wei, the reactionaries and capitulators. (*Unanimous applause.*) Why restrict the Communist Party, which is the most resolute in resisting Japan, the most revolutionary and the most progressive? It is absolutely wrong. We the people of Yenan voice our firm opposition and strong protest. (*Unanimous applause.*) We must oppose the "Measures for Restricting the Activities of Alien Parties", for such measures are at the very root of all kinds of criminal actions that wreck unity. We are holding this mass meeting today for the sake of continued resistance, unity and progress. To this end, the "Measures for Restricting the Activities of Alien Parties" must be abolished, the capitulators and reactionaries must be punished, and all revolutionary comrades, all the comrades and people resisting Japan must be protected. (*Warm applause and slogan shouting.*)

NOTES

[1] These reactionaries were Chiang Kai-shek and his henchmen. On June 12, 1939, acting on a secret order from Chiang Kai-shek, the Kuomintang's 27th Group Army dispatched troops to surround the New Fourth Army Liaison Office at Pingkiang, Hunan Province, and in cold blood murdered Comrade Tu Cheng-kun, staff officer of the New Fourth Army, Comrade Lo Tzu-ming, major and adjutant of the Eighth Route Army, and four other comrades. This massacre aroused indignation not only among the people in the anti-Japanese democratic base areas but also among honest people in the Kuomintang areas.

[2] Comrade Mao Tse-tung defined unification in order to counter the Kuomintang reactionaries' use of "unification" as a pretext for their schemes to liquidate the Communist-led anti-Japanese armed forces and base areas. After the renewed Kuomintang-Communist co-operation for joint resistance to Japan, the slogan of "unification" became the Kuomintang's chief weapon in attacking the Communist Party, which it accused of always seeking to be different and of obstructing unification and damaging the cause of resistance. This reactionary clamour increased after January 1939, when the Fifth Plenary Session of the Kuomintang's Fifth Central Executive Committee adopted the "Measures for Restricting the Activities of Alien Parties" on the proposal of Chiang Kai-shek. Comrade Mao Tse-tung wrested the slogan of "unification" from the Kuomintang reactionaries and turned it into a revolutionary slogan for opposing the Kuomintang's divisive activities against the people and the nation.

[3] After the fall of Wuhan in October 1938, Japan's main policy became one of employing political means to lure the Kuomintang into capitulation. International imperialism, including the British and U.S. imperialists, also repeatedly suggested to Chiang Kai-shek that he should negotiate peace, and Chamberlain, the British Prime Minister, indicated that Britain would take part in the so-called "reconstruction of the Far East". The Japanese aggressors and the international imperialists stepped up their conspiracies in 1939. In April of that year, Clark-Kerr, the British ambassador to China, acted as an intermediary between Chiang Kai-shek and the Japanese aggressors in arranging a peace parley. In July an agreement was reached between Britain and Japan under which the British government was prepared to recognize the "actual situation" Japan had brought about in China.

[4] The "Measures for Restricting the Activities of Alien Parties" were secretly issued by the central authorities of the Kuomintang in 1939. They imposed severe

restrictions on communist and all other progressive ideas, speech and action, with the aim of disrupting all the anti-Japanese organizations of the people. They also stipulated that in places where, in the opinion of the Kuomintang, "the Communists were most active", the "law of collective responsibility and collective punishment" was to be enforced and an "information network", or counter-revolutionary secret service, was to be generally established within the *pao-chia* organizations. *Pao* and *chia* were then the basic administrative units of the Kuomintang's fascist regime. Ten households formed a *chia* and ten *chia* a *pao*.

INTERVIEW
WITH A *NEW CHINA DAILY* CORRESPONDENT
ON THE NEW INTERNATIONAL SITUATION

September 1, 1939

Correspondent: What is the significance of the Treaty of Non-Aggression Between the Soviet Union and Germany?[1]

Mao Tse-tung: The Soviet-German non-aggression treaty is the result of the growing socialist strength of the Soviet Union and the policy of peace persistently followed by the Soviet government. The treaty has shattered the intrigues by which the reactionary international bourgeoisie represented by Chamberlain and Daladier sought to instigate a Soviet-German war, has broken the encirclement of the Soviet Union by the German-Italian-Japanese anti-Communist bloc, strengthened peace between the Soviet Union and Germany, and safeguarded the progress of socialist construction in the Soviet Union. In the East it deals a blow to Japan and helps China; it strengthens the position of China's forces of resistance to Japan and deals a blow to the capitulators. All this provides a basis for helping the people throughout the world to win freedom and liberation. Such is the full political significance of the Soviet-German non-aggression treaty.

Question: Some people do not realize yet that the Soviet-German non-aggression treaty is the result of the breakdown of the Anglo-French-Soviet talks, but think that the Soviet-German treaty caused the breakdown. Will you please explain why the Anglo-French-Soviet talks failed?

Answer: The talks failed purely because the British and French governments were insincere. In recent years the reactionary international bourgeoisie, and primarily that of Britain and France, have consistently pursued the reactionary policy of "non-intervention" towards aggression by fascist Germany, Italy and Japan. Their purpose is to connive at wars of aggression and to profit by them.

Thus Britain and France flatly rejected the Soviet Union's repeated proposals for a genuine front against aggression; standing on the side-lines, they took a "non-interventionist" position and connived at German, Italian and Japanese aggression. Their aim was to step forward and intervene when the belligerents had worn each other out. In pursuit of this reactionary policy they sacrificed half of China to Japan, and the whole of Abyssinia, Spain, Austria and Czechoslovakia to Italy and Germany.[2] Then they wanted to sacrifice the Soviet Union. This plot was clearly revealed in the recent Anglo-French-Soviet talks. They lasted for more than four months, from April 15 to August 23, during which the Soviet Union exercised the utmost patience. But, from start to finish, Britain and France rejected the principle of equality and reciprocity; they demanded that the Soviet Union provide safeguards for their security, but refused to do likewise for the Soviet Union and the small Baltic states, so as to leave a gap through which Germany could attack, and they also refused to allow the passage of Soviet troops through Poland to fight the aggressor. That is why the talks broke down. In the meantime, Germany indicated her willingness to stop her activities against the Soviet Union and abandon the so-called Agreement Against the Communist International[3] and recognized the inviolability of the Soviet frontiers; hence the conclusion of the Soviet-German non-aggression treaty. The policy of "non-intervention" pursued by international and primarily Anglo-French reaction is a policy of "sitting on top of the mountain to watch the tigers fight", a downright imperialist policy of profiting at others' expense. This policy was initiated when Chamberlain took office, reached its climax in the Munich agreement of September last year and finally collapsed in the recent Anglo-French-Soviet talks. From now on the situation will inevitably develop into one of direct conflict between the two big imperialist blocs, the Anglo-French bloc and the German-Italian bloc. As I said in October 1938 at the Sixth Plenary Session of the Sixth Central Committee of our Party, "The inevitable result of Chamberlain's policy will be like 'lifting a rock only to drop it on one's own toes'." Chamberlain started with the aim of injuring others only to end up by ruining himself. This is the law of development which governs all reactionary policies.

Question: In your opinion, how will the present situation develop?

Answer: The international situation has already entered a new phase. The one-sided situation in the second imperialist war which has existed for some time, in other words, the situation in which, as a result of the policy of "non-intervention", one group of imperialist states attacks while another sits tight and looks on, will inevitably be replaced by a situation of all-embracing war as far as Europe is concerned. The second imperialist war has entered a new stage.

In Europe, a large-scale imperialist war is imminent between the German-Italian and the Anglo-French imperialist blocs which are contending for domination over the colonial peoples. In this war, each of the belligerents will brazenly declare its own cause to be just and that of its opponents unjust in order to delude people and win the support of public opinion. Actually this is a swindle. The aims of both sides are imperialist, both are fighting for the domination of colonies and semi-colonies and for spheres of influence, and both are waging a predatory war. At present, they are fighting over Poland, the Balkans and the Mediterranean littoral. This war is not at all a just war. The only just wars are non-predatory wars, wars of liberation. Communists will in no circumstances support any predatory war. They will, however, bravely step forward to support every just and non-predatory war for liberation, and they will stand in the forefront of the struggle. With Chamberlain and Daladier practising intimidation and bribery, the social-democratic parties affiliated to the Second International are splitting up. One section, the reactionary upper stratum, is following the same old disastrous road as in the First World War and is ready to support the new imperialist war. But another section will join with the Communists in forming a popular front against war and fascism. Chamberlain and Daladier are following in the footsteps of Germany and Italy and are becoming more and more reactionary, taking advantage of the war mobilization to put the state structure in their countries on a fascist footing and to militarize the economy. In short, the two big imperialist blocs are feverishly preparing for war and millions of people are facing the danger of mass slaughter. Surely all this will arouse movements of resistance among the masses. Whether in Germany or in Italy, Britain or France, or anywhere else in Europe or the world at large, if the people do not want to be used as imperialist cannon-fodder, they will have to rise up and oppose the imperialist war in every possible way.

Besides these two big blocs, there is a third bloc in the capitalist world, headed by the United States and including a number of Central and South American countries. In its own interests, this bloc will not enter the war for the time being. In the name of neutrality, U.S. imperialism is temporarily refraining from joining either of the belligerents, so as to be able to come on the scene later and contend for the leadership of the capitalist world. The fact that the U.S. bourgeoisie is not yet prepared to discard democracy and a peace-time economy at home is favourable to the world peace movement.

Badly hit by the Soviet-German treaty, Japanese imperialism is facing a future beset with still greater difficulties. Two factions within Japan are fighting over foreign policy. The militarists are contemplating an alliance with Germany and Italy for the purpose of gaining exclusive control of China, invading Southeast Asia and expelling Britain, the United States and France from the East; on the other hand, one section of the bourgeoisie would prefer to make concessions to Britain, the United States and France in order to concentrate on plundering China. At present, there is a strong tendency towards a compromise with Britain. The British reactionaries will offer Japan the joint partition of China plus financial and economic help, in return for which Japan will have to serve as the watchdog of British interests in the East, suppress the Chinese national liberation movement and contain the Soviet Union. Therefore, whatever happens, Japan's basic aim of conquering China will never change. The possibility that Japan will launch large-scale frontal military offensives in China may not be very great, but it will step up its political offensive to "use Chinese to subdue Chinese"[4] and its economic plundering of China to "sustain the war by means of war",[5] while keeping up its frantic "mopping-up" campaigns[6] in the occupied areas; moreover, it will work through Britain to force China to surrender. At a favourable moment it will propose an Eastern Munich and, with some relatively big concessions as bait, will try to coax and bully China into accepting its terms for surrender, so as to attain its aim of subjugating China. No matter what cabinet changes the Japanese ruling class may make, this imperialist aim will remain unchanged until the Japanese people rise in revolution.

Outside the capitalist world there is a world of light, the socialist Soviet Union. The Soviet-German treaty enables the Soviet Union to give greater help to the world movement for peace and to China in her resistance to Japan.

This is my appraisal of the international situation.

Question: In these circumstances, what are the prospects for China?

Answer: There are two possibilities. One is perseverance in resistance, unity and progress, which would mean national rejuvenation. The other is compromise, a split and retrogression, which would mean national subjugation.

In the new international situation, as Japan comes up against increased difficulties and China firmly refuses to compromise, the stage of strategic retreat will end for us and that of strategic stalemate will begin. The latter stage is one of preparation for the counter-offensive.

However, stalemate along the front means the reverse of stalemate in the enemy's rear; with the emergence of a stalemate along the front lines, the struggle behind the enemy's lines will become intense. Thus the large-scale "mopping-up" campaigns the enemy has been conducting in the occupied areas — mainly in northern China — since the fall of Wuhan will not only continue but will be intensified from now on. Furthermore, since the enemy's main policy at present consists in his political offensive to "use Chinese to subdue Chinese" and in his economic aggression for "sustaining the war by means of war", and since a Far Eastern Munich is the objective of British policy in the East, the danger of the surrender of the greater part of China and of an internal split will increase enormously. China is still far weaker than the enemy, and unless the whole country unites in an arduous struggle, it will not be able to build up strength for the counter-offensive.

Therefore, the most serious task for our country is still perseverance in the war, and there must be no slackening.

Beyond any doubt, China must on no account miss the present opportunity or make a wrong decision but must take a firm political stand.

In other words: First, firm adherence to the stand of resistance to Japan and opposition to any moves towards compromise. Determined blows must be struck at all the open or undercover Wang Ching-weis. China must firmly reject any blandishments, whether from Japan or from Britain, and must never take part in an Eastern Munich.

Second, firm adherence to the stand of unity and opposition to any moves towards a split. Strict vigilance must be maintained against such moves whether they stem from the Japanese imperialists, from other foreign countries, or from the capitulators at home. All internal friction harmful to the War of Resistance must be sternly checked.

Third, firm adherence to the stand of progress and opposition to any retrogression. Whether in the military, political, financial or economic sphere, or in party affairs, or in the field of culture and education, or in the mass movement, every theory, every institution, every measure harmful to the war must be re-examined and effectively changed to serve the War of Resistance.

If all this is done, China will be able effectively to build up her strength for the counter-offensive.

From now on the whole country must make "preparation for the counter-offensive" its over-all task in the War of Resistance.

Today, it is necessary on the one hand earnestly to sustain our defence along the front lines and vigorously to help the fighting behind the enemy lines and on the other to institute political, military and other reforms and build up tremendous strength, so that when the moment comes, the whole might of the nation can be thrown into a large-scale counter-offensive for the recovery of our lost territories.

NOTES

[1] The Treaty of Non-Aggression Between the Soviet Union and Germany was signed on August 23, 1939.

[2] Aided and abetted by the "non-intervention" policy of the British and French governments, fascist Germany and Italy committed a series of acts of aggression and achieved their purpose. Italy began her armed aggression against Abyssinia in October 1935 and occupied the whole country in May 1936. In July 1936 Germany and Italy started their joint armed intervention in the internal affairs of Spain and supported the fascist Franco in his rebellion against the Popular Front Government. After a prolonged war with the German and Italian interventionists and Franco's rebel troops, the Popular Front Government was defeated in March 1939. German troops occupied Austria in March 1938 and invaded the Sudeten area of Czechoslovakia in October. In March 1939 the whole of Czechoslovakia came under German occupation.

[3] The Agreement Against the Communist International was concluded between Japan and Germany in November 1936; Italy joined it in November 1937.

[4] "Using Chinese to subdue Chinese" was a sinister device of the Japanese imperialists in their aggression against China. To create divisions within the country, they cultivated various Chinese elements to serve as their stooges. After the outbreak of the war, they not only employed the openly pro-Japanese clique within the Kuomintang headed by Wang Ching-wei but also made use of Chiang Kai-shek's clique, in order to check the Communist Party which was the most resolute in resisting Japan. In 1939, they ceased attacking Chiang Kai-shek's troops and gave him political encouragement in his anti-Communist activities.

[5] "Sustaining the war by means of war" refers to Japan's policy of ruthless plunder of the Chinese areas under her occupation to meet the expenses of her aggressive war.

[6] "Mopping-up" campaigns were the Japanese aggressors' euphemism for their barbarous policy of triple atrocity — burning all, killing all and looting all.

INTERVIEW WITH THREE CORRESPONDENTS FROM THE CENTRAL NEWS AGENCY, THE *SAO TANG PAO* AND THE *HSIN MIN PAO*[1]

September 16, 1939

Correspondent: May we ask for your views on a few questions? We have read your statement of September 1 in today's *New China News*; it covers some of our questions, but there are others on which we would like you to elaborate. Our written questions are divided into three groups and we would be glad if you would give us your views on each of them.

Mao Tse-tung: I shall deal with them according to your list.

You ask if the War of Resistance has reached the stage of stalemate. I think it has in a sense — in the sense that there is a new international situation and that Japan is facing greater difficulties while China has stood firm against compromise. This does not rule out the possibility that the enemy may still launch fairly big offensive campaigns; for instance, he may attack Pakhoi, Changsha or even Sian. When we say that the enemy's large-scale strategic offensive and our strategic retreat have in a sense largely come to an end, we do not altogether exclude the possibility of further offensives and retreats. As for the specific task in the new stage, it is to prepare for the counter-offensive, and this concept covers everything. That is to say, during the stage of stalemate China must build up all the strength required for the future counter-offensive. To prepare for the counter-offensive does not mean launching it immediately, since it cannot be done unless the conditions are ripe. What we are talking about is the strategic, and not the tactical, counter-offensive. Tactical counter-offensives, such as our repulse of the enemy's "mopping-up" campaigns in southeastern Shansi, are not only possible but absolutely necessary. But the time has not yet arrived for an all-out strategic counter-offensive, and we are now at the stage of actively preparing for it. At this stage we shall still have to repulse a certain number of offensive campaigns the enemy may launch at the front.

To itemize the tasks of the new stage, in the enemy's rear we must keep up guerrilla warfare, smash his "mopping-up" campaigns and defeat his economic aggression; at the front we must strengthen our military defences and repulse any offensive campaign the enemy may launch; in the Great Rear Area the main thing is to work hard for political reforms. All these form the specific content of our preparations for the counter-offensive.

Internal political reform is very important because at present the enemy is mainly carrying on a political offensive, and so we must strengthen our political resistance in particular. In other words, the problem of democracy must be solved as soon as possible, for only in this way can we increase our capacity for political resistance and build up our military strength. China has to rely mainly on her own efforts in the War of Resistance. We have stood for regeneration through our own efforts, and this has become even more important in the new international situation. The essence of such regeneration is democracy.

Question: You have just said that democracy is essential to winning victory in the War of Resistance through our own efforts. How can such a system be brought into being in the present circumstances?

Answer: Dr. Sun Yat-sen originally envisaged the three stages of military rule, political tutelage and constitutional government.[2] But in his "Statement on My Departure for the North"[3] issued shortly before his death, he no longer spoke of three stages, but said instead that a national assembly must be convened immediately. This shows that Dr. Sun himself modified his views many years ago in the light of changing circumstances. In the grave situation prevailing today, with the War of Resistance going on, both the early convening of a national assembly and the introduction of democratic government are imperative for averting the calamity of national subjugation and for driving out the enemy. Opinions differ on this question. Some say that the common people are ignorant and democratic government cannot be introduced. They are wrong. The common people have made very rapid progress in the war and, given leadership and proper policy, democratic government can certainly be introduced. For instance, it has been put into practice in northern China. Most of the heads of districts, townships and the *pao* and *chia* there are chosen by popular vote. Even some county magistrates have been chosen in this way, and progressive elements and promising young people have been elected. The question should be thrown open to public discussion.

In the second group on your list, you raise the question of "restricting alien parties", that is, the question of the friction in various localities. Your concern over this matter is justified. There has been some improvement recently, but fundamentally the situation remains unchanged.

Question: Has the Communist Party made its position on this question clear to the Central Government?

Answer: We have protested.

Question: In what way?

Answer: Our Party representative, Comrade Chou En-lai, wrote a letter to Generalissimo Chiang Kai-shek as early as July. Then again on August 1, people from all walks of life in Yenan sent a telegram to the Generalissimo and the National Government, demanding the withdrawal of the "Measures for Restricting the Activities of Alien Parties", which had been secretly circulated and which are at the very root of the "friction" in various places.

Question: Has there been any reply from the Central Government?

Answer: No. But it is said that there are also people in the Kuomintang who disapprove of these measures. As everybody knows, an army that participates in the common fight against Japan is a friendly army, not an "alien army", and similarly, a political party that participates in the common fight against Japan is a friendly party, not an "alien party". There are many parties and groups taking part in the War of Resistance and, while they vary in strength, they are fighting in the same cause; surely they must all unite and must in no circumstances "restrict" one another. Which party is an alien party? The party of the traitors headed by Wang Ching-wei, the running dog of Japan, because it has nothing in common politically with the anti-Japanese parties; that is the kind of party which should be restricted. Between the Kuomintang and the Communist Party there is common political ground, namely, resistance to Japanese aggression. Therefore, the problem is to concentrate all our strength on opposing and checking Japan and Wang Ching-wei, and not on opposing and checking the Communist Party. This is the only basis for formulating correct slogans.

Wang Ching-wei has three slogans: "Oppose Chiang Kai-shek", "Oppose the Communist Party", and "Be friends with Japan". Wang Ching-wei is the common enemy of the Kuomintang, the Communist Party and the entire people. But the Communist Party is not the enemy of the Kuomintang, nor is the Kuomintang the enemy of the Communist Party; they should unite and help each other rather than oppose or "restrict" each other. The slogans on our side must be different from Wang Ching-wei's, they must be the opposite of his and never be confused with them. If he says, "Oppose Chiang Kai-shek", everyone should support Chiang Kai-shek; if he says, "Oppose the Communist Party", everyone should unite with the Communist Party; and if he says, "Be friends with Japan", everyone should resist Japan. We should support whatever the enemy opposes and oppose whatever the enemy supports. In articles nowadays people often quote the saying, "Do not sadden your friends and gladden your enemies." It comes from a letter which Chu Fou, a general under Liu Hsiu of the Eastern Han Dynasty, wrote to Peng Chung, the prefect of Yuyang. In context it reads, "Whatever you do, you must be sure that you do not sadden your friends and gladden your enemies." Chu Fou's words express a clear-cut political principle which we must never forget.

In your list of questions you also ask about the Communist Party's attitude to what has come to be known as "friction". I tell you frankly that we are absolutely opposed to friction between the anti-Japanese parties, which cancels out their strength. But if anyone persists in using violence against us, tries to bully us and resorts to repression, the Communist Party will have to take a firm stand. Our attitude is: We will not attack unless we are attacked; if we are attacked, we will certainly counter-attack. But our stand is strictly one of self-defence; no Communist is permitted to go beyond the principle of self-defence.

Question: How about the friction in northern China?

Answer: Chang Yin-wu and Chin Chi-jung are the two expert friction-mongers there. Chang Yin-wu in Hopei and Chin Chi-jung in Shantung are simply violating all laws, human or divine, and are scarcely distinguishable from the traitors. They seldom fight the enemy but often attack the Eighth Route Army. We have already sent Generalissimo Chiang a mass of indisputable evidence, such as Chang Yin-wu's orders to his subordinates to attack the Eighth Route Army.

Question: Is there any friction with the New Fourth Army?

Answer: Yes, there is. The incident of the Pingkiang massacre has shocked the whole nation.

Question: Some people say that the united front is important but that the Border Region Government should be abolished for the sake of unification. What do you think of this?

Answer: Nonsense of all sorts is being talked everywhere, the so-called abolition of the Border Region being one example. The Shensi-Kansu-Ningsia Border Region is a democratic anti-Japanese base area and is politically the most progressive region in the whole country. What grounds are there for abolishing it? Moreover, Generalissimo Chiang long ago recognized the Border Region and the Executive Yuan of the National Government officially recognized it as long ago as the winter of the 26th year of the Republic (1937). China certainly needs to be unified, but it must be unified on the basis of resistance, unity and progress. If unification is sought on the opposite basis, the country will perish.

Question: Since there are different interpretations of unification, is there any possibility of a split between the Kuomintang and the Communist Party?

Answer: If we are merely talking of possibilities, we can envisage both the possibility of unity and the possibility of a split, depending on the attitudes of the Kuomintang and the Communist Party, and especially of the people throughout the country. As far as we Communists are concerned, we have long made it clear that our policy is co-operation, and that we not only hope for long-term co-operation but are working hard for it. It is said that at the Fifth Plenary Session of the Central Executive Committee of the Kuomintang, Generalissimo Chiang Kai-shek also declared that domestic problems should not be solved by force. Confronted with a formidable enemy and bearing in mind the lessons of the past, the Kuomintang and the Communist Party must each persist in long-term co-operation and avoid a split. But to avoid all possibility of a split, political guarantees for long-term co-operation must be found, namely, perseverance in the War of Resistance and the introduction of democratic government. With these, unity can be maintained and a split avoided; it depends on the common effort of the two parties and the whole nation and the effort must be made. "Persist in resistance and oppose capitulation", "Persist in unity and oppose a split" and "Persist in progress and oppose retrogression" — these are the three great political slogans our Party put forward in its Manifesto of July 7 this year. In our opinion, this is the only way China can avoid subjugation and drive out the enemy. There is no other way.

NOTES

[1] The Central News Agency was the official Kuomintang news agency, the *Sao Tang Pao* was a paper run by military circles in the Kuomintang government, and the *Hsin Min Pao* was one of the mouthpieces of the national bourgeoisie.

[2] See Dr. Sun Yat-sen's *Programme of National Reconstruction*. For a long time, the Kuomintang reactionary clique headed by Chiang Kai-shek sought to justify their ruthless counter-revolutionary dictatorship by representing it as either the stage of "military rule" or that of "political tutelage" as envisaged by Dr. Sun.

[3] This statement was made by Dr. Sun Yat-sen on November 10, 1924, two days before he left Canton for Peking at the invitation of Feng Yu-hsiang. In this statement, which won the support of the whole nation, Dr. Sun reiterated his opposition to imperialism and the warlords and urged that a national assembly be called to settle the problems facing the country. Feng Yu-hsiang originally belonged to the Chihli warlord clique, but in the winter of 1924, when war broke out for the second time between them and the Fengtien warlord clique, he refused to fight and led his troops back to Peking, thus causing the downfall of Wu Pei-fu, the actual leader of the Chihli warlords. It was then that he sent the telegram inviting Dr. Sun to Peking.

THE IDENTITY OF INTERESTS
BETWEEN THE SOVIET UNION AND
ALL MANKIND

September 28, 1939

With the approach of the twenty-second anniversary of the Great October Socialist Revolution, the Sino-Soviet Cultural Association has asked me for an article. On the basis of my own observations, I should like to elucidate a few problems concerning the Soviet Union and China. For they are being discussed by the people in China today and apparently no definite conclusions have yet been reached. It may be of some help if I take this opportunity to set forth my views for the consideration of those who are concerned about the war in Europe and about Sino-Soviet relations.

Some people say that the Soviet Union does not want the world to remain at peace because the outbreak of a world war is to its advantage, and that the present war was precipitated by the Soviet Union's conclusion of a non-aggression treaty with Germany instead of a treaty of mutual assistance with Britain and France. I consider this view incorrect. The foreign policy of the Soviet Union over a very long period of time has consistently been one of peace, a policy based on the close links between its own interests and those of the overwhelming majority of mankind. For its own socialist construction the Soviet Union has always needed peace, has always needed to strengthen its peaceful relations with other countries and prevent an anti-Soviet war; for the sake of peace on a world scale, it has also needed to check the aggression of the fascist countries, curb the war-mongering of the so-called democratic countries and delay the outbreak of an imperialist world war for as long as possible. The Soviet Union has long devoted great energy to the cause of world peace. For instance, it has joined the League of Nations,[1] signed treaties of mutual assistance with France and Czechoslovakia[2] and tried hard to conclude security pacts with Britain and all other countries that might be willing to have peace. After Germany and Italy jointly invaded Spain and when Britain, the United States and France adopted a policy of nominal "non-intervention" but of actual connivance at their aggression, the Soviet Union opposed the "non-intervention" policy and gave the Spanish republican forces active help in their resistance to Germany and Italy. After Japan invaded China and when the same three powers adopted the same kind of "non-intervention" policy, the Soviet Union not only concluded a non-aggression treaty with China but gave China active help in her resistance. When Britain and France connived at Hitler's aggression and sacrificed Austria and Czechoslovakia, the Soviet Union spared no effort in exposing the sinister aims behind the Munich policy and made proposals to Britain and France for checking further aggression. When Poland became the burning question in the spring and summer of this year and it was touch-and-go whether world war would break out, the Soviet Union negotiated with Britain and France for over four months, despite Chamberlain's and Daladier's complete lack of sincerity, in an endeavour to conclude a treaty of mutual assistance to prevent the outbreak of war. But all these efforts were blocked by the imperialist policy of the British and French governments, a policy of conniving at, instigating and spreading war, so that eventually the cause of world peace was thwarted and the imperialist world war broke out. The governments of Britain, the United States and France had no genuine desire to prevent this war; on the contrary, they helped to bring it about. Their refusal to come to terms with the Soviet Union and conclude a really effective treaty of mutual assistance based on equality and reciprocity proved that they wanted not peace but war. Everybody knows that in the contemporary world rejection of the Soviet Union means rejection of peace. Even Lloyd George, that typical representative of the British bourgeoisie, knows this.[3] It was in these circumstances, and when Germany agreed to stop her anti-Soviet activities, abandon the Agreement Against the Communist International and recognize the inviolability of the Soviet frontiers, that the Soviet-German non-aggression treaty was concluded. The plan of Britain, the United States and France was to egg Germany on to attack the Soviet Union, so that they themselves, "sitting on top of the mountain to watch the tigers fight", could come down and take over after the Soviet Union and Germany had worn each other out. The Soviet-German non-aggression treaty smashed this plot. In overlooking this plot and the schemes of the Anglo-French imperialists who connived at and instigated war and precipitated a world war, some of our fellow-countrymen have actually been taken in by the sugary propaganda of these schemers. These crafty politicians were not the least bit interested in checking aggression against Spain, against China, or against Austria and Czechoslovakia; on the contrary, they connived at aggression and instigated war, playing the proverbial role of the fisherman who set the snipe and clam at each other and then took advantage of both. They euphemistically described their actions as "non-intervention", but what they actually did was to "sit on top of the mountain to watch the tigers fight". Quite a number of people throughout the world have been fooled by the honeyed words of Chamberlain and his partners, failing to see the murderous intent behind their smiles, or to understand that the Soviet-German non-aggression treaty was concluded only after Chamberlain and Daladier had made up their minds to reject the Soviet Union and bring about the imperialist war. It is time for these people to wake up. The fact that the Soviet Union worked hard to preserve world peace to the very last minute proves that the interests of the Soviet Union are identical with those of the overwhelming majority of mankind. This is the first question I wanted to talk about.

Some people say that now that the second imperialist world war has broken out, the Soviet Union will probably take sides — in other words, the Soviet Red Army seems to be on the point of joining the German imperialist front. I consider this view incorrect. On whichever side, the Anglo-French or the German, the war that has just broken out is an unjust, predatory and imperialist war. The Communist Parties and the people of all countries should rise up against it and expose the imperialist character of both belligerents, for this imperialist war brings only harm and no benefit whatever to the people of the world, and they should expose the criminal acts of the social-democratic parties in supporting the imperialist war and betraying the interests of the proletariat. The Soviet Union is a socialist country, a country in which the Communist Party is in power, and it necessarily maintains a clear-cut twofold attitude towards wars: (1) It firmly refuses to take part in any unjust, predatory and imperialist war and maintains strict neutrality towards the belligerents. Hence the Soviet Red Army will never disregard principles and join either of the imperialist war fronts. (2) It actively supports just and non-predatory wars of liberation. For instance, it helped the Chinese people in their war of the Northern

Expedition thirteen years ago and the Spanish people in their war against Germany and Italy up to this last year; it has been helping the Chinese people in their War of Resistance Against Japan for the last two years and the Mongolian people in resisting Japan for the last few months; and it will certainly give help to any war for the liberation of the masses or of a nation which may break out in other countries in the future, and will certainly give help to any wars that contribute to the defence of peace. The history of the Soviet Union in the last twenty-two years has already proved this, and history will prove it again in the future. Some people regard the Soviet Union's trade with Germany, which is based on the Soviet-German commercial agreement, as an act of participation in the war on the German side. This view, too, is wrong, for it confuses trade with participation in war. Trade must not be confused with participation in war or with rendering assistance. For example, the Soviet Union traded with Germany and Italy during the Spanish war, yet nobody in the world said that the Soviet Union was helping Germany and Italy in their aggression against Spain; on the contrary, people said that it was helping Spain in resisting this aggression, the reason being that the Soviet Union actually did give help to Spain. Again, during the present Sino-Japanese war the Soviet Union is trading with Japan, but nobody in the world is saying that the Soviet Union is helping Japan in its aggression against China; on the contrary, people say that it is helping China to resist this aggression, the reason being that it actually is helping China. At present, both sides in the world war have trading relations with the Soviet Union, but this cannot be regarded as assistance to either, still less as taking part in the war. Only if the nature of the war changes, if the war in one or more countries undergoes certain necessary changes and becomes advantageous to the Soviet Union and the peoples of the world, will it be possible for the Soviet Union to help or participate; otherwise it will not. As for the fact that the Soviet Union is obliged to trade to a greater or lesser extent on more or less preferential terms with one or another of the belligerents according to how friendly or hostile it happens to be, that depends not on the Soviet Union but on the attitude of the belligerents. But even if one or several countries adopt an anti-Soviet attitude, the Soviet Union will not break off trade relations with them so long as they, like Germany before August 23, are willing to maintain diplomatic relations and conclude trade treaties with it, and do not declare war on it. It should be clearly understood that such commercial relations do not mean assistance, much less participation in war. This is the second question I wanted to talk about.

Many people in China are bewildered by the fact that Soviet troops have entered Poland.[4] The Polish question should be viewed from various angles, from that of Germany, of Britain and France, of the Polish government, of the Polish people and of the Soviet Union. Germany started the war in order to plunder the Polish people and smash one flank of the Anglo-French imperialist front. By its nature, Germany's war is imperialist and should be opposed, not approved. As for Britain and France, they have regarded Poland as an object of plunder for their finance capital, exploited her to thwart the German imperialist attempt at a world re-division of the spoils, and made her a flank of their own imperialist front. Thus their war is an imperialist war, their so-called aid to Poland being merely for the purpose of contending with Germany for the domination of Poland, and this war, too, should be opposed, not approved. As for the Polish government, it was a fascist, reactionary government of the Polish landlords and bourgeoisie which ruthlessly exploited the workers and peasants and oppressed the Polish democrats; moreover, it was a government of Greater Poland chauvinists which ruthlessly oppressed the non-Polish minority nationalities — the Ukrainians, Byelorussians, Jews, Germans, Lithuanians and others, who number more than ten million; it was itself an imperialist government. In the war, this reactionary Polish government willingly drove the Polish people to serve as cannon-fodder for British and French finance capital, and it willingly served as a sector of the reactionary front of international finance capital. For twenty years the Polish government consistently opposed the Soviet Union and, during the talks between Britain, France and the Soviet Union, it obstinately rejected the Soviet offer to help it with troops. Moreover, it was an utterly incompetent government, its huge army of over 1,500,000 collapsed at the first blow, and it brought the country to ruin in just two weeks, leaving the Polish people under the heel of German imperialism. Such were the towering crimes of the Polish government and it would be wrong for us to waste any sympathy on it. As for the Polish people, they are victims; they should rise up against the oppression of the German fascists and against their own reactionary landlord and bourgeois classes, and establish an independent, free and democratic Polish state. Without the slightest doubt, our sympathy must go out to the Polish people. As for the Soviet Union, its actions have been perfectly

just. It was confronted by two problems. The first problem was
whether to let the whole of Poland fall under the rule of German
imperialism or to help the minority nationalities of eastern Poland win
their liberation. It chose the second course. A vast stretch of territory
inhabited by Byelorussians and Ukrainians had been snatched from
the new-born Soviet state by the German imperialists as far back as
1918 when the Treaty of Brest-Litovsk was signed, and it was later
arbitrarily put under the rule of the reactionary Polish government by
the Treaty of Versailles. What the Soviet Union has now done is
merely to recover its lost territory, liberate the oppressed Byelorussians and Ukrainians and save them from German oppression. The
news dispatches of the last few days show how warmly these minority
nationalities are welcoming the Red Army with food and drink as
their liberator, while not a single report of this kind has come in
from western Poland which has been occupied by German troops or
from the places in western Germany which have been occupied by
French troops. This shows clearly that the Soviet Union's war is a
just and non-predatory war of liberation, a war helping to liberate
weak and small nations and free the people. On the other hand, the
war being waged by Germany and by Britain and France is an
unjust, predatory and imperialist war for the oppression of other
nations and peoples. The second problem confronting the Soviet Union
was Chamberlain's endeavour to continue his old anti-Soviet policy.
His policy was, first, to impose a large-scale blockade on Germany
and bring pressure on her from the west; second, to try to form an
alliance with the United States and to buy over Italy, Japan and the
countries of northern Europe so as to isolate Germany; and third, to
bribe Germany with the offer of Poland, and even of Hungary and
Rumania. In short, Chamberlain resorted to all kinds of intimidation
and bribery to get Germany to renounce the Soviet-German non-
aggression treaty and turn her guns on the Soviet Union. This intrigue
has been going on for some time and will continue. The powerful
Soviet army's entry into eastern Poland, with the aim of recovering
the Soviet Union's own territory and liberating the weak and small
nationalities there, was at the same time a practical move to prevent the
forces of German aggression from expanding eastward and to frustrate
Chamberlain's intrigue. Judging by the news reports of the last few
days, this Soviet policy has been most successful. It is a concrete
manifestation of the identity of the interests of the Soviet Union with
those of the overwhelming majority of mankind, including those of

the oppressed people under reactionary Polish rule. This is the third question I wanted to talk about.

The whole situation since the conclusion of the Soviet-German non-aggression treaty constitutes a great blow to Japan and a great help to China; it strengthens the position of those resisting Japan and weakens the capitulators. The Chinese people have rightly welcomed this treaty. However, since the signing of the Nomonhan truce agreement,[5] British and U.S. news agencies have been busy spreading the story that a Soviet-Japanese non-aggression treaty is about to be signed, and this has caused concern among some Chinese people, who think that the Soviet Union may no longer help China. I believe they are wrong. The nature of the Nomonhan truce agreement is the same as that of the previous Changkufeng truce agreement;[6] that is to say, the Japanese militarists, being compelled to admit defeat, have had to recognize the inviolability of the Soviet and Mongolian frontiers. These truce agreements will enable the Soviet Union to increase rather than decrease its aid to China. As for the talk about a Japanese-Soviet non-aggression treaty, the Soviet Union has been proposing it for many years but Japan has invariably rejected it. Now there is a section of the Japanese ruling class that wants such a treaty with the Soviet Union, but whether the Soviet Union will be willing depends on the basic principle of whether the treaty will accord with the interests of the Soviet Union and of the overwhelming majority of mankind. Specifically, it depends on whether the treaty will conflict with the interests of China's war of national liberation. Judging from Stalin's report to the Eighteenth Congress of the Communist Party of the Soviet Union on March 10 this year and Molotov's speech at the Supreme Soviet of the U.S.S.R. on May 30, I think the Soviet Union will not alter this basic principle. Even if such a treaty were to be concluded, the Soviet Union would certainly not agree to anything that would restrict its freedom of action in helping China. The interests of the Soviet Union will always conform and never conflict with the interests of China's national liberation. I hold this as absolutely beyond doubt. People who are prejudiced against the Soviet Union are capitalizing on the Nomonhan truce agreement and on the talk about a Japanese-Soviet non-aggression treaty in order to make trouble and stir up ill feeling between the two great nations of China and the Soviet Union. This is what the British, U.S. and French intriguers and the Chinese capitulators are doing; it is highly dangerous and we must thoroughly expose their dirty tricks. It is obvious that

China's foreign policy must be one of resistance to Japanese aggression. This policy means primarily relying on our own efforts, while not ignoring any possibility of securing help from abroad. Now that the imperialist world war has broken out, foreign help is coming chiefly from three sources: (1) the socialist Soviet Union, (2) the people of the capitalist countries, and (3) the oppressed nations in the colonies and semi-colonies. These are our only reliable sources of help. Anything else that might be called foreign help, even if it might become available, can only be regarded as supplementary and temporary. Of course, China should try to obtain such supplementary and temporary foreign help, but must never depend too much on it or consider it reliable. China should maintain strict neutrality towards the belligerents in the imperialist war and not join either side. To maintain that China should join the Anglo-French imperialist war front is a capitulator's view, which is harmful to the War of Resistance as well as to the independence and liberation of the Chinese nation, and it should be flatly rejected. This is the fourth question I wanted to talk about.

These four questions are being widely discussed by our fellow-countrymen. It is a very good thing that they are giving attention to the study of international problems, to the relations between the imperialist world war and China's War of Resistance and between the Soviet Union and China, because their aim is victory over Japanese aggression. Here I have given some of my basic views on these questions, and I hope that readers will not spare their comments.

NOTES

[1] The League of Nations was an organization formed by Britain, France, Japan and other imperialist powers after World War I for the re-division of the world through bargaining and temporary adjustments of conflicting interests. In 1931 the Japanese imperialists occupied China's Northeast and in 1933 Japan withdrew from the League of Nations in order to be able to extend her aggression more freely. In the same year the German fascists came to power, and later they, too, withdrew from the League of Nations to facilitate their preparations for a war of aggression. It was in 1934, when the threat of a fascist war of aggression was growing, that the Soviet Union joined the League of Nations; in this way the possibility arose of this imperialist organization for the re-division of the world being turned into one that might serve the cause of world peace. Italy withdrew from the League of Nations after her invasion of Abyssinia in 1935.

[2] The Treaty of Mutual Assistance Between the Union of Soviet Socialist Republics and France and the Treaty of Mutual Assistance Between the Union of Soviet Socialist Republics and the Czechoslovak Republic were concluded in 1935.

[3] The British bourgeois politician Lloyd George, who had been Prime Minister during World War I, declared in Parliament in November 1938 when Britain, France, Germany and Italy were going to negotiate, that peace could not be won by rejecting Soviet participation in the negotiations.

[4] On September 1, 1939, the Germans invaded Poland and occupied most of her territory. On the 17th the reactionary Polish government fled abroad. On the same day, the Soviet Union dispatched its troops to eastern Poland in order to recover its own lost territories, emancipate the oppressed Ukrainian and Byelorussian peoples and check the eastward drive of the German fascist troops.

[5] The Nomonhan truce agreement was concluded in Moscow in September 1939. In May 1939 the Japanese and the puppet "Manchukuo" troops had jointly attacked the troops of the Soviet Union and the People's Republic of Mongolia at Nomonhan, on the border between Mongolia and "Manchukuo", and were completely defeated by the Soviet and Mongolian forces in a heroic war of self-defence. The Japanese then sued for peace. The truce agreement provided for an immediate cease-fire and the formation of a commission of four, with two representatives from each side, to demarcate the frontier between the Mongolian People's Republic and the puppet state of "Manchukuo" at places where the conflict had taken place.

[6] The Changkufeng truce agreement was concluded in Moscow on August 11, 1938. At the end of July and the beginning of August 1938, the Japanese had committed acts of provocation against the Soviet troops in the Changkufeng district on the border between China, Korea and the Soviet Union and had been vigorously repulsed. The Japanese sued for peace. The truce agreement provided for an immediate cease-fire and the formation of a commission of four, with two representatives from the Soviet side and two from the Japanese-"Manchukuo" side, to investigate the boundary lines and make a final settlement.

INTRODUCING *THE COMMUNIST*

October 4, 1939

The Central Committee has long planned to publish an internal Party journal, and now at last the plan has materialized. Such a journal is necessary for building up a bolshevized Chinese Communist Party, a party which is national in scale and has a broad mass character, a party which is fully consolidated ideologically, politically and organizationally. This necessity is all the more obvious in the present situation, which has special features: on the one hand, the danger of capitulation, of a split and of retrogression within the Anti-Japanese National United Front is increasing daily, while on the other, our Party has stepped out of its narrow confines and become a major national party. The duty of the Party is to mobilize the masses to overcome the dangers of capitulation, a split and retrogression and prepare against all possible eventualities so that in case they occur, the Party and the revolution will not suffer unexpected losses. An internal Party journal is indeed most necessary at a time like this.

This internal Party journal is called *The Communist*. What is its purpose? What will it deal with? In what way will it differ from other Party publications?

Its purpose is to help build a bolshevized Chinese Communist Party which is national in scale, has a broad mass character, and is fully consolidated ideologically, politically and organizationally. The building of such a party is imperative for the victory of the Chinese revolution and on the whole the subjective and objective conditions for it are present; indeed this great undertaking is now in progress. A special Party periodical is needed to help achieve this great task, which is beyond the capability of an ordinary Party publication, and this is why *The Communist* is now being published.

To a certain extent our Party is already national in scale and has a broad mass character; and it is already a bolshevized party, consolidated ideologically, politically and organizationally, so far as its core of leadership, a part of its membership and its general line and revolutionary work are concerned.

That being so, why set a new task?

The reason is that we now have many new branches, which have a great many new members but which cannot yet be considered as having a broad mass character, as being ideologically, politically and organizationally consolidated, or as being bolshevized. At the same time, there is the problem of raising the political level of the older Party members and of making further progress in bolshevizing the older branches and consolidating them ideologically, politically and organizationally. The circumstances in which the Party now finds itself and the responsibilities it is shouldering are quite unlike those in the revolutionary civil war period; the circumstances are much more complex and the responsibilities much heavier.

This is the period of the national united front, and we have formed a united front with the bourgeoisie; this is the period of the War of Resistance Against Japan, and the armed forces of our Party are at the front, fighting a ruthless war against the enemy in co-ordination with the friendly armies; this is the period when our Party has become a major national party and is therefore no longer what it was before. If we take all these factors together, we shall understand how glorious and momentous is the task we have set ourselves, the task of "building up a bolshevized Chinese Communist Party, a party which is national in scale and has a broad mass character, a party fully consolidated ideologically, politically and organizationally".

It is this kind of party that we now want to build, but how shall we go about it? We cannot answer this question without going into the history of our Party and of its eighteen years of struggle.

It is fully eighteen years since our First National Congress in 1921. In these eighteen years our Party has gone through many great struggles. And the members of the Party, its cadres and organizations, have all tempered themselves in these great struggles. They have had the experience both of splendid victories and grave defeats in the revolution. The Party established a national united front with the bourgeoisie and, with the break-up of this united front, engaged in a bitter armed struggle with the big bourgeoisie and its allies. During the last three years, it has again entered into a period of a national united front with the bourgeoisie. It is through this kind of complex relationship with the Chinese bourgeoisie that the Chinese revolution and the Communist Party of China have progressed in their development. This is a special historical feature, a feature peculiar to the revolution in colonial and semi-colonial countries and not to be found in the revolutionary history of any capitalist country. Moreover, since China is a semi-colonial and semi-feudal country, since her political, economic and cultural development is uneven, since her economy is predominantly semi-feudal and since her territory is vast, it follows that the character of the Chinese revolution in its present stage is bourgeois-democratic, that its principal targets are imperialism and feudalism and that its basic motive forces are the proletariat, the peasantry and the urban petty bourgeoisie, with the national bourgeoisie taking part at certain times and to a certain extent; it also follows that the principal form of struggle in the Chinese revolution is armed struggle. Indeed, the history of our Party may be called a history of armed struggle. Comrade Stalin has said, "In China the armed revolution is fighting the armed counter-revolution. That is one of the specific features and one of the advantages of the Chinese revolution."[1] This is perfectly true. The specific feature peculiar to semi-colonial China is not present, or is not present in the same way, in the history of the revolutions led by Communist Parties in the capitalist countries. Thus, there are two basic specific features in the Chinese bourgeois-democratic revolution: (1) the proletariat either establishes a revolutionary national united front with the bourgeoisie, or is forced to break it up; and (2) armed struggle is the principal form of the revolution. Here we do not describe the Party's relations with the peasantry and the urban petty bourgeoisie as a basic specific feature, first, because these relations are in principle the same as those which confront Communist Parties all over the world, and secondly, because armed struggle in China is, in essence, peasant war and the Party's relations with the peasantry and its close relations with the peasant war are one and the same thing.

It is because of these two basic specific features, in fact precisely because of them, that the building up and bolshevization of our Party are proceeding in special circumstances. The Party's failures or successes, its retreats or advances, its contraction or expansion, its development and consolidation are inevitably linked up with its relations with the bourgeoisie and with armed struggle. When the Party takes a correct political line on the question of forming a united front with the bourgeoisie or of breaking it up when forced to do so, our Party moves a step forward in its development, consolidation and bolshevization; but when it takes an incorrect line on its relations with the bourgeoisie, then our Party moves a step backward. Similarly, when our Party handles the question of revolutionary armed struggle correctly, it moves a step forward in its development, consolidation and bolshevization; but when it handles the question incorrectly, it moves a step backward. Thus, for eighteen years, the building and bolshevization of the Party have been closely linked with its political line, with the correct or incorrect handling of the questions of the united front and armed struggle. This conclusion is clearly confirmed by the eighteen years of our Party's history. Or conversely, the more bolshevized the Party, the more correctly can it decide upon its political line and handle the questions of the united front and armed struggle. This conclusion, too, is clearly confirmed by the eighteen years of our Party's history.

Therefore the united front, armed struggle and Party building are the three fundamental questions for our Party in the Chinese revolution. Having a correct grasp of these three questions and their interrelations is tantamount to giving correct leadership to the whole Chinese revolution. We are now able to draw correct conclusions concerning these three questions by virtue of our abundant experience in the eighteen years of our Party's history, our rich and profound experience of failures and successes, retreats and advances, contraction and expansion. This means that we are now able to handle the questions of the united front, of armed struggle and of Party building in a correct way. It also means that our eighteen years of experience have taught us that the united front, armed struggle and Party building are the Chinese Communist Party's three "magic weapons", its three principal magic weapons for defeating the enemy in the Chinese revolution. This is a great achievement of the Chinese Communist Party and of the Chinese revolution.

Here let us briefly discuss each of the three magic weapons, each of the three questions.

In the last eighteen years, the united front of the Chinese proletariat with the bourgeoisie and other classes has developed under three different sets of circumstances or through three different stages: the First Great Revolution from 1924 to 1927, the War of Agrarian Revolution from 1927 to 1937, and the present War of Resistance Against Japan. The history of the three stages has confirmed the following laws:

(1) The Chinese national bourgeoisie will take part in the struggle against imperialism and the feudal warlords at certain

times and to a certain extent, because foreign oppression is the greatest oppression to which China is subjected. Therefore, at such times, the proletariat should form a united front with the national bourgeoisie and maintain it as far as possible. (2) In other historical circumstances, the Chinese national bourgeoisie will vacillate and defect because of its economic and political flabbiness. Therefore the composition of China's revolutionary united front will not remain constant at all times, but is liable to change. At one time the national bourgeoisie may take part in it, at another it may not. (3) The Chinese big bourgeoisie, which is comprador in character, is a class which directly serves imperialism and is fostered by it. Hence the comprador Chinese big bourgeoisie has always been a target of the revolution. However, different groups within this big bourgeoisie are backed by different imperialist powers, so that when contradictions among these powers become sharper and when the edge of the revolution is mainly directed against a particular power, the big bourgeois groups dependent upon the other powers may join the struggle against that particular imperialist power to a certain extent and for a certain time. At such times, in order to weaken the enemy and add to its own reserves, the Chinese proletariat may form a united front with these groups and should maintain it as far as possible, provided it is advantageous to the revolution. (4) The comprador big bourgeoisie continues to be most reactionary even when it joins the united front alongside the proletariat in struggling against the common enemy. It stubbornly opposes any ideological, political and organizational development of the proletariat and the proletarian party, tries to impose restrictions on them and employs disruptive tactics such as deception, blandishments, "corrosion" and savage attacks against them; moreover, it does all this to prepare for capitulating to the enemy and splitting the united front. (5) The peasantry is the firm ally of the proletariat. (6) The urban petty bourgeoisie is a reliable ally.

The validity of these laws was confirmed during the First Great Revolution and the Agrarian Revolution, and it is being confirmed again in the present War of Resistance. Therefore, in forming a united front with the bourgeoisie (and especially with the big bourgeoisie), the party of the proletariat must carry on a stern and resolute struggle on two fronts. On the one hand, it is necessary to combat the error of neglecting the possibility that the bourgeoisie may join in the revolutionary struggle at certain times and to a certain extent. It is an error of "Left" closed-doorism to regard the bourgeoisie in China as being the same as in the capitalist countries, and consequently to neglect the policy of forming a united front with the bourgeoisie and maintaining it for as long as possible. On the other hand, it is also necessary to combat the error of identifying the programme, policy, ideology, practice, etc. of the proletariat with those of the bourgeoisie, and neglecting the differences in principle between them. The error here consists in neglecting the fact that the bourgeoisie (and especially the big bourgeoisie) not only exerts an influence on the petty bourgeoisie and the peasantry, but does its utmost to influence the proletariat and the Communist Party in a strenuous effort to destroy their ideological, political and organizational independence, turn them into an appendage of the bourgeoisie and its political party, and ensure that it will reap the fruits of the revolution for itself or its political party alone; this error also consists in neglecting the fact that the bourgeoisie (and especially the big bourgeoisie) betrays the revolution whenever the revolution conflicts with its own selfish interests or with those of its own political party. To neglect all this is Right opportunism. The characteristic feature of Chen Tu-hsiu's Right opportunism was that it led the proletariat to accommodate itself to the selfish interests of the bourgeoisie and its political party, and this was the subjective cause of the failure of the First Great Revolution. The dual character of the Chinese bourgeoisie in the bourgeois-democratic revolution exerts a great effect on our political line and our Party building, and without grasping this dual character we cannot have a good grasp of our political line or of Party building. One important component of the political line of the Chinese Communist Party is the policy both of unity with the bourgeoisie and of struggle against it. In fact, the development and tempering of the Party through its unity and struggle with the bourgeoisie are an important component of Party building. Unity here means the united front with the bourgeoisie. Struggle here means the "peaceful" and "bloodless" struggle, ideological, political and organizational, which goes on when we are united with the bourgeoisie and which turns into armed struggle when we are forced to break with it. If our Party does not understand that it must unite with the bourgeoisie in certain periods, it cannot advance and the revolution cannot develop; if our Party does not understand that it must wage a stern and resolute "peaceful" struggle against the bourgeoisie while uniting with it, then our Party will disintegrate ideologically, politically and organizationally and the revolution will fail; and if our Party does not wage a stern and resolute armed struggle against the bourgeoisie when forced to break with it, our Party will likewise disintegrate and the revolution will likewise fail. The truth of all this has been confirmed by the events of the past eighteen years.

Armed struggle by the Chinese Communist Party takes the form of peasant war under proletarian leadership. The history of this armed struggle, too, falls into three stages. The first was the stage in which we took part in the Northern Expedition. Our Party had already begun to realize the importance of armed struggle, but did not understand it fully, it did not understand that armed struggle was the principal form of struggle in the Chinese revolution. The second stage was the War of the Agrarian Revolution. By that time our Party had already built up its own independent armed forces, learned the art of fighting independently, and established people's political power and base areas. Our Party was already able to achieve direct or indirect co-ordination of armed struggle, the principal form of struggle, with many other necessary forms, that is, to co-ordinate it on a national scale with the workers' struggle, the peasants' struggle (which was the main thing), the struggle of the youth, the women and all other sections of the people, the struggle for political power, the struggles on the economic, the anti-espionage and the ideological fronts, and other forms of struggle. And this armed struggle was the peasant agrarian revolution under the leadership of the proletariat. The third stage is the present stage, the War of Resistance. In this stage we are able to turn to good account our experience of armed struggle in the first and especially the second stage, and our experience of co-ordinating armed struggle with all other necessary forms of struggle. In general, armed struggle at the present time means guerrilla warfare.[2] What is guerrilla warfare? It is the indispensable and therefore the best form of struggle for the people's armed forces to employ over a long period in a backward country, a large semi-colonial country, in order to inflict defeats on the armed enemy and build up their own bases. So far both our political line and our Party building have been closely linked with this form of struggle. It is impossible to have a good understanding of our political line and, consequently, of our Party building in isolation from armed struggle, from guerrilla warfare. Armed struggle is an important component of our political line. For eighteen years our Party has gradually learned to wage armed struggle and has persisted in it. We have learned that without armed struggle neither the proletariat, nor the people, nor the Communist Party would have any standing at all in China and that it would be impossible for the revolution to triumph. In these years the development, consolidation and bolshevization of our Party have proceeded in the midst of revolutionary wars; without armed struggle the Communist Party would assuredly not be what it is today. Comrades throughout the Party must never forget this experience for which we have paid in blood.

Similarly, there have been three distinct stages in the building up of the Party, its development, consolidation and bolshevization.

The first stage was the Party's infancy. In the early and middle phases of this stage the Party's line was correct and the revolutionary zeal both of the rank and file and of the cadres was exceedingly high; hence the victories in the First Great Revolution. But after all, ours was then still an infant Party, it lacked experience concerning the three basic problems of the united front, armed struggle and Party building, it did not have much knowledge of Chinese history and Chinese society or of the specific features and laws of the Chinese revolution, and it lacked a comprehensive understanding of the unity between the theory of Marxism-Leninism and the practice of the Chinese revolution. Hence in the last phase of this stage, or at the critical juncture of this stage, those occupying a dominant position in the Party's leading body failed to lead the Party in consolidating the victories of the revolution and, as a result, they were deceived by the bourgeoisie and brought the revolution to defeat. The Party organizations expanded in this stage but they were not consolidated, and they failed to help Party members and cadres become firm and stable ideologically and politically. There were plenty of new members but they were not given the necessary Marxist-Leninist education. There was also abundant experience in work, but it was not summed up properly. Many careerists sneaked into the Party, but they were not combed out. The Party was caught in a maze of schemes and intrigues both of enemies and of allies, but it lacked vigilance. Within the Party, activists came forward in great numbers, but they were not turned into the mainstay of the Party in good time. The Party had some revolutionary armed units under its command, but it was unable to keep a tight grip on them. The reasons for all this were inexperience, insufficient depth of revolutionary understanding, and ineptitude in integrating the theory of Marxism-Leninism with the practice of the Chinese revolution. Such was the first stage of Party building.

The second stage was the War of the Agrarian Revolution. Our Party was able to wage a successful agrarian revolutionary struggle for ten years because of the experience it had gained in the first stage, because of its better understanding of Chinese history and society and of the specific features and laws of the Chinese revolution, and because its cadres had a better grasp of the theory of Marxism-Leninism and were better able to integrate it with the practice of the Chinese revolution. Although the bourgeoisie had turned traitor, our Party was able to rely firmly on the peasantry. The Party organization not only grew afresh but also became consolidated. Day in day out the enemy tried to sabotage our Party, but the Party drove out the saboteurs. Once again large numbers of cadres came forward in the Party, and this time they became its mainstay. The Party blazed the trail of people's political power and thus learned the art of government. The Party created strong armed forces and thus learned the art of war. These were momentous advances and achievements. Nevertheless, in the course of these great struggles some of our comrades sank into the quagmire of opportunism, or did so at least for a time, and again the reasons were that they did not learn modestly from the experience of the past, did not acquire an understanding of Chinese history and society and of the specific features and laws of the Chinese revolution, and did not have an understanding of the unity between the theory of Marxism-Leninism and the practice of the Chinese revolution. Hence throughout this stage certain people who held leading positions in the Party failed to adhere to correct political and organizational lines. At one time the Party and the revolution were damaged by Comrade Li Li-san's "Left" opportunism, at another by "Left" opportunism in the revolutionary war and in the work in the White areas. Not until the Tsunyi Meeting (the meeting of the Political Bureau at Tsunyi, Kweichow, in January 1935) did the Party definitively take the road of bolshevization and lay the foundations for its subsequent victory over Chang Kuo-tao's Right opportunism and for the establishment of an anti-Japanese national united front. This was the second stage in the Party's development.

The third stage is that of the Anti-Japanese National United Front. We have been in this stage for three years now and these years of struggle are extremely important. Drawing on its experience in the two preceding revolutionary stages, on its organizational strength and the strength of its armed forces, on its high political prestige among the people of the whole country, and on its deeper understanding of the unity between the theory of Marxism-Leninism and the practice of the Chinese revolution, our Party has not only established the Anti-Japanese National United Front but has also been conducting the great War of Resistance Against Japan. Organizationally, it has stepped out of its narrow confines and become a major national party. Its armed forces are again growing and are becoming still stronger in the struggle against the Japanese aggressors. Its influence among the whole people is becoming more extensive. These are all great achievements. However, many of our new Party members have not yet been given education, many of the new organizations have not yet been consolidated, and there is still a vast difference between them and the older members and organizations. Many of the new Party members and cadres have not yet had sufficient revolutionary experience. They still know little or nothing about Chinese history and society or about the specific features and laws of the Chinese revolution. Their understanding of the unity between the theory of Marxism-Leninism and the practice of the Chinese revolution is far from being comprehensive. During the expansion of the Party's organizations, a good many careerists and enemy saboteurs did succeed in sneaking in despite the fact that the Central Committee stressed the slogan "Expand the Party boldly, but do not let a single undesirable in". Although the united front was formed and has been maintained for three years now, the bourgeoisie, and especially the big bourgeoisie, has constantly been trying to destroy our Party, the big bourgeois capitulators and die-hards have been instigating serious friction throughout the country, and the anti-Communist clamour is incessant. All this is being used by the big bourgeois capitulators and die-hards to prepare the way for capitulating to Japanese imperialism, breaking up the united front and dragging China backwards. Ideologically, the big bourgeoisie is trying to "corrode" communism, whilst politically and organizationally it is trying to liquidate the Communist Party, the Border Region and the Party's armed forces. In these circumstances it is undoubtedly our task to overcome the dangers of capitulation, a split and retrogression, to maintain the national united front and Kuomintang-Communist co-operation as far as possible, to work for continued resistance to Japan and continued unity and progress, and at the same time to prepare against all possible eventualities so that in case they occur, the Party and the revolution will not suffer unexpected losses. To this end, we must strengthen the Party's organization and its armed forces, and mobilize the whole people for resolute struggle against capitulation, a split and retrogression. The accomplishment of this task depends upon the efforts of the whole Party, upon the unrelenting and persistent struggle of all Party members, cadres and organizations everywhere and at every level. We are confident that the Chinese Communist Party with its eighteen years of experience will be able to achieve these objectives by the joint efforts of its experienced older members and cadres and its vigorous and youthful newer members and cadres, by the joint efforts of its well-tried bolshevized Central Committee and its local organizations, and by the joint efforts of its powerful armed forces and the progressive masses.

We have set out the principal experiences and principal problems of our Party in its eighteen years of history.

Our eighteen years of experience show that the united front and armed struggle are the two basic weapons for defeating the enemy. The united front is a united front for carrying on armed struggle. And the Party is the heroic warrior wielding the two weapons, the united front and the armed struggle, to storm and shatter the enemy's positions. That is how the three are related to each other.

How are we to build up our Party today? How can we build up "a bolshevized Chinese Communist Party, a party which is national in scale and has a broad mass character, a party which is fully consolidated ideologically, politically and organizationally"? The answer can be found by studying the Party's history, by studying Party building in connection with the united front and armed struggle, in connection with the problem of both uniting and struggling with the bourgeoisie, and with that of persistence in guerrilla warfare against Japan by the Eighth Route and the New Fourth Armies and the establishment of anti-Japanese base areas.

To sum up our eighteen years of experience and our current new experience on the basis of our understanding of the unity between the theory of Marxism-Leninism and the practice of the Chinese revolution, and to spread this experience throughout the Party, so that our Party becomes as solid as steel and avoids repeating past mistakes — such is our task.

NOTES

[1] J. V. Stalin, "The Prospects of the Revolution in China", *Works*, Eng. ed., FLPH, Moscow, 1954, Vol. VIII, p. 379.

[2] In saying that in general, armed struggle in the Chinese revolution means guerrilla warfare, Comrade Mao Tse-tung is summing up China's experience of revolutionary war from the Second Revolutionary Civil War to the early days of the War of Resistance Against Japan. During the long period of the Second Revolutionary Civil War, all the armed struggles led by the Chinese Communist Party took the form of guerrilla warfare. In the latter phase of that period, as the strength of the Red Army grew, guerrilla warfare changed into mobile warfare of a guerrilla character which, as Comrade Mao Tse-tung defines it, is guerrilla warfare on a higher level. But in the War of Resistance Against Japan, with a different enemy and in different circumstances, there was a shift back to guerrilla warfare. In the early days of the anti-Japanese war, those Party comrades who committed the error of Right opportunism belittled the guerrilla warfare led by the Party and pinned their hopes on the operations of the Kuomintang army. Comrade Mao Tse-tung refuted their views in his "Problems of Strategy in Guerrilla War Against Japan", "On Protracted War" and "Problems of War and Strategy", and in the present article he gave a theoretical summing-up of the experience gained in waging the prolonged armed struggle of the Chinese revolution which took the form of guerrilla warfare. In the latter stage of the anti-Japanese war, and more particularly in the period of the Third Revolutionary Civil War (1945-49), guerrilla warfare changed into regular warfare as the main form of armed struggle under the leadership of the Chinese Communist Party, and this was due to the further growth of the revolutionary forces and the changes in the enemy's circumstances. The latter stage of the Third Revolutionary Civil War witnessed a further development, when operations were conducted by huge formations, which, equipped with heavy arms, were able to storm strongly fortified enemy positions.

THE CURRENT SITUATION AND
THE PARTY'S TASKS

October 10, 1939

1. The outbreak of the imperialist world war is the result of the attempt of the imperialist countries to extricate themselves from a new economic and political crisis. Whether on the German side or the Anglo-French, the war is unjust, predatory and imperialist in character. The Communist Parties throughout the world must firmly oppose this war and also the criminal action of the social-democratic parties in betraying the proletariat by supporting it. The socialist Soviet Union is persevering as before in its policy of peace, is maintaining strict neutrality towards both belligerents and, by sending its armed forces into Poland, has checked the eastward expansion of the German forces of aggression, strengthened peace in Eastern Europe, and liberated its brother nations in western Ukraine and Byelorussia from the oppression of the Polish rulers. The Soviet Union has concluded a number of pacts with neighbouring countries to prevent any possible attacks by the forces of international reaction and is endeavouring to restore world peace.

2. The policy of Japanese imperialism in this new international situation is to concentrate its attacks on China in order to settle the China question, in preparation for extending its international adventures in the future. The policy by which it is attempting to settle the China question is as follows:

(a) With regard to the occupied areas, its policy is to tighten its hold on them in preparation for subjugating the whole of China. To do this it has to "mop up" the anti-Japanese guerrilla base areas, exploit economic resources, set up puppet regimes and break the people's national spirit.

This was a decision drafted by Comrade Mao Tse-tung for the Central Committee of the Communist Party of China.

(b) With regard to China's rear areas, its policy is to launch mainly political offensives, supplemented by military offensives. Political offensives mean concentration not on launching large-scale military attacks but on disrupting the anti-Japanese united front, breaking up Kuomintang-Communist co-operation and inducing the Kuomintang government to capitulate.

In the present period the enemy is not likely to launch big strategic offensives like the one against Wuhan, because of the blows dealt by China's heroic resistance during the past two years and of the inadequacy of his armed strength and financial resources. In this sense, basically the War of Resistance has reached the stage of strategic stalemate. And the stage of strategic stalemate is the stage of preparation for our counter-offensive. But first, when we say that basically a stalemate has been reached, we do not rule out the possibility of further offensive campaigns by the enemy; Changsha is now being attacked and other places may be attacked later. Second, as the possibility of a stalemate at the front grows, the enemy will intensify his "mopping-up" operations against our guerrilla base areas. Third, if China should fail to disrupt the enemy's occupation of the areas he has seized and allow him to succeed in his attempts to tighten his hold on them and exploit them, if China should fail to repulse the enemy's political offensives and to persist in resistance, unity and progress and thus fail to accumulate strength for the counter-offensive, or if the Kuomintang government should capitulate of its own accord, then the enemy may still launch bigger offensives. In other words, the stalemate that has now been reached may still be broken by the enemy or by the capitulators.

3. The danger of capitulation, a split and retrogression within the anti-Japanese united front is still the greatest current danger, and the present anti-Communist and retrogressive actions of the big landlords and the big bourgeoisie continue to be preparatory steps to their capitulation. In order to build up strength for the counter-offensive, it is still our task, in co-operation with all Chinese patriots, to mobilize the masses for the effective application of the three great political slogans put forward in our Party's Manifesto of July 7: "Persist in resistance and oppose capitulation", "Persist in unity and oppose a split", and "Persist in progress and oppose retrogression". To achieve this objective, behind the enemy lines it is imperative to keep up guerrilla warfare, defeat the enemy's "mopping-up" opera-

tions, disrupt the enemy's occupation of the areas he has seized, and introduce radical political and economic changes beneficial to the masses who are resisting Japan. At the front, it is imperative to sustain military defence and repel any offensive campaigns the enemy may launch. In China's rear area, it is imperative to introduce speedy and genuine political reforms, end the Kuomintang's one-party dictatorship, convene a national assembly truly representative of the people's will and invested with real power, draw up and adopt a constitution, and put constitutional government into practice. Any vacillation or procrastination, any contrary policy, is absolutely wrong. At the same time the leading bodies of our Party at all levels and all Party members must exercise more vigilance in the present situation and do their utmost to achieve the ideological, political and organizational consolidation of our Party and of the armed forces and organs of political power under its leadership, in order to be ready for any emergency endangering the Chinese revolution and to prevent unexpected losses to the Party and the revolution.

RECRUIT LARGE NUMBERS OF INTELLECTUALS[1]

December 1, 1939

1. In the long and ruthless war of national liberation, in the great struggle to build a new China, the Communist Party must be good at winning intellectuals, for only in this way will it be able to organize great strength for the War of Resistance, organize the millions of peasants, develop the revolutionary cultural movement and expand the revolutionary united front. Without the participation of the intellectuals victory in the revolution is impossible.

2. Our Party and our army have made considerable efforts to recruit intellectuals during the last three years, and many revolutionary intellectuals have been absorbed into the Party, the army, the organs of government, the cultural movement and the mass movement, thus broadening the united front; this is a major achievement. But many of the army cadres are not yet alive to the importance of the intellectuals, they still regard them with some apprehension and are even inclined to discriminate against them or shut them out. Many of our training institutes are still hesitant about enrolling young students in large numbers. Many of our local Party branches are still reluctant to let intellectuals join. All this is due to failure to understand the importance of the intellectuals for the revolutionary cause, the difference between intellectuals in colonial and semi-colonial countries and those in capitalist countries and the difference between intellectuals who serve the landlords and the bourgeoisie and those who serve the working class and the peasantry, as well as the seriousness of the situation in which the bourgeois political parties are desperately contending with us for the intellectuals and in which the Japanese imperialists are also trying in every possible way to buy over Chinese

---

This was a decision drafted by Comrade Mao Tse-tung for the Central Committee of the Chinese Communist Party.

intellectuals or corrupt their minds; in particular, it is due to the failure to understand the favourable factor that our Party and our army have already developed a hard core of well-tested cadres and are thus capable of leading the intellectuals.

3. From now on attention should therefore be paid to the following:

(a) All Party organizations in the war areas and all army units led by the Party should recruit large numbers of intellectuals into our army, training institutes and organs of government. We should use various ways and means to recruit all intellectuals who are willing to fight Japan and who are fairly loyal, hard-working and able to endure hardship; we should give them political education and help them to temper themselves in war and work and to serve the army, the government and the masses; and, taking each case on its merits, we should admit into the Party those who measure up to the requirements of Party membership. As for those who do not qualify or do not wish to join the Party, we should have good working relations with them and give them guidance in their work with us.

(b) In applying the policy of recruiting intellectuals in large numbers, we must undoubtedly take great care to prevent the infiltration of those elements sent in by the enemy and the bourgeois political parties and to keep out other disloyal elements. We must be very strict about keeping out such elements. Those who have already sneaked into our Party, army or government organs must be firmly but discriminatingly combed out on the basis of conclusive evidence. But we must not on that account suspect reasonably loyal intellectuals, and we must be strictly on guard against the false accusation of innocent people by counter-revolutionaries.

(c) We should assign appropriate work to all intellectuals who are reasonably loyal and useful, and we should earnestly give them political education and guidance so that in the long course of the struggle they gradually overcome their weaknesses, revolutionize their outlook, identify themselves with the masses, and merge with the older Party members and cadres and the worker and peasant members of the Party.

(d) The necessity of admitting intellectuals into our work should be brought home to those cadres, and especially to certain cadres in the main forces of our army, who are opposed to their admission. At the same time, we should work effectively to encourage worker and peasant cadres to study hard and raise their cultural level. Thus worker and peasant cadres will at the same time become intellectuals, while the intellectuals will at the same time become workers and peasants.

(e) In the main the principles stated above are also applicable in the Kuomintang areas and in the Japanese-occupied areas, except that, on admitting intellectuals into the Party, more attention must be paid to their degree of loyalty, so as to ensure still tighter Party organization in those areas. We should maintain suitable contact with the huge numbers of non-Party intellectuals who sympathize with us and organize them in the great struggle for resistance to Japan and for democracy, and in the cultural movement and the work of the united front.

4. All our Party comrades must understand that a correct policy towards the intellectuals is an important prerequisite for victory in the revolution. There must be no repetition of the incorrect attitude towards intellectuals which Party organizations in many localities and army units adopted during the Agrarian Revolution; the proletariat cannot produce intellectuals of its own without the help of the existing intellectuals. The Central Committee hopes that the Party committees at all levels and all Party comrades will give this matter their serious attention.

NOTES

1 The term "intellectuals" refers to all those who have had middle school or higher education and those with similar educational levels. They include university and middle school teachers and staff members, university and middle school students, primary school teachers, professionals, engineers and technicians, among whom the university and middle school students occupy an important position.

THE CHINESE REVOLUTION AND THE CHINESE COMMUNIST PARTY

December 1939

CHAPTER I

CHINESE SOCIETY

1. THE CHINESE NATION

China is one of the largest countries in the world, her territory being about the size of the whole of Europe. In this vast country of ours there are large areas of fertile land which provide us with food and clothing; mountain ranges across its length and breadth with extensive forests and rich mineral deposits; many rivers and lakes which provide us with water transport and irrigation; and a long coastline which facilitates communication with nations beyond the seas. From ancient times our forefathers have laboured, lived and multiplied on this vast territory.

China borders on the Union of Soviet Socialist Republics in the northeast, the northwest and part of the west; the Mongolian People's Republic in the north; Afghanistan, India, Bhutan and Nepal in the southwest and part of the west; Burma and Indo-China in the south;

The Chinese Revolution and the Chinese Communist Party is a textbook which was written jointly by Comrade Mao Tse-tung and several other comrades in Yenan in the winter of 1939. The first chapter, "Chinese Society", was drafted by other comrades and revised by Comrade Mao Tse-tung. The second chapter, "The Chinese Revolution", was written by Comrade Mao Tse-tung himself. Another chapter, scheduled to deal with "Party Building", was left unfinished by the comrades working on it. The two published chapters, and especially Chapter II, have played a great educational role in the Chinese Communist Party and among the Chinese people. The views on New Democracy set out by Comrade Mao Tse-tung in Chapter II were considerably developed in his "On New Democracy", written in January 1940.

and Korea in the east, where she is also a close neighbour of Japan and the Philippines. China's geographical setting has its advantages and disadvantages for the Chinese people's revolution. It is an advantage to be adjacent to the Soviet Union and fairly distant from the major imperialist countries in Europe and America, and to have many colonial or semi-colonial countries around us. It is a disadvantage that Japanese imperialism, making use of its geographical proximity, is constantly threatening the very existence of all China's nationalities and the Chinese people's revolution.

China has a population of 450 million, or almost a quarter of the world total. Over nine-tenths of her inhabitants belong to the Han nationality. There are also scores of minority nationalities, including the Mongol, Hui, Tibetan, Uighur, Miao, Yi, Chuang, Chungchia and Korean nationalities, all with long histories though at different levels of cultural development. Thus China is a country with a very large population composed of many nationalities.

Developing along the same lines as many other nations of the world, the Chinese people (here we refer mainly to the Hans) went through many thousands of years of life in classless primitive communes. Some 4,000 years have gone by since the collapse of these primitive communes and the transition to class society, which took the form first of slave and then of feudal society. Throughout the history of Chinese civilization its agriculture and handicrafts have been renowned for their high level of development; there have been many great thinkers, scientists, inventors, statesmen, soldiers, men of letters and artists, and we have a rich store of classical works. The compass was invented in China very long ago.[1] The art of paper-making was discovered as early as 1,800 years ago.[2] Block-printing was invented 1,300 years ago,[3] and movable type 800 years ago.[4] The use of gunpowder was known to the Chinese before the Europeans.[5] Thus China has one of the oldest civilizations in the world; she has a recorded history of nearly 4,000 years.

The Chinese nation is known throughout the world not only for its industriousness and stamina, but also for its ardent love of freedom and its rich revolutionary traditions. The history of the Han people, for instance, demonstrates that the Chinese never submit to tyrannical rule but invariably use revolutionary means to overthrow or change it. In the thousands of years of Han history, there have been hundreds of peasant uprisings, great and small, against the dark rule of the landlords and the nobility. And most dynastic changes came about as a result of such peasant uprisings. All the nationalities of China have resisted foreign oppression and have invariably resorted to rebellion to shake it off. They favour a union on the basis of equality but are against the oppression of one nationality by another. During the thousands of years of recorded history, the Chinese nation has given birth to many national heroes and revolutionary leaders. Thus the Chinese nation has a glorious revolutionary tradition and a splendid historical heritage.

2. THE OLD FEUDAL SOCIETY

Although China is a great nation and although she is a vast country with an immense population, a long history, a rich revolutionary tradition and a splendid historical heritage, her economic, political and cultural development was sluggish for a long time after the transition from slave to feudal society. This feudal society, beginning with the Chou and Chin Dynasties, lasted about 3,000 years.

The main features of the economic and political system of China's feudal era were as follows:

(1) A self-sufficient natural economy predominated. The peasants produced for themselves not only agricultural products but most of the handicraft articles they needed. What the landlords and the nobility exacted from them in the form of land rent was also chiefly for private enjoyment and not for exchange. Although exchange developed as time went on, it did not play a decisive role in the economy as a whole.

(2) The feudal ruling class composed of landlords, the nobility and the emperor owned most of the land, while the peasants had very little or none at all. The peasants tilled the land of the landlords, the nobility and the royal family with their own farm implements and had to turn over to them for their private enjoyment 40, 50, 60, 70, or even 80 per cent or more of the crop. In effect the peasants were still serfs.

(3) Not only did the landlords, the nobility and the royal family live on rent extorted from the peasants, but the landlord state also exacted tribute, taxes and *corvée* services from them to support a horde of government officials and an army which was used mainly for their repression.

(4) The feudal landlord state was the organ of power protecting this system of feudal exploitation. While the feudal state was torn apart into rival principalities in the period before the Chin Dynasty,

it became autocratic and centralized after the first Chin emperor unified China, though some feudal separatism remained. The emperor reigned supreme in the feudal state, appointing officials in charge of the armed forces, the law courts, the treasury and state granaries in all parts of the country and relying on the landed gentry as the mainstay of the entire system of feudal rule.

It was under such feudal economic exploitation and political oppression that the Chinese peasants lived like slaves, in poverty and suffering, through the ages. Under the bondage of feudalism they had no freedom of person. The landlord had the right to beat, abuse or even kill them at will, and they had no political rights whatsoever. The extreme poverty and backwardness of the peasants resulting from ruthless landlord exploitation and oppression is the basic reason why Chinese society remained at the same stage of socio-economic development for several thousand years.

The principal contradiction in feudal society was between the peasantry and the landlord class.

The peasants and the handicraft workers were the basic classes which created the wealth and culture of this society.

The ruthless economic exploitation and political oppression of the Chinese peasants forced them into numerous uprisings against landlord rule. There were hundreds of uprisings, great and small, all of them peasant revolts or peasant revolutionary wars — from the uprisings of Chen Sheng, Wu Kuang, Hsiang Yu and Liu Pang[6] in the Chin Dynasty, those of Hsinshih, Pinglin, the Red Eyebrows, the Bronze Horses[7] and the Yellow Turbans[8] in the Han Dynasty, those of Li Mi and Tou Chien-teh[9] in the Sui Dynasty, those of Wang Hsien-chih and Huang Chao[10] in the Tang Dynasty, those of Sung Chiang and Fang La[11] in the Sung Dynasty, that of Chu Yuan-chang[12] in the Yuan Dynasty, and that of Li Tzu-cheng[13] in the Ming Dynasty, down to the uprising known as the War of the Taiping Heavenly Kingdom in the Ching Dynasty. The scale of peasant uprisings and peasant wars in Chinese history has no parallel anywhere else. The class struggles of the peasants, the peasant uprisings and peasant wars constituted the real motive force of historical development in Chinese feudal society. For each of the major peasant uprisings and wars dealt a blow to the feudal regime of the time, and hence more or less furthered the growth of the social productive forces. However, since neither new productive forces, nor new relations of production, nor new class forces, nor any advanced political party existed in those days, the peasant uprisings and wars did not have correct leadership such as the proletariat and the Communist Party provide today; every peasant revolution failed, and the peasantry was invariably used by the landlords and the nobility, either during or after the revolution, as a lever for bringing about dynastic change. Therefore, although some social progress was made after each great peasant revolutionary struggle, the feudal economic relations and political system remained basically unchanged.

It is only in the last hundred years that a change of a different order has taken place.

3.   PRESENT-DAY COLONIAL, SEMI-COLONIAL AND SEMI-FEUDAL SOCIETY

As explained above, Chinese society remained feudal for 3,000 years. But is it still completely feudal today? No, China has changed. After the Opium War of 1840 China gradually changed into a semi-colonial and semi-feudal society. Since the Incident of September 18, 1931, when the Japanese imperialists started their armed aggression, China has changed further into a colonial, semi-colonial and semi-feudal society. We shall now describe the course of this change.

As discussed in Section 2, Chinese feudal society lasted for about 3,000 years. It was not until the middle of the 19th century, with the penetration of foreign capitalism, that great changes took place in Chinese society.

As China's feudal society had developed a commodity economy, and so carried within itself the seeds of capitalism, China would of herself have developed slowly into a capitalist society even without the impact of foreign capitalism. Penetration by foreign capitalism accelerated this process. Foreign capitalism played an important part in the disintegration of China's social economy; on the one hand, it undermined the foundations of her self-sufficient natural economy and wrecked the handicraft industries both in the cities and in the peasants' homes, and on the other, it hastened the growth of a commodity economy in town and country.

Apart from its disintegrating effects on the foundations of China's feudal economy, this state of affairs gave rise to certain objective conditions and possibilities for the development of capitalist production in China. For the destruction of the natural economy created a

commodity market for capitalism, while the bankruptcy of large numbers of peasants and handicraftsmen provided it with a labour market.

In fact, some merchants, landlords and bureaucrats began investing
in modern industry as far back as sixty years ago, in the latter part
of the 19th century, under the stimulus of foreign capitalism and
because of certain cracks in the feudal economic structure. About
forty years ago, at the turn of the century, China's national capitalism
took its first steps forward. Then about twenty years ago, during the
first imperialist world war, China's national industry expanded, chiefly
in textiles and flour milling, because the imperialist countries in Europe
and America were preoccupied with the war and temporarily relaxed
their oppression of China.

The history of the emergence and development of national
capitalism is at the same time the history of the emergence and
development of the Chinese bourgeoisie and proletariat. Just as a
section of the merchants, landlords and bureaucrats were precursors
of the Chinese bourgeoisie, so a section of the peasants and handicraft
workers were the precursors of the Chinese proletariat. As distinct
social classes, the Chinese bourgeoisie and proletariat are new-born
and never existed before in Chinese history. They have evolved into
new social classes from the womb of feudal society. They are twins
born of China's old (feudal) society, at once linked to each other and
antagonistic to each other. However, the Chinese proletariat emerged
and grew simultaneously not only with the Chinese national bourgeoisie but also with the enterprises directly operated by the imperialists in China. Hence, a very large section of the Chinese proletariat
is older and more experienced than the Chinese bourgeoisie, and is
therefore a greater and more broadly based social force.

However, the emergence and development of capitalism is only
one aspect of the change that has taken place since the imperialist
penetration of China. There is another concomitant and obstructive
aspect, namely, the collusion of imperialism with the Chinese feudal
forces to arrest the development of Chinese capitalism.

It is certainly not the purpose of the imperialist powers invading
China to transform feudal China into capitalist China. On the contrary,
their purpose is to transform China into their own semi-colony or colony.

To this end the imperialist powers have used and continue to use
military, political, economic and cultural means of oppression, so that
China has gradually become a semi-colony and colony. They are
as follows:

(1) The imperialist powers have waged many wars of aggression against China, for instance, the Opium War launched by Britain in 1840, the war launched by the Anglo-French allied forces in 1857,[14] the Sino-French War of 1884,[15] the Sino-Japanese War of 1894, and the war launched by the allied forces of the eight powers in 1900.[16] After defeating China in war, they not only occupied many neighbouring countries formerly under her protection, but seized or "leased" parts of her territory. For instance, Japan occupied Taiwan and the Penghu Islands and "leased" the port of Lushun, Britain seized Hongkong and France "leased" Kwangchowwan. In addition to annexing territory, they exacted huge indemnities. Thus heavy blows were struck at China's huge feudal empire.

(2) The imperialist powers have forced China to sign numerous unequal treaties by which they have acquired the right to station land and sea forces and exercise consular jurisdiction in China,[17] and they have carved up the whole country into imperialist spheres of influence.[18]

(3) The imperialist powers have gained control of all the important trading ports in China by these unequal treaties and have marked off areas in many of these ports as concessions under their direct administration.[19] They have also gained control of China's customs, foreign trade and communications (sea, land, inland water and air). Thus they have been able to dump their goods in China, turn her into a market for their industrial products, and at the same time subordinate her agriculture to their imperialist needs.

(4) The imperialist powers operate many enterprises in both light and heavy industry in China in order to utilize her raw materials and cheap labour on the spot, and they thereby directly exert economic pressure on China's national industry and obstruct the development of her productive forces.

(5) The imperialist powers monopolize China's banking and finance by extending loans to the Chinese government and establishing banks in China. Thus they have not only overwhelmed China's national capitalism in commodity competition, they have also secured a stranglehold on her banking and finance.

(6) The imperialist powers have established a network of comprador and merchant-usurer exploitation right across China, from the trading ports to the remote hinterland, and have created a comprador and merchant-usurer class in their service, so as to facilitate their exploitation of the masses of the Chinese peasantry and other sections of the people.

(7) The imperialist powers have made the feudal landlord class as well as the comprador class the main props of their rule in China. Imperialism "first allies itself with the ruling strata of the previous social structure, with the feudal lords and the trading and money-lending bourgeoisie, against the majority of the people. Everywhere imperialism attempts to preserve and to perpetuate all those pre-capitalist forms of exploitation (especially in the villages) which serve as the basis for the existence of its reactionary allies".[20] "Imperialism, with all its financial and military might, is the force in China that supports, inspires, fosters and preserves the feudal survivals, together with their entire bureaucratic-militarist superstructure."[21]

(8) The imperialist powers supply the reactionary government with large quantities of munitions and a host of military advisers, in order to keep the warlords fighting among themselves and to suppress the Chinese people.

(9) Furthermore, the imperialist powers have never slackened their efforts to poison the minds of the Chinese people. This is their policy of cultural aggression. And it is carried out through missionary work, through establishing hospitals and schools, publishing news-papers and inducing Chinese students to study abroad. Their aim is to train intellectuals who will serve their interests and to dupe the people.

(10) Since September 18, 1931, the large-scale invasion of Japanese imperialism has turned a big chunk of semi-colonial China into a Japanese colony.

These facts represent the other aspect of the change that has taken place since the imperialist penetration of China — the blood-stained picture of feudal China being reduced to semi-feudal, semi-colonial and colonial China.

It is thus clear that in their aggression against China the imperialist powers have on the one hand hastened the disintegration of feudal society and the growth of elements of capitalism, thereby transforming a feudal into a semi-feudal society, and on the other imposed their ruthless rule on China, reducing an independent country to a semi-colonial and colonial country.

Taking both these aspects together, we can see that China's colonial, semi-colonial and semi-feudal society possesses the following characteristics:

(1) The foundations of the self-sufficient natural economy of feudal times have been destroyed, but the exploitation of the peasantry by the landlord class, which is the basis of the system of feudal

exploitation, not only remains intact but, linked as it is with exploitation by comprador and usurer capital, clearly dominates China's social and economic life.

(2) National capitalism has developed to a certain extent and has played a considerable part in China's political and cultural life, but it has not become the principal pattern in China's social economy; it is flabby and is mostly associated with foreign imperialism and domestic feudalism in varying degrees.

(3) The autocratic rule of the emperors and nobility has been overthrown, and in its place there have arisen first the warlord-bureaucrat rule of the landlord class and then the joint dictatorship of the landlord class and the big bourgeoisie. In the occupied areas there is the rule of Japanese imperialism and its puppets.

(4) Imperialism controls not only China's vital financial and economic arteries but also her political and military power. In the occupied areas everything is in the hands of Japanese imperialism.

(5) China's economic, political and cultural development is very uneven, because she has been under the complete or partial domination of many imperialist powers, because she has actually been in a state of disunity for a long time, and because her territory is immense.

(6) Under the twofold oppression of imperialism and feudalism, and especially as a result of the large-scale invasion of Japanese imperialism, the Chinese people, and particularly the peasants, have become more and more impoverished and have even been pauperized in large numbers, living in hunger and cold and without any political rights. The poverty and lack of freedom among the Chinese people are on a scale seldom found elsewhere.

Such are the characteristics of China's colonial, semi-colonial and semi-feudal society.

This situation has in the main been determined by the Japanese and other imperialist forces; it is the result of the collusion of foreign imperialism and domestic feudalism.

The contradiction between imperialism and the Chinese nation and the contradiction between feudalism and the great masses of the people are the basic contradictions in modern Chinese society. Of course, there are others, such as the contradiction between the bourgeoisie and the proletariat and the contradictions within the reactionary ruling classes themselves. But the contradiction between imperialism and the Chinese nation is the principal one. These contradictions and their intensification must inevitably result in the incessant growth of revolutionary movements. The great revolutions in modern and contemporary China have emerged and grown on the basis of these basic contradictions.

CHAPTER II

THE CHINESE REVOLUTION

1. THE REVOLUTIONARY MOVEMENTS IN THE LAST HUNDRED YEARS

The history of China's transformation into a semi-colony and colony by imperialism in collusion with Chinese feudalism is at the same time a history of struggle by the Chinese people against imperialism and its lackeys. The Opium War, the Movement of the Taiping Heavenly Kingdom, the Sino-French War, the Sino-Japanese War, the Reform Movement of 1898, the Yi Ho Tuan Movement, the Revolution of 1911, the May 4th Movement, the May 30th Movement, the Northern Expedition, the Agrarian Revolutionary War and the present War of Resistance Against Japan — all testify to the Chinese people's indomitable spirit in fighting imperialism and its lackeys.

Thanks to the Chinese people's unrelenting and heroic struggle during the last hundred years, imperialism has not been able to subjugate China, nor will it ever be able to do so.

The valiant Chinese people will certainly fight on, even though Japanese imperialism is now exerting its full strength in an all-out offensive and many landlord and big bourgeois elements, such as the overt and covert Wang Ching-weis, have already capitulated to the enemy or are preparing to do so. This heroic struggle will not cease until the Chinese people have driven Japanese imperialism out of China and achieved the complete liberation of the country.

The national revolutionary struggle of the Chinese people has a history of fully one hundred years counting from the Opium War of 1840, or of thirty years counting from the Revolution of 1911. It has not yet run its full course, nor has it yet performed its tasks with any signal success; therefore the Chinese people, and above all the Communist Party, must shoulder the responsibility of resolutely fighting on.

What are the targets of the revolution? What are its tasks? What are its motive forces? What is its character? And what are its perspectives? These are the questions we shall now deal with.

2. THE TARGETS OF THE CHINESE REVOLUTION

From our analysis in the third section of Chapter I, we know that present-day Chinese society is a colonial, semi-colonial and semi-feudal society. Only when we grasp the nature of Chinese society will we be able clearly to understand the targets, tasks, motive forces and character of the Chinese revolution and its perspectives and future transition. A clear understanding of the nature of Chinese society, that is, of Chinese conditions, is therefore the key to a clear understanding of all the problems of the revolution.

Since the nature of present-day Chinese society is colonial, semi-colonial and semi-feudal, what are the chief targets or enemies at this stage of the Chinese revolution?

They are imperialism and feudalism, the bourgeoisie of the imperialist countries and the landlord class of our country. For it is these two that are the chief oppressors, the chief obstacles to the progress of Chinese society at the present stage. The two collude with each other in oppressing the Chinese people, and imperialism is the foremost and most ferocious enemy of the Chinese people, because national oppression by imperialism is the more onerous.

Since Japan's armed invasion of China, the principal enemy of the revolution has been Japanese imperialism together with all the Chinese traitors and reactionaries in league with it, whether they have capitulated openly or are preparing to do so.

The Chinese bourgeoisie, which is also a victim of imperialist oppression, once led or played a principal role in revolutionary struggles such as the Revolution of 1911, and has participated in revolutionary struggles such as the Northern Expedition and the present War of Resistance Against Japan. In the long period from 1927 to 1937, however, its upper stratum, namely, the section represented by the reactionary clique within the Kuomintang, collaborated with imperialism, formed a reactionary alliance with the landlord class, betrayed the friends who had helped it — the Communist Party, the proletariat, the peasantry and other sections of the petty bourgeoisie — betrayed the Chinese revolution and brought about its defeat. At that time, therefore, the revolutionary people and the revolutionary political party (the Communist Party) could not but regard these bourgeois elements as one of the targets of the revolution. In the War of Resistance a section of the big landlord class and big bourgeoisie, represented by Wang Ching-wei, has turned traitor and deserted to the enemy. Consequently, the anti-Japanese people cannot but regard these big bourgeois elements who have betrayed our national interests as one of the targets of the revolution.

It is evident, then, that the enemies of the Chinese revolution are very powerful. They include not only powerful imperialists and powerful feudal forces, but also, at times, the bourgeois reactionaries who collaborate with the imperialist and feudal forces to oppose the people. Therefore, it is wrong to underestimate the strength of the enemies of the revolutionary Chinese people.

In the face of such enemies, the Chinese revolution cannot be other than protracted and ruthless. With such powerful enemies, the revolutionary forces cannot be built up and tempered into a power capable of crushing them except over a long period of time. With enemies who so ruthlessly suppress the Chinese revolution, the revolutionary forces cannot hold their own positions, let alone capture those of the enemy, unless they steel themselves and display their tenacity to the full. It is therefore wrong to think that the forces of the Chinese revolution can be built up in the twinkling of an eye, or that China's revolutionary struggle can triumph overnight.

In the face of such enemies, the principal means or form of the Chinese revolution must be armed struggle, not peaceful struggle. For our enemies have made peaceful activity impossible for the Chinese people and have deprived them of all political freedom and democratic rights. Stalin says, "In China the armed revolution is fighting the armed counter-revolution. That is one of the specific features and one of the advantages of the Chinese revolution."[22] This formulation is perfectly correct. Therefore, it is wrong to belittle armed struggle, revolutionary war, guerrilla war and army work.

In the face of such enemies, there arises the question of revolutionary base areas. Since China's key cities have long been occupied by the powerful imperialists and their reactionary Chinese allies, it is imperative for the revolutionary ranks to turn the backward villages into advanced, consolidated base areas, into great military, political, economic and cultural bastions of the revolution from which to fight their vicious enemies who are using the cities for attacks on the rural districts, and in this way gradually to achieve the complete victory of the revolution through protracted fighting; it is imperative for them to do so if they do not wish to compromise with imperialism and its lackeys but are determined to fight on, and if they intend to build up and temper their forces, and avoid decisive battles with a powerful enemy while their own strength is inadequate. Such being the case, victory in the Chinese revolution can be won first in the rural areas, and this is possible because China's economic development is uneven (her economy not being a unified capitalist economy), because her territory is extensive (which gives the revolutionary forces room to manoeuvre), because the counter-revolutionary camp is disunited and full of contradictions, and because the struggle of the peasants who are the main force in the revolution is led by the Communist Party, the party of the proletariat; but on the other hand, these very circumstances make the revolution uneven and render the task of winning complete victory protracted and arduous. Clearly then the protracted revolutionary struggle in the revolutionary base areas consists mainly in peasant guerrilla warfare led by the Chinese Communist Party. Therefore, it is wrong to ignore the necessity of using rural districts as revolutionary base areas, to neglect painstaking work among the peasants, and to neglect guerrilla warfare.

However, stressing armed struggle does not mean abandoning other forms of struggle; on the contrary, armed struggle cannot succeed unless co-ordinated with other forms of struggle. And stressing the work in the rural base areas does not mean abandoning our work in the cities and in the other vast rural areas which are still under the enemy's rule; on the contrary, without the work in the cities and in these other rural areas, our own rural base areas would be isolated and the revolution would suffer defeat. Moreover, the final objective of the revolution is the capture of the cities, the enemy's main bases, and this objective cannot be achieved without adequate work in the cities.

It is thus clear that the revolution cannot triumph either in the rural areas or in the cities without the destruction of the enemy's army, his chief weapon against the people. Therefore, besides annihilating the enemy's troops in battle, there is the important task of disintegrating them.

It is also clear that the Communist Party must not be impetuous and adventurist in its propaganda and organizational work in the urban and rural areas which have been occupied by the enemy and dominated by the forces of reaction and darkness for a long time, but that it must have well-selected cadres working underground, must accumulate strength and bide its time there. In leading the people in struggle against the enemy, the Party must adopt the tactics of advancing step by step slowly and surely, keeping to the principle of waging struggles on just grounds, to our advantage, and with restraint, and making use of such open forms of activity as are permitted by law, decree and social custom; empty clamour and reckless action can never lead to success.

3. THE TASKS OF THE CHINESE REVOLUTION

Imperialism and the feudal landlord class being the chief enemies of the Chinese revolution at this stage, what are the present tasks of the revolution?

Unquestionably, the main tasks are to strike at these two enemies, to carry out a national revolution to overthrow foreign imperialist oppression and a democratic revolution to overthrow feudal landlord oppression, the primary and foremost task being the national revolution to overthrow imperialism.

These two great tasks are interrelated. Unless imperialist rule is overthrown, the rule of the feudal landlord class cannot be terminated, because imperialism is its main support. Conversely, unless help is given to the peasants in their struggle to overthrow the feudal landlord class, it will be impossible to build powerful revolutionary contingents to overthrow imperialist rule, because the feudal landlord class is the main social base of imperialist rule in China and the peasantry is the main force in the Chinese revolution. Therefore the two fundamental tasks, the national revolution and the democratic revolution, are at once distinct and united.

In fact, the two revolutionary tasks are already linked, since the main immediate task of the national revolution is to resist the Japanese imperialist invaders and since the democratic revolution must be accomplished in order to win the war. It is wrong to regard the national revolution and the democratic revolution as two entirely different stages of the revolution.

4. THE MOTIVE FORCES OF THE CHINESE REVOLUTION

Given the nature of Chinese society and the present targets and tasks of the Chinese revolution as analysed and defined above, what are the motive forces of the Chinese revolution?

Since Chinese society is colonial, semi-colonial and semi-feudal, since the targets of the revolution are mainly foreign imperialist rule and domestic feudalism, and since its tasks are to overthrow these two oppressors, which of the various classes and strata in Chinese society constitute the forces capable of fighting them? This is the question of the motive forces of the Chinese revolution at the present stage. A clear understanding of this question is indispensable to a correct solution of the problem of the basic tactics of the Chinese revolution.

What classes are there in present-day Chinese society? There are the landlord class and the bourgeoisie, the landlord class and the upper stratum of the bourgeoisie constituting the ruling classes in Chinese society. And there are the proletariat, the peasantry, and the different sections of the petty bourgeoisie other than the peasantry, all of which are still the subject classes in vast areas of China.

The attitude and the stand of these classes towards the Chinese revolution are entirely determined by their economic status in society. Thus the motive forces as well as the targets and tasks of the revolution are determined by the nature of China's socio-economic system.

Let us now analyse the different classes in Chinese society.

1. The Landlord Class

The landlord class forms the main social base for imperialist rule in China; it is a class which uses the feudal system to exploit and oppress the peasants, obstructs China's political, economic and cultural development and plays no progressive role whatsoever.

Therefore, the landlords, as a class, are a target and not a motive force of the revolution.

In the present War of Resistance a section of the big landlords, along with one section of the big bourgeoisie (the capitulationists), has surrendered to the Japanese aggressors and turned traitor, while another section of the big landlords, along with another section of the big bourgeoisie (the die-hards), is increasingly wavering even though it is still in the anti-Japanese camp. But a good many of the enlightened gentry who are middle and small landlords and who have some capitalist colouration display some enthusiasm for the war, and we should unite with them in the common fight against Japan.

2. The Bourgeoisie

There is a distinction between the comprador big bourgeoisie and the national bourgeoisie.

The comprador big bourgeoisie is a class which directly serves the capitalists of the imperialist countries and is nurtured by them; countless ties link it closely with the feudal forces in the countryside. Therefore, it is a target of the Chinese revolution and never in the history of the revolution has it been a motive force.

However, different sections of the comprador big bourgeoisie owe allegiance to different imperialist powers, so that when the contradictions among the latter become very acute and the revolution is directed mainly against one particular imperialist power, it becomes possible for the sections of the comprador class which serve other imperialist groupings to join the current anti-imperialist front to a certain extent and for a certain period. But they will turn against the Chinese revolution the moment their masters do.

In the present war the pro-Japanese big bourgeoisie (the capitulationists) have either surrendered or are preparing to surrender. The pro-European and pro-American big bourgeoisie (the die-hards) are wavering more and more, even though they are still in the anti-Japanese camp, and they are playing the double game of simultaneously resisting Japan and opposing the Communist Party. Our policy towards the big bourgeois capitulationists is to treat them as enemies and resolutely strike them down. Towards the big bourgeois die-hards, we employ a revolutionary dual policy; on the one hand, we unite with them because they are still anti-Japanese and we should make use of their contradictions with Japanese imperialism, but on the other hand, we firmly struggle against them because they pursue a high-handed anti-Communist, reactionary policy detrimental to resistance and unity, both of which would be jeopardized without such a struggle.

The national bourgeoisie is a class with a dual character.

On the one hand, it is oppressed by imperialism and fettered by feudalism and consequently is in contradiction with both of them. In this respect it constitutes one of the revolutionary forces. In the course of the Chinese revolution it has displayed a certain enthusiasm for fighting imperialism and the governments of bureaucrats and warlords.

But on the other hand, it lacks the courage to oppose imperialism and feudalism thoroughly because it is economically and politically flabby and still has economic ties with imperialism and feudalism. This emerges very clearly when the people's revolutionary forces grow powerful.

It follows from the dual character of the national bourgeoisie that, at certain times and to a certain extent, it can take part in the revolution against imperialism and the governments of bureaucrats and warlords and can become a revolutionary force, but that at other times there is the danger of its following the comprador big bourgeoisie and acting as its accomplice in counter-revolution.

The national bourgeoisie in China, which is mainly the middle bourgeoisie, has never really held political power but has been restricted by the reactionary policies of the big landlord class and big bourgeoisie which are in power, although it followed them in opposing the revolution in the period from 1927 to 1931 (before the September 18th Incident). In the present war, it differs not only from the capitulationists of the big landlord class and big bourgeoisie but also from the big bourgeois die-hards, and so far has been a fairly good ally of ours. Therefore, it is absolutely necessary to have a prudent policy towards the national bourgeoisie.

3. The Different Sections of the Petty Bourgeoisie Other than the Peasantry

The petty bourgeoisie, other than the peasantry, consists of the vast numbers of intellectuals, small tradesmen, handicraftsmen and professional people.

Their status somewhat resembles that of the middle peasants, they all suffer under the oppression of imperialism, feudalism and the big bourgeoisie, and they are being driven ever nearer to bankruptcy or destitution.

Hence these sections of the petty bourgeoisie constitute one of the motive forces of the revolution and are a reliable ally of the proletariat. Only under the leadership of the proletariat can they achieve their liberation.

Let us now analyse the different sections of the petty bourgeoisie other than the peasantry.

First, the intellectuals and student youth. They do not constitute a separate class or stratum. In present-day China most of them may be placed in the petty-bourgeois category, judging by their family origin, their living conditions and their political outlook. Their numbers have grown considerably during the past few decades. Apart from that section of the intellectuals which has associated itself with the imperialists and the big bourgeoisie and works for them against the people, most intellectuals and students are oppressed by imperialism, feudalism and the big bourgeoisie, and live in fear of unemployment or of having to discontinue their studies. Therefore, they tend to be quite revolutionary. They are more or less equipped with bourgeois scientific knowledge, have a keen political sense and often play a vanguard role or serve as a link with the masses in the present stage of the revolution. The movement of the Chinese students abroad before the Revolution of 1911, the May 4th Movement of 1919, the May 30th Movement of 1925 and the December 9th Movement of 1935 are striking proofs of this. In particular, the large numbers of more or less impoverished intellectuals can join hands with the workers and peasants in supporting or participating in the revolution. In China, it was among the intellectuals and young students that Marxist-Leninist ideology was first widely disseminated and accepted. The revolutionary forces cannot be successfully organized and revolutionary work cannot be successfully conducted without the participation of revolutionary intellectuals. But the intellectuals often tend to be subjective and individualistic, impractical in their thinking and irresolute in action until they have thrown themselves heart and soul into mass revolutionary struggles, or made up their minds to serve the interests of the masses and become one with them. Hence although the mass of revolutionary intellectuals in China can play a vanguard role or serve as a link with the masses, not all of them will remain revolutionaries to the end. Some will drop out of the revolutionary ranks at critical moments and become passive, while a few may even become enemies of the revolution. The intellectuals can overcome their shortcomings only in mass struggles over a long period.

Second, the small tradesmen. Generally they run small shops and employ few or no assistants. They live under the threat of bankruptcy as a result of exploitation by imperialism, the big bourgeoisie and the usurers.

Third, the handicraftsmen. They are very numerous. They possess their own means of production and hire no workers, or only one or two apprentices or helpers. Their position is similar to that of the middle peasants.

Fourth, professional people. They include doctors and men of other professions. They do not exploit other people, or do so only to a slight degree. Their position is similar to that of the handicraftsmen.

These sections of the petty bourgeoisie make up a vast multitude of people whom we must win over and whose interests we must protect because in general they can support or join the revolution and are good allies. Their weakness is that some of them are easily influenced by the bourgeoisie; consequently, we must carry on revolutionary propaganda and organizational work among them.

4. The Peasantry

The peasantry constitutes approximately 80 per cent of China's total population and is the main force in her national economy today.

A sharp process of polarization is taking place among the peasantry.

First, the rich peasants. They form about 5 per cent of the rural population (or about 10 per cent together with the landlords) and constitute the rural bourgeoisie. Most of the rich peasants in China are semi-feudal in character, since they let a part of their land, practise usury and ruthlessly exploit the farm labourers. But they generally engage in labour themselves and in this sense are part of the peasantry. The rich-peasant form of production will remain useful for a definite period. Generally speaking, they might make some contribution to the anti-imperialist struggle of the peasant masses and stay neutral in the agrarian revolutionary struggle against the landlords. Therefore we should not regard the rich peasants as belonging to the same class as the landlords and should not prematurely adopt a policy of liquidating the rich peasantry.

Second, the middle peasants. They form about 20 per cent of China's rural population. They are economically self-supporting (they may have something to lay aside when the crops are good, and occasionally hire some labour or lend small sums of money at interest); and generally they do not exploit others but are exploited by imperialism, the landlord class and the bourgeoisie. They have no political rights. Some of them do not have enough land, and only a section (the well-to-do middle peasants) have some surplus land. Not only can the middle peasants join the anti-imperialist revolution and the Agrarian Revolution, but they can also accept socialism. Therefore the whole middle peasantry can be a reliable ally of the proletariat and is an important motive force of the revolution. The positive or negative attitude of the middle peasants is one of the factors determining victory or defeat in the revolution, and this is especially true after the agrarian revolution when they become the majority of the rural population.

Third, the poor peasants. The poor peasants in China, together with the farm labourers, form about 70 per cent of the rural population. They are the broad peasant masses with no land or insufficient land, the semi-proletariat of the countryside, the biggest motive force of the Chinese revolution, the natural and most reliable ally of the proletariat and the main contingent of China's revolutionary forces. Only under the leadership of the proletariat can the poor and middle peasants achieve their liberation, and only by forming a firm alliance with the poor and middle peasants can the proletariat lead the revolution to victory. Otherwise neither is possible. The term "peasantry" refers mainly to the poor and middle peasants.

5. The Proletariat

Among the Chinese proletariat, the modern industrial workers number from 2,500,000 to 3,000,000, the workers in small-scale industry and in handicrafts and the shop assistants in the cities total about 12,000,000, and in addition there are great numbers of rural proletarians (the farm labourers) and other propertyless people in the cities and the countryside.

In addition to the basic qualities it shares with the proletariat everywhere — its association with the most advanced form of economy, its strong sense of organization and discipline and its lack of private means of production — the Chinese proletariat has many other outstanding qualities.

What are they?

First, the Chinese proletariat is more resolute and thoroughgoing in revolutionary struggle than any other class because it is subjected to a threefold oppression (imperialist, bourgeois and feudal) which is marked by a severity and cruelty seldom found in other countries. Since there is no economic basis for social reformism in colonial and semi-colonial China as there is in Europe, the whole proletariat, with the exception of a few scabs, is most revolutionary.

Secondly, from the moment it appeared on the revolutionary scene, the Chinese proletariat came under the leadership of its own revolutionary party — the Communist Party of China — and became the most politically conscious class in Chinese society.

Thirdly, because the Chinese proletariat by origin is largely made up of bankrupted peasants, it has natural ties with the peasant masses, which facilitates its forming a close alliance with them.

Therefore, in spite of certain unavoidable weaknesses, for instance, its smallness (as compared with the peasantry), its youth (as compared with the proletariat in the capitalist countries) and its low educational level (as compared with the bourgeoisie), the Chinese proletariat is nonetheless the basic motive force of the Chinese revolution. Unless it is led by the proletariat, the Chinese revolution cannot possibly succeed. To take an example from the past, the Revolution of 1911 miscarried because the proletariat did not consciously participate in it and the Communist Party was not yet in existence. More recently, the revolution of 1924-27 achieved great success for a time because the proletariat consciously participated and exercised leadership and the Communist Party was already in existence; it ended in defeat because the big bourgeoisie betrayed its alliance with the proletariat and abandoned the common revolutionary programme, and also because the Chinese proletariat and its political party did not yet have enough revolutionary experience. Now take the present anti-Japanese war — because the proletariat and the Communist Party are exercising leadership in the Anti-Japanese National United Front, the whole nation has been united and the great War of Resistance has been launched and is being resolutely pursued.

The Chinese proletariat should understand that although it is the class with the highest political consciousness and sense of organization, it cannot win victory by its own strength alone. In order to win, it must unite, according to varying circumstances, with all classes and strata that can take part in the revolution, and must organize a revolutionary united front. Among all the classes in Chinese society, the peasantry is a firm ally of the working class, the urban petty bourgeoisie is a reliable ally, and the national bourgeoisie is an ally in certain periods and to a certain extent. This is one of the fundamental laws established by China's modern revolutionary history.

6. The Vagrants

China's status as a colony and semi-colony has given rise to a multitude of rural and urban unemployed. Denied proper means of making a living, many of them are forced to resort to illegitimate ones, hence the robbers, gangsters, beggars and prostitutes and the numerous people who live on superstitious practices. This social stratum is unstable; while some are apt to be bought over by the reactionary forces, others may join the revolution. These people lack constructive qualities and are given to destruction rather than construction; after joining the revolution, they become a source of roving-rebel and anarchist ideology in the revolutionary ranks. Therefore, we should know how to remould them and guard against their destructiveness.

The above is our analysis of the motive forces of the Chinese revolution.

5. THE CHARACTER OF THE CHINESE REVOLUTION

We have now gained an understanding of the nature of Chinese society, *i.e.*, of the specific conditions in China; this understanding is the essential prerequisite for solving all China's revolutionary problems. We are also clear about the targets, the tasks and the motive forces of the Chinese revolution; these are basic issues at the present stage of the revolution and arise from the special nature of Chinese society, *i.e.*, from China's specific conditions. Understanding all this, we can now understand another basic issue of the revolution at the present stage, *i.e.*, the character of the Chinese revolution.

What, indeed, is the character of the Chinese revolution at the present stage? Is it a bourgeois-democratic or a proletarian-socialist revolution? Obviously, it is not the latter but the former.

Since Chinese society is colonial, semi-colonial and semi-feudal, since the principal enemies of the Chinese revolution are imperialism and feudalism, since the tasks of the revolution are to overthrow these two enemies by means of a national and democratic revolution in which the bourgeoisie sometimes takes part, and since the edge of the revolution is directed against imperialism and feudalism and not against capitalism and capitalist private property in general even if the big bourgeoisie betrays the revolution and becomes its enemy — since all this is true, the character of the Chinese revolution at the present stage is not proletarian-socialist but bourgeois-democratic.[23]

However, in present-day China the bourgeois-democratic revolution is no longer of the old general type, which is now obsolete, but one of a new special type. We call this type the new-democratic revolution and it is developing in all other colonial and semi-colonial countries as well as in China. The new-democratic revolution is part of the

world proletarian-socialist revolution, for it resolutely opposes imperialism, *i.e.*, international capitalism. Politically, it strives for the joint
dictatorship of the revolutionary classes over the imperialists, traitors
and reactionaries, and opposes the transformation of Chinese society
into a society under bourgeois dictatorship. Economically, it aims
at the nationalization of all the big enterprises and capital of the
imperialists, traitors and reactionaries, and the distribution among the
peasants of the land held by the landlords, while preserving private
capitalist enterprise in general and not eliminating the rich-peasant
economy. Thus, the new type of democratic revolution clears the way
for capitalism on the one hand and creates the prerequisites for
socialism on the other. The present stage of the Chinese revolution is
a stage of transition between the abolition of the colonial, semi-colonial
and semi-feudal society and the establishment of a socialist society,
i.e., it is a process of new-democratic revolution. This process, begun
only after the First World War and the Russian October Revolution,
started in China with the May 4th Movement of 1919. A new-
democratic revolution is an anti-imperialist and anti-feudal revolution
of the broad masses of the people under the leadership of the proletariat. Chinese society can advance to socialism only through such
a revolution; there is no other way.

The new-democratic revolution is vastly different from the democratic revolutions of Europe and America in that it results not in a
dictatorship of the bourgeoisie but in a dictatorship of the united front
of all the revolutionary classes under the leadership of the proletariat.
In the present War of Resistance, the anti-Japanese democratic political power established in the base areas which are under the leadership of the Communist Party is the political power of the Anti-Japanese
National United Front; this is neither a bourgeois nor a proletarian
one-class dictatorship, but a joint dictatorship of the revolutionary
classes under the leadership of the proletariat. All who stand for
resistance to Japan and for democracy are entitled to share in this
political power, regardless of their party affiliation.

The new-democratic revolution also differs from a socialist
revolution in that it overthrows the rule of the imperialists, traitors
and reactionaries in China but does not destroy any section of capitalism which is capable of contributing to the anti-imperialist, anti-
feudal struggle.

The new-democratic revolution is basically in line with the revolution envisaged in the Three People's Principles as advocated by

Dr. Sun Yat-sen in 1924. In the Manifesto of the First National
Congress of the Kuomintang issued in that year, Dr. Sun stated:

> The so-called democratic system in modern states is usually
> monopolized by the bourgeoisie and has become simply an in-
> strument for oppressing the common people. On the other hand,
> the Kuomintang's Principle of Democracy means a democratic
> system shared by all the common people and not privately owned
> by the few.

He added:

> Enterprises, such as banks, railways and airlines, whether
> Chinese-owned or foreign-owned, which are either monopolistic
> in character or too big for private management, shall be operated
> and administrated by the state, so that private capital cannot
> dominate the livelihood of the people: this is the main principle
> of the regulation of capital.

And again in his Testament, Dr. Sun pointed out the fundamental
principle for domestic and foreign policy: "We must arouse the masses
of the people and unite in a common struggle with those nations of
the world which treat us as equals." The Three People's Principles of
the old democracy, which were adapted to the old international and
domestic conditions, were thus reshaped into the Three People's Principles of New Democracy, which are adapted to the new international
and domestic conditions. The Communist Party of China was referring
to the latter kind of Three People's Principles and to no other when,
in its Manifesto of September 22, 1937, it declared that "the Three
People's Principles being what China needs today, our Party is ready
to fight for their complete realization". These Three People's Principles
embody Dr. Sun Yat-sen's Three Great Policies — alliance with Russia,
co-operation with the Communist Party and assistance to the peasants
and workers. In the new international and domestic conditions, any
kind of Three People's Principles which departs from the Three Great
Policies is not revolutionary. (Here we shall not deal with the fact
that, while communism and the Three People's Principles agree on
the basic political programme for the democratic revolution, they
differ in all other respects.)

Thus, the role of the proletariat, the peasantry and the other
sections of the petty bourgeoisie in China's bourgeois-democratic
revolution cannot be ignored, either in the alignment of forces for the

struggle (that is, in the united front) or in the organization of state power. Anyone who tries to bypass these classes will certainly be unable to solve the problem of the destiny of the Chinese nation or indeed any of China's problems. The Chinese revolution at the present stage must strive to create a democratic republic in which the workers, the peasants and the other sections of the petty bourgeoisie all occupy a definite position and play a definite role. In other words, it must be a democratic republic based on a revolutionary alliance of the workers, peasants, urban petty bourgeoisie and all others who are against imperialism and feudalism. Only under the leadership of the proletariat can such a republic be completely realized.

6. THE PERSPECTIVES OF THE CHINESE REVOLUTION

Now that the basic issues — the nature of Chinese society and the targets, tasks, motive forces and character of the Chinese revolution at the present stage — have been clarified, it is easy to see its perspectives, that is, to understand the relation between the bourgeois-democratic and the proletarian-socialist revolution, or between the present and future stages of the Chinese revolution.

There can be no doubt that the ultimate perspective of the Chinese revolution is not capitalism but socialism and communism, since China's bourgeois-democratic revolution at the present stage is not of the old general type but is a democratic revolution of a new special type — a new-democratic revolution — and since it is taking place in the new international environment of the Nineteen Thirties and Forties characterized by the rise of socialism and the decline of capitalism, in the period of the Second World War and the era of revolution.

However, it is not at all surprising but entirely to be expected that a capitalist economy will develop to a certain extent within Chinese society with the sweeping away of the obstacles to the development of capitalism after the victory of the revolution, since the purpose of the Chinese revolution at the present stage is to change the existing colonial, semi-colonial and semi-feudal state of society, i.e., to strive for the completion of the new-democratic revolution. A certain degree of capitalist development will be an inevitable result of the victory of the democratic revolution in economically backward China. But that will be only one aspect of the outcome of the Chinese revolution and not the whole picture. The whole picture will show the development of socialist as well as capitalist factors. What will the socialist factors be? The increasing relative importance of the proletariat and the Communist Party among the political forces in the country; leadership by the proletariat and the Communist Party which the peasantry, intelligentsia and the urban petty bourgeoisie already accept or are likely to accept; and the state sector of the economy owned by the democratic republic, and the co-operative sector of the economy owned by the working people. All these will be socialist factors. With the addition of a favourable international environment, these factors render it highly probable that China's bourgeois-democratic revolution will ultimately avoid a capitalist future and enjoy a socialist future.

7. THE TWOFOLD TASK OF THE CHINESE REVOLUTION AND THE CHINESE COMMUNIST PARTY

Summing up the foregoing sections of this chapter, we can see that the Chinese revolution taken as a whole involves a twofold task. That is to say, it embraces both the bourgeois-democratic revolution (the new-democratic revolution) and the proletarian-socialist revolution, *i.e.*, both the present and future stages of the revolution. The leadership in this twofold revolutionary task devolves on the Chinese Communist Party, the party of the proletariat, without whose leadership no revolution can succeed.

To complete China's bourgeois-democratic revolution (the new-democratic revolution) and to transform it into a socialist revolution when all the necessary conditions are ripe — such is the sum total of the great and glorious revolutionary task of the Chinese Communist Party. Every Party member must strive for its accomplishment and must under no circumstances give up halfway. Some immature Communists think that our task is confined to the present democratic revolution and does not include the future socialist revolution, or that the present revolution or the Agrarian Revolution is actually a socialist revolution. It must be emphatically pointed out that these views are wrong. Every Communist ought to know that, taken as a whole, the Chinese revolutionary movement led by the Communist Party embraces the two stages, *i.e.*, the democratic and the socialist revolutions, which are two essentially different revolutionary processes, and that the second process can be carried through only after the first has been completed. The democratic revolution is the necessary preparation for the socialist revolution, and the socialist revolution is the inevitable sequel to the democratic revolution. The ultimate aim for which all communists strive is to bring about a socialist and communist society. A clear understanding of both the differences and the interconnections between the democratic and the socialist revolutions is indispensable to correct leadership in the Chinese revolution.

Except for the Communist Party, no political party (bourgeois or petty-bourgeois) is equal to the task of leading China's two great revolutions, the democratic and the socialist revolutions, to complete fulfilment. From the very day of its birth, the Communist Party has taken this twofold task on its own shoulders and for eighteen years has fought strenuously for its accomplishment.

It is a task at once glorious and arduous. And it cannot be accomplished without a bolshevized Chinese Communist Party which is national in scale and has a broad mass character, a party fully consolidated ideologically, politically and organizationally. Therefore every Communist has the duty of playing an active part in building up such a Communist Party.

NOTES

[1] With reference to the invention of the compass, the magnetic power of the loadstone was mentioned as early as the 3rd century B.C. by Lu Pu-wei in his *Almanac*, and at the beginning of the 1st century A.D., Wang Chung, the materialist philosopher, observed in his *Lun Heng* that the loadstone points to the south, which indicates that magnetic polarity was known by then. Works of travel written at the beginning of the 12th century show that the compass was already in general use among Chinese navigators at that time.

[2] It is recorded in ancient documents that Tsai Lun, a eunuch of the Eastern Han Dynasty (A.D. 25-220), invented paper, which he had made from bark, hemp, rags and worn-out fishing nets. In A.D. 105 (the last year of the reign of Emperor Ho Ti), Tsai Lun presented his invention to the emperor, and subsequently this method of making paper from plant fibre gradually spread in China.

[3] Block-printing was invented about A.D. 600, in the Sui Dynasty.

[4] Movable type was invented by Pi Sheng in the Sung Dynasty between 1041 and 1048.

[5] According to tradition, gunpowder was invented in China in the 9th century, and by the 11th century it was already in use for firing cannon.

[6] Chen Sheng, Wu Kuang, Hsiang Yu and Liu Pang were leaders of the first great peasant uprising in the Chin Dynasty. In 209 B.C. Chen Sheng and Wu Kuang,

who were among nine hundred conscripts on their way to take up garrison duty at a frontier post, organized a revolt in Chihsien County (now Suhsien County in Anhwei Province) against the tyranny of the Chin Dynasty. Hsiang Yu and Liu Pang were the most prominent of those who rose in response to this armed uprising all over the country. Hsiang Yu's army annihilated the main forces of Chin, and Liu Pang's troops took Chin's capital. In the ensuing struggle between Liu Pang and Hsiang Yu, Liu Pang defeated Hsiang Yu and founded the Han Dynasty.

[7] The Hsinshih, the Pinglin, the Red Eyebrows and the Bronze Horses are the names of peasant uprisings in the latter years of the Western Han Dynasty when peasant unrest was widespread. In A.D. 8, Wang Mang overthrew the reigning dynasty, ascended the throne and introduced a few reforms to stave off the peasant unrest. But the starving masses in Hsinshih (in what is now Chingshan County in Hupeh) and Pinglin (in what is now Suihsien County in Hupeh) rose in revolt. The Bronze Horses and the Red Eyebrows were the peasant forces which revolted during his reign in what are now central Hopei and central Shantung Provinces. The Red Eyebrows, the largest of the peasant forces, were so named because the soldiers painted their eyebrows red.

[8] The Yellow Turbans, a peasant force which revolted in A.D. 184, were named after their headgear.

[9] Li Mi and Tou Chien-teh were leaders of great peasant uprisings against the Sui Dynasty in Honan and Hopei respectively at the opening of the 7th century.

[10] Wang Hsien-chih organized an uprising in Shantung in A.D. 874. In the following year Huang Chao organized an uprising to support him.

[11] Sung Chiang and Fang La were famous leaders of peasant uprisings early in the 12th century; Sung Chiang was active along the borders between Shantung, Hopei, Honan and Kiangsu, while Fang La was active in Chekiang and Anhwei.

[12] In 1351, the people in many parts of the country rose in revolt against the rule of the Yuan (Mongol) Dynasty. In 1352, Chu Yuan-chang joined the rebel forces led by Kuo Tzu-hsing and became their commander upon the latter's death. In 1368, he finally succeeded in overthrowing the rule of the Mongol Dynasty, which had been tottering under the attacks of the people's forces, and founded the Ming Dynasty.

[13] Li Tzu-cheng, also called King Chuang (the Dare-All King), native of Michih, northern Shensi, was the leader of a peasant revolt which led to the overthrow of the Ming Dynasty. The revolt first started in northern Shensi in 1628. Li joined the forces led by Kao Ying-hsiang and campaigned through Honan and Anhwei and back to Shensi. After Kao's death in 1636, Li succeeded him, becoming King Chuang, and campaigned in and out of the provinces of Shensi, Szechuan, Honan and Hupeh. Finally he captured the imperial capital of Peking in 1644, whereupon the last Ming emperor committed suicide. The chief slogan he spread among the masses was "Support King Chuang, and pay no grain taxes". Another slogan of his to enforce discipline among his men ran: "Any murder means the killing of my father, any rape means the violation of my mother." Thus he won the support of the masses and his movement became the main current of the peasant revolts raging all over the country. As he, too, roamed about without ever establishing relatively consolidated base areas, he was eventually defeated by Wu San-kuei, a Ming general, who colluded with the Ching troops in a joint attack on Li.

[14] From 1856 to 1860 Britain and France jointly waged a war of aggression against China, with the United States and tsarist Russia supporting them from the side-lines. The government of the Ching Dynasty was then devoting all its energies

to suppressing the peasant revolution of the Taiping Heavenly Kingdom and adopted a policy of passive resistance towards the foreign aggressors. The Anglo-French forces occupied such major cities as Canton, Tientsin and Peking, plundered and burned down the Yuan Ming Yuan Palace in Peking and forced the Ching government to conclude the Treaties of Tientsin and Peking. Their main provisions included the opening of Tientsin, Newchwang, Tengchow, Taiwan, Tamsui, Chaochow, Chiungchow, Nanking, Chinkiang, Kiukiang and Hankow as treaty ports, and the granting to foreigners of special privileges for travel, missionary activities and inland navigation in China's interior. From then on, the foreign forces of aggression spread through all China's coastal provinces and penetrated deep into the hinterland.

[15] In 1882-83, the French aggressors invaded the northern part of Indo-China. In 1884-85 they extended their war of aggression to the Chinese provinces of Kwangsi, Taiwan, Fukien and Chekiang. Despite the victories gained in this war, the corrupt Ching government signed the humiliating Treaty of Tientsin.

[16] In 1900 eight imperialist powers, Britain, the United States, Germany, France, tsarist Russia, Japan, Italy and Austria, sent a joint force to attack China in their attempt to suppress the Yi Ho Tuan Movement of the Chinese people against aggression. The Chinese people resisted heroically. The allied forces of the eight powers captured Taku and occupied Tientsin and Peking. In 1901 the Ching government concluded a treaty with the eight imperialist countries; its main provisions were that China had to pay those countries the huge sum of 450 million taels of silver as war reparations and grant them the special privilege of stationing troops in Peking and in the area from Peking to Tientsin and Shanhaikuan.

[17] Consular jurisdiction was one of the special privileges provided in the unequal treaties which the imperialist powers forced on the governments of old China — beginning with the supplementary treaty to the Sino-British Treaty of Nanking, signed at Humen (the Bogue) in 1843, and with the Sino-American Treaty of Wanghia in 1844. It meant that, if a national of any country enjoying the privilege of consular jurisdiction in China became a defendant in a lawsuit, civil or criminal, he was not to be tried by a Chinese court but by the consul of his own country.

[18] Spheres of influence were different parts of China marked off at the end of the 19th century by the imperialist powers that committed aggression against China. Each of these powers marked off those areas which fell within its economic and military influence. Thus, the provinces in the lower and middle Yangtse valley were specified as the British sphere of influence; Yunnan, Kwangtung and Kwangsi as the French; Shantung as the German sphere; Fukien as the Japanese; and the three northeastern provinces (the present provinces of Liaoning, Kirin and Heilungkiang) as the tsarist Russian sphere. After the Russo-Japanese War of 1905 the southern part of the three northeastern provinces came under Japanese influence.

[19] The foreign concessions were areas which the imperialist powers seized in the treaty ports after compelling the Ching government to open these ports. In these so-called concessions they enforced an imperialist system of colonial rule entirely independent of Chinese law and administration. Through those concessions, the imperialists exercised direct or indirect political and economic control over the Chinese feudal and comprador regime. During the revolution of 1924-27 the revolutionary people led by the Chinese Communist Party started a movement to abolish the concessions, and in January 1927 they took over the British concessions in Hankow and Kiukiang. However, the imperialists retained various concessions after Chiang Kai-shek betrayed the revolution.

[20] "The Theses on the Revolutionary Movement in Colonial and Semi-Colonial Countries" adopted by the Sixth Comintern Congress, stenographic record of the Sixth Comintern Congress, issue No. 6, Russ. ed., Moscow, 1929, p. 128.

[21] J. V. Stalin, "The Revolution in China and the Tasks of the Comintern", *Works*, Eng. ed., FLPH, Moscow, 1954, Vol. IX, p. 292.

[22] J. V. Stalin, "The Prospects of the Revolution in China", *Works*, Eng. ed., FLPH, Moscow, 1954, Vol. VIII, p. 379.

[23] See V. I. Lenin, "The Agrarian Programme of Social-Democracy in the First Russian Revolution, 1905-1907", *Collected Works*, Eng. ed., FLPH, Moscow, 1962, Vol. XIII, pp. 219-429.

STALIN, FRIEND OF THE CHINESE PEOPLE

December 20, 1939

On the Twenty-first of December, Comrade Stalin will be sixty years old. We can be sure that his birthday will evoke warm and affectionate congratulations from the hearts of all revolutionary people throughout the world who know of the occasion.

Congratulating Stalin is not a formality. Congratulating Stalin means supporting him and his cause, supporting the victory of socialism, and the way forward for mankind which he points out, it means supporting a dear friend. For the great majority of mankind today are suffering, and mankind can free itself from suffering only by the road pointed out by Stalin and with his help.

Living in a period of the bitterest suffering in our history, we Chinese people most urgently need help from others. The *Book of Odes* says, "A bird sings out to draw a friend's response." This aptly describes our present situation.

But who are our friends?

There are so-called friends, self-styled friends of the Chinese people, whom even some Chinese unthinkingly accept as friends. But such friends can only be classed with Li Lin-fu,[1] the prime minister in the Tang Dynasty who was notorious as a man with "honey on his lips and murder in his heart". They are indeed "friends" with "honey on their lips and murder in their hearts". Who are these people? They are the imperialists who profess sympathy with China.

However, there are friends of another kind, friends who have real sympathy with us and regard us as brothers. Who are they? They are the Soviet people and Stalin.

No other country has renounced its privileges in China; the Soviet Union alone has done so.

All the imperialists opposed us during our First Great Revolution; the Soviet Union alone helped us.

No government of any imperialist country has given us real help since the outbreak of the War of Resistance Against Japan; the Soviet Union alone has helped China with its aviation and supplies.

Is not the point clear enough?

Only the land of socialism, its leaders and people, and socialist thinkers, statesmen and workers can give real help to the cause of liberation of the Chinese nation and the Chinese people, and without their help our cause cannot win final victory.

Stalin is the true friend of the cause of liberation of the Chinese people. No attempt to sow dissension, no lies and calumnies, can affect the Chinese people's whole-hearted love and respect for Stalin and our genuine friendship for the Soviet Union.

NOTES

[1] Li Lin-fu (8th century) was a prime minister under Emperor Hsuan Tsung of the Tang Dynasty. Although feigning friendship, he plotted the ruin of all those who surpassed him in ability and fame or found favour in the emperor's eyes. Hence he was known to his contemporaries as a man with "honey on his lips and murder in his heart".

IN MEMORY OF NORMAN BETHUNE

December 21, 1939

Comrade Norman Bethune,[1] a member of the Communist Party of Canada, was around fifty when he was sent by the Communist Parties of Canada and the United States to China; he made light of travelling thousands of miles to help us in our War of Resistance Against Japan. He arrived in Yenan in the spring of last year, went to work in the Wutai Mountains, and to our great sorrow died a martyr at his post. What kind of spirit is this that makes a foreigner selflessly adopt the cause of the Chinese people's liberation as his own? It is the spirit of internationalism, the spirit of communism, from which every Chinese Communist must learn. Leninism teaches that the world revolution can only succeed if the proletariat of the capitalist countries supports the struggle for liberation of the colonial and semi-colonial peoples and if the proletariat of the colonies and semi-colonies supports that of the proletariat of the capitalist countries.[2] Comrade Bethune put this Leninist line into practice. We Chinese Communists must also follow this line in our practice. We must unite with the proletariat of all the capitalist countries, with the proletariat of Japan, Britain, the United States, Germany, Italy and all other capitalist countries, for this is the only way to overthrow imperialism, to liberate our nation and people and to liberate the other nations and peoples of the world. This is our internationalism, the internationalism with which we oppose both narrow nationalism and narrow patriotism.

Comrade Bethune's spirit, his utter devotion to others without any thought of self, was shown in his great sense of responsibility in his work and his great warm-heartedness towards all comrades and the people. Every Communist must learn from him. There are not a few people who are irresponsible in their work, preferring the light and shirking the heavy, passing the burdensome tasks on to others and choosing the easy ones for themselves. At every turn they think of themselves before others. When they make some small contribution, they swell with pride and brag about it for fear that others will not know. They feel no warmth towards comrades and the people but are cold, indifferent and apathetic. In truth such people are not Communists, or at least cannot be counted as devoted Communists. No one who returned from the front failed to express admiration for Bethune whenever his name was mentioned, and none remained unmoved by his spirit. In the Shansi-Chahar-Hopei border area, no soldier or civilian was unmoved who had been treated by Dr. Bethune or had seen how he worked. Every Communist must learn this true communist spirit from Comrade Bethune.

Comrade Bethune was a doctor, the art of healing was his profession and he was constantly perfecting his skill, which stood very high in the Eighth Route Army's medical service. His example is an excellent lesson for those people who wish to change their work the moment they see something different and for those who despise technical work as of no consequence or as promising no future.

Comrade Bethune and I met only once. Afterwards he wrote me many letters. But I was busy, and I wrote him only one letter and do not even know if he ever received it. I am deeply grieved over his death. Now we are all commemorating him, which shows how profoundly his spirit inspires everyone. We must all learn the spirit of absolute selflessness from him. With this spirit everyone can be very useful to the people. A man's ability may be great or small, but if he has this spirit, he is already noble-minded and pure, a man of moral integrity and above vulgar interests, a man who is of value to the people.

NOTES

[1] The distinguished surgeon Norman Bethune was a member of the Canadian Communist Party. In 1936 when the German and Italian fascist bandits invaded Spain, he went to the front and worked for the anti-fascist Spanish people. In order to help the Chinese people in their War of Resistance Against Japan, he came to China at the head of a medical team and arrived in Yenan in the spring of 1938. Soon after he went to the Shansi-Chahar-Hopei border area. Imbued with ardent internationalism and the great communist spirit, he served the army and the people of the Liberated Areas for nearly two years. He contracted blood poisoning while operating on wounded soldiers and died in Tanghsien, Hopei, on November 12, 1939.

[2] See J. V. Stalin, "The Foundations of Leninism", *Problems of Leninism*, Eng. ed., FLPH, Moscow, 1954, pp. 70-79.

ON NEW DEMOCRACY

January 1940

I. WHITHER CHINA?

A lively atmosphere has prevailed throughout the country ever since the War of Resistance began, there is a general feeling that a way out of the impasse has been found, and people no longer knit their brows in despair. Of late, however, the dust and din of compromise and anti-communism have once again filled the air, and once again the people are thrown into bewilderment. Most susceptible, and the first to be affected, are the intellectuals and the young students. The question once again arises: What is to be done? Whither China? On the occasion of the publication of *Chinese Culture*,[1] it may therefore be profitable to clarify the political and cultural trends in the country. I am a layman in matters of culture; I would like to study them, but have only just begun to do so. Fortunately, there are many comrades in Yenan who have written at length in this field, so that my rough and ready words may serve the same purpose as the beating of the gongs before a theatrical performance. Our observations may contain a grain of truth for the nation's advanced cultural workers and may serve as a modest spur to induce them to come forward with valuable contributions of their own, and we hope that they will join in the discussion to reach correct conclusions which will meet our national needs. To "seek truth from facts" is the scientific approach, and presumptuously to claim infallibility and lecture people will never settle anything. The troubles that have befallen our nation are extremely serious, and only a scientific approach and a spirit of responsibility can lead it on to the road of liberation. There is but one truth, and the question of whether or not one has arrived at it depends not on subjective boasting but on objective practice. The only yardstick of truth is the revolutionary practice of millions of people. This, I think, can be regarded as the attitude of *Chinese Culture*.

II. WE WANT TO BUILD A NEW CHINA

For many years we Communists have struggled for a cultural revolution as well as for a political and economic revolution, and our aim is to build a new society and a new state for the Chinese nation. That new society and new state will have not only a new politics and a new economy but a new culture. In other words, not only do we want to change a China that is politically oppressed and economically exploited into a China that is politically free and economically prosperous, we also want to change the China which is being kept ignorant and backward under the sway of the old culture into an enlightened and progressive China under the sway of a new culture. In short, we want to build a new China. Our aim in the cultural sphere is to build a new Chinese national culture.

III. CHINA'S HISTORICAL CHARACTERISTICS

We want to build a new national culture, but what kind of culture should it be?

Any given culture (as an ideological form) is a reflection of the politics and economics of a given society, and the former in turn has a tremendous influence and effect upon the latter; economics is the base and politics the concentrated expression of economics.[2] This is our fundamental view of the relation of culture to politics and economics and of the relation of politics to economics. It follows that the form of culture is first determined by the political and economic form, and only then does it operate on and influence the given political and economic form. Marx says, "It is not the consciousness of men that determines their being, but, on the contrary, their social being that determines their consciousness."[3] He also says, "The philosophers have only *interpreted* the world, in various ways; the point, however, is to *change* it."[4] For the first time in human history, these scientific formulations correctly solved the problem of the relationship between consciousness and existence, and they are the basic concepts underlying the dynamic revolutionary theory of knowledge as the reflection of reality which was later elaborated so profoundly by Lenin. These basic concepts must be kept in mind in our discussion of China's cultural problems.

Thus it is quite clear that the reactionary elements of the old national culture we want to eliminate are inseparable from the old national politics and economics, while the new national culture which we want to build up is inseparable from the new national politics and economics. The old politics and economics of the Chinese nation form the basis of its old culture, just as its new politics and economics will form the basis of its new culture.

What are China's old politics and economics? And what is her old culture?

From the Chou and Chin Dynasties onwards, Chinese society was feudal, as were its politics and its economy. And the dominant culture, reflecting the politics and economy, was feudal culture.

Since the invasion of foreign capitalism and the gradual growth of capitalist elements in Chinese society, the country has changed by degrees into a colonial, semi-colonial and semi-feudal society. China today is colonial in the Japanese-occupied areas and basically semi-colonial in the Kuomintang areas, and it is predominantly feudal or semi-feudal in both. Such, then, is the character of present-day Chinese society and the state of affairs in our country. The politics and the economy of this society are predominantly colonial, semi-colonial and semi-feudal, and the predominant culture, reflecting the politics and economy, is also colonial, semi-colonial and semi-feudal.

It is precisely against these predominant political, economic and cultural forms that our revolution is directed. What we want to get rid of is the old colonial, semi-colonial and semi-feudal politics and economy and the old culture in their service. And what we want to build up is their direct opposite, *i.e.*, the new politics, the new economy and the new culture of the Chinese nation.

What, then, are the new politics and the new economy of the Chinese nation, and what is its new culture?

In the course of its history the Chinese revolution must go through two stages, first, the democratic revolution, and second, the socialist revolution, and by their very nature they are two different revolutionary

processes. Here democracy does not belong to the old category —
it is not the old democracy, but belongs to the new category — it is
New Democracy.

It can thus be affirmed that China's new politics are the politics
of New Democracy, that China's new economy is the economy of
New Democracy and that China's new culture is the culture of New
Democracy.

Such are the historical characteristics of the Chinese revolution
at the present time. Any political party, group or person taking part
in the Chinese revolution that fails to understand this will not be able
to direct the revolution and lead it to victory, but will be cast aside
by the people and left to grieve out in the cold.

IV.   THE CHINESE REVOLUTION IS PART OF
THE WORLD REVOLUTION

The historical characteristic of the Chinese revolution lies in its
division into the two stages, democracy and socialism, the first being
no longer democracy in general, but democracy of the Chinese type, a
new and special type, namely, New Democracy. How, then, has this
historical characteristic come into being? Has it been in existence for
the past hundred years, or is it of recent origin?

A brief study of the historical development of China and of the
world shows that this characteristic did not emerge immediately after
the Opium War, but took shape later, after the first imperialist world
war and the October Revolution in Russia. Let us now examine the
process of its formation.

Clearly, it follows from the colonial, semi-colonial and semi-feudal
character of present-day Chinese society that the Chinese revolution
must be divided into two stages. The first step is to change the colonial,
semi-colonial and semi-feudal form of society into an independent,
democratic society. The second is to carry the revolution forward and
build a socialist society. At present the Chinese revolution is taking
the first step.

The preparatory period for the first step began with the Opium
War in 1840, i.e., when China's feudal society started changing into a
semi-colonial and semi-feudal one. Then came the Movement of the
Taiping Heavenly Kingdom, the Sino-French War, the Sino-Japanese

War, the Reform Movement of 1898, the Revolution of 1911, the May 4th
Movement, the Northern Expedition, the War of the Agrarian Revolution and the present War of Resistance Against Japan. Together these
have taken up a whole century and in a sense they represent that
first step, being struggles waged by the Chinese people, on different
occasions and in varying degrees, against imperialism and the feudal
forces in order to build up an independent, democratic society and
complete the first revolution. The Revolution of 1911 was in a fuller
sense the beginning of that revolution. In its social character, this
revolution is a bourgeois-democratic and not a proletarian-socialist
revolution. It is still unfinished and still demands great efforts, because
to this day its enemies are still very strong. When Dr. Sun Yat-sen
said, "The revolution is not yet completed, all my comrades must
struggle on", he was referring to the bourgeois-democratic revolution.

A change, however, occurred in China's bourgeois-democratic
revolution after the outbreak of the first imperialist world war in 1914
and the founding of a socialist state on one-sixth of the globe as a
result of the Russian October Revolution of 1917.

Before these events, the Chinese bourgeois-democratic revolution
came within the old category of the bourgeois-democratic world revolution, of which it was a part.

Since these events, the Chinese bourgeois-democratic revolution
has changed, it has come within the new category of bourgeois-
democratic revolutions and, as far as the alignment of revolutionary
forces is concerned, forms part of the proletarian-socialist world
revolution.

Why? Because the first imperialist world war and the first
victorious socialist revolution, the October Revolution, have changed
the whole course of world history and ushered in a new era.

It is an era in which the world capitalist front has collapsed in
one part of the globe (one-sixth of the world) and has fully revealed
its decadence everywhere else, in which the remaining capitalist parts
cannot survive without relying more than ever on the colonies and
semi-colonies, in which a socialist state has been established and
has proclaimed its readiness to give active support to the liberation
movement of all colonies and semi-colonies, and in which the
proletariat of the capitalist countries is steadily freeing itself from
the social-imperialist influence of the social-democratic parties and
has proclaimed its support for the liberation movement in the colonies
and semi-colonies. In this era, any revolution in a colony or semi-colony

that is directed against imperialism, *i.e.*, against the international bourgeoisie or international capitalism, no longer comes within the old category of the bourgeois-democratic world revolution, but within the new category. It is no longer part of the old bourgeois, or capitalist, world revolution, but is part of the new world revolution, the proletarian-socialist world revolution. Such revolutionary colonies and semi-colonies can no longer be regarded as allies of the counter-revolutionary front of world capitalism; they have become allies of the revolutionary front of world socialism.

Although such a revolution in a colonial and semi-colonial country is still fundamentally bourgeois-democratic in its social character during its first stage or first step, and although its objective mission is to clear the path for the development of capitalism, it is no longer a revolution of the old type led by the bourgeoisie with the aim of establishing a capitalist society and a state under bourgeois dictatorship. It belongs to the new type of revolution led by the proletariat with the aim, in the first stage, of establishing a new-democratic society and a state under the joint dictatorship of all the revolutionary classes. Thus this revolution actually serves the purpose of clearing a still wider path for the development of socialism. In the course of its progress, there may be a number of further sub-stages, because of changes on the enemy's side and within the ranks of our allies, but the fundamental character of the revolution remains unchanged.

Such a revolution attacks imperialism at its very roots, and is therefore not tolerated but opposed by imperialism. However, it is favoured by socialism and supported by the land of socialism and the socialist international proletariat.

Therefore, such a revolution inevitably becomes part of the proletarian-socialist world revolution.

The correct thesis that "the Chinese revolution is part of the world revolution" was put forward as early as 1924-27 during the period of China's First Great Revolution. It was put forward by the Chinese Communists and endorsed by all those taking part in the anti-imperialist and anti-feudal struggle of the time. However, the significance of this thesis was not fully expounded in those days, and consequently it was only vaguely understood.

The "world revolution" no longer refers to the old world revolution, for the old bourgeois world revolution has long been a thing of the past; it refers to the new world revolution, the socialist world revolution. Similarly, to form "part of" means to form part not of the old bourgeois but of the new socialist revolution. This is a tremendous change unparalleled in the history of China and of the world.

This correct thesis advanced by the Chinese Communists is based on Stalin's theory.

As early as 1918, in an article commemorating the first anniversary of the October Revolution, Stalin wrote:

> The great world-wide significance of the October Revolution chiefly consists in the fact that:
>
> 1) It has widened the scope of the national question and converted it from the particular question of combating national oppression in Europe into the general question of emancipating the oppressed peoples, colonies and semi-colonies from imperialism;
>
> 2) It has opened up wide possibilities for their emancipation and the right paths towards it, has thereby greatly facilitated the cause of the emancipation of the oppressed peoples of the West and the East, and has drawn them into the common current of the victorious struggle against imperialism;
>
> 3) *It has thereby erected a bridge between the socialist West and the enslaved East,* having created a new front of revolutions *against* world imperialism, extending from the proletarians of the West, through the Russian Revolution, to the oppressed peoples of the East.[5]

Since writing this article, Stalin has again and again expounded the theory that revolutions in the colonies and semi-colonies have broken away from the old category and become part of the proletarian-socialist revolution. The clearest and most precise explanation is given in an article published on June 30, 1925, in which Stalin carried on a controversy with the Yugoslav nationalists of the time. Entitled "The National Question Once Again", it is included in a book translated by Chang Chung-shih and published under the title *Stalin on the National Question*. It contains the following passage:

> Semich refers to a passage in Stalin's pamphlet *Marxism and the National Question,* written at the end of 1912. There it says that "the national struggle under the conditions of *rising* capitalism is a struggle of the bourgeois classes among themselves". Evidently, by this Semich is trying to suggest that his formula defining the social significance of the national movement under the present

historical conditions is correct. But Stalin's pamphlet was written before the imperialist war, when the national question was not yet regarded by Marxists as a question of world significance, when the Marxists' fundamental demand for the right to self-determination was regarded not as part of the proletarian revolution, but as part of the bourgeois-democratic revolution. It would be ridiculous not to see that since then the international situation has radically changed, that the war, on the one hand, and the October Revolution in Russia, on the other, transformed the national question from a part of the bourgeois-democratic revolution into a part of the proletarian-socialist revolution. As far back as October 1916, in his article, "The Discussion on Self-Determination Summed Up", Lenin said that the main point of the national question, the right to self-determination, had ceased to be a part of the general democratic movement, that it had already become a component part of the general proletarian, socialist revolution. I do not even mention subsequent works on the national question by Lenin and by other representatives of Russian communism. After all this, what significance can Semich's reference to the passage in Stalin's pamphlet, written in the period of the *bourgeois*-democratic revolution in Russia, have at the present time, when, as a consequence of the new historical situation, we have entered a new epoch, the epoch of *proletarian* revolution? It can only signify that Semich quotes outside of space and time, without reference to the living historical situation, and thereby violates the most elementary requirements of dialectics, and ignores the fact that what is right for one historical situation may prove to be wrong in another historical situation.[6]

From this it can be seen that there are two kinds of world revolution, the first belonging to the bourgeois or capitalist category. The era of this kind of world revolution is long past, having come to an end as far back as 1914 when the first imperialist world war broke out, and more particularly in 1917 when the October Revolution took place. The second kind, namely, the proletarian-socialist world revolution, thereupon began. This revolution has the proletariat of the capitalist countries as its main force and the oppressed peoples of the colonies and semi-colonies as its allies. No matter what classes, parties or individuals in an oppressed nation join the revolution, and no matter whether they themselves are conscious of the point or understand it, so long as they oppose imperialism, their revolution becomes part of the proletarian-socialist world revolution and they become its allies.

Today, the Chinese revolution has taken on still greater significance. This is a time when the economic and political crises of capitalism are dragging the world more and more deeply into the Second World War, when the Soviet Union has reached the period of transition from socialism to communism and is capable of leading and helping the proletariat and oppressed nations of the whole world in their fight against imperialist war and capitalist reaction, when the proletariat of the capitalist countries is preparing to overthrow capitalism and establish socialism, and when the proletariat, the peasantry, the intelligentsia and other sections of the petty bourgeoisie in China have become a mighty independent political force under the leadership of the Chinese Communist Party. Situated as we are in this day and age, should we not make the appraisal that the Chinese revolution has taken on still greater world significance? I think we should. The Chinese revolution has become a very important part of the world revolution.

Although the Chinese revolution in this first stage (with its many sub-stages) is a new type of bourgeois-democratic revolution and is not yet itself a proletarian-socialist revolution in its social character, it has long become a part of the proletarian-socialist world revolution and is now even a very important part and a great ally of this world revolution. The first step or stage in our revolution is definitely not, and cannot be, the establishment of a capitalist society under the dictatorship of the Chinese bourgeoisie, but will result in the establishment of a new-democratic society under the joint dictatorship of all the revolutionary classes of China headed by the Chinese proletariat. The revolution will then be carried forward to the second stage, in which a socialist society will be established in China.

This is the fundamental characteristic of the Chinese revolution of today, of the new revolutionary process of the past twenty years (counting from the May 4th Movement of 1919), and its concrete living essence.

V.   THE POLITICS OF NEW DEMOCRACY

The new historical characteristic of the Chinese revolution is its division into two stages, the first being the new-democratic revolution.

How does this manifest itself concretely in internal political and economic relations? Let us consider the question.

Before the May 4th Movement of 1919 (which occurred after the first imperialist world war of 1914 and the Russian October Revolution of 1917), the petty bourgeoisie and the bourgeoisie (through their intellectuals) were the political leaders of the bourgeois-democratic revolution. The Chinese proletariat had not yet appeared on the political scene as an awakened and independent class force, but participated in the revolution only as a follower of the petty bourgeoisie and the bourgeoisie. Such was the case with the proletariat at the time of the Revolution of 1911.

After the May 4th Movement, the political leader of China's bourgeois-democratic revolution was no longer the bourgeoisie but the proletariat, although the national bourgeoisie continued to take part in the revolution. The Chinese proletariat rapidly became an awakened and independent political force as a result of its maturing and of the influence of the Russian Revolution. It was the Chinese Communist Party that put forward the slogan "Down with imperialism" and the thoroughgoing programme for the whole bourgeois-democratic revolution, and it was the Chinese Communist Party alone that carried out the Agrarian Revolution.

Being a bourgeoisie in a colonial and semi-colonial country and oppressed by imperialism, the Chinese national bourgeoisie retains a certain revolutionary quality at certain periods and to a certain degree — even in the era of imperialism — in its opposition to the foreign imperialists and the domestic governments of bureaucrats and warlords (instances of opposition to the latter can be found in the periods of the Revolution of 1911 and the Northern Expedition), and it may ally itself with the proletariat and the petty bourgeoisie against such enemies as it is ready to oppose. In this respect the Chinese bourgeoisie differs from the bourgeoisie of old tsarist Russia. Since tsarist Russia was a military-feudal imperialism which carried on aggression against other countries, the Russian bourgeoisie was entirely lacking in revolutionary quality. There, the task of the proletariat was to oppose the bourgeoisie, not to unite with it. But China's national bourgeoisie has a revolutionary quality at certain periods and to a certain degree, because China is a colonial and semi-colonial country which is a victim of aggression. Here, the task of the proletariat is to form a united front with the national bourgeoisie against imperialism and the bureaucrat and warlord governments without overlooking its revolutionary quality.

At the same time, however, being a bourgeois class in a colonial and semi-colonial country and so being extremely flabby economically and politically, the Chinese national bourgeoisie also has another quality, namely, a proneness to conciliation with the enemies of the revolution. Even when it takes part in the revolution, it is unwilling to break with imperialism completely and, moreover, it is closely associated with the exploitation of the rural areas through land rent; thus it is neither willing nor able to overthrow imperialism, and much less the feudal forces, in a thorough way. So neither of the two basic problems or tasks of China's bourgeois-democratic revolution can be solved or accomplished by the national bourgeoisie. As for China's big bourgeoisie, which is represented by the Kuomintang, all through the long period from 1927 to 1937 it nestled in the arms of the imperialists and formed an alliance with the feudal forces against the revolutionary people. In 1927 and for some time afterwards, the Chinese national bourgeoisie also followed the counter-revolution. During the present anti-Japanese war, the section of the big bourgeoisie represented by Wang Ching-wei has capitulated to the enemy, which constitutes a fresh betrayal on the part of the big bourgeoisie. In this respect, then, the bourgeoisie in China differs from the earlier bourgeoisie of the European and American countries, and especially of France. When the bourgeoisie in those countries, and especially in France, was still in its revolutionary era, the bourgeois revolution was comparatively thorough, whereas the bourgeoisie in China lacks even this degree of thoroughness.

Possible participation in the revolution on the one hand and proneness to conciliation with the enemies of the revolution on the other — such is the dual character of the Chinese bourgeoisie, it faces both ways. Even the bourgeoisie in European and American history had shared this dual character. When confronted by a formidable enemy, they united with the workers and peasants against him, but when the workers and peasants awakened, they turned round to unite with the enemy against the workers and peasants. This is a general rule applicable to the bourgeoisie everywhere in the world, but the trait is more pronounced in the Chinese bourgeoisie.

In China, it is perfectly clear that whoever can lead the people in overthrowing imperialism and the forces of feudalism can win the people's confidence, because these two, and especially imperialism, are the mortal enemies of the people. Today, whoever can lead the people in driving out Japanese imperialism and introducing democratic government will be the saviours of the people. History has proved that the Chinese bourgeoisie cannot fulfil this responsibility, which inevitably falls upon the shoulders of the proletariat.

Therefore, the proletariat, the peasantry, the intelligentsia and the other sections of the petty bourgeoisie undoubtedly constitute the basic forces determining China's fate. These classes, some already awakened and others in the process of awakening, will necessarily become the basic components of the state and governmental structure in the democratic republic of China, with the proletariat as the leading force. The Chinese democratic republic which we desire to establish now must be a democratic republic under the joint dictatorship of all anti-imperialist and anti-feudal people led by the proletariat, that is, a new-democratic republic, a republic of the genuinely revolutionary new Three People's Principles with their Three Great Policies.

This new-democratic republic will be different from the old European-American form of capitalist republic under bourgeois dictatorship, which is the old democratic form and already out of date. On the other hand, it will also be different from the socialist republic of the Soviet type under the dictatorship of the proletariat which is already flourishing in the U.S.S.R., and which, moreover, will be established in all the capitalist countries and will undoubtedly become the dominant form of state and governmental structure in all the industrially advanced countries. However, for a certain historical period, this form is not suitable for the revolutions in the colonial and semi-colonial countries. During this period, therefore, a third form of state must be adopted in the revolutions of all colonial and semi-colonial countries, namely, the new-democratic republic. This form suits a certain historical period and is therefore transitional; nevertheless, it is a form which is necessary and cannot be dispensed with.

Thus the numerous types of state system in the world can be reduced to three basic kinds according to the class character of their political power: (1) republics under bourgeois dictatorship; (2) republics under the dictatorship of the proletariat; and (3) republics under the joint dictatorship of several revolutionary classes.

The first kind comprises the old democratic states. Today, after the outbreak of the second imperialist war, there is hardly a trace of democracy in many of the capitalist countries, which have come or are coming under the bloody militarist dictatorship of the bourgeoisie.

Certain countries under the joint dictatorship of the landlords and the bourgeoisie can be grouped with this kind.

The second kind exists in the Soviet Union, and the conditions for its birth are ripening in capitalist countries. In the future, it will be the dominant form throughout the world for a certain period.

The third kind is the transitional form of state to be adopted in the revolutions of the colonial and semi-colonial countries. Each of these revolutions will necessarily have specific characteristics of its own, but these will be minor variations on a general theme. So long as they are revolutions in colonial or semi-colonial countries, their state and governmental structure will of necessity be basically the same, *i.e.*, a new-democratic state under the joint dictatorship of several anti-imperialist classes. In present-day China, the anti-Japanese united front represents the new-democratic form of state. It is anti-Japanese and anti-imperialist; it is also a united front, an alliance of several revolutionary classes. But unfortunately, despite the fact that the war has been going on for so long, the work of introducing democracy has hardly started in most of the country outside the democratic anti-Japanese base areas under the leadership of the Communist Party, and the Japanese imperialists have exploited this fundamental weakness to stride into our country. If nothing is done about it, our national future will be gravely imperilled.

The question under discussion here is that of the "state system". After several decades of wrangling since the last years of the Ching Dynasty, it has still not been cleared up. Actually it is simply a question of the status of the various social classes within the state. The bourgeoisie, as a rule, conceals the problem of class status and carries out its one-class dictatorship under the "national" label. Such concealment is of no advantage to the revolutionary people and the matter should be clearly explained to them. The term "national" is all right, but it must not include counter-revolutionaries and traitors. The kind of state we need today is a dictatorship of all the revolutionary classes over the counter-revolutionaries and traitors.

The so-called democratic system in modern states is usually monopolized by the bourgeoisie and has become simply an instrument for oppressing the common people. On the other hand, the Kuomintang's Principle of Democracy means a democratic system shared by all the common people and not privately owned by the few.

Such was the solemn declaration made in the Manifesto of the First
National Congress of the Kuomintang, held in 1924 during the period
of Kuomintang-Communist co-operation. For sixteen years the Kuomintang has violated this declaration and as a result it has created
the present grave national crisis. This is a gross blunder, which we
hope the Kuomintang will correct in the cleansing flames of the
anti-Japanese war.

As for the question of "the system of government", this is a matter
of how political power is organized, the form in which one social class
or another chooses to arrange its apparatus of political power to oppose
its enemies and protect itself. There is no state which does not have
an appropriate apparatus of political power to represent it. China may
now adopt a system of people's congresses, from the national people's
congress down to the provincial, county, district and township people's
congresses, with all levels electing their respective governmental bodies.
But if there is to be a proper representation for each revolutionary class
according to its status in the state, a proper expression of the people's
will, a proper direction for revolutionary struggles and a proper manifestation of the spirit of New Democracy, then a system of really
universal and equal suffrage, irrespective of sex, creed, property or
education, must be introduced. Such is the system of democratic
centralism. Only a government based on democratic centralism can
fully express the will of all the revolutionary people and fight the
enemies of the revolution most effectively. There must be a spirit of
refusal to be "privately owned by the few" in the government and the
army; without a genuinely democratic system this cannot be attained
and the system of government and the state system will be out of
harmony.

The state system, a joint dictatorship of all the revolutionary
classes and the system of government, democratic centralism — these
constitute the politics of New Democracy, the republic of New
Democracy, the republic of the anti-Japanese united front, the republic
of the new Three People's Principles with their Three Great Policies,
the Republic of China in reality as well as in name. Today we have
a Republic of China in name but not in reality, and our present task
is to create the reality that will fit the name.

Such are the internal political relations which a revolutionary
China, a China fighting Japanese aggression, should and must establish without fail; such is the orientation, the only correct orientation,
for our present work of national reconstruction.

VI. THE ECONOMY OF NEW DEMOCRACY

If such a republic is to be established in China, it must be new-democratic not only in its politics but also in its economy.

It will own the big banks and the big industrial and commercial enterprises.

> Enterprises, such as banks, railways and airlines, whether Chinese-owned or foreign-owned, which are either monopolistic in character or too big for private management, shall be operated and administered by the state, so that private capital cannot dominate the livelihood of the people: this is the main principle of the regulation of capital.

This is another solemn declaration in the Manifesto of the Kuomintang's First National Congress held during the period of Kuomintang-Communist co-operation, and it is the correct policy for the economic structure of the new-democratic republic. In the new-democratic republic under the leadership of the proletariat, the state enterprises will be of a socialist character and will constitute the leading force in the whole national economy, but the republic will neither confiscate capitalist private property in general nor forbid the development of such capitalist production as does not "dominate the livelihood of the people", for China's economy is still very backward.

The republic will take certain necessary steps to confiscate the land of the landlords and distribute it to those peasants having little or no land, carry out Dr. Sun Yat-sen's slogan of "land to the tiller", abolish feudal relations in the rural areas, and turn the land over to the private ownership of the peasants. A rich peasant economy will be allowed in the rural areas. Such is the policy of "equalization of landownership". "Land to the tiller" is the correct slogan for this policy. In general, socialist agriculture will not be established at this stage, though various types of co-operative enterprises developed on the basis of "land to the tiller" will contain elements of socialism.

China's economy must develop along the path of the "regulation of capital" and the "equalization of landownership", and must never be "privately owned by the few"; we must never permit the few capitalists and landlords to "dominate the livelihood of the people"; we must never establish a capitalist society of the European-American type or allow the old semi-feudal society to survive. Whoever dares to go counter to this line of advance will certainly not succeed but will run into a brick wall.

Such are the internal economic relations which a revolutionary China, a China fighting Japanese aggression, must and necessarily will establish.

Such is the economy of New Democracy.

And the politics of New Democracy are the concentrated expression of the economy of New Democracy.

VII. REFUTATION OF BOURGEOIS DICTATORSHIP

More than 90 per cent of the people are in favour of a republic of this kind with its new-democratic politics and new-democratic economy; there is no alternative road.

What about the road to a capitalist society under bourgeois dictatorship? To be sure, that was the old road taken by the European and American bourgeoisie, but whether one likes it or not, neither the international nor the domestic situation allows China to do the same.

Judging by the international situation, that road is blocked. In its fundamentals, the present international situation is one of a struggle between capitalism and socialism, in which capitalism is on the downgrade and socialism on the upgrade. In the first place international capitalism, or imperialism, will not permit the establishment in China of a capitalist society under bourgeois dictatorship. Indeed the history of modern China is a history of imperialist aggression, of imperialist opposition to China's independence and to her development of capitalism. Earlier revolutions failed in China because imperialism strangled them, and innumerable revolutionary martyrs died, bitterly lamenting the non-fulfilment of their mission. Today a powerful Japanese imperialism is forcing its way into China and wants to reduce her to a colony; it is not China that is developing Chinese capitalism but Japan that is developing Japanese capitalism in our country; and it is not the Chinese bourgeoisie but the Japanese bourgeoisie that is exercising dictatorship in our country. True enough, this is the period of the final struggle of dying imperialism — imperialism is "moribund capitalism".[7] But just because it is dying, it is all the more dependent on colonies and semi-colonies for survival and will certainly not allow any colony or semi-colony to establish anything like a capitalist society under the dictatorship of its own bourgeoisie. Just because Japanese imperialism is bogged down in serious economic and political crises, just because it is dying, it must invade China and reduce her to a colony, thereby blocking the road to bourgeois dictatorship and national capitalism in China.

In the second place, socialism will not permit it. All the imperialist powers in the world are our enemies, and China cannot possibly gain her independence without the assistance of the land of socialism and the international proletariat. That is, she cannot do so without the help of the Soviet Union and the help which the proletariat of Japan, Britain, the United States, France, Germany, Italy and other countries provide through their struggles against capitalism. Although no one can say that the victory of the Chinese revolution must wait upon the victory of the revolution in all of these countries, or in one or two of them, there is no doubt that we cannot win without the added strength of their proletariat. In particular, Soviet assistance is absolutely indispensable for China's final victory in the War of Resistance. Refuse Soviet assistance, and the revolution will fail. Don't the anti-Soviet campaigns from 1927 onwards[8] provide an extraordinarily clear lesson? The world today is in a new era of wars and revolutions, an era in which capitalism is unquestionably dying and socialism is unquestionably prospering. In these circumstances, would it not be sheer fantasy to desire the establishment in China of a capitalist society under bourgeois dictatorship after the defeat of imperialism and feudalism?

Even though the petty Kemalist dictatorship of the bourgeoisie[9] did emerge in Turkey after the first imperialist world war and the October Revolution owing to certain specific conditions (the bourgeoisie's success in repelling Greek aggression and the weakness of the proletariat), there can be no second Turkey, much less a "Turkey" with a population of 450 million, after World War II and the accomplishment of socialist construction in the Soviet Union. In the specific conditions of China (the flabbiness of the bourgeoisie with its proneness to conciliation and the strength of the proletariat with its revolutionary thoroughness), things just never work out so easily as in Turkey. Did not some members of the Chinese bourgeoisie clamour for Kemalism after the First Great Revolution failed in 1927? But where is China's Kemal? And where are China's bourgeois dictatorship and capitalist society? Besides, even Kemalist Turkey eventually had to throw herself into the arms of Anglo-French imperialism, becoming more and more of a semi-colony and part of the reactionary imperialist world. In the international situation of today, the "heroes" in the colonies and semi-colonies either line up on the imperialist front and become part of the forces of world counter-revolution, or they line up on the anti-imperialist front and become part of the forces of world revolution. They must do one or the other, for there is no third choice.

Judging by the domestic situation, too, the Chinese bourgeoisie should have learned its lesson by now. No sooner had the strength of the proletariat and of the peasant and other petty bourgeois masses brought the revolution of 1927 to victory than the capitalist class, headed by the big bourgeoisie, kicked the masses aside, seized the fruits of the revolution, formed a counter-revolutionary alliance with imperialism and the feudal forces, and strained themselves to the limit in a war of "Communist suppression" for ten years. But what was the upshot? Today, when a powerful enemy has penetrated deep into our territory and the anti-Japanese war has been going on for two years, is it possible that there are still people who want to copy the obsolete recipes of the European and American bourgeoisie? A decade was spent on "suppressing the Communists" out of existence, but no capitalist society under bourgeois dictatorship was "suppressed" into existence. Is it possible that there are still people who want to have another try? True, a "one-party dictatorship" was "suppressed" into existence through the decade of "Communist suppression", but it is a semi-colonial and semi-feudal dictatorship. What is more, at the end of four years of "Communist suppression" (from 1927 to the Incident of September 18, 1931), "Manchukuo" was "suppressed" into existence and in 1937, after another six years of such "suppression", the Japanese imperialists made their way into China south of the Great Wall. Today if anyone wants to carry on "suppression" for another decade, it would mean a new type of "Communist suppression", somewhat different from the old. But is there not one fleet-footed person who has already outstripped everyone else and boldly undertaken this new enterprise of "Communist suppression"? Yes, Wang Ching-wei, who has become the new-style anti-Communist celebrity. Anyone who wishes to join his gang can please himself; but wouldn't that turn out to be an added embarrassment when talking big about bourgeois dictatorship, capitalist society, Kemalism, a modern state, a one-party dictatorship, "one doctrine", and so on and so forth? And if, instead of joining the Wang Ching-wei gang, someone wants to come into the "fight Japan" camp of the people but imagines that once the war is won he will be able to kick aside the people fighting Japan, seize the fruits of the victory of the fight against Japan and establish a "perpetual one-party dictatorship", isn't he just day-dreaming? "Fight Japan!" "Fight Japan!" But who is doing the fighting? Without the workers and the peasants and other sections of the petty bourgeoisie, you cannot move a step. Anyone who still dares to try and kick them aside will himself be crushed. Hasn't this, too, become a matter of common sense? But the die-hards among the Chinese bourgeoisie (I am referring solely to the die-hards) seem to have learned nothing in the past twenty years. Aren't they still shouting: "Restrict communism", "Corrode communism" and "Combat communism"? Haven't we seen "Measures for Restricting the Activities of Alien Parties" followed by "Measures for Dealing with the Alien Party Problem" and still later by "Directives for Dealing with the Alien Party Problem"? Heavens! With all this "restricting" and "dealing with" going on, one wonders what kind of future they are preparing for our nation and for themselves! We earnestly and sincerely advise these gentlemen: Open your eyes, take a good look at China and the world, see how things stand inside as well as outside the country, and do not repeat your mistakes. If you persist in your mistakes, the future of our nation will of course be disastrous, but I am sure things will not go well with you either. This is absolutely true, absolutely certain. Unless the die-hards among the Chinese bourgeoisie wake up, their future will be far from bright — they will only bring about their own destruction. Therefore we hope that China's anti-Japanese united front will be maintained and that, with the co-operation of all instead of the monopoly of a single clique, the anti-Japanese cause will be brought to victory; it is the only good policy — any other policy is bad. This is the sincere advice we Communists are giving, and do not blame us for not having forewarned you.

"If there is food, let everyone share it." This old Chinese saying contains much truth. Since we all share in fighting the enemy, we should all share in eating, we should all share in the work to be done, and we should all share access to education. Such attitudes as "I and I alone will take everything" and "no one dare harm me" are nothing but the old tricks of feudal lords which simply will not work in the Nineteen Forties.

We Communists will never push aside anyone who is revolutionary; we shall persevere in the united front and practise long-term co-operation with all those classes, strata, political parties and groups and individuals that are willing to fight Japan to the end. But it will not do if certain people want to push aside the Communist Party; it will not do if they want to split the united front. China must keep on fighting Japan, uniting and moving forward, and we cannot tolerate anyone who tries to capitulate, cause splits or move backward.

VIII.   REFUTATION OF "LEFT" PHRASE-MONGERING

If the capitalist road of bourgeois dictatorship is out of the question, then is it possible to take the socialist road of proletarian dictatorship?

No, that is not possible either.

Without a doubt, the present revolution is the first step, which will develop into the second step, that of socialism, at a later date. And China will attain true happiness only when she enters the socialist era. But today is not yet the time to introduce socialism. The present task of the revolution in China is to fight imperialism and feudalism, and socialism is out of the question until this task is completed. The Chinese revolution cannot avoid taking the two steps, first of New Democracy and then of socialism. Moreover, the first step will need quite a long time and cannot be accomplished overnight. We are not utopians and cannot divorce ourselves from the actual conditions confronting us.

Certain malicious propagandists, deliberately confusing these two distinct revolutionary stages, advocate the so-called theory of a single revolution in order to prove that the Three People's Principles apply to all kinds of revolutions and that communism therefore loses its *raison d'être*. Utilizing this "theory", they frantically oppose communism and the Communist Party, the Eighth Route and New Fourth Armies, and the Shensi-Kansu-Ningsia Border Region. Their real purpose is to root out all revolution, to oppose a thoroughgoing bourgeois-democratic revolution and thoroughgoing resistance to Japan and to prepare public opinion for their capitulation to the Japanese aggressors. This is deliberately being fostered by the Japanese imperialists. Since their occupation of Wuhan, they have come to realize that military force alone cannot subjugate China and have therefore resorted to political offensives and economic blandishments. Their political offensives consist in tempting wavering elements in the anti-Japanese camp, splitting the united front and undermining Kuomintang-Communist co-operation. Their economic blandishments take the form of the so-called joint industrial enterprises. In central and southern China the Japanese aggressors are allowing Chinese capitalists to invest 51 per cent of the capital in such enterprises, with Japanese capital making up the other 49 per cent; in northern China they are allowing Chinese capitalists to invest 49 per cent of the capital, with Japanese capital making up the other 51 per cent. The Japanese invaders have also promised to restore the former assets of the Chinese capitalists to them in the form of capital shares in the investment. At the prospect of profits, some conscienceless capitalists forget all moral principles and itch to have a go. One section, represented by Wang Ching-wei, has already capitulated. Another section lurking in the anti-Japanese camp would also like to cross over. But, with the cowardice of thieves, they fear that the Communists will block their exit and, what is more, that the common people will brand them as traitors. So they have put their heads together and decided to prepare the ground in cultural circles and through the press. Having determined on their policy, they have lost no time in hiring some "metaphysics-mongers"[10] plus a few Trotskyites who, brandishing their pens like lances, are tilting in all directions and creating bedlam. Hence the whole bag of tricks for deceiving those who do not know what is going on in the world around them — the "theory of a single revolution", the tales that communism does not suit the national conditions of China, that there is no need for a Communist Party in China, that the Eighth Route and the New Fourth Armies are sabotaging the anti-Japanese war and are merely moving about without fighting, that the Shensi-Kansu-Ningsia Border Region is a feudal separatist regime, that the Communist Party is disobedient, dissident, intriguing and disruptive — and all for the purpose of providing the capitalists with good grounds for getting their 49 or 51 per cent and selling out the nation's interests to the enemy at the opportune moment. This is "stealing the beams and pillars and replacing them with rotten timbers" — preparing the public mind for their projected capitulation. Thus, these gentlemen who, in all apparent seriousness, are pushing the "theory of a single revolution" to oppose communism and the Communist Party are out for nothing but their 49 or 51 per cent. How they must have cudgelled their brains! The "theory of a single revolution" is simply a theory of no revolution at all, and that is the heart of the matter.

But there are other people, apparently with no evil intentions, who are misled by the "theory of a single revolution" and the fanciful notion of "accomplishing both the political revolution and the social revolution at one stroke"; they do not understand that our revolution is divided into stages, that we can only proceed to the next stage of revolution after accomplishing the first, and that there is no such thing as "accomplishing both at one stroke". Their approach is likewise very harmful because it confuses the steps to be taken in the revolution and weakens the effort directed towards the current task. It is correct and in accord with the Marxist theory of revolutionary development to say of the two revolutionary stages that the first provides the conditions for the second and that the two must be consecutive, without allowing any intervening stage of bourgeois dictatorship. However, it is a utopian view rejected by true revolutionaries to say that the democratic revolution does not have a specific task and period of its own but can be merged and accomplished simultaneously with another task, *i.e.*, the socialist task (which can only be carried out in another period), and this is what they call "accomplishing both at one stroke".

IX. REFUTATION OF THE DIE-HARDS

The bourgeois die-hards in their turn come forward and say: "Well, you Communists have postponed the socialist system to a later stage and have declared, 'The Three People's Principles being what China needs today, our Party is ready to fight for their complete realization.'11 All right then, fold up your communism for the time being." A fearful hullabaloo has recently been raised with this sort of argument in the form of the "one doctrine" theory. In essence it is the howl of the die-hards for bourgeois despotism. Out of courtesy, however, we may simply describe it as totally lacking in common sense.

Communism is at once a complete system of proletarian ideology and a new social system. It is different from any other ideology or social system, and is the most complete, progressive, revolutionary and rational system in human history. The ideological and social system of feudalism has a place only in the museum of history. The ideological and social system of capitalism has also become a museum piece in one part of the world (in the Soviet Union), while in other countries it resembles "a dying person who is sinking fast, like the sun setting beyond the western hills", and will soon be relegated to the museum. The communist ideological and social system alone is full of youth and vitality, sweeping the world with the momentum of an avalanche and the force of a thunderbolt. The introduction of scientific communism into China has opened new vistas for people and has changed the face of the Chinese revolution. Without communism to guide it, China's democratic revolution cannot possibly succeed, let alone move on to the next stage. This is the reason why the bourgeois die-hards are so loudly demanding that communism be "folded up". But it must not be "folded up", for once communism is "folded up", China will be doomed. The whole world today depends on communism for its salvation, and China is no exception.

Everybody knows that the Communist Party has an immediate and a future programme, a minimum and a maximum programme, with regard to the social system it advocates. For the present period, New Democracy, and for the future, socialism; these are two parts of an organic whole, guided by one and the same communist ideology. Is it not, therefore, in the highest degree absurd to clamour for communism to be "folded up" on the ground that the Communist Party's minimum programme is in basic agreement with the political tenets of the Three People's Principles? It is precisely because of this basic agreement between the two that we Communists find it possible to recognize "the Three People's Principles as the political basis for the anti-Japanese united front" and to acknowledge that "the Three People's Principles being what China needs today, our Party is ready to fight for their complete realization"; otherwise no such possibility would exist. Here we have a united front between communism and the Three People's Principles in the stage of the democratic revolution, the kind of united front Dr. Sun Yat-sen had in mind when he said: "Communism is the good friend of the Three People's Principles."[12] To reject communism is in fact to reject the united front. The die-hards have concocted absurd arguments for the rejection of communism just because they want to reject the united front and practise their one-party doctrine.

Moreover, the "one doctrine" theory is an absurdity. So long as classes exist, there will be as many doctrines as there are classes, and even various groups in the same class may have their different doctrines. Since the feudal class has a feudal doctrine, the bourgeoisie a capitalist doctrine, the Buddhists Buddhism, the Christians

Christianity and the peasants polytheism, and since in recent years, some people have also advocated Kemalism, fascism, vitalism,[13] the "doctrine of distribution according to labour",[14] and what not, why then cannot the proletariat have its communism? Since there are countless "isms", why should the cry of "Fold it up!" be raised at the sight of communism alone? Frankly, "folding it up" will not work. Let us rather have a contest. If communism is beaten, we Communists will admit defeat in good grace. But if not, then let all that stuff about "one doctrine", which violates the Principle of Democracy, be "folded up" as soon as possible.

To avoid misunderstanding and for the edification of the die-hards, it is necessary to show clearly where the Three People's Principles and communism do coincide and where they do not.

Comparison of the two reveals both similarities and differences.

First for the similarities. They are to be found in the basic political programme of both doctrines during the stage of the bourgeois-democratic revolution in China. The three political tenets of the revolutionary Three People's Principles of Nationalism, Democracy and the People's Livelihood as reinterpreted by Dr. Sun Yat-sen in 1924 are basically similar to the communist political programme for the stage of the democratic revolution in China. Because of these similarities and because of the carrying out of the Three People's Principles, the united front of the two doctrines and the two parties came into existence. It is wrong to ignore this aspect.

Next for the differences. (1) There is a difference in part of the programme for the stage of the democratic revolution. The communist programme for the whole course of the democratic revolution includes full rights for the people, the eight-hour working day and a thorough agrarian revolution, whereas the Three People's Principles do not. Unless these points are added to the Three People's Principles and there is the readiness to carry them out, the two democratic programmes are only basically the same and cannot be described as altogether the same. (2) Another difference is that one includes the stage of the socialist revolution, and the other does not. Communism envisages the stage of the socialist revolution beyond the stage of the democratic revolution, and hence, beyond its minimum programme it has a maximum programme, i.e., the programme for the attainment of socialism and communism. The Three People's Principles which envisage only the stage of the democratic revolution and not the stage of the socialist revolution have only a minimum programme and not a maximum programme, *i.e.*, they have no programme for the establishment of socialism and communism. (3) There is the difference in world outlook. The world outlook of communism is dialectical and historical materialism, while the Three People's Principles explain history in terms of the people's livelihood, which in essence is a dualist or idealist outlook; the two world outlooks are opposed to each other. (4) There is the difference in revolutionary thoroughness. With communists, theory and practice go together, *i.e.*, communists possess revolutionary thoroughness. With the followers of the Three People's Principles, except for those completely loyal to the revolution and to truth, theory and practice do not go together and their deeds contradict their words, *i.e.*, they lack revolutionary thoroughness. The above are the differences between the two. They distinguish communists from the followers of the Three People's Principles. It is undoubtedly very wrong to ignore this distinction and see only the aspect of unity and not of contradiction.

Once all this is understood, it is easy to see what the bourgeois die-hards have in mind when they demand that communism be "folded up". If it does not mean bourgeois despotism, then there is no sense to it at all.

X. THE THREE PEOPLE'S PRINCIPLES,
OLD AND NEW

The bourgeois die-hards have no understanding whatsoever of historical change; their knowledge is so poor that it is practically non-existent. They do not know the difference either between communism and the Three People's Principles or between the new Three People's Principles and the old.

We Communists recognize "the Three People's Principles as the political basis for the Anti-Japanese National United Front", we acknowledge that "the Three People's Principles being what China needs today, our Party is ready to fight for their complete realization", and we admit the basic agreement between the communist minimum programme and the political tenets of the Three People's Principles. But which kind of Three People's Principles? The Three People's Principles as reinterpreted by Dr. Sun Yat-sen in the Manifesto of the First National Congress of the Kuomintang, and no other. I wish the die-hard gentlemen would spare a moment from the work of "restricting communism", "corroding communism" and "combating communism", in which they are so gleefully engaged, to glance through this manifesto. In the manifesto Dr. Sun Yat-sen said: "Here is the true interpretation of the Kuomintang's Three People's Principles." Hence these are the only genuine Three People's Principles and all others are spurious. The only "true interpretation" of the Three People's Principles is the one contained in the Manifesto of the First National Congress of the Kuomintang, and all other interpretations are false. Presumably this is no Communist fabrication, for many Kuomintang members and I myself personally witnessed the adoption of the manifesto.

The manifesto marks off the two epochs in the history of the Three People's Principles. Before it, they belonged to the old category; they were the Three People's Principles of the old bourgeois-democratic revolution in a semi-colony, the Three People's Principles of old democracy, the old Three People's Principles.

After it, they came within the new category; they became the Three People's Principles of the new bourgeois-democratic revolution in a semi-colony, the Three People's Principles of New Democracy, the new Three People's Principles. These and these alone are the revolutionary Three People's Principles of the new period.

The revolutionary Three People's Principles of the new period, the new or genuine Three People's Principles, embody the Three Great Policies of alliance with Russia, co-operation with the Communist Party and assistance to the peasants and workers. Without each and every one of these Three Great Policies, the Three People's Principles become either false or incomplete in the new period.

In the first place, the revolutionary, new or genuine Three People's Principles must include alliance with Russia. As things are today, it is perfectly clear that unless there is the policy of alliance with Russia, with the land of socialism, there will inevitably be a policy of alliance with imperialism, with the imperialist powers. Is this not exactly what happened after 1927? Once the conflict between the socialist Soviet Union and the imperialist powers grows sharper, China will have to take her stand on one side or the other. This is an inevitable trend. Is it possible to avoid leaning to either side? No, that is an illusion. The whole world will be swept into one or the other of these two fronts, and "neutrality" will then be merely a deceptive term. Especially is this true of China which, fighting an imperialist power that has penetrated deep into her territory, cannot conceive of ultimate victory without the assistance of the Soviet Union. If alliance with Russia is sacrificed for the sake of alliance with imperialism, the word "revolutionary" will have to be expunged from the Three People's Principles, which will then become reactionary. In the last analysis, there can be no "neutral" Three People's Principles; they can only be either revolutionary or counter-revolutionary. Would it not be more heroic to "fight against attacks from both sides"[15] as Wang Ching-wei once remarked, and to have the kind of Three People's Principles that serves this "fight"? Unfortunately, even its inventor Wang Ching-wei himself has abandoned (or "folded up") this kind of Three People's Principles, for he has adopted the Three People's Principles of alliance with imperialism. If it is argued that there is a difference between Eastern and Western imperialism, and that, unlike Wang Ching-wei who has allied himself with Eastern imperialism, one should ally oneself with some of the Western imperialists to march eastward and attack, then would not such conduct be quite revolutionary? However, whether you like it or not, the Western imperialists are determined to oppose the Soviet Union and communism, and if you ally yourself with them, they will ask you to march northward and attack, and your revolution will come to nothing. All these circumstances make it essential for the revolutionary, new and genuine Three People's Principles to include alliance with Russia, and under no circumstances alliance with imperialism against Russia.

In the second place, the revolutionary, new and genuine Three People's Principles must include co-operation with the Communist Party. Either you co-operate with the Communist Party or you oppose it. Opposition to communism is the policy of the Japanese imperialists and Wang Ching-wei, and if that is what you want, very well, they will invite you to join their Anti-Communist Company. But wouldn't that look suspiciously like turning traitor? You may say, "I am not following Japan, but some other country." That is just ridiculous. No matter whom you follow, the moment you oppose the Communist Party you become a traitor, because you can no longer resist Japan. If you say, "I am going to oppose the Communist Party independently", that is arrant nonsense. How can the "heroes" in a colony or semi-colony tackle a counter-revolutionary job of this magnitude without depending on the strength of imperialism? For ten long years, virtually all the imperialist forces in the world were enlisted against the Communist Party, but in vain. How can you suddenly oppose it "independently"?

Some people outside the Border Region, we are told, are now saying: "Opposing the Communist Party is good, but you can never succeed in it." This remark, if it is not simply hearsay, is only half wrong, for what "good" is there in opposing the Communist Party? But the other half is true, you certainly can "never succeed in it". Basically, the reason lies not with the Communists but with the common people, who like the Communist Party and do not like "opposing" it. If you oppose the Communist Party at a juncture when our national enemy is penetrating deep into our territory, the people will be after your hide; they will certainly show you no mercy. This much is certain, whoever wants to oppose the Communist Party must be prepared to be ground to dust. If you are not keen on being ground to dust, you had certainly better drop this opposition. This is our sincere advice to all the anti-Communist "heroes". Thus it is as clear as can be that the Three People's Principles of today must include co-operation with the Communist Party, or otherwise those Principles will perish. It is a question of life and death for the Three People's Principles. Co-operating with the Communist Party, they will survive; opposing the Communist Party, they will perish. Can anyone prove the contrary?

In the third place, the revolutionary, new and genuine Three People's Principles must include the policy of assisting the peasants and workers. Rejection of this policy, failure whole-heartedly to assist the peasants and workers or failure to carry out the behest in Dr. Sun Yat-sen's Testament to "arouse the masses of the people", amounts to preparing the way for the defeat of the revolution, and one's own defeat into the bargain. Stalin has said that "*in essence*, the national question is a peasant question".[16] This means that the Chinese revolution is essentially a peasant revolution and that the resistance to Japan now going on is essentially peasant resistance. Essentially, the politics of New Democracy means giving the peasants their rights. The new and genuine Three People's Principles are essentially the principles of a peasant revolution. Essentially, mass culture means raising the cultural level of the peasants. The anti-Japanese war is essentially a peasant war. We are now living in a time when the "principle of going up into the hills"[17] applies; meetings, work, classes, newspaper publication, the writing of books, theatrical performances — everything is done up in the hills, and all essentially for the sake of the peasants. And essentially it is the peasants who provide everything that sustains the resistance to Japan and keeps us going. By "essentially" we mean basically, not ignoring the other sections of the people, as Stalin himself has explained. As every schoolboy knows, 80 per cent of China's population are peasants. So the peasant problem becomes the basic problem of the Chinese revolution and the strength of the peasants is the main strength of the Chinese revolution. In the Chinese population the workers rank second to the peasants in number. There are several million industrial workers in China and several tens of millions of handicraft workers and agricultural labourers. China cannot live without her workers in the various industries, because they are the producers in the industrial sector of the economy. And the revolution cannot succeed without the modern industrial working class, because it is the leader of the Chinese revolution and is the most revolutionary class. In these circumstances, the revolutionary, new and genuine Three People's Principles must include the policy of assisting the peasants and workers. Any other kind of Three People's Principles which lack this policy, do not give the peasants and workers whole-hearted assistance or do not carry out the behest to "arouse the masses of the people", will certainly perish.

Thus it is clear that there is no future for any Three People's Principles which depart from the Three Great Policies of alliance with Russia, co-operation with the Communist Party and assistance to the peasants and workers. Every conscientious follower of the Three People's Principles must seriously consider this point.

The Three People's Principles comprising the Three Great Policies — in other words, the revolutionary, new and genuine Three People's Principles — are the Three People's Principles of New Democracy, a development of the old Three People's Principles, a great contribution of Dr. Sun Yat-sen's and a product of the era in which the Chinese revolution has become part of the world socialist revolution. It is only these Three People's Principles which the Chinese Communist Party regards as "being what China needs today" and for whose "complete realization" it declares itself pledged "to fight". These are the only Three People's Principles which are in basic agreement with the Communist Party's political programme for the stage of democratic revolution, namely, with its minimum programme.

As for the old Three People's Principles, they were a product of the old period of the Chinese revolution. Russia was then an imperialist power, and naturally there could be no policy of alliance with her; there was then no Communist Party in existence in our country, and naturally there could be no policy of co-operation with it; the movement of the workers and peasants had not yet revealed its full political significance and aroused people's attention, and naturally there could be no policy of alliance with them. Hence the Three People's Principles of the period before the reorganization of the Kuomintang in 1924 belonged to the old category, and they became obsolete. The Kuomintang could not have gone forward unless it had developed them into the new Three People's Principles. Dr. Sun Yat-sen in his wisdom saw this point, secured the help of the Soviet Union and the Chinese Communist Party and reinterpreted the Three People's Principles so as to endow them with new characteristics suited to the times; as a result, a united front was formed between the Three People's Principles and communism, Kuomintang-Communist co-operation was established for the first time, the sympathy of the people of the whole country was won, and the revolution of 1924-27 was launched.

The old Three People's Principles were revolutionary in the old period and reflected its historical features. But if the old stuff is repeated in the new period after the new Three People's Principles have been established, or alliance with Russia is opposed after the socialist state has been established, or co-operation with the Communist Party is opposed after the Communist Party has come into existence, or the policy of assisting the peasants and workers is opposed after they have awakened and demonstrated their political strength, then that is reactionary and shows ignorance of the times. The period of reaction after 1927 was the result of such ignorance. The old proverb says, "Whosoever understands the signs of the times is a great man." I hope the followers of the Three People's Principles today will bear this in mind.

Were the Three People's Principles to fall within the old category, then they would have nothing basically in common with the communist minimum programme, because they would belong to the past and be obsolete. Any sort of Three People's Principles that oppose Russia, the Communist Party or the peasants and workers are definitely reactionary; they not only have absolutely nothing in common with the communist minimum programme but are the enemy of communism, and there is no common ground at all. This, too, the followers of the Three People's Principles should carefully consider.

In any case, people with a conscience will never forsake the new Three People's Principles until the task of opposing imperialism and feudalism is basically accomplished. The only ones who do are people like Wang Ching-wei. No matter how energetically they push their spurious Three People's Principles which oppose Russia, the Communist Party and the peasants and workers, there will surely be no lack of people with a conscience and sense of justice who will continue to support Sun Yat-sen's genuine Three People's Principles. Many followers of the genuine Three People's Principles continued the struggle for the Chinese revolution even after the reaction of 1927, and their numbers will undoubtedly swell to tens upon tens of thousands now that the national enemy has penetrated deep into our territory. We Communists will always persevere in long-term co-operation with all the true followers of the Three People's Principles and, while rejecting the traitors and the sworn enemies of communism, will never forsake any of our friends.

XI. THE CULTURE OF NEW DEMOCRACY

In the foregoing we have explained the historical characteristics of Chinese politics in the new period and the question of the new-democratic republic. We can now proceed to the question of culture.

A given culture is the ideological reflection of the politics and economics of a given society. There is in China an imperialist culture which is a reflection of imperialist rule, or partial rule, in the political and economic fields. This culture is fostered not only by the cultural organizations run directly by the imperialists in China but by a number of Chinese who have lost all sense of shame. Into this category falls all culture embodying a slave ideology. China also has a semi-feudal culture which reflects her semi-feudal politics and economy, and whose exponents include all those who advocate the worship of Confucius, the study of the Confucian canon, the old ethical code and the old ideas in opposition to the new culture and new ideas. Imperialist culture and semi-feudal culture are devoted brothers and have formed a reactionary cultural alliance against China's new culture. This kind of reactionary culture serves the imperialists and the feudal class and must be swept away. Unless it is swept away, no new culture of any kind can be built up. There is no construction without destruction, no flowing without damming and no motion without rest; the two are locked in a life-and-death struggle.

As for the new culture, it is the ideological reflection of the new politics and the new economy which it sets out to serve.

As we have already stated in Section 3, Chinese society has gradually changed in character since the emergence of a capitalist economy in China; it is no longer an entirely feudal but a semi-feudal society, although the feudal economy still predominates. Compared with the feudal economy, this capitalist economy is a new one. The political forces of the bourgeoisie, the petty bourgeoisie and the pro- letariat are the new political forces which have emerged and grown simultaneously with this new capitalist economy. And the new culture reflects these new economic and political forces in the field of ideology and serves them. Without the capitalist economy, without the bour- geoisie, the petty bourgeoisie and the proletariat, and without the political forces of these classes, the new ideology or new culture could not have emerged.

These new political, economic and cultural forces are all revolu- tionary forces which are opposed to the old politics, the old economy and the old culture. The old is composed of two parts, one being China's own semi-feudal politics, economy and culture, and the other the politics, economy and culture of imperialism, with the latter head- ing the alliance. Both are bad and should be completely destroyed. The struggle between the new and the old in Chinese society is a struggle between the new forces of the people (the various revolu- tionary classes) and the old forces of imperialism and the feudal class. It is a struggle between revolution and counter-revolution. This struggle has lasted a full hundred years if dated from the Opium War, and nearly thirty years if dated from the Revolution of 1911.

But as already indicated, revolutions too can be classified into old and new, and what is new in one historical period becomes old in another. The century of China's bourgeois-democratic revolution can be divided into two main stages, a first stage of eighty years and a second of twenty years. Each has its basic historical characteristics: China's bourgeois-democratic revolution in the first eighty years be- longs to the old category, while in the last twenty years, owing to the change in the international and domestic political situation, it belongs to the new category. Old democracy is the characteristic of the first eighty years. New Democracy is the characteristic of the last twenty. This distinction holds good in culture as well as in politics.

How does it manifest itself in the field of culture? We shall explain this next.

XII. THE HISTORICAL CHARACTERISTICS OF
CHINA'S CULTURAL REVOLUTION

On the cultural or ideological front, the two periods preceding and following the May 4th Movement form two distinct historical periods.

Before the May 4th Movement, the struggle on China's cultural front was one between the new culture of the bourgeoisie and the old culture of the feudal class. The struggles between the modern school system and the imperial examination system,[18] between the new learning and the old learning, and between Western learning and Chinese learning, were all of this nature. The so-called modern schools or new learning or Western learning of that time concentrated mainly (we say mainly, because in part pernicious vestiges of Chinese feudalism still remained) on the natural sciences and bourgeois social and political theories, which were needed by the representatives of the bourgeoisie. At the time, the ideology of the new learning played a revolutionary role in fighting the Chinese feudal ideology, and it served the bourgeois-democratic revolution of the old period. However, because the Chinese bourgeoisie lacked strength and the world had already entered the era of imperialism, this bourgeois ideology was only able to last out a few rounds and was beaten back by the reactionary alliance of the enslaving ideology of foreign imperialism and the "back to the ancients" ideology of Chinese feudalism; as soon as this reactionary ideological alliance started a minor counter-offensive, the so-called new learning lowered its banners, muffled its drums and beat a retreat, retaining its outer form but losing its soul. The old bourgeois-democratic culture became enervated and decayed in the era of imperialism, and its failure was inevitable.

But since the May 4th Movement things have been different. A brand-new cultural force came into being in China, that is, the communist culture and ideology guided by the Chinese Communists, or the communist world outlook and theory of social revolution. The May 4th Movement occurred in 1919, and in 1921 came the founding of the Chinese Communist Party and the real beginning of China's labour movement — all in the wake of the First World War and the October Revolution, *i.e.*, at a time when the national problem and the colonial revolutionary movements of the world underwent a change, and the connection between the Chinese revolution and the world

revolution became quite obvious. The new political force of the
proletariat and the Communist Party entered the Chinese political
arena, and as a result, the new cultural force, in new uniform and
with new weapons, mustering all possible allies and deploying its
ranks in battle array, launched heroic attacks on imperialist culture
and feudal culture. This new force has made great strides in the
domain of the social sciences and of the arts and letters, whether of
philosophy, economics, political science, military science, history, literature or art (including the theatre, the cinema, music, sculpture and
painting). For the last twenty years, wherever this new cultural force
has directed its attack, a great revolution has taken place both in
ideological content and in form (for example, in the written language).
Its influence has been so great and its impact so powerful that it is
invincible wherever it goes. The numbers it has rallied behind it have
no parallel in Chinese history. Lu Hsun was the greatest and the most
courageous standard-bearer of this new cultural force. The chief commander of China's cultural revolution, he was not only a great man
of letters but a great thinker and revolutionary. Lu Hsun was a man
of unyielding integrity, free from all sycophancy or obsequiousness;
this quality is invaluable among colonial and semi-colonial peoples.
Representing the great majority of the nation, Lu Hsun breached and
stormed the enemy citadel; on the cultural front he was the bravest
and most correct, the firmest, the most loyal and the most ardent
national hero, a hero without parallel in our history. The road he took
was the very road of China's new national culture.

Prior to the May 4th Movement, China's new culture was a culture
of the old-democratic kind and part of the capitalist cultural revolution of the world bourgeoisie. Since the May 4th Movement, it has
become new-democratic and part of the socialist cultural revolution
of the world proletariat.

Prior to the May 4th Movement, China's new cultural movement,
her cultural revolution, was led by the bourgeoisie, which still had a
leading role to play. After the May 4th Movement, its culture and
ideology became even more backward than its politics and were incapable of playing any leading role; at most, they could serve to a
certain extent as an ally during revolutionary periods, while inevitably
the responsibility for leading the alliance rested on proletarian culture
and ideology. This is an undeniable fact.

The new-democratic culture is the anti-imperialist and anti-feudal
culture of the broad masses; today it is the culture of the anti-Japanese

united front. This culture can be led only by the culture and ideology of the proletariat, by the ideology of communism, and not by the culture and ideology of any other class. In a word, new-democratic culture is the proletarian-led, anti-imperialist and anti-feudal culture of the broad masses.

XIII. THE FOUR PERIODS

A cultural revolution is the ideological reflection of the political and economic revolution and is in their service. In China there is a united front in the cultural as in the political revolution.

The history of the united front in the cultural revolution during the last twenty years can be divided into four periods. The first covers the two years from 1919 to 1921, the second the six years from 1921 to 1927, the third the ten years from 1927 to 1937, and the fourth the three years from 1937 to the present.

The first period extended from the May 4th Movement of 1919 to the founding of the Chinese Communist Party in 1921. The May 4th Movement was its chief landmark.

The May 4th Movement was an anti-imperialist as well as an anti-feudal movement. Its outstanding historical significance is to be seen in a feature which was absent from the Revolution of 1911, namely, its thorough and uncompromising opposition to imperialism as well as to feudalism. The May 4th Movement possessed this quality because capitalism had developed a step further in China and because new hopes had arisen for the liberation of the Chinese nation as China's revolutionary intellectuals saw the collapse of three great imperialist powers, Russia, Germany and Austria-Hungary, and the weakening of two others, Britain and France, while the Russian proletariat had established a socialist state and the German, Hungarian and Italian proletariat had risen in revolution. The May 4th Movement came into being at the call of the world revolution, of the Russian Revolution and of Lenin. It was part of the world proletarian revolution of the time. Although the Communist Party had not yet come into existence, there were already large numbers of intellectuals who approved of the Russian Revolution and had the rudiments of communist ideology. In the beginning the May 4th Movement was the revolutionary movement of a united front of three sections of people — communist intellectuals, revolutionary petty-bourgeois intellectuals and bourgeois intellectuals (the last forming the right wing of the movement). Its shortcoming was that it was confined to the intellectuals and that the workers and peasants did not join in. But as soon as it developed into the June 3rd Movement,[19] not only the intellectuals but the mass of the proletariat, the petty bourgeoisie and the bourgeoisie joined in, and it became a nation-wide revolutionary movement. The cultural revolution ushered in by the May 4th Movement was uncompromising in its opposition to feudal culture; there had never been such a great and thoroughgoing cultural revolution since the dawn of Chinese history. Raising aloft the two great banners of the day, "Down with the old ethics and up with the new!" and "Down with the old literature and up with the new!", the cultural revolution had great achievements to its credit. At that time it was not yet possible for this cultural movement to become widely diffused among the workers and peasants. The slogan of "Literature for the common people" was advanced, but in fact the "common people" then could only refer to the petty-bourgeois and bourgeois intellectuals in the cities, that is, the urban intelligentsia. Both in ideology and in the matter of cadres, the May 4th Movement paved the way for the founding of the Chinese Communist Party in 1921 and for the May 30th Movement in 1925 and the Northern Expedition. The bourgeois intellectuals, who constituted the right wing of the May 4th Movement, mostly compromised with the enemy in the second period and went over to the side of reaction.

In the second period, whose landmarks were the founding of the Chinese Communist Party, the May 30th Movement and the Northern Expedition, the united front of the three classes formed in the May 4th Movement was continued and expanded, the peasantry was drawn into it and a political united front of all these classes, the first instance of Kuomintang-Communist co-operation, was established. Dr. Sun Yat-sen was a great man not only because he led the great Revolution of 1911 (although it was only a democratic revolution of the old period), but also because, "adapting himself to the trends of the world and meeting the needs of the masses", he had the capacity to bring forward the revolutionary Three Great Policies of alliance with Russia, co-operation with the Communist Party and assistance to the peasants and workers, give new meaning to the Three People's Principles and thus institute the new Three People's Principles with their Three Great Policies. Previously, the Three People's Principles had

exerted little influence on the educational and academic world or
with the youth, because they had not raised the issues of opposition
to imperialism or to the feudal social system and feudal culture and
ideology. They were the old Three People's Principles which people
regarded as the time-serving banner of a group of men bent on seizing
power, in other words, on securing official positions, a banner used
purely for political manoeuvring. Then came the new Three People's
Principles with their Three Great Policies. The co-operation between
the Kuomintang and the Communist Party and the joint efforts of the
revolutionary members of the two parties spread the new Three
People's Principles all over China, extending to a section of the educational and academic world and the mass of student youth. This was
entirely due to the fact that the original Three People's Principles had
developed into the anti-imperialist, anti-feudal and new-democratic
Three People's Principles with their Three Great Policies. Without
this development it would have been impossible to disseminate the
ideas of the Three People's Principles.

During this period, the revolutionary Three People's Principles
became the political basis of the united front of the Kuomintang and
the Communist Party and of all the revolutionary classes, and since
"communism is the good friend of the Three People's Principles",
a united front was formed between the two of them. In terms of
social classes, it was a united front of the proletariat, the peasantry,
the urban petty bourgeoisie and the bourgeoisie. Using the Communist
Weekly Guide, the Kuomintang's *Republican Daily News* of Shanghai
and other newspapers in various localities as their bases of operations,
the two parties jointly advocated anti-imperialism, jointly combated
feudal education based upon the worship of Confucius and upon the
study of the Confucian canon and jointly opposed feudal literature
and the classical language and promoted the new literature and the
vernacular style of writing with an anti-imperialist and anti-feudal
content. During the wars in Kwangtung and during the Northern
Expedition, they reformed China's armed forces by the inculcation of
anti-imperialist and anti-feudal ideas. The slogans, "Down with the
corrupt officials" and "Down with the local tyrants and evil gentry",
were raised among the peasant millions, and great peasant revolutionary struggles were aroused. Thanks to all this and to the assistance
of the Soviet Union, the Northern Expedition was victorious. But no
sooner did the big bourgeoisie climb to power than it put an end to
this revolution, thus creating an entirely new political situation.

The third period was the new revolutionary period of 1927-37. As a change had taken place within the revolutionary camp towards the end of the second period, with the big bourgeoisie going over to the counter-revolutionary camp of the imperialist and feudal forces and the national bourgeoisie trailing after it, only three of the four classes formerly within the revolutionary camp remained, i.e., the proletariat, the peasantry and the other sections of the petty bourgeoisie (including the revolutionary intellectuals), and consequently the Chinese revolution inevitably entered a new period in which the Chinese Communist Party alone gave leadership to the masses. This period was one of counter-revolutionary campaigns of "encirclement and suppression", on the one hand, and of the deepening of the revolution, on the other. There were two kinds of counter-revolutionary campaigns of "encirclement and suppression", the military and the cultural. The deepening of the revolution was of two kinds; both the agrarian and the cultural revolutions were deepened. At the instigation of the imperialists, the counter-revolutionary forces of the whole country and of the whole world were mobilized for both kinds of campaigns of "encirclement and suppression", which lasted no less than ten years and were unparalleled in their ruthlessness; hundreds of thousands of Communists and young students were slaughtered and millions of workers and peasants suffered cruel persecution. The people responsible for all this apparently had no doubt that communism and the Communist Party could be "exterminated once and for all". However, the outcome was different; both kinds of "encirclement and suppression" campaigns failed miserably. The military campaign resulted in the northern march of the Red Army to resist the Japanese, and the cultural campaign resulted in the outbreak of the December 9th Movement of the revolutionary youth in 1935. And the common result of both was the awakening of the people of the whole country. These were three positive results. The most amazing thing of all was that the Kuomintang's cultural "encirclement and suppression" campaign failed completely in the Kuomintang areas as well, although the Communist Party was in an utterly defenceless position in all the cultural and educational institutions there. Why did this happen? Does it not give food for prolonged and deep thought? It was in the very midst of such campaigns of "encirclement and suppression" that Lu Hsun, who believed in communism, became the giant of China's cultural revolution.

The negative result of the counter-revolutionary campaigns of "encirclement and suppression" was the invasion of our country by

Japanese imperialism. This is the chief reason why to this very day the people of the whole country still bitterly detest those ten years of anti-communism.

In the struggles of this period, the revolutionary side firmly upheld the people's anti-imperialist and anti-feudal New Democracy and their new Three People's Principles, while the counter-revolutionary side, under the direction of imperialism, imposed the despotic regime of the coalition of the landlord class and the big bourgeoisie. That despotic regime butchered Dr. Sun Yat-sen's Three Great Policies and his new Three People's Principles both politically and culturally, with catastrophic consequences to the Chinese nation.

The fourth period is that of the present anti-Japanese war. Pursuing its zigzag course, the Chinese revolution has again arrived at a united front of the four classes; but the scope of the united front is now much broader because its upper stratum includes many members of the ruling classes, its middle stratum includes the national bourgeoisie and the petty bourgeoisie, and its lower stratum includes the entire proletariat, so that the various classes and strata of the nation have become members of the alliance resolutely resisting Japanese imperialism. The first stage of this period lasted until the fall of Wuhan. During that stage, there was a lively atmosphere in the country in every field; politically there was a trend towards democracy and culturally there was fairly widespread activity. With the fall of Wuhan the second stage began, during which the political situation has undergone many changes, with one section of the big bourgeoisie capitulating to the enemy and another desiring an early end to the War of Resistance. In the cultural sphere, this situation has been reflected in the reactionary activities of Yeh Ching,[20] Chang Chun-mai and others, and in the suppression of freedom of speech and of the press.

To overcome this crisis, a firm struggle is necessary against all ideas opposed to resistance, unity and progress, and unless these reactionary ideas are crushed, there will be no hope of victory. How will this struggle turn out? This is the big question in the minds of the people of the whole country. Judging by the domestic and international situation, the Chinese people are bound to win, however numerous the obstacles on the path of resistance. The progress achieved during the twenty years since the May 4th Movement exceeds not only that of the preceding eighty years but virtually surpasses that achieved in the thousands of years of Chinese history. Can we not visualize what further progress China will make in another twenty years? The unbridled violence of all the forces of darkness, whether domestic or foreign, has brought disaster to our nation; but this very violence indicates that while the forces of darkness still have some strength left, they are already in their death throes, and that the people are gradually approaching victory. This is true of China, of the whole East and of the entire world.

XIV.   SOME WRONG IDEAS ABOUT THE NATURE OF CULTURE

Everything new comes from the forge of hard and bitter struggle. This is also true of the new culture which has followed a zigzag course in the past twenty years, during which both the good and the bad were tested and proved in struggle.

The bourgeois die-hards are as hopelessly wrong on the question of culture as on that of political power. They neither understand the historical characteristics of this new period in China, nor recognize the new-democratic culture of the masses. Their starting point is bourgeois despotism, which in culture becomes the cultural despotism of the bourgeoisie. It seems that a section (and I refer only to a section) of educated people from the so-called European-American school[21] who in fact supported the Kuomintang government's "Communist suppression" campaign on the cultural front in the past are now supporting its policy of "restricting" and "corroding" the Communist Party. They do not want the workers and the peasants to hold up their heads politically or culturally. This bourgeois die-hard road of cultural despotism leads nowhere; as in the case of political despotism, the domestic and international pre-conditions are lacking. Therefore this cultural despotism, too, had better be "folded up".

So far as the orientation of our national culture is concerned, communist ideology plays the guiding role, and we should work hard both to disseminate socialism and communism throughout the working class and to educate the peasantry and other sections of the people in socialism properly and step by step. However, our national culture as a whole is not yet socialist.

Because of the leadership of the proletariat, the politics, the economy and the culture of New Democracy all contain an element of socialism, and by no means a mere casual element but one with a decisive role. However, taken as a whole, the political, economic and cultural situation so far is new-democratic and not socialist. For the Chinese revolution in its present stage is not yet a socialist revolution for the overthrow of capitalism but a bourgeois-democratic revolution, its central task being mainly that of combating foreign imperialism and domestic feudalism. In the sphere of national culture, it is wrong to assume that the existing national culture is, or should be, socialist in its entirety. That would amount to confusing the dissemination of communist ideology with the carrying out of an immediate programme of action, and to confusing the application of the communist standpoint and method in investigating problems, undertaking research, handling work and training cadres with the general policy for national education and national culture in the democratic stage of the Chinese revolution. A national culture with a socialist content will necessarily be the reflection of a socialist politics and a socialist economy. There are socialist elements in our politics and our economy, and hence these socialist elements are reflected in our national culture; but taking our society as a whole, we do not have a socialist politics and a socialist economy yet, so that there cannot be a wholly socialist national culture. Since the present Chinese revolution is part of the world proletarian-socialist revolution, the new culture of China today is part of the world proletarian-socialist new culture and is its great ally. While this part contains vital elements of socialist culture, the national culture as a whole joins the stream of the world proletarian-socialist new culture not entirely as a socialist culture, but as the anti-imperialist and anti-feudal new-democratic culture of the broad masses. And since the Chinese revolution today cannot do without proletarian leadership, China's new culture cannot do without the leadership of proletarian culture and ideology, of communist ideology. At the present stage, however, this kind of leadership means leading the masses of the people in an anti-imperialist and anti-feudal political and cultural revolution, and therefore, taken as a whole, the content of China's new national culture is still not socialist but new-democratic.

Beyond all doubt, now is the time to spread communist ideas more widely and put more energy into the study of Marxism-Leninism, or otherwise we shall not only be unable to lead the Chinese revolution forward to the future stage of socialism, but shall also be unable to guide the present democratic revolution to victory. However, we must keep the spreading of communist ideas and propaganda about the communist social system distinct from the practical application of the new-democratic programme of action; we must also keep the communist theory and method of investigating problems, undertaking research, handling work and training cadres distinct from the new-democratic line for national culture as a whole. It is undoubtedly inappropriate to mix the two up.

It can thus be seen that the content of China's new national culture at the present stage is neither the cultural despotism of the bourgeoisie nor the socialism of the proletariat, but the anti-imperialist and anti-feudal New Democracy of the masses, under the leadership of proletarian-socialist culture and ideology.

XV. A NATIONAL, SCIENTIFIC AND MASS CULTURE

New-democratic culture is national. It opposes imperialist oppression and upholds the dignity and independence of the Chinese nation. It belongs to our own nation and bears our own national characteristics. It links up with the socialist and new-democratic cultures of all other nations and they are related in such a way that they can absorb something from each other and help each other to develop, together forming a new world culture; but as a revolutionary national culture it can never link up with any reactionary imperialist culture of whatever nation. To nourish her own culture China needs to assimilate a good deal of foreign progressive culture, not enough of which was done in the past. We should assimilate whatever is useful to us today not only from the present-day socialist and new-democratic cultures but also from the earlier cultures of other nations, for example, from the culture of the various capitalist countries in the Age of Enlightenment. However, we should not gulp any of this foreign material down uncritically, but must treat it as we do our food — first chewing it, then submitting it to the working of the stomach and intestines with their juices and secretions, and separating it into nutriment to be absorbed and waste matter to be discarded — before it can nourish us. To advocate "wholesale westernization"[22] is wrong. China has suffered a great deal from the mechanical absorption of foreign material. Similarly, in applying Marxism to China, Chinese communists must fully and properly integrate the universal truth of Marxism with the concrete practice of the Chinese revolution, or in other words, the universal truth of Marxism must be combined with specific national characteristics and acquire a definite national form if it is to be useful, and in no circumstances can it be applied subjectively as a mere formula. Marxists who make a fetish of formulas are simply playing the fool with Marxism and the Chinese revolution, and there is no room for them in the ranks of the Chinese revolution. Chinese culture should have its own form, its own national form. National in form and new-democratic in content — such is our new culture today.

New-democratic culture is scientific. Opposed as it is to all feudal and superstitious ideas, it stands for seeking truth from facts, for objective truth and for the unity of theory and practice. On this point, the possibility exists of a united front against imperialism, feudalism and superstition between the scientific thought of the Chinese proletariat and those Chinese bourgeois materialists and natural scientists who are progressive, but in no case is there a possibility of a united front with any reactionary idealism. In the field of political action Communists may form an anti-imperialist and anti-feudal united front with some idealists and even religious people, but we can never approve of their idealism or religious doctrines. A splendid old culture was created during the long period of Chinese feudal society. To study the development of this old culture, to reject its feudal dross and assimilate its democratic essence is a necessary condition for developing our new national culture and increasing our national self-confidence, but we should never swallow anything and everything uncritically. It is imperative to separate the fine old culture of the people which had a more or less democratic and revolutionary character from all the decadence of the old feudal ruling class. China's present new politics and new economy have developed out of her old politics and old economy, and her present new culture, too, has developed out of her old culture; therefore, we must respect our own history and must not lop it off. However, respect for history means giving it its proper place as a science, respecting its dialectical development, and not eulogizing the past at the expense of the present or praising every drop of feudal poison. As far as the masses and the young students are concerned, the essential thing is to guide them to look forward and not backward.

New-democratic culture belongs to the broad masses and is therefore democratic. It should serve the toiling masses of workers and peasants who make up more than 90 per cent of the nation's population and should gradually become their very own. There is a difference of degree, as well as a close link, between the knowledge imparted to the revolutionary cadres and the knowledge imparted to the revolutionary masses, between the raising of cultural standards and popularization. Revolutionary culture is a powerful revolutionary weapon for the broad masses of the people. It prepares the ground ideologically before the revolution comes and is an important, indeed essential, fighting front in the general revolutionary front during the revolution. People engaged in revolutionary cultural work are the commanders at various levels on this cultural front. "Without revolutionary theory there can be no revolutionary movement";[23] one can thus see how important the cultural movement is for the practical revolutionary movement. Both the cultural and practical movements must be of the masses. Therefore all progressive cultural workers in the anti-Japanese war must have their own cultural battalions, that is, the broad masses. A revolutionary cultural worker who is not close to the people is a commander without an army, whose fire-power cannot bring the enemy down. To attain this objective, written Chinese must be reformed, given the requisite conditions, and our spoken language brought closer to that of the people, for the people, it must be stressed, are the inexhaustible source of our revolutionary culture.

A national, scientific and mass culture — such is the anti-imperialist and anti-feudal culture of the people, the culture of New Democracy, the new culture of the Chinese nation.

Combine the politics, the economy and the culture of New Democracy, and you have the new-democratic republic, the Republic of China both in name and in reality, the new China we want to create.

Behold, New China is within sight. Let us all hail her!

Her masts have already risen above the horizon. Let us all cheer in welcome!

Raise both your hands. New China is ours!

NOTES

[1] *Chinese Culture* was a magazine founded in January 1940 in Yenan; the present article appeared in the first number.

[2] See V. I. Lenin, "Once Again on the Trade Unions, the Present Situation and the Mistakes of Trotsky and Bukharin", *Selected Works*, Eng. ed., International Publishers, New York, 1943, Vol. IX, p. 54.

[3] Karl Marx, "Preface to *A Contribution to the Critique of Political Economy*", *Selected Works of Marx and Engels*, Eng. ed., FLPH, Moscow, 1958, Vol. I, p. 363.

[4] Karl Marx, "Theses on Feuerbach", *Selected Works of Marx and Engels*, Eng. ed., FLPH, Moscow, 1958, Vol. II, p. 405.

[5] J. V. Stalin, "The October Revolution and the National Question", *Works*, Eng. ed., FLPH, Moscow, 1953, Vol. IV, pp. 169-70.

[6] J. V. Stalin, "The National Question Once Again", *Works*, Eng. ed., FLPH, Moscow, 1954, Vol. VII, pp. 225-27.

[7] V. I. Lenin, "Imperialism, the Highest Stage of Capitalism", *Selected Works*, Eng. ed., FLPH, Moscow, 1950, Vol. I, Part 2, p. 566.

[8] These anti-Soviet campaigns were instigated by the Kuomintang government following Chiang Kai-shek's betrayal of the revolution. On December 13, 1927, the Kuomintang murdered the Soviet vice-consul in Canton and on the next day its government in Nanking issued a decree breaking off relations with Russia, withdrawing official recognition from Soviet consuls in the provinces and ordering Soviet commercial establishments to cease activity. In August 1929 Chiang Kai-shek, under the instigation of the imperialists, organized acts of provocation in the Northeast against the Soviet Union, which resulted in armed clashes.

[9] After World War I the British imperialists instigated their vassal Greece to commit aggression against Turkey, but the Turkish people, with the help of the Soviet Union, defeated the Greek troops in 1922. In 1923, Kemal was elected President of Turkey. Stalin said:

> A Kemalist revolution is a revolution of the top stratum, a revolution of the national merchant bourgeoisie, arising in a struggle against the foreign imperialists, and whose subsequent development is essentially directed against the peasants and workers, against the very possibility of an agrarian revolution. ("Talk with Students of the Sun Yat-sen University", *Works*, Eng. ed., FLPH, Moscow, 1954, Vol. IX, p. 261.)

[10] The "metaphysics-mongers" were Chang Chun-mai and his group. After the May 4th Movement, Chang openly opposed science and advocated metaphysics, or what he called "spiritual culture", and thus came to be known as a "metaphysics-monger". In order to support Chiang Kai-shek and the Japanese aggressors, he published an "Open Letter to Mr. Mao Tse-tung" in December 1938 at Chiang Kai-shek's bidding, wildly demanding the abolition of the Eighth Route Army, the New Fourth Army and the Shensi-Kansu-Ningsia Border Region.

[11] See the manifesto of the Central Committee of the Chinese Communist Party on the establishment of Kuomintang-Communist co-operation, issued in September 1937.

[12] See Dr. Sun Yat-sen, *Lectures on the Principle of People's Livelihood*, 1924, Lecture II.

[13] *Vitalism* was an exposition of Kuomintang fascism, a hotch-potch ghost-written by a number of reactionary hacks for Chen Li-fu, one of the notorious chiefs of Chiang Kai-shek's secret service.

[14] The "doctrine of distribution according to labour" was a high-sounding slogan shamelessly put forward by Yen Hsi-shan, warlord and representative of the big landlords and big compradors in Shansi Province.

[15] "Fight Against Attacks from Both Sides" was the title of an article written by Wang Ching-wei after his betrayal of the revolution in 1927.

[16] J. V. Stalin, "Concerning the National Question in Yugoslavia", a speech delivered in the Yugoslav Commission of the E.C.C.I., March 30, 1925. Stalin said:

> . . . the peasantry constitutes the main army of the national movement, . . . there is no powerful national movement without the peasant army, nor can

there be. That is what is meant when it is said that, *in essence*, the national question is a peasant question. (*Works*, Eng. ed., FLPH, Moscow, 1954, Vol. VII, pp. 71-72.)

[17] The "principle of going up into the hills" was a dogmatist gibe against Comrade Mao Tse-tung for his emphasis on rural revolutionary bases. He makes use of the expression to explain the importance of the role played by the rural revolutionary bases.

[18] The modern school system was the educational system modelled on that of capitalist countries in Europe and America. The imperial examination system was the old examination system in feudal China. Towards the end of the 19th century, enlightened Chinese intellectuals urged the abolition of the old competitive examination system and the establishment of modern schools.

[19] The June 3rd Movement marked a new stage in the patriotic movement of May 4. On June 3, 1919, students in Peking held public meetings and made speeches in defiance of persecution and repression by the army and police. They went on strike and the strike spread to the workers and merchants in Shanghai, Nanking, Tientsin, Hangchow, Wuhan and Kiukiang and in the provinces of Shantung and Anhwei. Thus the May 4th Movement grew into a broad mass movement in which the proletariat, the urban petty bourgeoisie and the national bourgeoisie all participated.

[20] Yeh Ching was a renegade Communist who became a hired hack in the Kuomintang secret service.

[21] The spokesman of the so-called European-American school was the counter-revolutionary Hu Shih.

[22] Wholesale westernization was the view held by a number of westernized Chinese bourgeois intellectuals who unconditionally praised the outmoded individualist bourgeois culture of the West and advocated the servile imitation of capitalist Europe and America.

[23] V. I. Lenin, "What Is to Be Done?", *Collected Works*, Eng. ed., FLPH, Moscow, 1961, Vol. V, p. 369.

OVERCOME THE DANGER OF CAPITULATION
AND
STRIVE FOR A TURN FOR THE BETTER

January 28, 1940

Current developments confirm the correctness of the Central Committee's appraisals. The line of capitulation taken by the big landlord class and the big bourgeoisie runs sharply counter to the line of armed resistance taken by the proletariat, the peasantry, the urban petty bourgeoisie and the middle bourgeoisie, and there is a struggle between the two. Both lines exist at present, and one or the other can win out in the future. What all our Party comrades must realize in this connection is that the serious cases of capitulation, anti-communism and retrogression which have occurred in various places should not be viewed in isolation. We should realize their seriousness, combat them resolutely and not be overwhelmed by their impact. If we lack this spirit and a correct policy for dealing firmly with these incidents, if we let the Kuomintang die-hards continue their "military and political restriction of the Communist Party" and are in constant dread at the thought of the break-up of the united front, then the War of Resistance will be jeopardized, capitulation and anti-communism will spread throughout the country, and there will be a real danger of the break-up of the united front. But it must be made abundantly clear that many objective conditions favourable to our struggle for continued resistance, unity and progress are still present both at home and abroad. For example, Japan's policy towards China remains as tough as ever; it is very difficult to rig up a Far Eastern Munich conference because there has been no real reconciliation between Japan on the one hand and Britain, the United States and France on the other despite some lessening of the contradictions between them, and because the British and

---

This was an inner-Party directive written by Comrade Mao Tse-tung on behalf of the Central Committee of the Chinese Communist Party.

French positions in the East have been weakened by the European war; and the Soviet Union is actively helping China. These are the international factors which render it difficult for the Kuomintang to capitulate or compromise, or to launch a nation-wide anti-Communist war. At home, the Communist Party and the Eighth Route and New Fourth Armies are firmly opposing capitulation and upholding the policy of resistance and unity; the intermediate classes, too, are against capitulation; and the capitulators and the die-hards within the Kuomintang, though in power, are numerically a minority. These are the domestic factors which render it difficult for the Kuomintang to capitulate or compromise, or to launch a nation-wide anti-Communist war. In these circumstances, our Party has a twofold task. On the one hand, it must resolutely resist the military and political offensives of the capitulators and die-hards. On the other, it must actively develop the united front of the political parties, the government organs, the armed forces, the civilian population and the intellectuals; it must do its utmost to win over the majority of the Kuomintang, the intermediate classes and sympathizers in the armies fighting Japan, to deepen the mass movement, to win over the intellectuals, to consolidate the anti-Japanese base areas, expand the anti-Japanese armed forces and the organs of anti-Japanese political power, and consolidate our Party and ensure its progress. If we do both these tasks simultaneously, we shall be able to overcome the danger of capitulation by the big landlords and the big bourgeoisie and to bring about a turn for the better in the whole situation. Therefore, the present general policy of the Party is to strive for a turn for the better and at the same time to be on guard against any emergencies (such emergencies, so far, being on a limited and local scale).

Now that Wang Ching-wei has announced his traitorous pact[1] and Chiang Kai-shek has published his message to the nation, it is beyond doubt that the agitation for peace will suffer a setback and that the forces favouring resistance will grow; on the other hand, the "military and political restriction of the Communist Party" will continue, there will be more local incidents, and the Kuomintang may stress so-called "unification against the foreign enemy" in order to attack us. The reason is that the forces supporting resistance and progress cannot build up enough strength in the immediate future to overwhelm the forces supporting capitulation and retrogression. Our policy is to spare no effort in extending the propaganda campaign against Wang Ching-wei's traitorous pact in all parts of the country having Communist Party organizations. In his message, Chiang Kai-shek states that he will carry on the War of Resistance, but he does not stress the need to strengthen national unity, nor does he mention any policy for persevering in resistance and progress, without which it would be impossible to persist in the war. Hence in the campaign against Wang Ching-wei we should stress the following points: (1) support the national policy of waging the War of Resistance to the very end and oppose Wang Ching-wei's traitorous pact; (2) the whole country must unite and overthrow the traitor Wang Ching-wei and his puppet central government; (3) support Kuomintang-Communist co-operation and crush Wang Ching-wei's anti-Communist policy; (4) down with the hidden traitors of the Wang Ching-wei brand, anti-communism being Wang Ching-wei's plot for splitting the anti-Japanese united front; (5) strengthen national unity and eliminate internal "friction"; (6) introduce political reforms, unfold the movement for constitutionalism and institute democracy; (7) lift the ban on political parties and grant legal status to anti-Japanese parties and groups; (8) guarantee the people freedom of speech and assembly in order to combat the Japanese and the traitors; (9) consolidate the anti-Japanese base areas and oppose the disruptive plots of the Wang Ching-wei brand of traitors; (10) support the troops who are fighting really well in the war and give adequate supplies to the fronts; and (11) promote cultural activities which help the cause of resistance, protect the progressive youth and proscribe all expression of collaborationist views. The above slogans should be widely publicized. Large numbers of articles, manifestoes, leaflets and pamphlets should be published and speeches delivered, and other slogans suitable to local circumstances should be added.

A mass rally to denounce Wang Ching-wei's traitorous pact is scheduled to be held on February 1 in Yenan. Together with the people of all circles and with the anti-Japanese members of the Kuomintang, we should organize similar mass rallies in all areas in the early part or the middle of February in order to create a nation-wide upsurge against capitulation, against the collaborators and against "friction".

NOTES

[1] Wang Ching-wei signed a traitorous secret pact, called the "Programme for Readjusting Sino-Japanese Relations", with the Japanese aggressors at the end of 1939. According to its main provisions:

(1) Northeastern China was to be ceded to Japan and the "Mongolian Territory" (*i.e.*, what was at that time Suiyuan, Chahar and northern Shansi), northern China, the lower Yangtse valley and the islands in southern China were to be marked off as "zones for close Sino-Japanese collaboration", that is, as zones permanently occupied by Japanese troops.

(2) From its central government down to the local governments, the puppet regime was to be under the supervision of Japanese advisors and officials.

(3) The puppet troops and police were to be trained by Japanese military instructors and their equipment was to be supplied by Japan.

(4) The puppet government's fiscal and economic policies, its industrial and agricultural enterprises and its means of communication were to be controlled by Japan, and China's natural resources were to be freely exploited by Japan.

(5) All anti-Japanese activities were to be prohibited.

UNITE ALL ANTI-JAPANESE FORCES
AND
COMBAT THE ANTI-COMMUNIST DIE-HARDS

February 1, 1940

Why are we, the people of all circles in Yenan, meeting here today? We are here to denounce the traitor Wang Ching-wei, we are here to unite all anti-Japanese forces and to combat the anti-Communist die-hards.

Time and again we Communists have pointed out that Japanese imperialism is set in its policy of subjugating China. Whatever cabinet changes there may be in Japan, she will not change her basic policy of subjugating China and reducing it to a colony. Frightened out of his wits by this fact, Wang Ching-wei, the political representative of the pro-Japanese faction of the Chinese big bourgeoisie, grovels before Japan and concludes a traitorous pact, betraying China to Japanese imperialism. Moreover, he wants to set up a puppet government and army in opposition to the anti-Japanese government and army. Of late he has hardly mentioned opposition to Chiang Kai-shek and is said to have shifted over to "alliance with Chiang". Anti-communism is the main objective both of Japan and of Wang Ching-wei. Knowing that the Communist Party is the most resolute in fighting Japan and that Kuomintang-Communist co-operation means greater strength for resistance, they are trying their hardest to break up this co-operation and to separate the two parties, or better still, to set them to fighting each other. Hence they have used the die-hards within the Kuomintang to create trouble everywhere. In Hunan, there was the Pingkiang massacre;[1] in Honan, the Chuehshan massacre;[2] in Shansi, the old army attacked the new army;[3] in Hopei, Chang Yin-wu attacked

---

Comrade Mao Tse-tung delivered this speech at a mass rally in Yenan to denounce Wang Ching-wei.

the Eighth Route Army;[4] in Shantung, Chin Chi-jung attacked the
guerrillas;[5] in eastern Hupeh, Cheng Ju-huai killed between five and
six hundred Communists;[6] and as for the Shensi-Kansu-Ningsia Border
Region, the die-hards are trying to set up a spy network from within
and enforce a "blockade" from without, and are preparing an armed
attack.[7] In addition, they have arrested a large number of progressive
young people and put them in concentration camps;[8] they have hired
that metaphysics-monger Chang Chun-mai to make reactionary proposals for the liquidation of the Communist Party, the abolition of the
Shensi-Kansu-Ningsia Border Region and the disbandment of the
Eighth Route and New Fourth Armies; and they have hired the
Trotskyite Yeh Ching and others to write articles abusing the Communist Party. All this has one purpose only — to disrupt resistance to
Japan and turn the Chinese people into colonial slaves.[9]

Thus, the Wang Ching-wei clique and the anti-Communist die-
hards in the Kuomintang have been working in collusion, one from
without and the other from within, and have created pandemonium.

This state of affairs has infuriated large numbers of people who
think that the resistance to Japan is now finished and done for and
that the members of the Kuomintang are all scoundrels who ought
to be opposed. We must say that their fury is entirely justified, for
how can anybody help becoming infuriated in the face of such a grave
situation? But resistance to Japan is not finished and done for, nor
are all Kuomintang members scoundrels. Different policies should be
adopted towards the different sections of the Kuomintang. Those
conscienceless scoundrels who had the audacity to stab the Eighth
Route and New Fourth Armies in the back, to perpetrate the massacres
at Pingkiang and Chuehshan, to disrupt the Border Region and to
attack progressive armies and organizations and progressive individuals — these scoundrels must not be tolerated but must be dealt
counterblows; any concession to them is out of the question. For they
are so utterly devoid of conscience that they are even creating "friction"
and perpetrating massacres and splits after our national enemy has
penetrated deep into our territory. Whatever they may think, they
are actually helping Japan and Wang Ching-wei, and some of them
have been undercover traitors from the very outset. Failure to punish
them would be a mistake; it would be an encouragement to the collaborators and traitors, it would be disloyalty to the national resistance
and to our motherland, and an invitation to the scoundrels to disrupt
the united front. It would be a violation of the policy of our Party.

However, the sole purpose of the policy of dealing blows to the capitulators and the anti-Communist die-hards is to keep up the resistance to Japan and safeguard the anti-Japanese united front. Therefore, we should show goodwill towards those Kuomintang members who are not capitulators or anti-Communist die-hards but are loyal to the War of Resistance; we should unite with them, respect them and be willing to continue our long-term co-operation with them so as to put our country in order. Whoever does otherwise is also violating the policy of the Party.

The policy of our Party is twofold: on the one hand to unite all the progressive forces and all people loyal to the cause of resisting Japan, and on the other to oppose all the heartless scoundrels, the capitulators and the anti-Communist die-hards. Both these aspects of our policy have a single objective — to bring about a turn for the better and defeat Japan. The task of the Communist Party and the people all over the country is to unite all the forces of resistance and progress, to combat all the forces of capitulation and retrogression, and to work hard to stop the present deterioration and change the situation for the better. This is our basic policy. We are optimistic, we shall never become pessimistic or despairing. We are not afraid of any attacks by the capitulators or the anti-Communist die-hards. We must smash them, and we certainly shall. China will surely achieve national liberation; China will never perish. China will surely achieve progress, the present retrogression is only a temporary phenomenon.

In our meeting today we also want to make it clear to the people throughout the country that the unity and progress of the whole nation are essential to the War of Resistance. Some people emphasize resistance alone and are reluctant to emphasize unity and progress, or even fail to mention them. This is wrong. How can the War of Resistance be maintained without genuine and firm unity, without rapid and solid progress? The anti-Communist die-hards within the Kuomintang emphasize unification, but their so-called unification is not genuine but a sham, not a rational but an irrational unification, not a unification in substance but in form. They howl for unification, but what they really want is to liquidate the Communist Party, the Eighth Route and New Fourth Armies and the Shensi-Kansu-Ningsia Border Region, on the pretext that China cannot be unified so long as these exist. They want to turn everything over to the Kuomintang and not merely to continue but to extend their one-party dictatorship. If this were to occur, what unification could there be? Truth to tell, if the

Communist Party, the Eighth Route and New Fourth Armies and the Shensi-Kansu-Ningsia Border Region had not stepped forth and sincerely advocated ending the civil war and uniting for resistance to Japan, there would have been nobody to initiate the Anti-Japanese National United Front or to take the lead in the peaceful settlement of the Sian Incident, and there would have been no possibility at all of resisting Japan. And if today the Communist Party, the Eighth Route and New Fourth Armies, the Shensi-Kansu-Ningsia Border Region and the anti-Japanese democratic base areas did not step forth and sincerely sustain the resistance to Japan and combat the dangerous tendencies towards capitulation, a split and retrogression, the situation would indeed be in a terrible mess. The several hundred thousand troops of the Eighth Route and New Fourth Armies are holding two-fifths of the enemy forces in check by engaging seventeen out of the forty Japanese divisions.[10] Why should these armies be disbanded? The Shensi-Kansu-Ningsia Border Region is the most progressive region in the country, it is a democratic anti-Japanese base area. Here there are, first, no corrupt officials; second, no local tyrants and evil gentry; third, no gambling; fourth, no prostitutes; fifth, no concubines; sixth, no beggars; seventh, no narrow self-seeking cliques; eighth, no atmosphere of dejection and laxity; ninth, no professional friction-mongers; and tenth, no war profiteers. Why then should the Border Region be abolished? Only people without any sense of shame dare suggest anything so shameful. What right have these die-hards to breathe a word against us? No, Comrades! What needs to be done is not to abolish the Border Region but to get the whole country to follow its example, not to disband the Eighth Route and New Fourth Armies but to get the whole country to follow their example, not to liquidate the Communist Party but to get the whole country to follow its example, not to pull progressive people back to the level of backward people but to get the latter to catch up with the former. We Communists are the staunchest advocates of unification; it is we who have initiated and maintained the united front and who have put forward the slogan for a unified democratic republic. Who else could have proposed these things? Who else could have put them into effect? Who else could be content with a monthly allowance of only five yuan?[11] Who else could have formed such a clean and incorruptible government? There is unification and unification. The capitulators have their idea of unification, they want to unify us into capitulating; the anti-Communist die-hards have their idea of unification, they want to unify us into splitting and retrogression. Could we ever accept these ideas of theirs? Can any unification that is not based on resistance, unity and progress be considered genuine? Or rational? Or real unification? What a pipe dream! It is to put forward our own idea of unification that we are meeting here today. Our idea of unification is identical with that of all the people of China, of every man and woman with a conscience. It is based on resistance, unity and progress. Only through progress can we achieve unity; only through unity can we resist Japan; and only through progress, unity and resistance can the country be unified. This is our idea of unification, a genuine, rational, real unification. The idea of a sham, irrational and formal unification is one which would lead to national subjugation and which is held by persons utterly devoid of conscience. These people want to destroy the Communist Party, the Eighth Route and New Fourth Armies and the anti-Japanese democratic base areas, and wipe out all the local anti-Japanese forces, in order to establish unification under the Kuomintang. This is a plot, an attempt to perpetuate autocratic rule under the guise of unification, to sell the dog-meat of their one-party dictatorship under the label of the sheep's head of unification; it is a plot of brazen-faced braggarts who are lost to all sense of shame. We are meeting here today precisely to punch holes in this paper tiger of theirs. Let us relentlessly combat these anti-Communist die-hards.

NOTES

[1] For the Pingkiang massacre, see "The Reactionaries Must Be Punished", Note 1, p. 260 of this volume.

[2] The Chuehshan massacre occurred on November 11, 1939, when more than 1,800 Kuomintang secret agents and soldiers attacked the liaison offices of the New Fourth Army in the town of Chukou, Chuehshan County, Honan. Over two hundred people were murdered, including New Fourth Army officers and soldiers who had been wounded in the anti-Japanese war and members of their families.

[3] The old army refers to the troops under Yen Hsi-shan, the Kuomintang warlord in Shansi; the new army, known as the Anti-Japanese Dare-to-Die Corps, was the people's anti-Japanese army of Shansi which grew up under the influence and leadership of the Communist Party. In December 1939 Chiang Kai-shek and Yen Hsi-shan concentrated six army corps in western Shansi to attack the corps, but met with a smashing defeat. At the same time, Yen's troops in southeastern Shansi attacked the anti-Japanese democratic county governments and mass organizations in the Yangcheng-Chincheng area and murdered a great number of Communists and progressives.

[4] Chang Yin-wu, commander of the peace preservation corps of the Kuomintang brigands in Hopei, sprang a surprise attack on the liaison offices of the Eighth Route Army in Shenhsien County, Hopei, in June 1939 and slaughtered more than four hundred of its cadres and soldiers.

[5] In April 1939, on the instructions of Shen Hung-lieh, the Kuomintang governor of Shantung, Chin Chi-jung's bandit troops attacked the Third Guerrilla Detachment of the Shantung Column of the Eighth Route Army at Poshan, killing four hundred men, including regimental officers.

[6] In September 1939, Cheng Ju-huai, a Kuomintang military commander in eastern Hupeh, attacked the liaison offices of the New Fourth Army and killed between five and six hundred Communists.

[7] From the winter of 1939 to the spring of 1940 the Kuomintang troops seized the county towns of Chunhua, Hsunyi, Chengning, Ninghsien and Chenyuan in the Shensi-Kansu-Ningsia Border Region.

[8] Imitating the German and Italian fascists, the Kuomintang reactionaries established during the anti-Japanese war many concentration camps which extended from Lanchow and Sian in the Northwest to Kanchow and Shangjao in the Southeast. Large numbers of Communists, patriots and progressive youth were interned in them.

[9] After the fall of Wuhan in October 1938, the Kuomintang intensified its anti-Communist activities. In February 1939 Chiang Kai-shek secretly issued such documents as "Measures for Dealing with the Communist Problem" and "Measures for Guarding Against Communist Activities in the Japanese-Occupied Areas", and stepped up his political repression of the Communist Party in the Kuomintang-controlled areas and his military attacks on it in central and northern China. The culmination was the first large-scale anti-Communist onslaught of December 1939-March 1940.

[10] The Eighth Route and New Fourth Armies later engaged an even larger number of Japanese troops. By 1943 they were fighting 64 per cent of Japan's forces of aggression and 95 per cent of the puppet troops.

[11] Five yuan was the average monthly allowance for all men serving in the anti-Japanese armed forces and in the anti-Japanese government offices under Communist leadership.

TEN DEMANDS ON THE KUOMINTANG

February 1, 1940

This mass rally against Wang Ching-wei, held in Yenan on February 1, unanimously resolves, in righteous indignation, to denounce his treason and capitulation and to wage the War of Resistance Against Japan to the very end. To overcome the present crisis and ensure victory in the War of Resistance, we hereby submit ten major points for saving the country, in the hope that the National Government, all political parties and groups, all officers and men fighting in the War of Resistance and all our fellow-countrymen will accept them and act upon them.

1. *Let the whole nation denounce the Wang Ching-weis.* Now that the traitor Wang Ching-wei has gathered his gang together, betrayed his country, attached himself to the enemy and signed traitorous secret pacts, playing the jackal to the tiger, all our countrymen demand his death. But this only takes care of the open Wang Ching-weis and leaves out the undercover ones. The latter are either craftily seizing key posts and swaggering about, or working obscurely and worming their way into all walks of life. In effect, the corrupt officials are part of the Wang Ching-wei gang and all the friction-mongers are its underlings. Unless there is a national campaign to denounce the Wang Ching-weis, a campaign in town and country and from top to bottom in which everyone is mobilized, including all political parties, government organs, armed forces, civilian bodies, the press and the educational institutions, the Wang Ching-wei gang will never be eradicated but will persist in its nefarious activities, doing incalculable damage by opening the door to the enemy from without and by subversion from within. The government should issue a decree calling on the whole people to repudiate the Wang Ching-weis. Wherever the

---

This was an open telegram drafted by Comrade Mao Tse-tung on behalf of the Yenan mass rally denouncing Wang Ching-wei.

decree is not carried out, the officials should be called to account. The Wang Ching-wei gang must be extirpated. This is the first point which we urge you to accept and act upon.

2. *Strengthen unity.* Nowadays some people talk not of unity but of unification, and the implication is that unification means nothing short of liquidating the Communist Party, disbanding the Eighth Route and New Fourth Armies, abolishing the Shensi-Kansu-Ningsia Border Region and demolishing the anti-Japanese forces everywhere. What this kind of talk ignores is the fact that the Communist Party, the Eighth Route and New Fourth Armies and the Shensi-Kansu-Ningsia Border Region are the staunchest advocates of unification in all China. Was it not they who recommended the peaceful settlement of the Sian Incident? Is it not they who have initiated the Anti-Japanese National United Front, proposed a unified democratic republic and worked really hard for both? Is it not they who are standing at the forefront of the nation's defences, resisting seventeen enemy divisions, shielding the Central Plains and the Northwest and defending northern China and the regions south of the lower Yangtse, and resolutely applying the Three People's Principles and the Programme of Armed Resistance and National Reconstruction? Yet the moment Wang Ching-wei openly came out against the Communists and sided with the Japanese, sorcerers like Chang Chun-mai and Yeh Ching chimed in with tendentious articles, and the anti-Communist and die-hard cliques joined in by stirring up "friction". Autocratic rule has been imposed in the name of unification. The principle of unity has been discarded and the thin end of the wedge of disruption driven in. This Szuma Chao trick is obvious to every man in the street.[1] The Communist Party, the Eighth Route and New Fourth Armies and the Border Region stand firmly for genuine and against sham unification, for rational and against irrational unification, and for unification in substance and against unification in form. They advocate unification for resistance and not for capitulation, for unity and not for division, for progress and not for retrogression. Unification on the basis of these three — resistance, unity and progress — is genuine, rational and real unification. To seek unification on any other basis, whatever intrigues or tricks are used, is like "going south by driving the chariot north"; with that we beg to disagree. All the local anti-Japanese forces should be looked after equally well, without discriminating against some and favouring others; all of them should be trusted, provisioned, supported,

and encouraged with rewards. There should be sincerity and not hypocrisy, large-mindedness and not pettiness, in dealing with people. If things are really done in this way, all except those with ulterior motives will unite and take the road of national unification. It is an unalterable truth that unification must be based on unity and unity in its turn must be based on progress, and that only progress can bring unity and only unity can bring unification. This is the second point which we urge you to accept and act upon.

3. *Put constitutional government into effect.* The long years of "political tutelage" have yielded nothing. "A thing turns into its opposite if pushed too far"; hence constitutional government is now on the order of the day. There is still no freedom of speech, the ban on political parties has not been lifted, and constitutionalism is violated everywhere. If the constitution is drawn up on these lines, it will be a mere scrap of official paper. Such constitutionalism will be no different from one-party dictatorship. Now that there is a profound national crisis, with the Japanese and Wang Ching-wei harassing us from without and the traitors disrupting us from within, our existence as a nation and people will be placed in jeopardy unless there is a change of policy. The government should immediately lift the ban on the political parties and encourage freedom of opinion to show that it sincerely intends to put constitutionalism into practice. Nothing is more urgent for winning the full confidence of the people and shaping the destiny of the nation anew. This is the third point which we urge you to accept and act upon.

4. *Put an end to the "friction".* Since the "Measures for Restricting the Activities of Alien Parties" were introduced in March last year, the clamour for "restricting", "corroding" and "combating" the Communist Party has reverberated throughout the country, there has been one tragic incident after another, and blood has flown freely. As if this were not enough, the additional "Measures for Dealing with the Alien Party Problem" were introduced in October last year. Then there are the "Directives for Dealing with the Alien Party Problem" in northwestern, northern and central China. People have been saying, and quite justifiably, that "political restriction" of the Communist Party has been succeeded by "military restriction". In fact, restricting communism equals anti-communism. And anti-communism is the cunning and pernicious scheme used by the Japanese and Wang Ching-wei for subjugating China. That is why the people are suspicious and

shocked and are telling one another about it, and are afraid that the bitter tragedy of a decade ago is being re-enacted. Matters have gone far enough, with the Pingkiang Massacre in Hunan, the Chuehshan Massacre in Honan, the attack on the Eighth Route Army by Chang Yin-wu in Hopei, the attack on the guerrillas by Chin Chi-jung in Shantung, the ruthless slaughter of between five and six hundred Communists by Cheng Ju-huai in eastern Hupeh, the large-scale assaults on the garrison forces of the Eighth Route Army by the Central Army in eastern Kansu and, more recently, the tragedy in Shansi where the old army attacked the new army and invaded positions held by the Eighth Route Army. If such incidents are not immediately prohibited, both sides will be doomed, and what hope will there be then of victory over Japan? For the sake of unity in the War of Resistance, the government should order the punishment of all the perpetrators of these massacres and announce to the whole nation that no such incident will be allowed to recur. This is the fourth point which we urge you to accept and act upon.

5. *Protect the youth.* Concentration camps have recently been set up near Sian, and people have been horrified to learn that more than seven hundred progressive young people from the northwestern and central provinces have already been interned there, subjected to mental and physical bondage and treated like convicts. What crime have they committed to deserve such cruelty? Young people are the cream of the nation, and the progressive ones in particular are our most precious asset in the War of Resistance. Everyone should enjoy freedom of belief; ideas can never be suppressed by force of arms. The crime of the ten years of "cultural suppression" is known to everyone; why should anyone desire to repeat it today? The government should immediately issue a nation-wide order for the protection of youth, for the abolition of the concentration camps near Sian and for the strict prohibition of the outrageous attacks on young people in various places. This is the fifth point which we urge you to accept and act upon.

6. *Support the front.* Troops who are fighting in the very front line and with fine records of service, such as the Eighth Route Army, the New Fourth Army and certain other units, are receiving the worst treatment; they are thinly clad, badly fed and kept short of ammunition and medicines. Yet unscrupulous traitors are allowed to slander them. There is a deafening din of countless absurd slanders against them. Merit goes unrewarded and distinguished service uncited, while false

charges and malicious plots become more and more brazen. This fantastic state of affairs dampens the ardour of our officers and men and wins applause only from the enemy; on no account must it be allowed to continue. To lift up the hearts of the troops and so help the war, the government should adequately provision the front-line troops who have good service records and at the same time strictly prohibit the treacherous slanders and accusations against them. This is the sixth point which we urge you to accept and act upon.

7. *Proscribe the secret service.* People are comparing the secret service agents to Chou Hsing and Lai Chun-chen[2] of the Tang Dynasty and Wei Chung-hsien and Liu Chin[3] of the Ming Dynasty because of their lawlessness and violence. Ignoring the enemy and concentrating on our own countrymen, they are committing innumerable murders and insatiably taking bribes; in fact the secret service is the head-quarters of the rumour-mongers and a breeding ground of treason and evil. Ordinary people everywhere recoil and turn away in fear from these fiendish brutes of agents. To preserve its own prestige, the government should immediately proscribe these activities of the secret service and reorganize it, defining its duties as exclusively directed against the enemy and the traitors, so that the people's confidence may be restored and the foundations of the state strengthened. This is the seventh point which we urge you to accept and act upon.

8. *Dismiss corrupt officials.* Since the beginning of the War of Resistance, there have been cases of officials netting up to 100 million yuan out of the national crisis and taking as many as eight or nine concubines. Conscription, government bonds, economic controls, famine relief and war relief, all without exception have become money-making opportunities for corrupt officials. With such a pack of wolves running wild, no wonder the country's affairs are in chaos. The people are seething with discontent and anger, yet none dare expose the ruth-lessness of these officials. To save the country from collapse, drastic and effective steps should immediately be taken to clear out all corrupt officials. This is the eighth point which we urge you to accept and act upon.

9. *Put the Testament of Dr. Sun Yat-sen into effect.* The Testament says:

> For forty years I have devoted myself to the cause of the national revolution with the aim of winning freedom and equality for China. My experiences during these forty years have firmly

convinced me that to achieve this aim we must arouse the masses
of the people. . . .

A most remarkable statement indeed, and we the 450 million people
of China are all familiar with it. But the Testament is more often
chanted than carried out. Desecrators of the Testament are rewarded
while those who honour it in their acts are punished. What could be
more preposterous? The government should decree that anyone who
dares to violate the Testament and who tramples on the masses of the
people instead of arousing them will be punished for profaning Dr. Sun
Yat-sen's memory. This is the ninth point which we urge you to accept
and act upon.

10. *Put the Three People's Principles into effect.* The Three People's Principles are the platform of the Kuomintang. Yet many people,
making anti-communism their first duty, are giving up the war effort
and doing everything possible to suppress and hold back the people
as they rise to resist Japan, which is tantamount to abandoning the
Principle of Nationalism; officials are depriving the people of all
democratic rights, which is tantamount to abandoning the Principle
of Democracy; they are ignoring the people's sufferings, which is
tantamount to abandoning the Principle of the People's Livelihood.
Such persons pay only lip-service to the Three People's Principles and
either ridicule those who seriously try to put them into effect as busy-
bodies or severely punish them. Thus, all sorts of fantastic abuses have
sprung up and the government's prestige has reached rock bottom.
An unequivocal order should immediately be issued for the strict
carrying out of the Three People's Principles throughout the country.
Those who violate the order should be severely punished and all who
carry it out amply encouraged. It is only in this way that the Three
People's Principles can at long last be put into effect and the foundations
laid for victory in the war. This is the tenth point which we urge you
to accept and act upon.

These ten proposals are essential measures for saving the nation
and winning the war. Now that the enemy is stepping up his
aggression against China and traitor Wang Ching-wei is running wild,
we dare not remain silent on what we feel to be crucial issues. Please
accept and act upon these proposals, and great advantage will ensue
to the War of Resistance and the cause of national liberation. It is with
a keen sense of urgency that we state our views, and we await your
considered opinion.

NOTES

[1] Szuma Chao was a prime minister of the state of Wei (220-265) who nursed a secret ambition to ascend the throne. The emperor once remarked: "Szuma Chao's intention is obvious to every man in the street."

[2] Chou Hsing and Lai Chun-chen were notoriously cruel inquisitors in the Tang Dynasty. They organized a network of spies who wantonly arrested people they disliked and subjected these people to all kinds of torture.

[3] Liu Chin and Wei Chung-hsien were eunuchs in the Ming Dynasty. The first was a favourite of Emperor Wu Tsung (in the 16th century), and the second of Emperor Hsi Tsung (in the 17th century). They made use of large secret services to persecute and murder those who opposed them.

NOTES.

INTRODUCING *THE CHINESE WORKER*

February 7, 1940

The publication of *The Chinese Worker*[1] meets a need. Led by its own political party, the Communist Party of China, the Chinese working class has waged heroic struggles for the past twenty years and become the most politically awakened section of the people and the leader of the Chinese revolution. Rallying the peasantry and all revolutionary people against imperialism and feudalism, it has fought to establish a new-democratic China and to drive out Japanese imperialism, and its contribution has been outstanding. But the Chinese revolution has not yet triumphed and great efforts are still needed to unite the working class itself and to unite the peasantry and the other sections of the petty bourgeoisie, the intellectuals, and the entire revolutionary people. This is a tremendous political and organizational task. The responsibility for its accomplishment rests on the Communist Party of China, on the progressive workers and on the entire working class. The ultimate liberation of the working class and the people as a whole will be achieved only under socialism, which is the final goal the Chinese proletariat must struggle to attain. But before we can enter the stage of socialism, we must pass through the stage of the anti-imperialist and anti-feudal democratic revolution. The immediate task of the Chinese working class, therefore, is to strengthen unity in its own ranks and unite the people, to oppose imperialism and feudalism, and to struggle for a new China, a China of New Democracy. *The Chinese Worker* is being published with just this task in view.

Using simple language, *The Chinese Worker* will explain the hows and whys of many issues to the workers, report the realities of the working-class struggle in the War of Resistance and sum up the experience gained, and in this way it will endeavour to fulfil its task.

The Chinese Worker should become a school for educating the workers and for training cadres from their midst, and the readers will be its students. It is necessary to educate many cadres from among the workers, knowledgeable and capable cadres who do not seek empty fame but are ready for honest work. It is impossible for the working class to attain liberation without large numbers of such cadres.

The working class should welcome the help of the revolutionary intellectuals and never refuse it. For without their help the working class itself cannot go forward nor can the revolution succeed.

I hope that the journal will be well edited and that it will publish a good deal of lively writing, carefully avoiding wooden and trite articles which are flat, insipid and unintelligible.

Once started, a journal must be run conscientiously and well. This is the responsibility of the readers as well as of the staff. It is very important for the readers to send in suggestions and write brief letters and articles indicating what they like and what they dislike, for this is the only way to make the journal a success.

With these few words I express my hopes; let them serve as an introduction to *The Chinese Worker*.

NOTES

[1] *The Chinese Worker* was a monthly founded in February 1940 in Yenan and published under the auspices of the Trade Union Commission of the Central Committee of the Chinese Communist Party.

WE MUST STRESS UNITY AND PROGRESS

February 10, 1940

Resistance, unity and progress — these are the three major principles which the Communist Party put forward last July 7 on the second anniversary of the War of Resistance. The three form an organic whole, and not one of them can be dispensed with. If the stress is solely on resistance to the exclusion of unity and progress, then such "resistance" will be neither dependable nor enduring. Without a programme for unity and progress, resistance must sooner or later turn into capitulation or end in defeat. We Communists hold that the three must be integrated. For the sake of the War of Resistance, it is necessary to fight against capitulation, against Wang Ching-wei's traitorous pact with Japan, against his puppet regime, and against all the traitors and capitulators concealed in the anti-Japanese ranks. For the sake of unity, it is necessary to oppose splitting activities and internal "friction", to oppose the stabbing of the Eighth Route and New Fourth Armies and other progressive anti-Japanese groups in the back, to oppose the disruption of the anti-Japanese base areas behind the enemy lines and of the Shensi-Kansu-Ningsia Border Region which is the rear area of the Eighth Route Army, to oppose the denial of legal status to the Communist Party and the avalanche of documents for "restricting the activities of alien parties". For the sake of progress, it is necessary to oppose retrogression and the shelving of the Three People's Principles and of the Programme of Armed Resistance and National Reconstruction, to oppose the refusal to carry out the injunction in Dr. Sun Yat-sen's Testament to "arouse the masses of the people", to oppose the internment of progressive young people in concentration camps, to oppose the suppression of what little freedom of speech and of the press there was in the early days of the War of Resistance, to oppose

---

This article was written by Comrade Mao Tse-tung for the *New China News* of Yenan on the occasion of its first anniversary.

the scheme to turn the movement for constitutional government into
the private concern of a few bureaucrats, to oppose the attacks on the
new army, the persecution of the League of Self-Sacrifice and the
massacre of progressives in Shansi,[1] to oppose the activities of the
Three People's Principles Youth League in kidnapping people along
the Hsienyang-Yulin Highway and the Lunghai Railway,[2] to oppose
such shameless practices as taking nine concubines and making
fortunes of 100 million yuan out of the national crisis, and to oppose
the unbridled brutality of the corrupt officials and the local tyrants
and evil gentry. Without opposing all these and without unity and
progress, "resistance" will be just empty talk and victory a vain hope.
What will be the political orientation of the *New China News* in its
second year? It will be to stress unity and progress and oppose all the
vicious practices which are detrimental to the war, so that further
successes can be achieved in our cause of resistance to Japan.

NOTES

[1] The League of Self-Sacrifice for National Salvation in Shansi was a local
anti-Japanese mass organization formed in 1936 which co-operated closely with the
Communist Party. It played an important role in the anti-Japanese fighting there. In
December 1939 Yen Hsi-shan, the Kuomintang warlord-governor of Shansi, openly
began to suppress the league in the western part of the province and brutally killed
a great number of Communists, officers of the league and other progressives.

[2] In 1939 the Kuomintang drew a cordon along the Hsienyang-Yulin Highway
and the Lunghai (Kansu-Haichow) Railway by setting up a number of check-posts
in the guise of "hostels" of the Three People's Principles Youth League. Secret
agents posted at these hostels, working together with the Kuomintang troops, arrested
progressive young people and intellectuals entering or leaving the Shensi-Kansu-
Ningsia Border Region and interned them in concentration camps, where they were
either cruelly murdered or compelled to turn informer against the Communist Party.

NEW-DEMOCRATIC
CONSTITUTIONAL GOVERNMENT

February 20, 1940

It is highly significant that representatives of the people of all circles in Yenan are meeting here today to inaugurate the Association for the Promotion of Constitutional Government and that everybody has become interested in constitutionalism. What is the purpose of our meeting? It is to facilitate the full expression of the popular will, the defeat of Japan and the building of a new China.

Armed resistance to Japan, which we all support, is already being carried out, and the question now is only one of persevering in it. But there is something else, namely, democracy, which is not being carried out. Both are of paramount importance to China today. To be sure, China lacks many things, but the main ones are independence and democracy. In the absence of either, China's affairs will not go well. And while there are two things lacking, there are also two superfluous ones. What are they? Imperialist oppression and feudal oppression. It is because of these two superfluous things that China has become a colonial, semi-colonial and semi-feudal country. The principal demands of the nation today are for independence and democracy, and therefore imperialism and feudalism must be destroyed. They must be destroyed resolutely, thoroughly, and without the least mercy. Some say that only

---

Comrade Mao Tse-tung delivered this speech before the Yenan Association for the Promotion of Constitutional Government. Confused by Chiang Kai-shek's deceptive propaganda at the time, many comrades in the Party thought that perhaps the Kuomintang really would establish a constitutional government. Comrade Mao Tse-tung here exposed Chiang Kai-shek's deceit, wrested the propaganda weapon of "constitutional government" from his hands and turned it into a weapon for awakening the people to demand freedom and democracy from Chiang Kai-shek. Thereupon, Chiang Kai-shek immediately packed up this bag of tricks, and never again throughout the whole War of Resistance Against Japan did he dare to propagate his so-called constitutional government.

construction is needed, not destruction. Well, we should like to ask: Shouldn't Wang Ching-wei be destroyed? Shouldn't Japanese imperialism be destroyed? Shouldn't the feudal system be destroyed? Construction is certainly out of the question unless you destroy these evils. Only by destroying them can China be saved and construction be set going; otherwise, it will all be an idle dream. Only by destroying the old and the rotten can we build the new and the sound. Combine independence and democracy and you have resistance on the basis of democracy, or democracy in the service of resistance. Without democracy, resistance will fail. Without democracy, resistance cannot be maintained. With democracy, we shall certainly win even if we have to go on resisting for eight or ten years.

What is constitutional government? It is democratic government. I agree with what our old Comrade Wu[1] has just said. What kind of democratic government do we need today? New-democratic government, the constitutional government of New Democracy. Not the old, outmoded, European-American type of so-called democracy which is bourgeois dictatorship, nor as yet the Soviet type of democracy which is the dictatorship of the proletariat.

Democracy of the old type, practised in other countries, is on its way out and has become reactionary. Under no circumstances should we accept such a reactionary thing. The sort of constitutional government which the Chinese die-hards are talking about is the old type of bourgeois democracy found abroad. But while they talk about it, they do not really want even that; they are using such talk to deceive the people. What they really want is a one-party fascist dictatorship. The Chinese national bourgeoisie, on the other hand, does want this type of constitutional government and would like to establish a bourgeois dictatorship in China, but it can never succeed. For the Chinese people do not want such a government and would not welcome a one-class dictatorship by the bourgeoisie. China's affairs must be decided by the vast majority of the Chinese people, and the monopoly of government by the bourgeoisie alone must be absolutely rejected. Then what about socialist democracy? Of course, it is very good, and will eventually prevail throughout the world. But today this type of democracy is not yet practicable in China, and we must therefore do without it for the time being. Not until certain conditions are present will it be possible to have socialist democracy. The kind of democratic government we need today is neither democracy of the old type nor yet democracy of the socialist type, but New Democracy which is suited to the conditions of present-day China. The constitutional government to be promoted is new-democratic constitutional government.

What is new-democratic constitutional government? It is the joint dictatorship of several revolutionary classes over the traitors and reactionaries. Someone once said, "If there is food, let everyone share it." I think this can serve to illustrate New Democracy. Just as everyone should share what food there is, so there should be no monopoly of power by a single party, group or class. This idea was well expressed by Dr. Sun Yat-sen in the Manifesto of the First National Congress of the Kuomintang:

> The so-called democratic system in modern states is usually monopolized by the bourgeoisie and has become simply an instrument for oppressing the common people. On the other hand, the Kuomintang's Principle of Democracy means a democratic system shared by all the common people and not privately owned by the few.

Comrades, in studying constitutional government we shall read various books, but above all, we must study this manifesto, and this passage should be learned by heart. "Shared by all the common people and not privately owned by the few" — this is the substance of what we describe as new-democratic constitutional government, as the joint democratic dictatorship of several revolutionary classes over the traitors and reactionaries; such is the constitutional government we need today. And it is the form which a constitutional government of the anti-Japanese united front should take.

The purpose of our meeting today is to promote or urge the establishment of constitutional government. Why do we have to "urge" it? If everybody were marching forward, then nobody would need to be urged. Why do we trouble to hold this meeting? Because some people, instead of marching forward, are lying down and refusing to move on. Not only do they refuse to move forward, they actually want to go back. You call on them to go forward, but they would rather die than do so; these people are die-hards. They are so stubborn that we have to hold this meeting to give them an "urging". Where does the term "urge" come from? Who first applied it in this connection? Not we, but that great and venerated man, Dr. Sun Yat-sen, who said: "For forty years I have devoted myself to the cause of the national revolution. . . ." Read his Testament and you will find the following words: "Most recently I have recommended the convocation of the national assembly . . . and its realization in the shortest possible time must in particular be urged. This is my heartfelt charge to you." Comrades, not an ordinary "charge" but a "heartfelt charge". A "heartfelt charge" is not just the usual kind of charge, so how can it be lightly ignored? Again, "the shortest possible time"; first, not the longest time, second, not a relatively long time, and third, not just a short time but "the shortest possible time". If we want the national assembly to come into being in the shortest possible time, then we have to "urge" it. Dr. Sun Yat-sen has been dead for fifteen years, but to this day the national assembly he recommended has not been convened. Fiddling every day with political tutelage, certain people have senselessly fiddled away the time, turning "the shortest possible time" into the longest time, and yet they are for ever invoking Dr. Sun Yat-sen's name. How Dr. Sun's ghost would rebuke these unworthy followers of his! It is perfectly clear that without "urging", there will be no moving forward; "urging" is needed because many are moving back and many others are not yet awakened.

As some people are not moving forward, we have to urge them. We have to urge others because they are slow. That is why we are calling many meetings to urge the establishment of constitutional government. The youth have held such meetings, and so have the women, the workers, the schools, government organizations and army units. It is all very lively and very good. And now we are holding this general meeting for the same purpose, so that all of us can go into action to urge the speedy enforcement of constitutional government and the immediate application of Dr. Sun Yat-sen's teachings.

Some say: "You are in Yenan while those people are in various other places. What is the use of your urging them if they take no notice?" Yes, there is some use. For things are moving and they will have to take notice. If we hold more meetings, write more articles, make more speeches and send more telegrams, they will find it impossible not to take notice. I think our numerous meetings in Yenan to promote constitutional government have a twofold purpose. One is to study the problem and the other is to push people forward. Why do we have to study? Because supposing they do not go forward and you urge them, and they then ask why you are pushing, it is necessary to be able to answer. To do so, we have to make a serious study of the hows and whys of constitutional government. This is exactly what our old Comrade Wu has been talking about in some detail. All schools, government organizations and army units and all sections of the people should study the problem of constitutional government confronting us.

Once we have studied it, we can push people forward. To push them forward is to urge them on and, as we push in all fields, things will all gradually move ahead. The many little streams will merge into a great river to wash away all that is rotten and filthy, and new-democratic constitutional government will emerge. The effect of such pushing will be very great. What we do in Yenan is bound to influence the whole country.

Comrades, do you imagine that once the meetings have been held and the telegrams dispatched, the die-hards will be bowled over, will start moving forward, will submit to our orders? No, they will not be as docile as that. A great many of them are graduates of special training schools for die-hards. Die-hards they are today, and die-hards they will remain tomorrow and even the day after. What does die-hard mean? "Hard" means to be inflexible and "die" means to be dead set against progress today, tomorrow and even the day after. Such are the people we call die-hards. To make them listen to us is no easy matter.

As far as the constitutional governments the world has so far known are concerned, whether in Britain, France, the United States or the Soviet Union, a body of basic laws, that is, a constitution, has generally been promulgated after a successful revolution to give recognition to the actual establishment of democracy. But China's case is different. In China the revolution has not yet succeeded and, except in areas like our Border Region, democratic government is not yet a fact. The fact is that China today is under semi-colonial and semi-feudal rule, and even if a good constitution were promulgated, it would inevitably be hindered by the feudal forces and obstructed by the die-hards, so that it would be impossible to carry it out smoothly. Thus the present movement for constitutional government has to strive for a democracy that is not yet achieved, rather than to affirm a democracy that has already become a fact. This means a major struggle, and it is certainly no light or easy matter.

Those who have all along opposed constitutional government[2] are now paying it lip-service. Why? Because they are under pressure from the people, who want to fight Japan, and they have to temporize a little. They are even shouting at the top of their voices, "We have always stood for constitutional government!" and making a terrific din. For years we have been hearing the words "constitutional government", but so far we have seen no trace of it. These people say one thing and do another and may be called double-dealers in constitutional government. Their "always stood for" is truly an example of their double-dealing. The die-hards of today are precisely such double-dealers. Their constitutional government is a swindle. In the not too distant future you may get a constitution, and a president into the bargain. But as for democracy and freedom, heaven alone knows when they will give you that. China has already had a constitution. Did not Tsao Kun promulgate one?[3] But where were democracy and freedom to be found? As for presidents, there have been a number of them. The first, Sun Yat-sen, was good, but he was edged out by Yuan Shih-kai. The second was Yuan Shih-kai, the third Li Yuan-hung,[4] the fourth Feng Kuo-chang[5] and the fifth Hsu Shih-chang,[6] indeed a great many, but were they any different from the despotic emperors? Both the constitution and the presidents were fakes. At the present time the so-called constitutional and democratic governments of countries like Britain, France and the United States are in fact man-eating governments. The same is true of Central and South America where many countries display the republican signboard but in fact have no trace of democracy. Similarly with China's present-day die-hards. Their talk of constitutional government is only "selling dog-meat under the label of a sheep's head". They display the sheep's head of constitutional government while selling the dog-meat of one-party dictatorship. I am not attacking them groundlessly; my words are well-founded, because for all their talk about constitutional government they do not give the people a particle of freedom.

Comrades, real constitutional government will never come easily; it can only be obtained through hard struggle. Therefore you must not expect that it will come immediately after we have held our meetings, sent our telegrams and written our articles. Nor must you expect that once the People's Political Council[7] passes a resolution, the National Government issues a decree, and the national assembly[8] meets on November 12, promulgates a constitution and even elects a president, everything will be fine and all will be right with the world. That is impossible, so don't get confused. This needs to be explained to the common people so that they will not be confused either. Things will never be that easy.

Should we then lament the cause as lost? Things are so difficult that it seems hopeless. But that is not so either. There is still hope for constitutional government, and great hope at that, and China will certainly become a new-democratic state. Why? The difficulties arise because of trouble-making by the die-hards, but they cannot go on being die-hards for ever, and that is why we still have high hopes. The die-hards of the world may be die-hards today and remain so tomorrow and even the day after, but not for ever; in the end they will have to change. Wang Ching-wei, for example, was a die-hard for a very long time, yet he could not keep on acting the die-hard within the anti-Japanese ranks and had to go over to the Japanese. Chang Kuo-tao, to take another example, was also a die-hard for a very long time, but he, too, took to his heels after we held a number of meetings and struggled repeatedly against him. Actually, the die-hards may be hard, but they are not hard unto death, and in the end they change — into something filthy and contemptible, like dog's dung. Some change for the better and that is also the result of our repeated struggles against them — they come to see their mistakes and change for the better. In short, die-hards do change eventually. They always have many schemes in hand, schemes for profiting at others' expense, for double-dealing, and so on. But they always get the opposite of what they want. They invariably start by doing others harm but end by ruining themselves. We once said that Chamberlain was "lifting a rock only to drop it on his own toes", and this has now come to pass. Chamberlain had set his heart on using Hitler as the rock with which to crush the toes of the Soviet people, but since that September day last year when war broke out between Germany on the one side and Britain and France on the other, the rock in his hands has fallen on his own toes. To this day he is still smarting from it. Similar instances abound in China. Yuan Shih-kai wanted to crush the toes of the common people but in the event hurt himself, and he died just a few months after becoming emperor.[9] Tuan Chi-jui, Hsu Shih-chang, Tsao Kun, Wu Pei-fu and all the rest wanted to repress the people, but finally they were all overthrown by the people. Whoever tries to profit at others' expense will come to no good end.

I think that, unless they move forward, the anti-Communist die-hards of today can be no exception to this rule. On the high-sounding pretext of unification, they are planning to liquidate the progressive Shensi-Kansu-Ningsia Border Region, the progressive Eighth Route and New Fourth Armies, the progressive Communist Party and mass organizations. They have any number of schemes of this sort. But I believe the outcome will be not the liquidation of progress by die-hardism but the liquidation of die-hardism by progress. Indeed, to escape liquidation the die-hards have no alternative but to move forward. Hence we have often advised them not to attack the Eighth Route Army, the Communist Party and the Border Region. If they must, they had better make a resolution starting as follows: "Determined as we are to liquidate ourselves and provide the Communist Party with ample opportunity to expand, we, the die-hards, assume the responsibility for attacking the Communist Party and the Border Region." The die-hards have had plenty of experience in "suppressing the Communists", and should they now want to have another go, they are free to do so. If after eating their fill and having a good sleep, they feel like doing some "suppression", that is up to them. However, they must be prepared for the above resolution to go into effect, for it is unalterable. The "suppression of the Communists" in the past ten years invariably turned out in conformity with this resolution. Any further "suppression" will also conform to it. Hence I advise them not to go in for "suppression". For what the whole nation wants is not "suppression of the Communists" but resistance, unity and progress. Therefore, anyone who tries to "suppress the Communists" is bound to fail.

In short, retrogression eventually produces the reverse of what its promoters intend. There is no exception to this rule either in modern or in ancient times, in China or elsewhere.

The same is true of constitutional government today. If the die-hards keep on opposing it, the result will certainly be the reverse of what they intend. The movement for constitutional government will never follow the course decided on by the die-hards, but will run counter to their intentions, and it will inevitably take the course decided on by the people. This is certain, for the people throughout the country demand it, and so do the current of China's historical development and the whole trend of world affairs. Who can resist it? The wheel of history cannot be pushed back. However, the work we have undertaken requires time and cannot be accomplished overnight; it requires effort and cannot be done in a slipshod way; it requires the mobilization of the great masses of the people and cannot be done effectively by a single pair of hands. It is a very good thing that we are holding this meeting here today; after our meeting we shall write articles and send telegrams, and we shall also hold similar meetings in the Wutai Mountains, the Taihang Mountains, northern China, central China and all over the country. If we go on doing this and keep it up for several years, that will be just about right. We must make a good job of it, we must win democracy and freedom, we must establish new-democratic constitutional government. If this is not done and the die-hards are allowed to have their way, the nation will perish. This is the way we must work to avoid national subjugation. For this purpose everybody must exert himself. If we do so, there is great hope for our cause. It must further be understood that after all the die-hards are only a minority, while the majority consists not of die-hards but of people capable of moving forward. With the majority pitted against the minority, plus the efforts we exert, the hope will be even greater. That is why I say that, difficult though the task may be, there is great hope.

NOTES

[1] Old Comrade Wu is Comrade Wu Yu-chang, who was then Chairman of the Yenan Association for the Promotion of Constitutional Government.

[2] "Those" refers to the Kuomintang reactionary clique headed by Chiang Kai-shek.

[3] In 1923 Tsao Kun, a big Northern warlord, had himself elected President of the Republic by bribing 590 members of parliament with 5,000 silver dollars each. He then promulgated a constitution, which came to be known as the "Tsao Kun Constitution" or the "Constitution of Bribery".

[4] Li Yuan-hung was originally commander of a brigade in the armed forces of the Ching Dynasty. He was compelled by his officers and men to side with the revolution during the Wuchang Uprising in 1911 and was made military governor of Hupeh Province. He later became Vice-President and then President of the Republic under the regime of the Northern warlord clique.

[5] Feng Kuo-chang was one of Yuan Shih-kai's underlings. After Yuan's death, he became the leader of the Chihli (Hopei) group of the Northern warlord clique. In 1917 he got rid of Li Yuan-hung and became President himself.

[6] Hsu Shih-chang was a politician in the service of the Northern warlord clique. He was elected President in 1918 by the parliament controlled by Tuan Chi-jui.

[7] The People's Political Council was a mere advisory body reluctantly set up by the Kuomintang government after the outbreak of the anti-Japanese war. The members were all "invited" by the Kuomintang government. Nominally it included the representatives of all anti-Japanese political parties and groups, but it was actually dominated by the Kuomintang majority. It had no power to influence the policies or the measures adopted by the Kuomintang government. As Chiang Kai-shek and the Kuomintang became more and more reactionary, the number of Kuomintang and other reactionaries on the council increased while the number of democrats decreased and their freedom of speech was severely curtailed, until the council increasingly became a mere tool of Kuomintang reaction. After the Southern Anhwei Incident of 1941, the Communist members of the council boycotted its meetings several times in protest against the Kuomintang's reactionary measures.

[8] A resolution demanding that the Kuomintang government convene a national assembly and establish a constitutional government at a fixed date was passed at the Fourth Session of the People's Political Council in September 1939, on the proposal of the Communist Party and the democrats of other parties and groups. In November 1939 the Sixth Plenary Session of the Central Executive Committee of the Kuomintang announced that the national assembly would be convened on November 12, 1940. Though much publicized to dupe the people, this pledge came to nothing.

[9] Yuan Shih-kai proclaimed himself emperor on December 12, 1915, but was forced to give up the title on March 22, 1916.

ON THE QUESTION OF POLITICAL POWER
IN THE ANTI-JAPANESE BASE AREAS

March 6, 1940

1. This is a time when the anti-Communist die-hards of the Kuomintang are doing all they can to prevent us from setting up organs of anti-Japanese democratic political power in northern and central China and other places, while we on our part must set them up, and in the major anti-Japanese base areas it is already possible for us to do so. Our struggle with the anti-Communist die-hards over this issue in northern, central and northwestern China can help to promote the establishment of united front organs of political power over the whole country and it is being followed attentively by the whole nation. Therefore, this issue must be handled carefully.

2. The political power we are establishing during the anti-Japanese war is of a united front character. It is the political power of all those who support both resistance and democracy; it is the joint democratic dictatorship of several revolutionary classes over the traitors and reactionaries. It differs from the counter-revolutionary dictatorship of the landlord class and the bourgeoisie as well as from the worker-peasant democratic dictatorship of the Agrarian Revolution period. A clear understanding of the character of this political power and conscientious efforts to put it into practice will greatly help to spread democracy through the country. Any deviation, either to the "Left" or the Right, will create a very bad impression on the whole nation.

3. The convening of the Hopei Provincial Assembly and the elections to the Hopei Administrative Council, preparations for which have just been started, will be of exceptional importance. Equally important will be the establishment of the new organs of political power in northwestern Shansi, in Shantung, in areas north of the Huai

This inner-Party directive was written by Comrade Mao Tse-tung on behalf of the Central Committee of the Communist Party of China.

River, in the counties of Suiteh and Fuhsien, and in eastern Kansu.
We must proceed according to the united front principle and do our
utmost to avoid any Right or "Left" tendencies. At the moment the
"Left" tendency of neglecting to win over the middle bourgeoisie and
the enlightened gentry is the more serious danger.

4. In accordance with the united front principle concerning the
organs of political power, the allocation of places should be one-third
for Communists, one-third for non-Party left progressives, and one-
third for the intermediate sections who are neither left nor right.

5. We must make sure that the Communists play the leading role
in the organs of political power, and therefore the Party members
who occupy one-third of the places must be of high calibre. This will be
enough to ensure the Party's leadership without a larger representation.
Leadership is neither a slogan to be shouted from morning till night
nor an arrogant demand for obedience; it consists rather in using the
Party's correct policies and the example we set by our own work to
convince and educate people outside the Party so that they willingly
accept our proposals.

6. The non-Party progressives must be allocated one-third of the
places because they are linked with the broad masses of the petty
bourgeoisie. This will be of tremendous importance in winning the
latter over.

7. Our aim in allocating one-third of the places to the intermediate
sections is to win over the middle bourgeoisie and the enlightened
gentry. Winning over these sections is an important step in isolating
the die-hards. At the present time, we must not fail to take the strength
of these sections into account and must be circumspect in our relations
with them.

8. Our attitude to the non-Communists must be one of co-
operation, whether or not they have party affiliations and whatever
these may be, so long as they favour resistance to Japan and are
willing to co-operate with the Communist Party.

9. The allocation of places described above represents the genuine
policy of the Party, and we must on no account be half-hearted about
it. To execute this policy, we must educate the Party members who
work in the organs of political power, overcome the narrowness
manifested in their reluctance and uneasiness in co-operating with
non-Communists, and encourage a democratic style of work, that is,
consultation with the non-Party people and winning majority approval
before taking action. At the same time, we must do all we can to

encourage the non-Party people to express their views on various problems and must lend an attentive ear to their suggestions. We must never think that because we hold military and political power we can force unconditional compliance with our decisions, and on that account shun the effort to win the non-Party people over to our views so that they carry them out gladly and whole-heartedly.

10. The above figures for the allocation of places are not rigid quotas to be filled mechanically; they are in the nature of a rough proportion which every locality must apply according to its specific circumstances. At the lowest level, the ratio may be somewhat modified to prevent the landlords and evil gentry from sneaking into the organs of political power. Where such organs have been in existence for some time, as in the Shansi-Chahar-Hopei border area, the central Hopei area, the Taihang mountain area and the southern Hopei area, there should be a re-examination of policy in the light of this principle. And this principle should be observed whenever a new organ of political power is set up.

11. The united front policy on suffrage should be that every Chinese who reaches the age of eighteen and is in favour of resistance and democracy should enjoy the right to elect and to be elected, irrespective of class, nationality, sex, creed, party affiliation or educational level. The organs of political power of the anti-Japanese united front must be elected by the people. Their form of organization should be based on democratic centralism.

12. The fundamental point of departure for all major policy measures in the united front organs of political power should be opposition to Japanese imperialism, protection of the people who are resisting Japan, proper adjustment of the interests of all the anti-Japanese social strata, improvement of the livelihood of the workers and peasants and suppression of traitors and reactionaries.

13. The non-Party people who work in our organs of political power should not be required to live, talk and act like Communists, or otherwise they may feel dissatisfied or ill at ease.

14. All regional and sub-regional bureaus of the Central Committee, all area Party committees and all heads of army units are hereby instructed to give a clear explanation of this directive to Party members, and ensure that it is fully carried out in the work of our organs of political power.

CURRENT PROBLEMS OF TACTICS IN
THE ANTI-JAPANESE UNITED FRONT

March 11, 1940

1. The present political situation is as follows:

(a) Japanese imperialism has been dealt a heavy blow by China's War of Resistance and is already incapable of launching any more large-scale military offensives, so that the relation of forces between the enemy and ourselves has now reached the stage of strategic stalemate. But the enemy is still holding fast to his basic policy of subjugating China and is pursuing it by such means as undermining our anti-Japanese united front, intensifying his "mopping-up" campaigns in the rear areas and stepping up his economic aggression.

(b) Britain and France are finding their positions in the East weakened by the war in Europe, while the United States is continuing its policy of "sitting on top of the mountain and watching the tigers fight", so that an Eastern Munich[1] conference is out of the question for the moment.

(c) The Soviet Union has gained new successes in its foreign policy and is maintaining its policy of giving active support to China's War of Resistance.

(d) The pro-Japanese section of the big bourgeoisie, having completely capitulated to Japan, is ready to play the puppet. The pro-European and pro-American big bourgeoisie may continue to resist Japan, but its proneness to conciliation remains serious. It follows a dual policy. While desiring to remain united with the various non-Kuomintang forces to cope with Japan, it is doing all it can to suppress them, and especially the Communist Party

---

Comrade Mao Tse-tung wrote this outline for the report he made at a meeting of the Party's senior cadres in Yenan.

and the other progressive forces. It forms the die-hard section of the anti-Japanese united front.

(e) The intermediate forces, including the middle bourgeoisie, the enlightened gentry and the regional power groups, often take a middle position between the progressives and the die-hards because of their contradictions with the main ruling sections of the big landlords and the big bourgeoisie on the one hand, and with the working class and the peasantry on the other. They form the middle section of the anti-Japanese united front.

(f) Recently, the Communist-led progressive forces of the proletariat, the peasantry and the urban petty bourgeoisie have grown much stronger and in the main have succeeded in creating base areas in which anti-Japanese democratic political power has been established. Their influence is very great among the workers, peasants and urban petty bourgeoisie throughout the country and is also quite considerable among the middle forces. On the battlefield the Communists are fighting roughly as many Japanese troops as is the Kuomintang. They form the progressive section of the anti-Japanese united front.

This is the present political situation in China. In these circumstances the possibility still exists of preventing the situation from deteriorating and of changing it for the better; the Central Committee's resolutions of February 1 are entirely correct.

2. The basic condition for victory in the War of Resistance is the extension and consolidation of the anti-Japanese united front. The tactics required for this purpose are to develop the progressive forces, win over the middle forces and combat the die-hard forces; these are three inseparable links, and the means to be used to unite all the anti-Japanese forces is struggle. In the period of the anti-Japanese united front, struggle is the means to unity and unity is the aim of struggle. If unity is sought through struggle, it will live; if unity is sought through yielding, it will perish. This truth is gradually being grasped by Party comrades. However, there are still many who do not understand it; some think that struggle will split the united front or that struggle can be employed without restraint, and others use wrong tactics towards the middle forces or have mistaken notions about the die-hard forces. All this must be corrected.

3. Developing the progressive forces means building up the forces of the proletariat, the peasantry and the urban petty bourgeoisie, boldly

expanding the Eighth Route and New Fourth Armies, establishing anti-Japanese democratic base areas on an extensive scale, building up Communist organizations throughout the country, developing national mass movements of the workers, peasants, youth, women and children, winning over the intellectuals in all parts of the country, and spreading the movement for constitutional government among the masses as a struggle for democracy. Steady expansion of the progressive forces is the only way to prevent the situation from deteriorating, to forestall capitulation and splitting, and to lay a firm and indestructible foundation for victory in the War of Resistance. But the expansion of the progressive forces is a serious process of struggle, which must be ruthlessly waged not only against the Japanese imperialists and the traitors but also against the die-hards. For the latter are opposed to the growth of the progressive forces, while the middle section is sceptical. Unless we engage in resolute struggle against the die-hards and, moreover, get tangible results, we shall be unable to resist their pressure or dispel the doubts of the middle section. In that case the progressive forces will have no way of expanding.

4. Winning over the middle forces means winning over the middle bourgeoisie, the enlightened gentry and the regional power groups. They are three distinct categories, but as things are, they all belong to the middle forces. The middle bourgeoisie constitutes the national bourgeoisie as distinct from the comprador class, *i.e.*, from the big bourgeoisie. Although it has its class contradictions with the workers and does not approve of the independence of the working class, it still wants to resist Japan and, moreover, would like to grasp political power for itself, because it is oppressed by the Japanese imperialists in the occupied areas and kept down by the big landlords and big bourgeoisie in the Kuomintang areas. When it comes to resisting Japan, it is in favour of united resistance; when it comes to winning political power, it is in favour of the movement for constitutional government and tries to exploit the contradictions between the progressives and the die-hards for its own ends. This is a stratum we must win over. Then there are the enlightened gentry who are the left-wing of the landlord class, that is, the section with a bourgeois colouration, whose political attitude is roughly the same as that of the middle bourgeoisie. Although they have class contradictions with the peasants, they also have their contradictions with the big landlords and big bourgeoisie. They do not support the die-hards and they, too, want to exploit the

contradictions between us and the die-hards for their own political ends. On no account should we neglect this section either, and our policy must be to win them over. As for the regional power groups, they are of two kinds — the forces which control certain regions as their own, and the troops of miscellaneous brands which do not. Although these groups are in contradiction with the progressive forces, they also have their contradictions with the Kuomintang Central Government because of the self-seeking policy it pursues at their expense; they, too, want to exploit the contradictions between us and the die-hards for their own political ends. Most of the leaders of the regional power groups belong to the big landlord class and the big bourgeoisie and, therefore, progressive as they may appear at certain times during the war, they soon turn reactionary again; nevertheless, because of their contradictions with the Kuomintang central authorities, the possibility exists of their remaining neutral in our struggle against the die-hards, provided we pursue a correct policy. Our policy towards the three categories of middle forces described above is to win them over. However, this policy differs from that of winning over the peasants and the urban petty bourgeoisie, and, moreover, it varies for each category of the middle forces. While the peasants and the urban petty bourgeoisie should be won over as basic allies, the middle forces should be won over as allies against imperialism. Among the middle forces, it is possible for the middle bourgeoisie and the enlightened gentry to join us in the common fight against Japan and also in the setting up of anti-Japanese democratic political power, but they fear agrarian revolution. In the struggle against the die-hards, some may join in to a limited degree, others may observe a benevolent neutrality, and still others a rather reluctant neutrality. But, apart from joining us in the war, the regional power groups will at most observe a temporary neutrality in our struggle against the die-hards; they are unwilling to join us in establishing democratic political power since they themselves belong to the big landlord class and the big bourgeoisie. The middle forces tend to vacillate and are bound to break up, and we should educate and criticize them appropriately, with special reference to their vacillating attitude.

The winning over of the middle forces is an extremely important task for us in the period of the anti-Japanese united front, but it can only be accomplished given certain conditions. These are: (1) that we have ample strength; (2) that we respect their interests; and (3) that we are resolute in our struggle against the die-hards and steadily win victories. If these conditions are lacking, the middle forces will vacillate or even become allies of the die-hards in the latter's attacks on us, because the die-hards are also doing their best to win over the middle forces in order to isolate us. The middle forces carry considerable weight in China and may often be the decisive factor in our struggle against the die-hards; we must therefore be prudent in dealing with them.

5. The die-hard forces at the present time are the big landlord class and the big bourgeoisie. Divided at the moment into the group that has capitulated to Japan and the group that favours resistance, these classes will gradually become still further differentiated. Within the big bourgeoisie, the group favouring resistance is now different from the group that has already capitulated. It pursues a dual policy. It still stands for unity against Japan, but at the same time it follows the extremely reactionary policy of suppressing the progressive forces in preparation for its eventual capitulation. As it still favours unity against Japan, we can still try and keep it in the anti-Japanese united front, and the longer the better. It would be wrong to neglect our policy of winning over this group and co-operating with it and to regard it as having already capitulated and as being on the verge of launching an anti-Communist war. But at the same time, we must adopt tactics of struggle to combat its reactionary policy and carry on a determined ideological, political and military fight against it, because all over the country it pursues the reactionary policy of suppressing the progressive forces, because instead of carrying out the common programme of the revolutionary Three People's Principles it stubbornly opposes our efforts to do so, and because it works hard to prevent us from going beyond the limits it has set for us, *i.e.*, it tries to confine us to the passive resistance it itself practises, and, moreover, it tries to assimilate us, failing which it applies ideological, political and military pressure against us. Such is our revolutionary dual policy to meet the dual policy of the die-hards, and such is our policy of seeking unity through struggle. If in the ideological sphere we can put forward correct revolutionary theory and strike hard at their counter-revolutionary theory, if in the political sphere we adopt tactics suited to the times and strike hard at their anti-Communist and anti-progressive policies, and if in the military sphere we take appropriate measures and strike back hard at their attacks, then we shall be able to restrict the effective range of their reactionary policy and compel

them to recognize the status of the progressive forces, and we shall be able to expand the progressive forces, win over the middle forces and isolate the die-hard forces. What is more, we shall be able to induce those die-hards who are still willing to resist Japan to prolong their participation in the anti-Japanese united front, and shall thus be able to avert a large-scale civil war of the kind that broke out before. Thus the purpose of our struggle against the die-hards in the period of the anti-Japanese united front is not only to parry their attacks in order to protect the progressive forces and enable the latter to go on growing, it is also to prolong the die-hards' resistance to Japan and to preserve our co-operation with them in order to avert large-scale civil war. Without struggle, these progressive forces would be exterminated by the die-hard forces, the united front would cease to exist, there would be nothing to hinder the die-hards from capitulating to the enemy, and civil war would break out. Therefore, struggle against the die-hards is an indispensable means of uniting all the anti-Japanese forces, achieving a favourable turn in the situation and averting large-scale civil war. All our experience confirms this truth.

However, there are several principles which we must observe in our struggle against the die-hards in the period of the anti-Japanese united front. First, the principle of self-defence. We will not attack unless we are attacked; if we are attacked, we will certainly counter-attack. That is to say, we must never attack others without provocation, but once attacked we must never fail to return the blow. Herein lies the defensive nature of our struggle. The military attacks of the die-hards must be smashed — resolutely, thoroughly, wholly and completely. Second, the principle of victory. We will not fight unless we are sure of victory; we must never fight without a plan, without preparation, and without certainty of success. We must know how to exploit the contradictions among the die-hards and must not take on too many of them at a single time, but must direct our blows at the most reactionary of them first. Herein lies the limited nature of the struggle. Third, the principle of a truce. After repulsing one die-hard attack, we should know when to stop and bring that particular fight to a close before another attack is made on us. A truce should be made in the interval. We should then take the initiative in seeking unity with the die-hards and, if they concur, we should make a peace agreement with them. On no account should we fight on day after day without cease, or be carried away by success. Herein lies the temporary nature of each struggle. Only when the die-hards launch a new attack should we counter with a new struggle. In other words, the three principles are to fight "on just grounds", "to our advantage" and "with restraint". By keeping to this kind of struggle, waged on just grounds, to our advantage and with restraint, we can develop the progressive forces, win over the middle forces and isolate the die-hard forces, and we can also make the die-hards think twice before attacking us, compromising with the enemy or starting large-scale civil war. Thus a favourable turn in the situation will become possible.

6. The Kuomintang is a heterogeneous party which includes die-hards, middle elements and progressives; taken as a whole, it must not be equated with the die-hards. Some people regard the Kuomintang as consisting entirely of die-hards because its Central Executive Committee has promulgated such counter-revolutionary friction-mongering decrees as the "Measures for Restricting the Activities of Alien Parties" and has mobilized every ounce of its strength for counter-revolutionary friction-mongering in the ideological, political, and military spheres throughout the country. But this is a mistaken view. The die-hards in the Kuomintang are still in a position to dictate its policies, but numerically they are in a minority, while the majority of the membership (many are members only in name) are not necessarily die-hards. This point must be clearly recognized if we are to take advantage of the contradictions within the Kuomintang, follow a policy of differentiating between its different sections and do our utmost to unite with its middle and progressive sections.

7. On the question of political power in the anti-Japanese base areas, we must make sure that the political power established there is that of the Anti-Japanese National United Front. No such political power exists as yet in the Kuomintang areas. It is the political power of all who support both resistance and democracy, *i.e.*, the joint democratic dictatorship of several revolutionary classes over the traitors and reactionaries. It is different from the dictatorship of the landlord class and the bourgeoisie, and is also somewhat different from a strictly worker-peasant democratic dictatorship. Places in the organs of political power should be allocated as follows: one-third to the Communists, representing the proletariat and the poor peasantry; one-third to the left progressives, representing the petty bourgeoisie; and the remaining one-third to the middle and other elements, representing the middle bourgeoisie and the enlightened gentry. Traitors

and anti-Communist elements are the only people disqualified from participation in these organs of political power. This general rule for the allocation of places is necessary, or otherwise it will not be possible to maintain the principle of united front political power. This allocation of places represents the genuine policy of our Party and must be carried out conscientiously; there must be no half-heartedness about it. It provides a broad rule which has to be applied according to the specific conditions, and there must be no mechanical filling up of quotas. At the lowest level the ratio may have to be somewhat modified to prevent domination by the landlords and evil gentry, but the fundamental spirit of this policy must not be violated. We should not labour the question of whether the non-Communists in these organs have party affiliations, or what their party affiliations are. In areas under the political power of the united front, all political parties, whether the Kuomintang or any other, must be granted legal status so long as they co-operate with and do not oppose the Communist Party. On the question of suffrage, the policy is that every Chinese who reaches the age of eighteen and is in favour of resistance and democracy should have the right to elect and to be elected, irrespective of class, nationality, party affiliation, sex, creed or educational level. The organs of united front political power should be elected by the people and then apply to the National Government for confirmation. Their form of organization must be based on democratic centralism. The fundamental point of departure for all major policy measures in the united front organs of political power should be opposition to Japanese imperialism, opposition to confirmed traitors and reactionaries, protection of the people who are resisting Japan, proper adjustment of the interests of all the anti-Japanese social strata and improvement of the livelihood of the workers and peasants. The establishment of this anti-Japanese united front political power will exert a great influence on the whole country and serve as a model for united front political power on a national scale; therefore this policy should be fully understood and resolutely carried out by all Party comrades.

8. In our struggle to develop the progressive forces, win over the middle forces and isolate the die-hard forces, we must not overlook the role of the intellectuals, whom the die-hards are doing their utmost to win over; therefore it is an important and indeed an essential policy to win over all progressive intellectuals and bring them under the influence of the Party.

9. In our propaganda we should stress the following programme:

(a) carry out the Testament of Dr. Sun Yat-sen by arousing the masses for united resistance to Japan;

(b) carry out the Principle of Nationalism by firmly resisting Japanese imperialism and striving for complete national liberation and the equality of all the nationalities within China;

(c) carry out the Principle of Democracy by granting the people absolute freedom to resist Japan and save the nation, by enabling them to elect governments at all levels, and by establishing the revolutionary democratic political power of the Anti-Japanese National United Front;

(d) carry out the Principle of the People's Livelihood by abolishing exorbitant taxes and miscellaneous levies, reducing land rent and interest, enforcing the eight-hour working day, developing agriculture, industry and commerce, and improving the livelihood of the people; and

(e) carry out Chiang Kai-shek's declaration that "every person, young or old, in the north or in the south, must take up the responsibility of resisting Japan and defending our homeland".

All these points are in the Kuomintang's own published programme, which is also the common programme of the Kuomintang and the Communist Party. But the Kuomintang has failed to carry out any part of this programme other than resistance to Japan; only the Communist Party and the progressive forces are able to carry it out. It is a simple enough programme and is widely known, yet many Communists fail to use it as a weapon for mobilizing the masses and isolating the die-hards. From now on we should keep attention focussed on the five points of this programme and popularize them through public notices, manifestoes, leaflets, articles, speeches, statements, and so on. In the Kuomintang areas it is still only a propaganda programme, but in the areas reached by the Eighth Route Army and the New Fourth Army it is already a programme of action. In acting according to this programme we are within the law, and when the die-hards oppose our carrying it out, it is they who are outside the law. In the stage of the bourgeois-democratic revolution, this programme of the Kuomintang's is basically the same as ours, but the ideology of the Kuomintang is entirely different from that of the Communist Party. It is this common programme of the democratic revolution that we should put

into practice, but on no account should we follow the ideology of
the Kuomintang.

NOTES

¹ For the Eastern Munich, see "Oppose Capitulationist Activity", Note 3, p. 255
of this volume.

FREELY EXPAND THE ANTI-JAPANESE FORCES AND RESIST THE ONSLAUGHTS OF THE ANTI-COMMUNIST DIE-HARDS

May 4, 1940

1. In all regions behind the enemy lines and in all the war zones, stress should be laid not on particularity, but on identity; to do otherwise would be a gross error. While each region has its individual peculiarities, they are all identical in that all are confronted by the enemy and all are engaged in the War of Resistance, whether in northern, central or southern China, in the areas north or south of the Yangtse River, or in the plains, the mountain or lake regions, and whether the force involved is the Eighth Route Army, the New Fourth Army or the South China Guerrilla Column.[1] It follows that in all cases we can and should expand. The Central Committee has pointed out this policy of expansion to you time and again. To expand means to reach out into all enemy-occupied areas and not to be bound by the Kuomintang's restrictions but to go beyond the limits allowed by the Kuomintang, not to expect official appointments from them or depend on the higher-ups for financial support but instead to expand the armed forces freely and independently, set up base areas unhesitatingly, independently arouse the masses in those areas to action and build up united front organs of political power under the leadership of the Communist Party. In Kiangsu Province, for example, despite the verbal attacks and the restrictions and oppression by anti-Communist elements

This directive was written by Comrade Mao Tse-tung on behalf of the Central Committee of the Chinese Communist Party and addressed to its Southeast Bureau. At the time of writing, Comrade Hsiang Ying, member of the Central Committee and secretary of its Southeast Bureau, held strong Rightist views and was irresolute in carrying out the line of the Central Committee. He did not dare fully to arouse the masses to action and to expand the Liberated Areas and the people's army in the Japanese-occupied areas, did not sufficiently realize the seriousness of the possibility of reactionary attacks by the Kuomintang, and was therefore unprepared

431

such as Ku Chu-tung, Leng Hsin and Han Teh-chin,[2] we should gain control of as many districts as possible from Nanking in the west to the seacoast in the east and from Hangchow in the south to Hsuchow in the north, and do so as fast as possible and yet steadily and systematically; and we should independently expand the armed forces, establish organs of political power, set up fiscal offices to levy taxes for resistance to Japan and economic agencies to promote agriculture, industry and commerce, and open up schools of various kinds to train large numbers of cadres. The Central Committee previously instructed you to enlarge the anti-Japanese armed forces to 100,000 men, with as many rifles, and to set up organs of political power promptly in the regions behind the enemy lines in Kiangsu and Chekiang Provinces before the end of this year. What concrete measures have you taken? Opportunities have been missed before, and if this year they are missed again, things will become still more difficult.

2. At a time when the anti-Communist die-hards in the Kuomintang are obstinately persisting in their policy of containing, restricting and combating the Communist Party in preparation for capitulation to Japan, we must stress struggle and not unity; to do otherwise would be a gross error. Therefore, whether in the theoretical, the political, or the military sphere, we should as a matter of principle firmly resist all the verbal attacks, propaganda, orders and laws of the anti-Communist die-hards designed to contain, restrict and oppose the Communist Party, and our attitude towards them should be one of firm struggle. This struggle must be based on the principle of fighting on just grounds, to our advantage, and with restraint, that is, on the principles of self-defence, victory and truce, which means that every concrete struggle is defensive, limited and temporary in nature. We must take tit-for-tat action and conduct a determined struggle against all the reactionary verbal attacks, propaganda, orders and laws of the anti-Communist die-hards. For instance, when they demanded that our Fourth and Fifth Detachments[3] be moved to the south, we countered

---

for them mentally and organizationally. When the directive reached the Southeast Bureau, Comrade Chen Yi, member of the Southeast Bureau and commander of the First Detachment of the New Fourth Army, immediately put it into effect, but Comrade Hsiang Ying was reluctant to do so. He made no preparations against the attacks of the Kuomintang reactionaries so that he was in a weak and helpless position when Chiang Kai-shek staged the Southern Anhwei Incident in January 1941, in which nine thousand of our troops were annihilated and Comrade Hsiang Ying himself was killed.

by insisting that it was absolutely impossible to do so; when they demanded that the units under Yeh Fei and Chang Yun-yi[4] be moved to the south, we countered by asking permission for a part of these units to move to the north; when they charged us with having undermined their conscription plans, we asked them to enlarge the recruiting area for the New Fourth Army; when they said we were carrying on wrong propaganda, we asked them to stop all their anti-Communist propaganda and to rescind all decrees and orders which cause "friction"; and whenever they launch military attacks against us, we should smash them by counter-attacks. We are on just grounds in carrying out this tit-for-tat policy. And it is not only the Central Committee of our Party that should take action whenever we are on just grounds, but every unit of our army should do so. What Chang Yun-yi did to Li Pin-hsien and what Li Hsien-nien did to Li Tsung-jen[5] are both good examples of strong protests from the lower levels to the higher-ups. This kind of strong attitude towards the die-hards and the policy of struggling against them on just grounds, to our advantage, and with restraint are the only way to make the die-hards somewhat afraid of repressing us, to reduce the scope of their activities in containing, restricting and combating the Communist Party, to force them to recognize our legal status, and to make them think twice before causing a split. Therefore, struggle is by far the most important means of averting the danger of capitulation, of achieving a turn for the better in the situation and of strengthening Kuomintang-Communist co-operation. Within our own Party and army, persistence in the struggle against the die-hards is the only way to heighten our fighting spirit, give full play to our courage, unite our cadres, increase our strength and consolidate our army and Party. In our relations with the intermediate sections, persistence in the struggle against the die-hards is the only way to win over the waverers and give support to our sympathizers — there is no other way. Similarly, struggle is the only policy which can ensure that the whole Party and the whole army are mentally on the alert against a possible nation-wide emergency and are prepared for it in their work. Otherwise, the mistake of 1927[6] will be repeated.

3. In appraising the present situation, we should clearly understand that while the danger of capitulation has greatly increased, it is still possible to avert it. The present military clashes are still local and not national. They are acts of strategic reconnaissance by our opponents and not yet "Communist suppression" on a large scale; they are steps preparatory to capitulation and not yet steps immediately preceding

capitulation. Our task is persistently and vigorously to carry out the threefold policy laid down by the Central Committee, which is the only correct policy, namely, to develop the progressive forces, win over the middle forces and isolate the die-hard forces, for the purpose of averting the danger of capitulation and bringing about a turn for the better in the situation. It would be perilous not to point out and correct any "Left" or Right deviations in appraising the situation and in defining our tasks.

4. The battles of self-defence fought by the Fourth and the Fifth Detachments against the attacks of Han Teh-chin and Li Tsung-jen in eastern Anhwei and those fought by Li Hsien-nien's column against the die-hards' attacks in central and eastern Hupeh, the determined struggle carried on by Peng Hsueh-feng's detachment north of the Huai River, the expansion of Yeh Fei's forces north of the Yangtse River, and the southward movement of over 20,000 men of the Eighth Route Army to areas north of the Huai River and to eastern Anhwei and northern Kiangsu[7] — all these were not only absolutely necessary and correct in themselves, but were indispensable for making Ku Chu-tung think twice before attacking you in southern Anhwei and southern Kiangsu. That is to say, the more victories we win and the more we expand north of the Yangtse River, the more will Ku Chu-tung be afraid to act rashly south of the Yangtse River, and the easier will it be for you to play your role in southern Anhwei and southern Kiangsu. Similarly, the more the Eighth Route Army, the New Fourth Army and the South China Guerrilla Column expand in northwestern, northern, central and southern China, and the more the Communist Party grows throughout the country, the greater will be the possibility of averting the danger of capitulation and bringing about a turn for the better in the situation, and the easier will it be for our Party to play its role in all parts of the country. It is wrong to make the opposite appraisal or adopt the opposite tactics in the belief that the more our forces expand, the more the die-hards will tend towards capitulation, that the more concessions we make, the more they will resist Japan, or that the whole country is on the verge of a split and Kuomintang-Communist co-operation is no longer possible.

5. The Anti-Japanese National United Front is our policy for the whole country in the War of Resistance. The establishment of democratic anti-Japanese base areas in the enemy rear is part of this policy. You should firmly carry out the Central Committee's decisions on the question of political power.

6. Our policy in the Kuomintang areas is different from that in the war zones and the areas behind the enemy lines. In the Kuomintang areas our policy is to have well-selected cadres working underground for a long period, to accumulate strength and bide our time, and to avoid rashness and exposure. In conformity with the principle of waging struggles on just grounds, to our advantage, and with restraint, our tactics in combating the die-hards are to wage steady and sure struggles and to build up our strength by utilizing all Kuomintang laws and decrees that can serve our purpose as well as everything permitted by social custom. If a member of our Party is forced to join the Kuomintang, let him do so; our members should penetrate the *pao chia*[8] and the educational, economic and military organizations everywhere; they should develop extensive united front work, *i.e.*, make friends, in the Central Army and among the troops of miscellaneous brands.[9] In all the Kuomintang areas the Party's basic policy is likewise to develop the progressive forces (the Party organizations and the mass movements), to win over the middle forces (seven categories in all, namely, the national bourgeoisie, the enlightened gentry, the troops of miscellaneous brands, the intermediate sections in the Kuomintang, the intermediate sections in the Central Army, the upper stratum of the petty bourgeoisie, and the small political parties and groups) and to isolate the die-hard forces, in order to avert the danger of capitulation and bring about a favourable turn in the situation. At the same time we should be fully prepared to deal with any emergency on a local or national scale. Our Party organizations in the Kuomintang areas must be kept strictly secret. In the Southeast Bureau[10] and in all the provincial, special, county and district committees, the whole personnel (from Party secretaries to cooks) must be strictly scrutinized one by one, and no one open to the slightest suspicion should be allowed to remain in any of these leading bodies. Great care must be taken to protect our cadres, and whoever is in danger of being arrested and killed by the Kuomintang while working in an open or semi-open capacity should either be sent to some other locality and go underground or be transferred to the army. In the Japanese-occupied areas (in Shanghai, Nanking, Wuhu or Wusih, or in any other city, large or small, and also in the countryside), our policy is basically the same as in the Kuomintang areas.

7. The present tactical directive was decided upon by the Political Bureau of the Central Committee at its recent meeting, and comrades of the Southeast Bureau and the military sub-commission are requested

to discuss it, relay it to all cadres in the Party organizations and the army, and firmly carry it out.

8. Comrade Hsiang Ying is instructed to relay this directive in southern Anhwei and Comrade Chen Yi to relay it in southern Kiangsu. Discussion and relaying should be completed within a month of receiving this telegram. Comrade Hsiang Ying has the over-all responsibility for arranging Party and army work in the whole area in accordance with the line of the Central Committee and should report the results to the Central Committee.

NOTES

[1] The South China Guerrilla Column was a general name given to a number of anti-Japanese guerrilla units in southern China led by the Chinese Communist Party.

[2] Ku Chu-tung, Leng Hsin and Han Teh-chin were reactionary Kuomintang generals stationed in Kiangsu, Chekiang, southern Anhwei, Kiangsi and other places.

[3] The Fourth and Fifth Detachments of the New Fourth Army were then building up an anti-Japanese base area in the Huai River valley on the Kiangsu-Anhwei provincial border.

[4] The units of the New Fourth Army under Yeh Fei and Chang Yun-yi were then carrying on anti-Japanese guerrilla warfare and building up an anti-Japanese base area north of the Yangtse River in central Kiangsu and eastern Anhwei.

[5] During March and April 1940, Li Pin-hsien, the Kuomintang provincial governor of Anhwei, and Li Tsung-jen, the Kuomintang commander of the 5th War Zone, both warlords of the Kwangsi clique, launched large-scale offensives on the New Fourth Army in the Anhwei-Hupeh border area. Comrade Chang Yun-yi, commander of New Fourth Army units north of the Yangtse River, and Comrade Li Hsien-nien, commander of the Army's Hupeh-Honan Assault Troops, lodged strong protests and repulsed the offensives.

[6] The mistake of 1927 refers to Chen Tu-hsiu's Right opportunism.

[7] In January 1940 the Central Committee of the Chinese Communist Party dispatched more than 20,000 men of the Eighth Route Army from northern China to reinforce the New Fourth Army in its anti-Japanese warfare north of the Huai River and in eastern Anhwei and northern Kiangsu.

[8] *Pao chia* was the administrative system by which the Kuomintang reactionary clique enforced its fascist rule at the primary level.

[9] Chiang Kai-shek's clique called its own armed forces the Central Army and those belonging to other cliques troops of miscellaneous brands. It discriminated against the latter and did not treat them on an equal footing with the Central Army.

[10] The Southeast Bureau directed the work in southeastern China (including the provinces of Kiangsu, Chekiang, Anhwei, Kiangsi, Hupeh and Hunan) on behalf of the Central Committee of the Chinese Communist Party in the period 1938-41.

UNITY TO THE VERY END

July 1940

The third anniversary of the outbreak of the War of Resistance Against Japan and the nineteenth anniversary of the founding of the Communist Party of China occur within a few days of each other. In commemorating the anniversary of the resistance today we Communists feel our responsibility all the more keenly. To fight for the survival of the Chinese nation is a responsibility which falls on all the anti-Japanese political parties and groups and the whole people, but as we see it an even heavier responsibility falls on us as Communists. The Central Committee of our Party has issued a statement on the present situation, the essence of which is a call for resistance and unity to the very end. This statement, we hope, will meet with the approval of the friendly parties and armies and the whole nation, and Communists in particular must conscientiously carry out the line it has laid down.

All Communists must realize that only through resistance to the very end can there be unity to the very end, and vice versa. Therefore, Communists must set an example in both resistance and unity. Our opposition is directed solely against the enemy and against the determined capitulators and anti-Communists; with all others we must unite in earnest. In every place the determined capitulators and anti-Communists are only a minority. I made an investigation of one local government and found that out of 1,300 staff members, only 40 to 50, or less than 4 per cent, were confirmed anti-Communists, while all the rest wanted unity and resistance. Of course we cannot tolerate these capitulators and anti-Communists, because that would amount to allowing them to sabotage resistance and wreck unity; we must resolutely oppose the capitulators and, in self-defence, firmly repel the attacks of the anti-Communist elements. Failure to do so would be Right opportunism and would harm unity and resistance. However,

437

our policy must be one of unity with all those who are not absolutely set in their capitulation and anti-communism. For some face both ways, others are acting under compulsion, and still others have temporarily gone astray; for the sake of continued unity and resistance we must win over all these people. Failure to do so would be "Left" opportunism and this, too, would harm unity and resistance. All Communists should realize that, having initiated the Anti-Japanese National United Front, we must maintain it. Now that the national crisis is deepening and the world situation is undergoing a great change, we must shoulder the very heavy responsibility of saving the Chinese nation. We must defeat Japanese imperialism and build China into an independent, free and democratic republic, and to do so we must unite the greatest possible number of people, with or without party affiliations. Communists should not enter into unprincipled united fronts and must therefore oppose all such schemes as corroding, restricting, containing and repressing the Communist Party as well as oppose the Right opportunism within the Party. But at the same time Communists should not fail to respect the Party's united front policy and must therefore unite, on the principle of resistance, with all those who are still willing to resist Japan and must oppose "Left" opportunism within the Party.

Thus, as far as political power is concerned, we stand for united front organs of political power; we do not favour one-party dictatorship either by the Communist Party or by any other party, but we stand for the joint dictatorship of all political parties and groups, people in all walks of life and all armed forces, that is, for united front political power. Whenever we establish organs of anti-Japanese political power in the enemy rear after destroying the enemy and the puppet regimes there, we should adopt the "three thirds system" as decided upon by the Central Committee of our Party, so that Communists take only one-third of the places in all government or people's representative bodies, while the remaining two-thirds are taken by people who stand for resistance and democracy whether or not they are members of other parties or groups. Anybody may take part in the work of the government so long as he is not in favour of capitulation or is not an anti-Communist. Every political party or group shall have the right to exist and carry on its activities under the anti-Japanese political power, so long as it is not in favour of capitulation and is not anti-Communist.

In regard to the question of the armed forces, our Party's statement has made it clear that we shall continue to observe the decision "not to extend our Party organizations to any friendly army". Local Party organizations which have not strictly observed this decision should immediately put the matter right. A friendly attitude should be taken towards all armed units that do not start armed clashes with the Eighth Route or New Fourth Armies. Friendly relations should be restored even with those troops that have created "friction", once they stop doing so. This is our united front policy with regard to the armed forces.

As for our policies on other matters, whether financial, economic, cultural or educational or anti-espionage, for the sake of resistance we must follow the united front policy by adjusting the interests of the different classes and must oppose both Right and "Left" opportunism.

Internationally the imperialist war is becoming world-wide and the extremely grave political and economic crises to which it has given rise will inevitably cause revolutions to break out in many countries. We are in a new era of wars and revolutions. The Soviet Union, which has not been drawn into the maelstrom of this imperialist war, is the supporter of all the oppressed people and all the oppressed nations of the world. These factors are favourable to China's War of Resistance. But at the same time the danger of capitulation is more serious than ever before because Japanese imperialism is intensifying its attacks on China in preparation for its aggression against Southeast Asia, and this will certainly induce some of the vacillating elements to surrender. The fourth year of the war is going to be a most difficult one. Our task is to unite all anti-Japanese forces, oppose the capitulators, surmount all the difficulties and persist in nation-wide resistance. All Communists must unite with the friendly parties and armies to accomplish this task. We are confident that, through the united efforts of all members of our Party, of the friendly parties and armies and the whole people, we shall succeed in preventing capitulation, in conquering the difficulties, in driving out the Japanese aggressors and in recovering our lost territories. The prospects for our War of Resistance are indeed bright.

ON POLICY

December 25, 1940

In the present high tide of anti-Communist attacks, the policy we adopt is of decisive importance. But many of our cadres fail to realize that the Party's present policy must be very different from its policy during the Agrarian Revolution. It has to be understood that in no circumstances will the Party change its united front policy for the entire period of the War of Resistance Against Japan, and that many of the policies adopted during the ten years of the Agrarian Revolution cannot just be duplicated today. In particular, many ultra-Left policies of the latter period of the Agrarian Revolution are not merely totally inapplicable today in the War of Resistance, but were wrong even then, arising as they did from the failure to understand two fundamental points — that the Chinese revolution is a bourgeois-democratic revolution in a semi-colonial country, and that it is a protracted revolution. For example, there was the thesis that the Kuomintang's fifth "encirclement and suppression" campaign and our counter-campaign constituted the decisive battle between counter-revolution and revolution; there was the economic elimination of the capitalist class (the ultra-Left policies on labour and taxation) and of the rich peasants (by allotting them poor land); the physical elimination of the landlords (by not allotting them any land); the attack on the intellectuals; the "Left" deviation in the suppression of counter-revolutionaries; the monopolizing by Communists of the organs of political power; the focussing on communism as the objective in popular education; the ultra-Left military policy (of attacking the big cities and denying the role of guerrilla warfare); the putschist policy in the work in the White areas; and the policy within the Party of attacks on comrades through the abuse of disciplinary measures. These

This inner-Party directive was written by Comrade Mao Tse-tung on behalf of the Central Committee of the Communist Party of China.

ultra-Left policies were manifestations of the error of "Left" opportunism, or exactly the reverse of the Right opportunism of Chen
Tu-hsiu in the latter period of the First Great Revolution. It was all
alliance and no struggle in the latter period of the First Great Revolution, and all struggle and no alliance (except with the basic sections
of the peasantry) in the latter period of the Agrarian Revolution —
truly striking demonstrations of the two extremist policies. Both
extremist policies caused great losses to the Party and the revolution.

Today our Anti-Japanese National United Front policy is neither
all alliance and no struggle nor all struggle and no alliance, but
combines alliance and struggle. Specifically, it means:

(1) All people favouring resistance (that is, all anti-Japanese
workers, peasants, soldiers, students and intellectuals, and businessmen) must unite in the Anti-Japanese National United Front.

(2) Within the united front our policy must be one of independence
and initiative, *i.e.*, both unity and independence are necessary.

(3) As far as military strategy is concerned, our policy is guerrilla
warfare waged independently and with the initiative in our own hands
within the framework of a unified strategy; guerrilla warfare is basic,
but no chance of waging mobile warfare should be lost when the
conditions are favourable.

(4) In the struggle against the anti-Communist die-hards, our
policy is to make use of contradictions, win over the many, oppose the
few and crush our enemies one by one, and to wage struggles on just
grounds, to our advantage, and with restraint.

(5) In the enemy-occupied and Kuomintang areas our policy is,
on the one hand, to develop the united front to the greatest possible
extent and, on the other, to have well-selected cadres working underground. With regard to the forms of organization and struggle, our
policy is to have well-selected cadres working underground for a long
period, to accumulate strength and bide our time.

(6) With regard to the alignment of the various classes within the
country, our basic policy is to develop the progressive forces, win over
the middle forces and isolate the anti-Communist die-hard forces.

(7) With respect to the anti-Communist die-hards, ours is a revolutionary dual policy of uniting with them, in so far as they are still
in favour of resisting Japan, and of isolating them, in so far as they
are determined to oppose the Communist Party. Moreover, the die-
hards have a dual character with regard to resistance to Japan, and
our policy is to unite with them, in so far as they are still in favour

of resistance, and to struggle against them and isolate them in so far as they vacillate (for instance, when they collude with the Japanese aggressors and show reluctance in opposing Wang Ching-wei and other traitors). As their opposition to the Communist Party has also a dual character, our policy, too, should have a dual character; in so far as they are still unwilling to break up Kuomintang-Communist co-operation altogether, it is one of alliance with them, but in so far as they are high-handed and launch armed attacks on our Party and the people, it is one of struggling against them and isolating them. We make a distinction between such people with a dual character and the traitors and pro-Japanese elements.

(8) Even among the traitors and pro-Japanese elements there are people with a dual character, towards whom we should likewise employ a revolutionary dual policy. In so far as they are pro-Japanese, our policy is to struggle against them and isolate them, but in so far as they vacillate, our policy is to draw them nearer to us and win them over. We make a distinction between such ambivalent elements and the out-and-out traitors like Wang Ching-wei, Wang Yi-tang[1] and Shih Yu-san.[2]

(9) The pro-Japanese big landlords and big bourgeoisie who are against resistance must be distinguished from the pro-British and pro-American big landlords and big bourgeoisie who are for resistance; similarly, the ambivalent big landlords and big bourgeoisie who are for resistance but vacillate, and who are for unity but are anti-Communist, must be distinguished from the national bourgeoisie, the middle and small landlords and the enlightened gentry, the duality of whose character is less pronounced. We build our policy on these distinctions. The diverse policies mentioned above all stem from these distinctions in class relations.

(10) We deal with imperialism in the same way. The Communist Party opposes all imperialism, but we make a distinction between Japanese imperialism which is now committing aggression against China and the imperialist powers which are not doing so now, between German and Italian imperialism which are allies of Japan and have recognized "Manchukuo" and British and U.S. imperialism which are opposed to Japan, and between the Britain and the United States of yesterday which followed a Munich policy in the Far East and undermined China's resistance to Japan, and the Britain and the United States of today which have abandoned this policy and are now in favour of China's resistance. Our tactics are guided by one and

the same principle: to make use of contradictions, win over the many, oppose the few and crush our enemies one by one. Our foreign policy differs from that of the Kuomintang. The Kuomintang claims, "There is only one enemy and all the rest are friends"; it appears to treat all countries other than Japan alike, but in fact it is pro-British and pro-American. On our part we must draw certain distinctions, first, between the Soviet Union and the capitalist countries, second, between Britain and the United States on the one hand and Germany and Italy on the other, third, between the people of Britain and the United States and their imperialist governments, and fourth, between the policy of Britain and the United States during their Far Eastern Munich period and their policy today. We build our policy on these distinctions. In direct contrast to the Kuomintang our basic line is to use all possible foreign help, subject to the principle of independent prosecution of the war and reliance on our own efforts, and not, as the Kuomintang does, to abandon this principle by relying entirely on foreign help or hanging on to one imperialist bloc or another.

To correct the lop-sided views of many Party cadres on the question of tactics and their consequent vacillations between "Left" and Right, we must help them to acquire an all-round and integrated understanding of the changes and developments in the Party's policy, past and present. The ultra-Left viewpoint is creating trouble and is still the main danger in the Party. In the Kuomintang areas, there are many people who cannot seriously carry out the policy of having well-selected cadres working underground for a long period, of accumulating strength and biding our time, because they underestimate the gravity of the Kuomintang's anti-Communist policy. At the same time, there are many others who cannot carry out the policy of expanding the united front, because they over-simplify matters and consider the entire Kuomintang to be quite hopeless and are therefore at a loss what to do. A similar state of affairs exists in the Japanese-occupied areas.

In the Kuomintang areas and the anti-Japanese base areas, the Rightist views which were once prevalent to a serious extent have now been basically overcome; those who held such views used to stress alliance to the exclusion of struggle and overestimate the Kuomintang's inclination to resist Japan, and they therefore blurred the difference in principle between the Kuomintang and the Communist Party, rejected the policy of independence and initiative within the united front, appeased the big landlords and big bourgeoisie and the Kuomintang, and tied their own hands instead of boldly expanding the anti-Japanese revolutionary forces and conducting resolute struggle against the Kuomintang's policy of opposing and restricting the Communist Party. But since the winter of 1939 an ultra-Left tendency has cropped up in many places as a result of the anti-Communist "friction" engineered by the Kuomintang and of the struggles we have waged in self-defence. This tendency has been corrected to some extent but not altogether, and it still finds expression in concrete policies in many places. It is therefore most necessary for us to examine and define our concrete policies now.

As the Central Committee has already issued a series of directives on concrete policies, now only a few points are given here by way of summary.

The organs of political power. The "three thirds system", under which Communists have only one-third of the places in the organs of political power and many non-Communists are drawn into participation, must be carried out resolutely. In areas like northern Kiangsu, where we have just begun to establish anti-Japanese democratic political power, the proportion of Communists may be even less than one-third. The representatives of the petty bourgeoisie, the national bourgeoisie and the enlightened gentry who are not actively opposed to the Communist Party must be drawn into participation both in the government and in the people's representative bodies, and those Kuomintang members who do not oppose the Communist Party must also be allowed to participate. Even a small number of right-wingers may be allowed to join the people's representative bodies. On no account should our Party monopolize everything. We are not destroying the dictatorship of the big comprador bourgeoisie and the big landlord class in order to replace it with a one-party dictatorship of the Communist Party.

Labour policy. The livelihood of the workers must be improved if their enthusiasm in the fight against Japan is to be fully aroused. But we must strictly guard against being ultra-Leftist; there must not be excessive increases in wages or excessive reductions in working hours. Under present conditions, the eight-hour working day cannot be universally introduced in China and a ten-hour working day should still be permitted in certain branches of production. In other branches of production the working day should be fixed according to the circumstances. Once a contract between labour and capital is concluded, the workers must observe labour discipline and the capitalists must be allowed to make some profit. Otherwise factories will close down, which will neither help the war nor benefit the workers. Particularly in the rural areas, the living standards and wages of the workers should not be raised too high, or it will give rise to complaints from the peasants, create unemployment among the workers and result in a decline in production.

Land policy. It must be explained to Party members and to the peasants that this is not the time for a thorough agrarian revolution and that the series of measures taken during the Agrarian Revolution cannot be applied today. On the one hand, our present policy should stipulate that the landlords shall reduce rent and interest, for this serves to arouse the enthusiasm of the basic peasant masses for resistance to Japan, but the reductions should not be too great. In general, land rent should be reduced by 25 per cent, and if the masses demand a greater reduction, the tenant-farmer may keep up to 60 or 70 per cent of his crop, but not more. The reduction in interest on loans should not be so great as to render credit transactions impossible. On the other hand, our policy should stipulate that the peasants shall pay rent and interest and that the landlords shall retain their owner-ship of land and other property. Interest should not be so low as to make it impossible for the peasants to obtain loans, nor the settlement of old accounts be such as to enable the peasants to get back their mortgaged land gratis.

Tax policy. Taxes must be levied according to income. Except for the very poor who should be exempt, all people with an income shall pay taxes to the state, which means that the burden shall be carried by more than 80 per cent of the population, including the workers and peasants, and not be placed entirely on the landlords and the capitalists. Arresting people and imposing fines on them as a means of financing the army must be forbidden. We may use the existing Kuomintang system of taxation with appropriate alterations until we have devised a new and more suitable one.

Anti-espionage policy. We must firmly suppress the confirmed traitors and anti-Communists, or otherwise we shall not be able to protect the anti-Japanese revolutionary forces. But there must not be too much killing, and no innocent person should be incriminated. Vacillating elements and reluctant followers among the reactionaries should be dealt with leniently. Corporal punishment must be abolished in trying criminals; the stress must be on the weight of evidence and confessions should not be taken on trust. Our policy towards prisoners captured from the Japanese, puppet or anti-Communist troops is to set them all free, except for those who have incurred the bitter hatred of the masses and must receive capital punishment and whose death sentence has been approved by the higher authorities. Among the prisoners, those who were coerced into joining the reactionary forces but who are more or less inclined towards the revolution should be won over in large numbers to work for our army. The rest should be released and, if they fight us and are captured again, should again be set free. We should not insult them, take away their personal effects or try to exact recantations from them, but without exception should treat them sincerely and kindly. This should be our policy, however reactionary they may be. It is a very effective way of isolating the hard core of reaction. As for renegades, except for those who have committed heinous crimes, they should be given a chance to turn over a new leaf provided they discontinue their anti-Communist activities; and if they come back and wish to rejoin the revolution they may be accepted, but must not be re-admitted into the Party. The general run of Kuomintang intelligence agents must not be identified with the Japanese spies and Chinese traitors; the two should be differentiated and handled accordingly. An end should be put to the state of confusion in which any governmental or non-governmental organization can make arrests. To establish revolutionary order in the interests of the war, it must be stipulated that, with the exception of army units in combat action, only government judicial or public security agencies shall be empowered to make arrests.

The rights of the people. It must be laid down that all landlords and capitalists not opposed to the War of Resistance shall enjoy the same rights of person and property, the same right to vote and the same freedom of speech, assembly, association, political conviction and religious belief as the workers and peasants. The government shall take action only against saboteurs and those who organize riots in our base areas, and shall protect all others and not molest them.

Economic policy. We must actively develop industry and agriculture and promote the circulation of commodities. Capitalists should be encouraged to come into our anti-Japanese base areas and start enterprises here if they so desire. Private enterprise should be encouraged and state enterprise regarded as only one sector of the economy. The purpose in all this is to achieve self-sufficiency. Care must be taken not to damage any useful enterprise. Both our tariff and our monetary policies should conform to our basic line of expanding agriculture, industry and commerce, and not run counter to it. The essential factor in maintaining the base areas over a long period is the achievement of self-sufficiency through a conscientious and meticulous, not a crude and careless, organization of the economy.

Cultural and educational policy. This should centre on promoting and spreading the knowledge and skills needed for the war and a sense of national pride among the masses of the people. Bourgeois-liberal educators, men of letters, journalists, scholars and technical experts should be allowed to come to our base areas and co-operate with us in running schools and newspapers and doing other work. We should accept into our schools all intellectuals and students who show enthusiasm for resisting Japan, give them short-term training, and then assign them to work in the army, the government, or mass organizations; we should boldly draw them in, give them work and promote them. We should not be over-cautious or too afraid of reactionaries sneaking in. Unavoidably, some such elements will creep in, but there will be time to comb them out in the course of study and work. Every base area must establish printing shops, publish books and newspapers and organize distribution and delivery agencies. Every base area must also, as far as possible, set up big schools for training cadres, and the more and bigger, the better.

Military policy. There must be maximum expansion of the Eighth Route and New Fourth Armies, because they are the most reliable armed forces of the Chinese people in pressing on with the national war of resistance. We should continue our policy of never attacking the Kuomintang troops unless attacked and do all we can to make friends with them. In order to help the building up of our army, no effort should be spared to draw those officers who are sympathetic to us into the Eighth Route and New Fourth Armies, whether they are members of the Kuomintang or are without party affiliation. Something must be done now to change the situation where Communists dominate everything in our armies by sheer numbers. Of course, the "three thirds system" should not be introduced into our main forces, but so long as the leadership of the army is kept in the hands of the Party (this is an absolute and inviolable necessity), we need not be afraid of drawing large numbers of sympathizers into the work of building up the military and technical departments of our army. Now that the ideological and organizational foundations of our Party and our army have been firmly laid, not only is there no danger in drawing in large numbers of sympathizers (not saboteurs of course) but it is indeed an indispensable policy, for otherwise it will be impossible to win the sympathy of the whole country and expand our revolutionary forces.

All these tactical principles for the united front and the concrete policies formulated in accordance with them must be firmly applied by the whole Party. At a time when the Japanese invaders are intensifying their aggression against China and when the big landlords and big bourgeoisie are pursuing high-handed policies and launching armed attacks against the Communist Party and the people, the application of the tactical principles and concrete policies outlined above is the only way to press on with the War of Resistance, broaden the united front, win the sympathy of the whole people and bring about a turn for the better in the situation. In rectifying errors, however, we must proceed step by step, and must not be so hasty as to cause discontent among the cadres, suspicion among the masses, counter-attacks by the landlords, or other undesirable developments.

NOTES

[1] Wang Yi-tang was a big bureaucrat in the period of the Northern warlords and a pro-Japanese traitor. He was recalled from retirement by Chiang Kai-shek after the Northern China Incident of 1935 to serve in the Kuomintang government. In 1938, he served as a Japanese puppet in northern China and was made chairman of the bogus Northern China Political Council.

[2] Shih Yu-san was a Kuomintang warlord who frequently changed sides. He was commander-in-chief of the Kuomintang's 10th Army Group after the outbreak of the War of Resistance, collaborated with the Japanese armed forces in southern Hopei and did nothing but attack the Eighth Route Army, destroy organs of anti-Japanese democratic political power and slaughter Communists and progressives.

ORDER AND STATEMENT
ON THE SOUTHERN ANHWEI INCIDENT

January 1941

ORDER OF
THE REVOLUTIONARY MILITARY COMMISSION OF
THE CENTRAL COMMITTEE OF
THE COMMUNIST PARTY OF CHINA

Yenan, January 20, 1941

The New Fourth Army of the National Revolutionary Army has won fame both at home and abroad by its distinguished service in the War of Resistance. Commander Yeh Ting has an outstanding record in leading the army against the enemy. Recently, however, while it was moving northward in accordance with instructions, this army was treacherously attacked by the pro-Japanese clique, and Commander Yeh, wounded and exhausted in the fighting, was thrown into jail. Informed of the whole course of the Southern Anhwei Incident by telegrams from Chen Yi, the Commander of the First Detachment of the army, and Chang Yun-yi, the army's Chief of Staff, the Commission expresses its great wrath and its deep solicitude for our comrades. In addition to the adoption of measures to deal with the towering crime of the pro-Japanese clique in sabotaging the War of Resistance, attacking the people's armed forces and launching civil war, the Commission hereby appoints Chen Yi as Acting Commander of the New Fourth Army of the National Revolutionary Army, Chang Yun-yi as Deputy Commander, Lai Chuan-chu as Chief of Staff, and Teng Tzu-hui as Director of the Political Department. Acting Commander Chen Yi and his associates are hereby instructed to devote their efforts to strengthening the army, reinforcing unity within its ranks, ensuring good relations with the people, carrying out the Three People's Principles, adhering

to the Testament of Dr. Sun Yat-sen, and consolidating and expanding
the Anti-Japanese National United Front in the struggle to defend
our people and our country, to carry the War of Resistance forward
to the end and to guard against attacks by the pro-Japanese clique.

STATEMENT BY THE SPOKESMAN OF THE REVOLUTIONARY MILITARY COMMISSION OF THE CENTRAL COMMITTEE OF THE COMMUNIST PARTY OF CHINA TO A CORRESPONDENT OF THE HSINHUA NEWS AGENCY

January 22, 1941

The recent anti-Communist Southern Anhwei Incident had been
brewing for a long time. Present developments are but the opening
phase of a national emergency. Since the formation of their triple
alliance[1] with Germany and Italy, the Japanese aggressors have
redoubled their efforts to engineer changes within China so as to find
a quick solution to the Sino-Japanese war. Their purpose is to use
the Chinese themselves to suppress the anti-Japanese movement and
consolidate the rear for Japan's southward drive, so that she will be
free to drive south in co-ordination with Hitler's offensive against
Britain. A considerable number of ringleaders from the pro-Japanese
clique have long entrenched themselves in the party, government and
army organizations of the Kuomintang and have been carrying on
agitation day and night. The preparations for their plot were completed by the end of last year. The attack on the New Fourth Army
units in southern Anhwei and the reactionary Order of January 17[2] are
only the first open signs of this plot. Incidents of the gravest nature will
now be staged one after another. What are the details of the plot of the
Japanese aggressors and the pro-Japanese clique? They are as follows:

(1) To publish the two telegrams of October 19 and December 8[3] to
Chu Teh, Peng Teh-huai, Yeh Ting and Hsiang Ying over the signatures
of Ho Ying-chin and Pai Chung-hsi, in order to arouse public opinion.

(2) To start a press campaign on the importance of observing
military discipline and military orders in preparation for launching
civil war.

(3) To wipe out the New Fourth Army units in southern Anhwei.

(4) To declare that the New Fourth Army has "mutinied" and cancel its official designation.

These four steps have already been taken.

(5) To appoint Tang En-po, Li Pin-hsien, Wang Chung-lien and Han Teh-chin as "Communist suppression" commanders of the various route armies in central China, with Li Tsung-jen as supreme commander, in order to attack the New Fourth Army units under Peng Hsueh-feng, Chang Yun-yi and Li Hsien-nien and, if this comes off, to make further attacks on the Eighth Route Army and the New Fourth Army units in Shantung and northern Kiangsu, with the Japanese troops acting in close co-ordination.

This step is now being taken.

(6) To find a pretext to declare that the Eighth Route Army has "mutinied", cancel its official designation, and order the arrest of Chu Teh and Peng Teh-huai.

This move is now in preparation.

(7) To close down the liaison offices of the Eighth Route Army in Chungking, Sian and Kweilin, and arrest Chou En-lai, Yeh Chien-ying, Tung Pi-wu and Teng Ying-chao.

This move has begun with the closing down of the liaison office in Kweilin.

(8) To close down the *New China Daily*.

(9) To launch attacks on the Shensi-Kansu-Ningsia Border Region and seize Yenan.

(10) To make wholesale arrests of prominent people favouring resistance to Japan and suppress the anti-Japanese movement in Chungking and in the provinces.

(11) To destroy Communist Party organizations in all provinces and make wholesale arrests of Communists.

(12) To proclaim "the recovery of lost territories" by the Kuomintang government upon the withdrawal of Japanese troops from central and southern China, and at the same time to carry out propaganda on the necessity of concluding a so-called "peace with honour".

(13) Japan to launch most ferocious attacks on the Eighth Route Army by bringing up her troops from central and southern China as reinforcements to the north, and to co-operate with the Kuomintang forces in order to annihilate the whole Eighth Route and New Fourth Armies.

(14) The Kuomintang to continue last year's state of cease-fire with Japan on all fronts in order to turn it into one of general truce and peace negotiations while ceaselessly attacking the Eighth Route Army and the New Fourth Army.

(15) The Kuomintang government to sign a peace treaty with Japan and join the triple alliance.

Active preparations are now being made for these moves.

Such in general outline is the treacherous plot of Japan and the pro-Japanese clique. The Central Committee of the Communist Party of China pointed out in its Manifesto of July 7, 1939: "Capitulation presents the greatest danger in the current situation, and anti-communism is the preparatory step to capitulation." Its Manifesto of July 7, 1940 stated: "The danger of capitulation has never been so serious and the difficulties in the war have never been so great as they are today." Chu Teh, Peng Teh-huai, Yeh Ting and Hsiang Ying pointed this out even more concretely in their telegram of November 9 of last year:

> Certain people at home are engineering a new anti-Communist onslaught in an attempt to clear the way for capitulation. . . . They want to put an end to the War of Resistance by what they call Sino-Japanese co-operation in "suppressing the Communists". They want to substitute civil war for the War of Resistance, capitulation for independence, a split for unity and darkness for light. Their activities are sinister and their designs pernicious. People are telling each other the news and are horrified. Indeed, the situation has never been so critical as it is today.

Thus the Southern Anhwei Incident and the Order of January 17 of the Military Council in Chungking are merely the beginning of a series of incidents. The Order of January 17 in particular is full of grave political implications. The fact that those who issued this counter-revolutionary order dared to do so openly, risking universal condemnation, shows that they must have determined upon a complete split and out-and-out capitulation. For without their wire-pulling masters the political representatives of the flabby class of big landlords and big bourgeoisie in China cannot move an inch, let alone embark on an undertaking such as this which has shocked the whole world. In the present circumstances, it seems very difficult to make those who issued the order change their minds and it will probably be impossible to do so without emergency action by the whole nation and strong diplomatic pressure from abroad. Hence the urgent task of the whole nation now is to watch developments with the utmost vigilance and prepare itself against any sinister eventuality that the reactionaries may precipitate; there must not be the slightest negligence. As for China's future, the matter is quite clear. Even if the Japanese aggressors and the pro-Japanese clique are able to succeed in their plots, we Chinese Communists and the people will never allow them to keep up their tyranny indefinitely; not only are we duty bound to step forward and take control of the situation, we are also confident of our ability to do so. However dark the situation, however thorny the road, and whatever the price that road exacts (the loss of the New Fourth Army units in southern Anhwei is part of that price), the Japanese aggressors and the pro-Japanese clique are certainly doomed. The reasons are as follows:

(1) The Communist Party of China can no longer be easily deceived and crushed, as it was in 1927. It is now a major party standing firmly on its own feet.

(2) Many members of other parties and groups (including the Kuomintang) who are apprehensive of the disaster of national subjugation certainly have no wish to capitulate and fight a civil war. Some of them are hoodwinked for the moment, but they may come to their senses in due course.

(3) The same is true of the troops. Most of them oppose the Communist Party under compulsion.

(4) The vast majority of the Chinese people have no desire to be colonial slaves.

(5) The imperialist war is on the eve of a great change. However rampant they may be for the moment, the parasites who depend on imperialism will soon find out that their bosses are not reliable. The whole situation will change when the tree falls and the monkeys scatter.

(6) The outbreak of revolution in many countries is only a question of time, and it is certain that these revolutions and the Chinese revolution will support one another in the joint struggle for victory.

(7) The Soviet Union is the strongest force in the world and will definitely help China fight the War of Resistance to the very end.

For all these reasons we hope that those who are playing with fire will not get too dizzy. We now serve them with this formal warning: Better be careful. This fire is not a plaything. Look out for your own skins! If you calm down and give the matter some thought, you will have to take the following steps promptly and in earnest:

(1) Rein in on the brink of the precipice and stop your provocations.

(2) Rescind the reactionary Order of January 17 and publicly admit that you have been completely wrong.

(3) Punish Ho Ying-chin, Ku Chu-tung and Shangkuan Yun-hsiang, the chief culprits in the Southern Anhwei Incident.

(4) Release Yeh Ting and reinstate him as Commander of the New Fourth Army.

(5) Return all the men and arms captured in southern Anhwei to the New Fourth Army.

(6) Compensate all the officers and men of the New Fourth Army who were wounded and the families of those who were killed in southern Anhwei.

(7) Withdraw the troops sent to central China for "Communist suppression".

(8) Demolish the blockade line in the Northwest.[4]

(9) Release all patriotic political prisoners.

(10) Abolish the one-party dictatorship and introduce democratic government.

(11) Carry out the Three People's Principles and observe Dr. Sun Yat-sen's Testament.

(12) Arrest the ringleaders of the pro-Japanese clique and bring them to trial in accordance with the law of the land.

There will, of course, be a return to normal if these twelve points are put into effect, and we Communists and the whole people will certainly not push matters to extremes. Otherwise, "Chi Sun's troubles, I am afraid, will not come from Chuanyu but will arise at home";[5] in other words, the reactionaries will be lifting a rock only to drop it on their own toes, and then we will not be able to help them even if we would like to. We value co-operation, but they ought to set store by it, too. To be frank, there is a limit to our concessions; the stage of concessions is over as far as we are concerned. They have inflicted the first gash, and a very deep one at that. If they still care for their own future, they should come forward of their own accord and dress the wound. "It is not too late to mend the fold even after some of the sheep have been lost." It is a matter of life and death for them, and we feel obliged to give them this final piece of advice. But if they remain impenitent and keep up their wrongdoing, the people of China, having reached the end of their forbearance, will dump them on the muck heap and then it will be too late for repentance. As for the New Fourth Army, the Revolutionary Military Commission of the Central Committee of the Communist Party of China issued an order on

January 20, appointing Chen Yi as Acting Commander, Chang Yun-yi as Deputy Commander, Lai Chuan-chu as Chief of Staff and Teng Tzu-hui as Director of the Political Department. With more than 90,000 troops remaining in central China and the southern part of Kiangsu, the New Fourth Army, though subjected to pincer attacks by the Japanese aggressors and the anti-Communist troops, will certainly fight on despite all hardships and will never cease to render loyal service to the nation. Meanwhile, the units of its brother army, the Eighth Route Army, will not sit by and watch it suffer these pincer attacks, but will certainly take steps to give the necessary assistance — this I can say bluntly. As for the statement made by the spokesman of the Military Council in Chungking, the only possible comment is that it is self-contradictory. While the Chungking Military Council stated in its Order that the New Fourth Army had "mutinied", the spokesman said that its aim was to move into the Nanking-Shanghai-Hangchow triangle in order to establish a base there. Now, suppose we accept what he says. Can a move into the Nanking-Shanghai-Hangchow triangle be regarded as a "mutiny"? That blockhead of a Chungking spokesman did not stop to think. Against whom would the New Fourth Army be mutinying in that area? Is it not an area under Japanese occupation? Then why should you prevent the New Fourth Army from moving into that area and try to wipe it out while it was still in southern Anhwei? Ah, of course! After all that is what loyal servants of Japanese imperialism would do. Hence their plan to mass seven divisions in an annihilation campaign, hence their Order of January 17, and hence their trial of Yeh Ting. However, I still say that the Chungking spokesman is an idiot, for without being pressed he has let the cat out of the bag and revealed the plans of Japanese imperialism to the whole people.

NOTES

[1] The triple alliance refers to the tripartite pact between Germany, Italy and Japan signed in Berlin on September 27, 1940.

[2] The counter-revolutionary Order of January 17 for the disbandment of the New Fourth Army was issued by Chiang Kai-shek in the name of the Military Council of the National Government.

[3] These two notorious telegrams were sent late in 1940 by Chiang Kai-shek when he launched the second anti-Communist onslaught, and they were signed by

Ho Ying-chin and Pai Chung-hsi, Chief and Deputy Chief of the General Staff of the Military Council of the Kuomintang government. The telegram of October 19 contained outrageous calumnies against the Eighth Route Army and the New Fourth Army which were fighting in the enemy-occupied areas and peremptorily ordered their units operating against the Japanese south of the Yellow River to be shifted to the north by a specified date. In the interest of unity for armed resistance, Comrades Chu Teh, Peng Teh-huai, Yeh Ting and Hsiang Ying, in a joint reply on November 9, consented to shift the troops in southern Anhwei to the north, at the same time rebutting the slanders. The telegram of December 8 signed by Ho Ying-chin and Pai Chung-hsi, which was a reply to the telegram of November 9, represented a further attempt to turn public opinion against the Communists.

4 The blockade line in the Northwest was built by the Kuomintang reactionaries around the Shensi-Kansu-Ningsia Border Region. From 1939 onward they pressed the local people into service and built five lines of blockhouses, stone walls and trenches. The line started from Ningsia in the west, ran along the Chingshui River in the south and terminated at the Yellow River in the east. On the eve of the Southern Anhwei Incident the Kuomintang troops surrounding the Border Region were increased to more than 200,000.

5 The quotation is from *Confucian Analects*, Book XVI, Chapter I. Confucius made this remark when Chi Sun, minister of the state of Lu, was about to attack Chuanyu, a small neighbouring state.

THE SITUATION
AFTER THE REPULSE OF
THE SECOND
ANTI-COMMUNIST ONSLAUGHT

March 18, 1941

1. The second anti-Communist onslaught,[1] which was touched off by the telegram of Ho Ying-chin and Pai Chung-hsi (dated October 19 last year), reached its climax in the Southern Anhwei Incident and Chiang Kai-shek's Order of January 17; the rearguard actions are his anti-Communist speech of March 6 and the anti-Communist resolution of the People's Political Council.[2] From now on there may be some temporary easing of the situation. With the world's two major imperialist blocs on the eve of a decisive struggle, that section of China's big bourgeoisie which is pro-British and pro-American and which is still opposed to the Japanese aggressors finds it necessary to seek a slight temporary relaxation in the present strained relations between the Kuomintang and the Communist Party. Besides, the Kuomintang cannot keep these relations strained to the pitch of the past five months, because of the situation within the Kuomintang (there are contradictions between its central and local authorities, between the C.C. Clique and the Political Science Group, between the C.C. Clique and the Fu Hsing Society[3] and between the die-hards and the intermediate sections, and also contradictions within the C.C. Clique and the Fu Hsing Society themselves), because of the domestic situation (the broad masses of the people are opposed to the Kuomintang's tyranny and sympathize with the Communist Party) and because of our Party's own policy (of continuing the protest campaign). At the moment, therefore, Chiang Kai-shek needs a slight temporary easing of the tension.

This inner-Party directive was written by Comrade Mao Tse-tung on behalf of the Central Committee of the Communist Party of China.

2. The recent struggle points to a decline in the standing of the Kuomintang and a rise in that of the Communist Party, and this is the key factor in certain changes that have occurred in the relative strength of the two parties. All this has compelled Chiang Kai-shek to reconsider his own position and attitude. In stressing national defence and preaching that party politics are out of date, he is posing as a "national leader" who is above domestic contradictions and feigning impartiality to class and party, his aim being to preserve the rule of the big landlord class and big bourgeoisie and the Kuomintang. But this attempt of his will certainly prove futile, if it is only a subterfuge and means no real change in policy.

3. At the beginning of the recent anti-Communist onslaught, the policy of conciliation and concession which our Party adopted out of consideration for the general interest (as indicated in the telegram of November 9 last year) won the sympathy of the people, and we again won the support of the whole people when, after the Southern Anhwei Incident, we turned to a vigorous counter-offensive (as indicated by our two sets of twelve demands,[4] our refusal to attend the People's Political Council, and the country-wide protest campaign). This policy of ours, the policy of waging struggle on just grounds, to our advantage, and with restraint, was entirely necessary for repulsing the latest anti-Communist onslaught, and it has already proved fruitful. Until there is a reasonable settlement of the major points at issue between the Kuomintang and the Communist Party, we must not show any slackening in our campaign of stern protest against the Southern Anhwei Incident, which was engineered by the pro-Japanese and anti-Communist cliques in the Kuomintang, and against their political and military oppression in all its forms, and must intensify our propaganda for the first twelve demands.

4. The Kuomintang will never relax its policy of oppression of our Party and other progressives or its anti-Communist propaganda in the areas under its rule; therefore our Party must heighten its vigilance. The Kuomintang will continue its attacks on the areas north of the Huai River, in eastern Anhwei and in central Hupeh, and our armed forces must not hesitate to repulse them. All base areas must strictly carry out the Central Committee's directive of December 25 last year,[5] intensify inner-Party education on tactics and rectify ultra-Left views, so that we can unfalteringly maintain the anti-Japanese democratic base areas. Throughout the country, including, of course, all the base areas, we must reject the erroneous estimate that a final split

between the Kuomintang and the Communist Party has either already occurred or is about to occur, together with the many incorrect views arising therefrom.

NOTES

[1] For a fuller account of the second anti-Communist onslaught, see "A Comment on the Sessions of the Kuomintang Central Executive Committee and of the People's Political Council", *Selected Works of Mao Tse-tung*, Eng. ed., FLP, Peking, 1965, Vol. III, pp. 137-51.

[2] On March 6, 1941, Chiang Kai-shek delivered an anti-Communist speech at a meeting of the People's Political Council. Harping on his old theme that the "direction of all military and political affairs" must be "unified", he declared that the organs of anti-Japanese democratic political power in the enemy's rear should be abolished and that the people's armed forces led by the Chinese Communist Party must be "concentrated in specified areas" according to his "orders and plans". On the same day, the People's Political Council, which was dominated by the Kuomintang reactionaries, passed a resolution whitewashing Chiang Kai-shek's anti-Communist and anti-popular activities and violently attacking the Communist members of the People's Political Council for their refusal to attend the council's session in protest against the Southern Anhwei Incident.

[3] For the Political Science Group, see "Problems of War and Strategy", Note 14, p. 234 of this volume. For the C.C. Clique and the Fu Hsing Society, see "The Situation and Tasks in the Anti-Japanese War After the Fall of Shanghai and Taiyuan", Note 10, p. 74 of this volume.

[4] The first set of "twelve demands", proposed by the Communist members of the People's Political Council at its session of February 15, 1941, were similar to those listed in the "Order and Statement on the Southern Anhwei Incident". The second set were put to Chiang Kai-shek on March 2, 1941 by the Communist members of the People's Political Council as a condition for their attendance of the council's sessions and were as follows:

(1) Immediately stop the anti-Communist military attacks all over the country.

(2) Immediately stop the nation-wide political persecution of the Chinese Communist Party and of all other democratic parties and groups, recognize their legal status, and release all their members arrested in Sian, Chungking, Kweiyang and other places.

(3) Lift the ban on the bookshops which have been closed down in various places, and rescind the order for impounding anti-Japanese books and newspapers in post offices.

(4) Immediately stop all restrictions on the *New China Daily*.

(5) Recognize the legal status of the Shensi-Kansu-Ningsia Border Region.

(6) Recognize the organs of anti-Japanese democratic political power in the enemy's rear.

(7) Maintain the *status quo* in the division of garrison areas in central, northern and northwestern China.

(8) Let the Communist-led armed forces form another group army in addition to the Eighteenth Group Army, making a total of six army corps.

(9) Release all the cadres arrested during the Southern Anhwei Incident and provide funds for the relief of the victims' families.

(10) Release all officers and men taken prisoner during the Southern Anhwei Incident and return all their arms.

(11) Form a joint committee of all the parties and groups, with one representative from each, and appoint the Kuomintang and the Communist Party representatives to be its chairman and vice-chairman respectively.

(12) Include Communist representatives in the presidium of the People's Political Council.

5 The directive of December 25 is included as the article "On Policy", pp. 441-49 of this volume.

CONCLUSIONS ON THE REPULSE
OF THE
SECOND ANTI-COMMUNIST ONSLAUGHT

May 8, 1941

As the Central Committee's directive of March 18, 1941, has stated, the second anti-Communist onslaught has come to an end. What has followed since is the continuance of the War of Resistance Against Japan in new circumstances, international as well as domestic. The additional factors in these new circumstances are the spread of the imperialist war, the upsurge of the international revolutionary movement, the neutrality pact between the Soviet Union and Japan,[1] the defeat of the Kuomintang's second anti-Communist onslaught and the consequent decline in the political standing of the Kuomintang and rise in that of the Communist Party, and, furthermore, the latest preparations by Japan for a new large-scale offensive against China. It is absolutely necessary for us to study and learn the lessons of our Party's heroic and victorious struggle against the recent anti-Communist onslaught, for the purpose of uniting the people throughout the country to persevere in the War of Resistance and for the purpose of continuing effectively to overcome the danger of capitulation and the anti-Communist counter-current of the big landlords and the big bourgeoisie.

1. Of China's two major contradictions, the national contradiction between China and Japan is still primary and the internal class contradiction in China is still subordinate. The fact that a national enemy has penetrated deep into our country is all-decisive. As long as the contradiction between China and Japan remains acute, even if the entire big landlord class and big bourgeoisie turn traitor and

---

This inner-Party directive was written by Comrade Mao Tse-tung for the Central Committee of the Communist Party of China.

surrender, they can never bring about another 1927 situation, with a repetition of the April 12th[2] and the May 21st Incidents[3] of that year. The first anti-Communist onslaught[4] was appraised as another May 21st Incident by some comrades, and the second onslaught as a repetition of the April 12th and the May 21st Incidents, but objective facts have proved these appraisals wrong. The mistake of these comrades lies in forgetting that the national contradiction is the primary one.

2. In the circumstances, the pro-British and pro-American big landlords and big bourgeoisie, who direct all Kuomintang government policy, remain classes with a dual character. On the one hand they are opposed to Japan, and on the other they are opposed to the Communist Party and the broad masses of the people represented by the Party. And both their resistance to Japan and their anti-communism bear a dual character. With regard to their resistance to Japan, while they are opposed to Japan, they are not actively waging war or actively opposing Wang Ching-wei and the other traitors, and sometimes they even flirt with Japan's peace emissaries. With regard to their anti-communism, they are opposed to the Communist Party, having gone so far as to create the Southern Anhwei Incident and to issue the Order of January 17, but at the same time they do not want a final split and still maintain their stick-and-carrot policy. These facts have been confirmed once again in the recent anti-Communist onslaught. Chinese politics, which are extremely complex, demand our comrades' deepest attention. Since the pro-British and pro-American big landlords and big bourgeoisie are still resisting Japan and are still using the stick and carrot in dealing with our Party, the policy of our Party is to "do unto them as they do unto us",[5] stick for stick and carrot for carrot. Such is the revolutionary dual policy. So long as the big landlords and the big bourgeoisie do not completely turn traitor, this policy of ours will not change.

3. A whole range of tactics is needed to combat the Kuomintang's anti-Communist policy, and there must be absolutely no carelessness or negligence. The enmity and brutality of the big landlords and the big bourgeoisie represented by Chiang Kai-shek towards the people's revolutionary forces were not only demonstrated by the ten years of anti-Communist war, but they have been fully demonstrated in the midst of the war against Japan by two anti-Communist onslaughts, and particularly by the Southern Anhwei Incident during the second anti-Communist onslaught. If a people's

revolutionary force is to avoid extermination by Chiang Kai-shek and to compel him to acknowledge its existence, it has no alternative but to wage a tit-for-tat struggle against his counter-revolutionary policies. The defeat resulting from Comrade Hsiang Ying's opportunism during the recent anti-Communist onslaught should serve as a grave warning to the whole Party. But the struggle must be waged on just grounds, to our advantage, and with restraint; if any of the three is lacking, we shall suffer setbacks.

4. In the struggle against the Kuomintang die-hards, the big comprador bourgeoisie must be distinguished from the national bourgeoisie, which has little or no comprador character, and the most reactionary big landlords must be distinguished from the enlightened gentry and the general run of landlords. This is the theoretical basis of our Party's endeavour to win over the intermediate sections and establish organs of political power on the "three thirds system", and it has been repeatedly stressed by the Central Committee since March last year. Its correctness was proved afresh during the recent anti-Communist onslaught. The stand we took before the Southern Anhwei Incident, as expressed in our November 9 telegram,[6] was entirely necessary for our shift to the political counter-attack after the incident; otherwise we could not have won over the intermediate sections. For unless they had been taught time and again by experience, the intermediate sections would have been unable to understand why our Party must wage resolute struggles against the Kuomintang die-hards, why unity can be gained only through struggle and why there can be no unity whatsoever if struggle is abandoned. Although the leading elements in the regional power groups belong to the big landlord class and the big bourgeoisie, generally they should also be regarded and treated as intermediate sections, since there are contradictions between them and the big landlords and big bourgeois who control the central government. Yen Hsi-shan who was most active in the first anti-Communist onslaught took a middle stand in the second, and although the Kwangsi clique which took a middle stand in the first onslaught came in on the anti-Communist side in the second, it is still in contradiction with the Chiang Kai-shek clique and not to be identified with it. This applies with still greater force to other regional power groups. Many of our comrades, however, still lump the different landlord and bourgeois groups together, as though the entire landlord class and bourgeoisie had turned traitor after the Southern Anhwei Incident; this is an over-simplification of

China's complex politics. Were we to adopt this view and identify all the landlords and the bourgeoisie with the Kuomintang die-hards, we would isolate ourselves. It must be realized that Chinese society is big in the middle and small at both ends[7] and that the Communist Party cannot solve China's problems unless it wins over the masses of the intermediate classes and unless it enables them to play their proper role according to their circumstances.

5. Because some comrades have wavered on the point that the contradiction between China and Japan is the primary one and hence have wrongly appraised class relations in China, they have at times wavered on the policy of the Party. Proceeding from their appraisal of the Southern Anhwei Incident as another April 12th or May 21st Incident, these comrades now seem to think that the Central Committee's policy directive of December 25 last year is no longer applicable, or at least not altogether applicable. They believe that we no longer need the kind of state power that includes all who stand for resistance and democracy but need a so-called state power of the workers, peasants and urban petty bourgeoisie, and that we no longer need the united front policy of the period of the War of Resistance but need a policy of agrarian revolution as during the ten years' civil war. The Party's correct policy has become blurred in the minds of these comrades, at any rate for the time being.

6. When these comrades were instructed by the Central Committee of our Party to be prepared against a possible split by the Kuomintang, that is, against the worst possible development, they forgot the other possibilities. They do not understand that while it is absolutely necessary to prepare for the worst possibility, this does not mean ignoring the favourable possibilities; on the contrary, such preparation for the worst is precisely a condition for creating favourable possibilities and turning them into reality. On this occasion, we were fully prepared against a split by the Kuomintang, and so the Kuomintang dared not bring about a split lightly.

7. There are even more comrades who fail to understand the unity of the national struggle and the class struggle, and who fail to understand united front policy and class policy, and consequently the unity of united front education and class education. They hold that after the Southern Anhwei Incident special emphasis should be placed on class education as distinct from united front education. Even now they do not understand that for the whole period of the anti-Japanese war the Party has a single integral policy — the national united front

policy (a dual policy) which integrates the two aspects, unity and struggle — towards all those in the upper and middle strata who are still resisting Japan, whether they belong to the big landlord class and big bourgeoisie or the intermediate classes. This dual policy should be applied even to the puppet troops, the traitors and the pro-Japanese elements, except for those who are absolutely unrepentant, whom we must resolutely crush. The education which our Party conducts among its own members and the people in general likewise embraces both these aspects, that is, it teaches the proletariat and the peasantry and other sections of the petty bourgeoisie how to unite, in different ways, with the different strata of the bourgeoisie and the landlord class for resistance to Japan, and at the same time how to conduct struggles against them in varying degrees according to the varying degrees in which they compromise, vacillate and are anti-Communist. United front policy *is* class policy and the two are inseparable; whoever is unclear on this will be unclear on many other problems.

8. Other comrades do not understand that the social character of the Shensi-Kansu-Ningsia Border Region and the anti-Japanese base areas in northern and central China is already new-democratic. The main criterion in judging whether an area is new-democratic in character is whether representatives of the broad masses of the people participate in the political power there and whether this political power is led by the Communist Party. Therefore, united front political power under Communist leadership is the chief mark of a new-democratic society. Some people think that New Democracy can be considered as accomplished only if there is an agrarian revolution like that of the ten years' civil war, but they are wrong. At present the political system in the base areas is a political system of the united front of all the people who are for resistance and democracy, the economy is one from which the elements of semi-colonialism and semi-feudalism have been basically eliminated, and the culture is an anti-imperialist and anti-feudal culture of the broad masses of the people. Therefore, whether viewed politically, economically or culturally, both the anti-Japanese base areas which have only enforced the reduction of rent and interest and the Shensi-Kansu-Ningsia Border Region which has gone through a thorough agrarian revolution are new-democratic in character. When the example of the anti-Japanese base areas is extended throughout the country, then the whole of China will become a new-democratic republic.

NOTES

[1] The neutrality pact between the Soviet Union and Japan, concluded on April 13, 1941, ensured peace on the eastern border of the Soviet Union, thus crushing the plot for a joint German, Italian and Japanese attack on the Soviet Union. It marked a major victory for the Soviet Union's peaceful foreign policy.

[2] The April 12th Incident was the counter-revolutionary coup d'état staged by Chiang Kai-shek in Shanghai on April 12, 1927, during which a great number of Communists and revolutionary workers, peasants and students and intellectuals were massacred.

[3] Instigated by Chiang Kai-shek and Wang Ching-wei, the counter-revolutionary Kuomintang army commanders in Hunan, including Hsu Keh-hsiang and Ho Chien, ordered a raid on the provincial headquarters of the trade unions, the peasant associations and other revolutionary organizations in Changsha on May 21, 1927. Communists and revolutionary workers and peasants were arrested and killed en masse. This signalized the open collaboration of the two counter-revolutionary Kuomintang cliques, the Wuhan clique headed by Wang Ching-wei and the Nanking clique headed by Chiang Kai-shek.

[4] The first anti-Communist onslaught during the anti-Japanese war was conducted by Chiang Kai-shek in the winter of 1939 and the spring of 1940.

[5] The quotation is from the commentary by Chu Hsi (1130-1200), a philosopher of the Sung Dynasty, on the *Confucian Doctrine of the Mean*, Chapter 13.

[6] The telegram of November 9, 1940 was sent by Chu Teh and Peng Teh-huai, Commander-in-Chief and Deputy Commander-in-Chief of the Eighteenth Group Army (Eighth Route Army), and Yeh Ting and Hsiang Ying, Commander and Deputy Commander of the New Fourth Army, in reply to the telegram of the Kuomintang generals Ho Ying-chin and Pai Chung-hsi, dated October 19, 1940. Exposing the plot by the Kuomintang reactionaries to attack the Communist Party and capitulate to Japan, they denounced Ho Ying-chin's and Pai Chung-hsi's absurd proposal that the New Fourth Army and the Eighth Route Army should shift from the south to the north of the Yellow River. However, in a spirit of conciliation and compromise for the sake of maintaining unity against Japan, they agreed to shift their forces from the south to the north of the Yangtse River, while demanding the solution of a number of major outstanding issues between the Kuomintang and the Communist Party. The telegram won the sympathy of the intermediate sections and served to isolate Chiang Kai-shek.

[7] Comrade Mao Tse-tung's remark about Chinese society means that the Chinese industrial proletariat which led the revolution formed only a minority of China's population, as did also the reactionary big landlords and big bourgeoisie.

毛 泽 东 选 集

第 二 卷

*

外文出版社出版（北京）

一九六五年第一版

一九六七年第二次印刷

编号：（英）1050—386